Orchestration for the theatre
The traditional and national music of Scotland
Hebridean folksongs, vol. 1 *with J. L. Campbell of Canna*

Francis Collinson

# The Bagpipe
## The history of a musical instrument

**Routledge & Kegan Paul**

London and Boston

First published in 1975
by Routledge & Kegan Paul Ltd
Broadway House, 68–74 Carter Lane,
London EC4V 5EL and
9 Park Street,
Boston, Mass. 02108, USA
Set in Monotype Modern Ext. No. 7
and printed in Great Britain by
T. and A. Constable Ltd, Edinburgh

ISBN 0 7100 7913 3

# Contents

# Illustrations

## Plates

# Figures

Dedicated in retrospect to Miss Grant
of Balvenie ('Aunt Meta') in happy
memory of a wonderful old Highland lady

'I like them best at a distance'
(frequent saying)

# Preface

This book has turned out to be quite different from the one I set out to write. My intention was to write a book about the Scottish Highland bagpipe which would amplify the chapters on the subject in my book, *The Traditional and National Music of Scotland*. This will be clear from my original opening paragraph, which read:

> This book sets out to be an account of Scotland's national musical instrument, the great Highland bagpipe. To see the subject in proper perspective however, one must take a backward glance at the general history of the bagpipe itself, and its location as an indigenous instrument in other countries of the world. One should look particularly at the pipes in those countries in which the earliest records and depictions of the instrument are to be found, to see if one can discern any ordered evolution of our own Scottish bagpipe from earlier roots.

I envisaged what I called 'a cosy preliminary chapter' to deal with this. It should take perhaps a month to do.

A year and a half later I found myself still working at this chapter, having in the writing of it had to make daring exploratory incursions into archaeology and the history of ancient Egypt and Mesopotamia; having renewed and augmented my sketchy recollections of the literature of Greece and Rome; having read up the subject of Britain under the Romans and seen for myself the remains of their artefacts at the museums along Hadrian's Wall, as well as at Edinburgh, London, Gloucester and elsewhere; having examined the carved stone crosses at Iona and the plaster casts of the Irish crosses of Monasterboice and Clonmacnoise at the Victoria and Albert Museum; having brushed up my modest knowledge of the Celts and Celtic Ireland, of Wales and of twelfth-century Britain; and visited the Pitt Rivers and Horniman Museums in Oxford and London with their wealth of musical pipes of many nations and counrties – all for the purpose of my preliminary chapter, my 'backward glance'.

I early discovered one important fact, namely that the term for the players of the ancient wind-instruments beloved of the translators of the Latin and Greek classics, 'flute-players', which I remembered from my schooldays, was a mistranslation – one which persists up to the present day on which I write. It is a mistranslation which has befogged the whole picture. These 'flute-players' were in fact *pipers*, who played, not upon the 'double-flute' as the translators have it, but upon *reed-sounded pipes* – double-pipes.

To be sure, the streets of ancient Rome must have been as full of the sound of pipes as Oban on a Saturday evening – not quite the same pipes certainly, for the bag-component had not yet been invented, and the inflated cheeks were used instead – but nevertheless *reed-pipes* and not flutes.

The pipes in the days of ancient Rome were already a very ancient instrument, nearly twice as ancient then as the days of ancient Rome are to us now. The realization came to me quite suddenly that the history of the pipes stretched back unbroken for a period of nearly five thousand years. In point of fact, it extended backwards to the days when, in ancient Mesopotamia, civilization commenced again after Noah's Flood, which archaeologists place at about 4000 B.C.;[1] for, incredible as it may seem, the crumpled remains of a set of pipes, the ancient mouth-blown double-pipes of the period of this post-Deluge civilization (of *c.* 2800 B.C.), have actually been found, at the site of the city of Ur in Babylonia, a city built literally upon the silt of the Deluge.* These pipes, which are of silver, are now on view in Philadelphia Museum, U.S.A.

As regards the book I had set out to write, it became obvious in the end that my preliminary chapter had become a considerable part – almost the main part – of the book itself; a book which must perforce be of very much wider scope than I had dreamed of, and of which the Scottish Highland bagpipe could only occupy the last part, though not an unimportant one. It is a canvas across which, whether in historical fact, tradition, or fable, move some of the great figures of the world's history, ranging from Homer, Xenophon, Julius Caesar, Cleopatra, the Emperors Nero and Hadrian, to Jesus of Nazareth.

I should make it clear however that my ultimate target, in this now greatly enlarged quest, was still the Scottish Highland bagpipe; but instead of glancing back into the past as a prelude to the subject, I now saw that I must begin at the beginning and work towards my objective – five thousand years ahead!

There can have been fewer subjects about which greater nonsense has been written than that of the Scottish bagpipe. In this book I have tried to avoid the kind of woolly statement (to cite an actual quotation) that 'one of the Roman historians tells us that he heard the instrument, still strange to the Romans, played upon by the Celts'; or that the Greek musicologist Aristides Quintilianus (*c.* A.D. 150) stated that (to quote again) 'this instrument was known to the Scottish Highlanders in his

---

* C. Leonard Woolley, *Ur of the Chaldees*. Ur is between five and six hundred miles south of Mount Ararat of Noah's Ark.

day' (he did not say any such thing); with the grandiloquent comment, 'what does it matter to us whether he gained his knowledge *while travelling in this country* [i.e. Scotland!], or while watching the daily processions from his parlour window in Rome?'!

I have tried wherever possible to give rather more exact references for my statements.

I referred in my original opening paragraph, quoted above, to the various locations of the bagpipe as an *indigenous* instrument. The distinction is necessary, because in the course of the last two hundred years or so, the Scottish Highland bagpipe, with its mingled aura of panache, romance and nostalgia, has travelled so widely through the world, and has achieved such wide popularity in doing so, whether by the Scottish Highland regiments, or at the hands of the lone Highlander in exile, that it has remained and flourished as a 'scape' in many of the lands it has visited. This is notably so for instance in India, where at Sialkot in the Punjab, as I have been informed by a former member of the old Indian Army, one can find the Scottish Highland bagpipe being manufactured for the use of the present military forces of the sub-continent – a legacy from their former Scottish comrades in arms. It is to be found too in many of the African countries formerly under British administration. Now it has seemingly begun to appear as a rival, if only in the courtesy sense, of the native instrument, in such unexpected places as Brittany, which has its own ancient *biniou* and (bagless) *bombarde*. It is a rivalry that has been brought about by the visiting Scots piper, abroad on friendly competitive occasions.

In the former British Dominions of Canada, Australia and New Zealand, as well as in South Africa, it is of course as much a national instrument as in Scotland itself.

In tracing the development of the bagpipe in the British Isles from the first possible cryptic reference to it in one of a series of riddles in an eleventh-century Anglo-Saxon manuscript, to the arrival of the fully-fledged three-droned Scottish Highland bagpipe of modern times, I have adopted the method of dealing with the growth of the instrument chronologically *in all four countries simultaneously*, until one by one the various forms became extinct and drop out of the story, leaving the Scottish Highland bagpipe and its small cousin the Northumbrian pipes as the sole survivors.

There is a considered reason for the use of such chronological method, which is that the early use of musical instruments of a portable character such as the pipe, harp and lute, lay largely in the hands of the ancient minstrels, who travelled freely across the borders of the countries of Europe, including those of the British Isles. One may reasonably assume that these minstrels would not only assimilate and make use of the latest refinements and techniques of the musical instruments they observed in the countries in which they travelled, but would also enrich the instrumental resources of these countries by their acquired knowledge, and enable them in some measure to keep pace with each other.

It is possible that the Highlands of Scotland were *terra incognita* to the minstrels because of their difficulty of access, and because of the fierceness and frequent lawlessness of their inhabitants. The Lowlands of Scotland however were fully open to the minstrels, as historical records indicate. There is little doubt, as is suggested in these pages, that the Scottish Highlander knew very well what was going on in the Lowlands, in music as in most other things. This was partly through the frequent visits of the Highland chiefs and, more to the point, their attendants, on official business to the capital city; and partly also through the incursions into the Lowlands of the famed Highland reivers on cattle raids and for other booty, or (from the fourteenth century onwards) the legitimate journeyings of the cattle-traders and drovers, duly documented in these pages.

It has to be admitted indeed that there is a scarcity of evidence and documentation of the bagpipe in Scotland up to and beyond its first appearance in stone carvings on religious buildings in the Lowlands, in the late fourteenth and early fifteenth century. But where there is a paucity of evidence in one of the four countries of the British Isles at a particular period, it is not unreasonable, from a study of the subject, to assume a more or less parallel development in all four.

On this count it seems to me that the chronological sequence of presentation in the four countries at once is necessary. Such treatment has entailed the crossing and recrossing of the political borders, particularly of the border between England and Scotland, right up to the final disappearance of the English bagpipe in the eighteenth century (with the exception of the Northumbrian pipes, which are a special case). While this may be confusing at times (though I hope not unduly so) it is to my mind preferable for the purpose of keeping an idea of the general picture throughout, than to deal with the bagpipe of each country at a time.

Finally I wish to make it clear that this book does not attempt to trace the parallel development of the bagpipe in other countries of the world, except in the evolution of the instrument itself in prehistory and antiquity. Such comparative research has been capably undertaken and set out by Anthony Baines in his authoritative book, *Bagpipes*, of which I gratefully acknowledge that I have availed myself at many points throughout my book. I have however given brief particulars of the names of other bagpipes and the countries of their use in an appendix, with references to sources where fuller details and illustrations of the pipes may be found.

Let me therefore state again that the theme of my book is the evolution and story of the Scottish Highland bagpipe. The evolutionary part of it is a long tale that stretches far afield and takes many chapters in the telling.

F. C.

# Acknowledgments

A great many people have helped me in various ways in the preparation of this book, and to all of them I am deeply grateful. In particular I wish to record my most sincere gratitude to my friend Dr J. L. Campbell of Canna for his constant and unfailing help with references and suggestions; for much useful information about the bagpipe in Scottish, particularly Gaelic, history and literature; also for reading the text and later the proofs of the section of the book dealing with the Scottish Highland bagpipe. I am under a similar debt to Professor Ian Campbell, Professor of Humanity at Edinburgh, for reading and correcting the text and proofs of the section dealing with the periods of classical Greece and Rome, and to Dr E. K. Borthwick, lecturer in Greek at Edinburgh, who is an authority on Greek and Roman music and musical instruments, for his assistance in this task; to Dr Winnington Ingram for the previous translation of a passage of Greek text from Aristides Quintilianus; to my friend G. Lyndesay Langwill for putting into my hands his MS notes on The Waits, the Stock-and-horn, and much other material bearing on the subject, for his readiness to help at all times, and for reading through and making useful comments on my text; to the Librarian and staff of the National Library of Scotland for their constant and willing help in a variety of ways; to Dr J. Imrie, Keeper of the Records of Scotland, for his personal interest and help, particularly concerning records of the Scottish cattle-drovers, and to his staff for their searches of the Records on the subject. My thanks are also due to the Trustees, Keepers and staff of the British Museum for supplying pictures, for permission to quote from British Museum publications and to reproduce Plates 6, 11, 12 and 19, for assistance in locating manuscripts and prints, and for help in other ways; to the London proprietors and to Harvard University Press for permission to use translations and quotations from the Loeb Classical Library; to the Librarian, London Library, for his readiness to suggest and send books on various subjects; to the Keeper and staff of the National Museum of Antiquities of Scotland for information on Scottish bagpipes and other Scottish musical instruments; to the Keepers of The Scottish National Portrait Gallery and The National Gallery of Scotland for advice and information on pictures of bagpipes and pipers by Scottish artists and for permission to reproduce these (Plates 22 and 24); to the Librarian and Keeper of Manuscripts at Edinburgh University for help and information on Scottish MSS bearing on my subject; to the School of Scottish Studies, Edinburgh University, in particular to Professor John MacQueen, the School's Director, for glossing a long passage from Barbour's *Bruce*; to Fred Kent, chief technician, for making photographing expeditions with me; and to the School's delineator, Ralph Morton, for making numerous drawings for the book and for providing photographs for reproduction; to Mr Seumas MacNeill, Principal of the College of Piping, Glasgow, for his generous permission to quote from articles and to use illustrative material from the *Piping Times*, and also for personal information; and to the Trustees of the late Mrs Magdalene Sharpe Erskine, Dunimarle Castle Museum, Culross, Fife, for permission to reproduce Plate 23.

My grateful thanks and acknowledgments are also due to the following libraries, museums, art galleries and publishers in addition to those already mentioned, for permission to quote or produce copyright material and for other help: The University Museum, Pennsylvania (Plate 1); The University Museum, Philadelphia; The Royal Irish Academy, Dublin (Plate 15, and for help in dating an Irish manuscript); The City Museum, Carlisle; The City Museum, Gloucester; The Society of Antiquaries, Newcastle-upon-Tyne; The City Library, York; The Royal College of Music, London (for information about the researches of A. H. Frere, former Curator of the Musical Instruments) also Mr E. K. Ridley for help on the same subject; The London Museum for producing from store Roman 'flutes' (i.e. reed-pipes) for my inspection; The Royal Scottish Museum, Edinburgh, for allowing me to inspect the Duncan Fraser collection of bagpipes not generally on exhibit, and for help in tracing an Asiatic sculpture; The Royal Commission on Ancient and Historical Monuments (Scotland); The Department of the Environment (Plate 10: Crown copyright) and the Department's Library, Edinburgh; The Librarian, East Lothian County Council; The National Museum of Wales and the Welsh Folk Museum; The Archivist, Winchester College; The Dean and Chapter of Westminster (Plate 14) and the Keeper of the Muniments, Westminster Abbey; The Master of the Armouries, The Tower of London; The Librarian, Ripon Cathedral; the verger, Hexham Abbey, the head verger, Beverley Minster; H. G. The Duke of Wellington's Loan Collection, Reading Museum and Art Gallery (Plate 8); The Newton Port Museum and Public Library (Plate 21); The Director, Museo Nazionale, Rome (Plate 4); The Director, National Museum of Greece, Athens (Plate 7); The Department of Antiquities and Museums, Israel (Plate 3); The Director of the Kunst Historischen Museum, Vienna (Plate 17); Deutscher Verlag für Musik, Leipzig (Plate 5).

My grateful thanks are also due to the following persons: Dr Kenneth Steer, for information on the Lethendy slab, and on the Glen bagpipes; Mr Claude Blair, for information on Henry VIII's armour; Alexander MacAuley for information regarding an Irish *piob mhór* said to have been deposited at the Musée de Cluny, Paris; Madame la Comtesse de Chambure, Neuilly-sur-Seine, and Miss Patricia Boshell, Paris, for pursuing enquiries at the Musée de Cluny regarding these pipes; Dr Vidor Luithlen, Vienna, for help regarding the Dürer engraving of *Der Dudelsackpfeifer*; Mr A. B. Haldane for information regarding the Scottish cattle drovers; Mrs J. Ball, proprietoress of the 'Cat and Bagpipe', East Harley, for information on the same subject regarding the inn of that name; Miss Georgina Masson for help regarding Roman sculpture at Rome, Munich and Paris; Mr John Boardman, Oxford, for his opinion concerning the engraving of a bagpiper on a Hellenic gem; the late William Cocks, for his unsparing help on the whole subject of bagpipes; the late Professor Sidney T. M. Newman, Reid Professor of Music, Edinburgh, for inspecting a Roman altar to Atys at Gloucester for me; Professor J. M. C. Toynbee for much help on Romano-British and Roman archaeology, and for visiting Gloucester Museum with me to inspect the Roman altar mentioned above; The Rev. Tom and Mrs Griffiths for bringing to me from Rome a photograph and information about the Ludovisi Throne; Mr J. C. Corson, Honorary Librarian at Abbotsford, for supplying a reference to an observation on the bagpipe by Sir Walter Scott; Robin Lorimer, for information on pibroch and on the MacCrimmons; Angus MacPherson, son of *Calum Piobaire*, for information on the use of nasal inhalation by Scottish pipers in playing the practice chanter, and on the subject of the MacCrimmon *canntaireachd*; Mr Stewart Sanderson for locating and making a rubbing of the Piper's Stone in Ford church, Northumberland; Professor Stuart Piggott for sending me a dating of the stone; the Rev. William Matheson for translating a Gaelic motto inscribed on the Black Chanter of the Clan MacPherson; the late Canon Deighton for a long written account of the *ambubaiae*, and of the temple women in ancient eastern religions; Mr John Prebble for a reference concerning the execution of James Reid, Jacobite piper, after the 1745 Rising; Mrs Margaret Macdonald (Sheriff Kidd) for kind and useful introductions to various authorities; to Dame Flora MacLeod of Dunvegan and her daughter, Mrs Joan Wolrige Gordon, for bringing the MacCrimmon pipes to Edinburgh to be photographed and for permission to use them for Plate 20; to Capt. John A. MacLellan of the Army School of Piping for recording the sound of the MacCrimmon pipes at the School of Scottish Studies; Mr Anthony Baines, for information on early bag-hornpipes in the Mediterranean area and Near East; Dr Colin Renfrew, for supplying a reference to the figurine of a player of the double pipes in antiquity; to Seton Gordon, for kindly letting me have his source reference for a statement in *The Charm of Skye* on the 'MacCrimmon diploma'; Tom Scott, photographer, Edinburgh, for providing photographs for illustrations; Walter Scott (Bradford) Ltd, photographers, for Plate 13; Mr R. W. Feacham, Archaeology officer, Ordnance Survey, for a photocopy of an early account of the finding of the Richborough figure of a bagpiper in brass; Dr Anne Ross for drawing my attention to the

Silchester 'Flute-girl'; Mr Melville Mason, Honorary Secretary of the
Galpin Society, for facilitating inspection of an old account book of a
bagpipe maker; Andrew Ross senior and Andrew Ross junior, of the firm
of J. & R. Glen, instrument makers, Edinburgh, for information on woods
used in bagpipe making.

To my nephew, Major Euan Gordon, the Gordon Highlanders, for
obtaining for me the picture of Pipe-major Robert Burns of the Royal
Scots for the book jacket, and to the Royal Scots for permission to use the
picture.

To my wife's cousin, Mrs Margaret Gilchrist, for facilitating my
researches in the Midlands by her hospitality, and for the loan of books;
to Mrs Eve Collinson, my sister-in-law, for similarly facilitating by her
hospitality my researches in Oxford; and last but not least, to my wife
for her unfailing support and encouragement throughout the long task.

With so many helpers, it is all too likely that I may have omitted
someone whom I would have liked to thank, and I can assure any such
kind person that the omission is unintentional.

# Chapter one

# Antiquity

## The earliest pipes

If we examine the general principle of the bagpipe as it is today, we may reduce it, in its simplest terms, to an inflatable bag of skin which provides under pressure of the arm a stream of air to one, two or more reed-sounded pipes. Usually one of these plays the melody, and the others the accompaniment. Such accompaniment is most often in the form of a continuous fixed drone; though there are numerous instances among the different species of bagpipe of the accompaniment taking the form of a variable drone or simple harmony part, or even of a rudimentary counter-point to the melody. In one instance, indeed, that of the Cheremiss bagpipe in Russia, it is observed by Anthony Baines in his book *Bagpipes* (p. 49) that the players of it achieve all these three elements of accompaniment together, in 'a rich mixture of drone, harmony and true polyphony'.

This is not the place to describe in detail the construction and technique of the modern bagpipe. The reader is referred to chapter 1 of Anthony Baines's *Bagpipes* for a full description and to the glossary of names of the component parts at the back of this book. But by looking here at the general principle of the bagpipe, we may see that the invention of the bag did not in itself constitute a new musical instrument, but merely an addition to an existing one. This was the more ancient reed-sounded single- or double-pipe blown by the mouth. In the double-pipes, one of the pipes probably sounded the melody and the other the accompaniment, just as with the bag-blown instrument we know.

These reed-pipes are very ancient indeed. They are known to have been in use for nearly three thousand years before the bag was invented – and that was certainly not later than the first century B.C., as we shall see.

## The reed

The basic means of producing the sound in the pipes, the reed, is a discovery belonging to prehistory – to that far distant moment in time when some unnamed youth found that by pinching flat the end of a straw or plant-stalk and blowing into it with compressed lips, he could produce

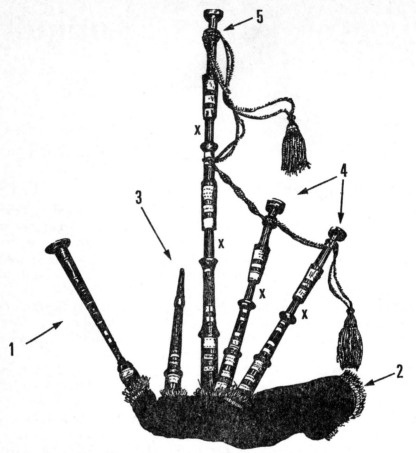

*Figure 1*  The Scottish Highland bagpipe

(1) The chanter
(2) The bag, with cloth cover (often of tartan)
(3) The blow-pipe ('blow-stick') or insufflation tube
(4) The tenor drones
(5) The bass drone
X X X tuning slides for the drones

a more or less musical sound. He had stumbled upon the principle of the *double reed*, so called from the fact that the squeezing of the end of the straw naturally produces *two* flattened surfaces or 'blades' at the squeezed part. These two blades vibrate with the pressure of the breath and produce the sound.

Such a simple discovery as this could have occurred (and probably did occur) in any number of places in any part of the world independently. It is as well to state this at once, for though it is possible to say where the earliest specimens of the reed-sounded pipe or pipes have been found, namely in Babylonia and ancient Egypt, such finds may have depended as much on natural conditions for their preservation through time, as on any priority of construction or invention in the countries of their discovery.

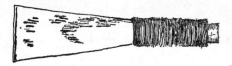

*Figure 2* Double reed

For this reason, it is impossible to dogmatize upon any theory of evolution of the reed-pipes based upon geography. One can only say that reed-sounded pipes have been known to be in use in certain countries of the East at a certain period of time. One cannot say that they had not already been invented and in use elsewhere. We know very little, for instance, about the music or musical instruments of the early Celtic races before about A.D. 500, though they must have had music long before that.

So much for the hypothetical discovery of the double reed. The process of construction of the *single* reed was slightly more complicated. For this a knife was necessary. It was found that if a tongue was cut a little way along the length of the straw, either towards or away from one of the knots or natural nodes, and the player inserted the straw into his mouth to the full length of the cut and blew, a musical sound could be produced. With such fragile material as a corn-stalk the single reed would be less liable to become clogged or sodden with the moisture of the mouth than would the crushed end of the straw of the double reed. It would be more dependable and easily controlled.

Such an imagined picture of the discovery of the principle of the reed may be thought to be over-fanciful; but in fact musical pipes of earlier millennia have been found in the excavated tombs of Egypt having just such reeds of straw as we have described, sometimes with unused straws beside them for their replacement. The reeds have been found in position in the pipes, with spare straws in the protective cases in which the pipes were found.* These will be discussed in detail.

When the tongue or 'blade' of the single reed is cut towards the knot or node of the straw or cane, it is known as an 'up-cut' reed. When the blade is cut away from the node, the reed is called 'down-cut'.

The *double* reed made of cane is the type used in the chanter of the Scottish bagpipe. It is the type also used in the instruments of the oboe and bassoon families of the symphony orchestra. The *single* reed is the type used in the drones of the Scottish bagpipe. It is also to be found, in more sophisticated form, in the orchestral clarinet.

It would have been convenient for the purpose of easy identification if

* Fragments of these straw reeds still remaining in the ancient musical pipes from Egyptian tombs are said to have been identified as of barley-straw, notably in specimens now at the museum at Turin and at Leyden. Cf. *Musical Times*, December 1890.

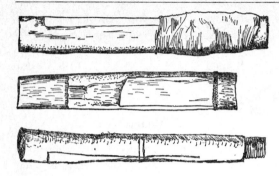

*Figure 3*  Single reed

(a) single 'beating' reed, down-cut

(b) single beating reed, up-cut (both (a) and (b) are enlarged to show detail)

(c) reed of bass drone of Scottish Highland bag-pipe (down-cut)

one could have referred to the double reed as a 'chanter reed' and the single as a 'drone reed', as in the Scottish bagpipe; but in dealing with the general history of the instrument this will not do, for in the pipes of other countries, both ancient and modern, we find that either type of reed may be found in use for chanter or drone according to its particular country and species. The well-known musicologist, the late Curt Sachs, refers to the pipes of whatever age simply as 'oboes' or 'clarinets' according to their type of reed (double or single, respectively) which for clarity has a good deal to recommend it.*

### The chanter

It seems logical to suppose that the use of a single pipe, playing the melody only, must have come before the twin or double pipes which, with the possibility of a harmony part on the second pipe, appear to represent an enormous advance in musical resource and sophistication. The curious fact is, however, that the earliest known specimens of the reed-pipe yet discovered, and even the earliest depictions of it upon the stone or terra cotta steles and inscriptions of Egypt and the middle-east, are all of the *double* pipe. There is one exception which will be described in its place. This means that the addition of the second pipe, presumably for accompanying the melody, must have been very early indeed. A number of such double-pipes have been discovered in ancient Egyptian tombs, whose age is to be reckoned in thousands of years. These are on view in the museums of Cairo[1] and elsewhere.

There was however a curious intermediate stage between the single pipe playing melody only and the addition of a second pipe for accompaniment. This was the use of two duplicate pipes *closely bound together*, with the

---

* Sachs, *The History of Musical Instruments*, pp. 91, 98. But see James MacGillivray's contention in 'The cylindrical reed pipe from antiquity to the 20th century', *Music Libraries and Instruments*, that the classification of oboe and clarinet and the tonal characteristics of each depends not upon the type of reed used, but upon whether the pipe is conical or cylindrical in bore. He contends that a cylindrical pipe fitted with a double reed must clearly be regarded as a double-reed clarinet.

fingerholes corresponding in position in each pipe, and therefore both intended to play the melody simultaneously. Each finger covered the corresponding holes in both pipes and *produced the same note from each pipe at every finger position.*

*Figure 4*   Ancient Egyptian parallel pipes fastened together with wax. The reeds, which would almost certainly have been single reeds, are missing (drawing from a specimen in Cairo Museum)

One may well ask what musical advantage there could have been in adding a second pipe for the sole purpose of doubling the melody. There were two possible reasons. One was that two pipes played together in unison would obviously produce twice the volume of sound that a single pipe would – on the principle of the old proverb that 'two pigs under a gate make more noise than one pig'. It is also possible, by putting one pipe ever so slightly out of tune with the other, to produce a 'beat' or wave effect in the sound. This can be not unattractive, as the modern organ-builder has found and developed in the organ stop known as 'waves of the sea' or *unda maris.*

The two pipes, voicing the same note in this fashion, were sometimes contained within a single tube possessing twin bores throughout its length. Each bore had its own reed and fingerholes. The fingerholes, corresponding in position and lying close together in pairs, could as a general rule only be played by the same finger covering both holes at once. This species, found largely in central Europe, notably in Croatia (see Baines, *Bagpipes*, p. 71), is known as the *diple* (i.e. double) pipe. It may be seen in a Scottish example, in the exquisitely made stock and horn in the National Museum of Antiquities of Scotland in Edinburgh.

The typical and perhaps clearest example of the parallel mouth-blown pipes are the ancient Egyptian *zummara*, with corresponding fingerholes in each pipe. *Zummaras* of obvious antiquity are displayed in the plates of the illustrated catalogue of the Cairo Museum; but probably because of the less meticulous documentation of exhibits at the time of their discovery, their period is stated as 'unknown'; Curt Sachs in his *History of Musical Instruments* mentions a pair of *zummaras*, or 'double clarinets' as he calls them, excavated from Egyptian tombs of the first century B.C., though he does not give a reference. He has also (ibid., p. 92) recognized parallel pipes on a relief known to be as early as 2700 B.C.

These parallel pipes seem to have been played with the single reed, the reed roughly similar to the drone-reed of the Scottish bagpipe. Unfortunately the reed has not been found in any of the specimens of antiquity in the Cairo Museum, but the *zummara* of ancient times corresponds so closely with the modern one in its general design that we can fairly safely assume that the type of reed was the same.* The reeds of the modern *zummara* are of cane, like the pipes themselves, and are 'up-cut'. In the Cairo Museum also however is an instrument almost identical with the *zummara* but with the reeds down-cut; this is listed under the name of *mashourah*.[2]

The pipes of the common modern *zummara* are usually unornamented, though the several coils of fine black string binding them together form a characteristic ornamentation of its own sort. The catalogue describes a pair of *zummaras* of which, to quote, 'Les tubes sont décorés de quelques decoratives [sic] à dessins simples se composant soit de traits parallèles soit de signes géométriques.'

*Figure 5*   Egyptian pipes

(a) *Zummarah* or *zummara* (modern Egyptian); note up-cut reeds from a specimen in Cairo Museum)

(b) *Mashourah* (ancient Egyptian); down-cut reeds (from specimen in Cairo Museum)

Coincident with these parallel pipes, though not necessarily in use in the same countries at the same time, were the divergent pipes. These were two separate pipes; they were not bound together but one was held in each hand. The end of each, containing the reed, was inserted in the mouth, the two pipes diverging from the lips of the player at an acute angle to each other.

It is generally thought, though one cannot be certain in all cases, that the divergent pipes were fitted with the double reed (the oboe type). Sachs says:[3] 'Geminated clarinets [i.e. double-pipes with single reed] always were closely tied together without forming an angle; geminated oboes [i.e. double-pipes with double-reeds] were divergent.'†

Obviously the divergent pipes, because they were held one in each hand and only one hand could finger each pipe, could not have more than four fingerholes in each. Many of them, including a number of those of ancient Egypt, had four fingerholes in the right-hand pipe and three in the left.

---

* A pair of *zummaras* found by Flinders Petrie at Illahun in 1890, reproduced in Baines, *Bagpipes*, p. 34, Fig. 12(a), shows one of the two reeds surviving. This is the same pattern as in the modern instrument; but this is listed by Baines as of Coptic period, about A.D. 800.

† On the other hand, Kathleen Schlesinger, writing of the Greek *aulos* in the *Encyclopaedia Britannica* (11th ed.), says there is no conclusive evidence as to whether the *aulos* was a single- or double-reed instrument.

*Figure 6* Divergent double-pipes
Shown issuing from the player's
mouth in the form of a V, the apex
being at the player's mouth (after
Engel, 1864, who calls it an Assyrian
double-pipe)

We cannot tell which came first: the parallel 'double-clarinet', possessing what in Scotland would be called drone-type (single) reeds, or the divergent 'double-oboe' with its chanter-type (double) reeds. What we do know is that the oldest set of pipes ever found, which will be described presently, were of the separate, divergent pattern.

## The drone

From the double-pipe in which both pipes, being stopped by the same finger, sounded the same note and doubled the melody, it was but a step that players should experiment in making one of the pipes sound a different note from the other, to make a rudimentary harmony with it. Some enterprising player hit upon the idea of stopping several of the holes in the second pipe with wax, thus leaving the fingers concerned free for playing the other pipe. The simplest procedure was to stop *all except one* of the fingerholes in the second pipe with wax in this way, which would result in a continuous drone upon the pitch of the hole thus left unstopped. We find this very process used in fact in antiquity. One such pipe with stopped fingerholes was found by the Earl of Carnarvon and Howard Carter in their excavations in Egypt in 1910. In a tomb at the mouth of the Der el Bahari valley, lying beside a mummy case, was found a wooden cylinder covered with leather, containing six musical reed-pipes. One of these had three of its five fingerholes 'intentionally blocked up with resinous material', to quote the account.[4] These are now in the Cairo Museum. Of this particular pipe with the stopped fingerholes, Hans Hickmann observes, 'Le fait que deux trous sont bouchés fait entrevoir l'emploi de cet instrument comme bourdon d'un double hautbois'.[5] The term *hautbois* here denotes that the pipe had a double reed, i.e. of the 'oboe type'.

In this particular specimen, two of the fingerholes of the second pipe were left unstopped by the resinous material. With both holes thus left uncovered by the fingers, a drone-note would result at the pitch of the upper of the two holes. This drone could of course be lowered to the pitch of the bottom hole by covering the higher of the two open holes with the finger, thus leaving only the bottom hole unstopped. It could be lowered still further, to the pitch of the full length of the pipe itself, by covering both holes. The drone-note could thus be varied by the fingers in the course of the music without difficulty.

One could also of course vary the drone by the cumbersome process of extracting the wax and changing the stopping of the holes. This seems sometimes actually to have been done, for pipes exist with a hook hanging on the end of a chain or ribbon for the purpose of extracting the wax stopping.[6]

The same process of stopping some of the holes with wax was also used, though more rarely, with the divergent 'double-oboe', just as it was with the 'double-clarinets'. When all three of the fingerholes in the second pipe of the divergent pipes were unstopped with wax and in use, however, this second pipe presumably had, or at least could have had, a more complicated part to play than a mere drone. What sort of part it was, we do not know.

Examples of this stopping of the fingerholes of a pipe with resin or wax to sound a drone are found at the present day, for example in the *s'ruti upanga* of south India; in the *toomeri* or *tubri*, the double hornpipe of the Deccan and in the bagpipe of Gwalior, central India; and in the *tulum* of Turkey.[7]

Yet a further development of the drone was to increase the length of the pipe of the drone so that it sounded *below* the pitch of the bottom note of the melody pipe. Among the mouth-blown parallel pipes we are discussing, the best-known which possesses this feature is the modern Egyptian instrument, the *arghul*. In this the pipe of the drone is extended by means of detachable extensions to twice the length of the melody-pipe, and therefore to the pitch of the octave below its bottom note. Here we see a parallel to the great drone of the Scottish Highland bagpipe. The *arghul* is clearly a descendant of the ancient Egyptian *zummara*.

### Nasal inhalation

The method of blowing all these reed-sounded pipes was to puff out the cheeks and use them as a kind of air reservoir – using the cheeks, in fact, as a precursor of the bag principle. Air was taken into the distended cheeks through the nose and blown out in a continuous stream through the mouth into the reed of the pipe. This enabled the player to play a continuous melody without breaks, as in the later bagpipe.

This same method, devised in antiquity, is still in use in many countries, in India, Morocco, Iraq, Turkestan and Albania and probably elsewhere. Anthony Baines in *Bagpipes* writes that the Near Eastern herdsman playing his double pipe in this way 'can be quite easily mistaken for a bagpiper, while the historical implication is that wind music no different in sound from the more primitive kinds of bagpiping may have been familiar in the countrysides of the Near East perhaps two thousand years before the bag idea is first recorded' (p. 35). Curt Sachs tells that today in teaching the playing of the native triple-pipe, the *launeddas*, in Sardinia, the method is imparted to the pupil by means of a straw and a bowl of water. The pupil dips the end of the straw into the water, producing a stream of bubbles. If the stream is broken, the teacher gives the pupil a box on the ear. Sachs adds that he was told that at Cairo 'Egyptian-oboe' players are still trained in this way.[8]

# Sumeria

### The silver pipes of Ur

In 1926-7, in the Royal Cemetery of the ancient Sumerian city of Ur, there was found in the course of archaeological excavations by Sir Leonard Woolley,[9] a pair of slender pipes made of silver, probably of the double-oboe, divergent variety.[10] Ur, which lies some 240 miles north of the head of the Persian Gulf and about 140 miles roughly south of Baghdad and Babylon, will be known from its biblical reference as Ur of the Chaldees,* the city from which the patriarch Abraham set out upon his journey to find the Promised Land, and to settle in it the people of the Children of Israel, as told in the Book of Genesis.† The Chaldees were, however, late-comers upon the Ur scene compared to the period of the silver pipes, and Sir Leonard Woolley observes that Abraham's journey came fifteen centuries later than the earliest period concerned in his archaeological finds in this particular part of the cemetery.[11] This was the Pre-dynastic sector, which Woolley dates at between 3500 and 3200 B.C.; and as the pipes were found in the oldest part of this sector of the cemetery, we can include them amongst the earliest of the objects found in the Ur excavations. Woolley does say, however, that 'so far as the actual dates were concerned [i.e. of his chronological schedule] I have of course recognised that there was room for differences of opinion'. Later estimates, notably those based upon the work of Albright,[12] have dated the Ur cemeteries from about 2800 B.C. onwards; and this is the approximate period assigned to the silver pipes by Curt Sachs,[13] though Henry Farmer would put them three centuries later, i.e. about 2500 B.C.[14]

---

* The Chaldean people first appeared in Babylonia during the Aramaean invasions (*c.* 1050–950 B.C.); *Encyclopaedia Britannica* (11th ed.).

† Archaeologists and biblical historians now believe that Abraham came from Haran in north-west Mesopotamia, and not from Ur; see W. Keller, *The Bible as History*, p. 68.

It is a near miracle that these pipes could have survived the five thousand years or so since their burial: they were found, not in a hollow burial-chamber of the Egyptian type in which even pipes of cane have been recovered in good and sometimes playable condition, but in an earthen grave. The finding of such an important landmark in the history of the pipes deserves to be told in the words of its discoverer. This is how Sir Leonard Woolley recounts it:[15]

> In P.G. 333* there were found what seemed to be bars of silver wantonly twisted and bent. These were scientifically cleaned in the University Museum† and proved to be of great interest. The apparently meaningless mass consists of silver tubing with a total length of 0.408 metres [roughly 16½ inches]; it is broken into five pieces, but may have consisted of two parts, each of approximate length of 0.250 metres [about 10¾ inches]. Along one side of each there are five (?) holes 0.006 m. in diameter placed at intervals of 0.025 m. [roughly 1 inch]; the last hole comes at 0.025 m. from the end of the tube; and the first at 0.14 m. from the unbroken end which may be the mouthpiece. At 0.07 m. from the [complete] end of one tube there is a double incised band, and a similar band on the second tube close to its broken end.
>
> There can be no question but that we have here the remains of one of the double pipes figured on Sumerian carvings, e.g. to take a late instance, on the great stela of the Nammu.[16] The slenderness of the pipe suggests that it was inspired by its original – the reed of the marshes.

From the drawing which accompanies the account, the double incised band referred to would almost certainly seem to be a stylization of the node or knot of the reed or cane of its prototype.

Whatever may be the date of the silver pipes of Ur, therefore, it can be assumed that they were almost certainly modelled on an earlier progenitor of reed or cane. Such a cane pipe could easily have been in use for quite a few centuries before it began to be fabricated in silver. The city of Ur existed, according to the archaeological evidence, before the Deluge. No musical pipes were found in the more ancient pre-Flood strata which Sir Leonard Woolley also uncovered and examined; but then pipes of cane could hardly have survived from that period of time in the drowned land beneath the Flood. It is sufficient for our purpose to say that the whole picture of the Ur discovery does without doubt point to the extreme antiquity of the reed-sounded pipe itself, from which, several thousand years later, the modern bagpipe was to evolve.

So much for the pipes. What of the player of them – the first piper

* P.G. 333 is the reference number of the grave. P.G. presumably stands for Pre-dynastic grave.
† The University Museum, Philadelphia, where the pipes are now kept.

known in the world's history, whose mortal remains were brought into
the light of day in this century after their interment of nearly five
thousand years? We can, strange to say, still learn or deduce a surprising
amount about him from the objects found in his grave. This was note-
worthy, to quote Woolley, for having 'a greater number of offerings than
found with any other clay-coffin burial'. To understand more fully the
significance of these offerings, we may read what Woolley has to say
about the custom and ritual of these ancient burials.[17]

The dead, whether wrapped in matting or placed inside a coffin,
were buried in their clothes. In all cases the fabric had perished,
and at the best some fragment has left its impression and perhaps
something of its substance on the oxidised surface of a copper
vessel or on the base of a clay jar – enough to show that various
styles of woollen and linen cloth were used. There is no evidence of
any winding sheet, but none is to be expected. On the body
therefore, we find such personal belongings as the man or woman
would have worn with the ordinary costume of the time. Pins to
fasten the dress, finger rings and bracelets, earrings and necklaces,
these went with the body to the grave; and although special finery
may have been used to do honour to the corpse, yet such things
are not what can be called distinctive grave-furniture. Similarly the
knife or dagger, the toilet case, the cylinder seal, the weapons of the
warrior, may have reference to the continuance of life in another world,
but taken by themselves they might also be nothing more than the
personal and private effects of the dead which are placed with him
not so much that he may need them as because they are peculiarly
his and nobody has any right to or wish for them. The more imper-
sonal offerings are those most informative for the beliefs of the age.
    In every undisturbed grave the dead man holds between his
hands, in front of his face, a cup or drinking vessel of metal, stone,
or clay; in practically every grave there is some kind of jar or
bottle, presumably for the replenishing of the cup, and in most if
not all, there is a saucer for solid food; of these essential articles
the first is always, and the others are generally placed inside the
coffin or the matting roll. Here quite definitely we have witness to
a belief in a future life; the food and drink are needed by the man
himself, and a dead man needs neither.
    These are the essential things, but they could be multiplied
indefinitely in the case of a wealthy person, and to them would be
added cooking-pots, arms, vessels of luxury, spare jewels, musical
instruments, and what not. Some of them might be put into the
coffin, but where the offerings were numerous there would be no
room for them, and other accommodation had to be provided.*

* I.e. outside the coffin but within the grave.

    . . . For the offerings, there was no ritual order; they were put as
the space allowed, often piled one on top of another, and of the
vessels many must have been empty, though others contained food
or drink; bird and animal bones are commonly found in the open
bowls or saucers, the jars frequently contain a sediment of a
vegetable character such as would come from a beer brewed from
barley, and whole wheat or barley grains and date-stones are also
found, the last sometimes in baskets. . . . All the offerings are
strictly utilitarian; food, utensils for cooking and eating, weapons,
games, they are what a man had used in this life and would wish
to continue using in the next; the belief is personal, but that is all
to which the graves bear witness; of deistic religion connected
with the dead there is astonishingly little sign.

To what extent does all this help to visualize our piper? From the
reference to the occasional inclusion of musical instruments among such
offerings, it might seem not impossible that the silver pipes did not belong
in life to the occupant of the grave, but were the last tribute of one of his
obviously many admirers. Admittedly that could be so, but as Woolley
tells us, such offerings are of the kind 'used by the deceased in this life, and
which he would wish to continue using in the next'. This would confirm
that the occupant of the grave was indeed himself a piper. Let us see
what else of interest his grave contained.

In addition to the pipes, and to the usual ritual vessels to be found in
every grave as described above, there were: a saw and two chisels, all of
copper; a needle and a small arrowhead of the same metal; a whetstone
for sharpening these tools, and some cockle-shells. Within the clay coffin,
or *larnax*, were found: a silver pin, of a type thought to be designed to
hold a feather in the head-dress; some silver rings, a small axe and a razor;
a number of very small beads of lapis-lazuli; one faceted date-shaped
bead of gold and a similar bead of cornelian, with a few beads of conoid
shape also of cornelian. No article of clothing survived.

From these personal belongings it does not seem too much to say that
something of the piper himself begins to emerge. Of the copper needle, the
official account notes that 'needles are rare, because they are out of place
in a grave'. This might indicate that it served some purpose connected
with the pipes themselves. Could the piper have used it perhaps for
removing wax from stopped-up fingerholes in one of the pipes (probably
the left-hand one) so as to change to pitch of the drone? – or, heated red-
hot, for boring through the nodes of a cane in the making of a work-a-day
cane pipe? Of the small copper arrowhead, it seems just as likely, in the
circumstances, that this may also have been used as a piper's tool rather
than as the tip of an offensive weapon to be shot from a bow. From its
shape as typified in the catalogue, it could well have been used as a reaming
tool (perhaps for boring holes in cane?). The axe, saw, chisels and whet-

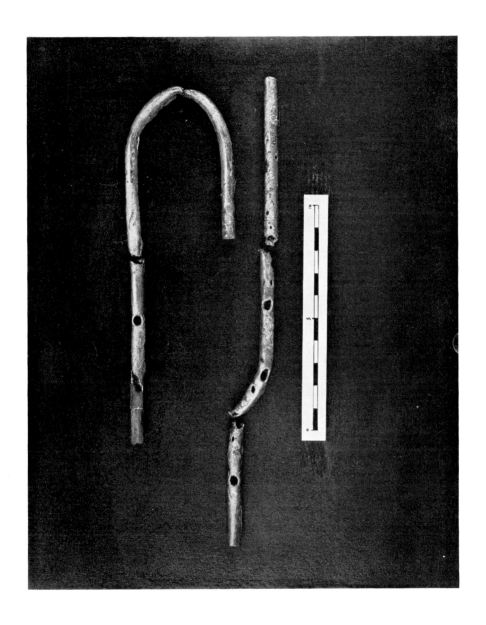

*Plate 1*  The silver pipes of Ur.
Discovered by Sir Leonard Woolley in 1926–7, in the Royal Cemetery at Ur in
Babylonia. Authoritative opinion dates these at c. 2800 B.C. (see p. 9).
University Museum, Pennsylvania, No. P.CBS. 17554.

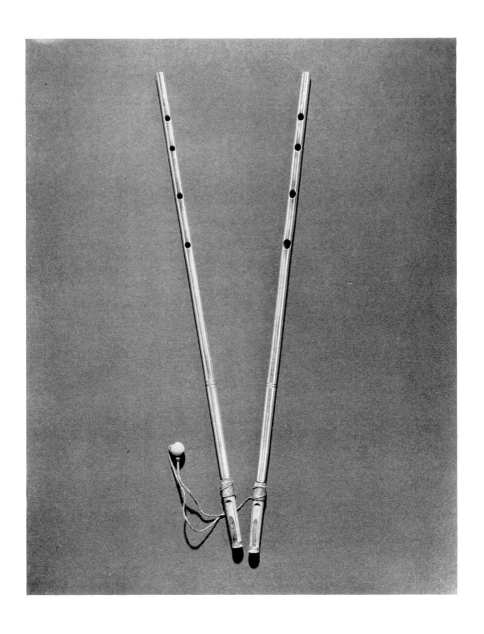

*Plate 2* A reconstruction of the silver pipes of Ur, fitted with 'single' reeds. It seems doubtful if both pipes would have four fingerholes. The pipes of antiquity more often have four holes in one pipe and three in the other.

stone *might* of course betoken that he was a wood-worker by trade, and so possibly an amateur at piping; but they could all also have been used in the making of cane pipes, which presumably a piper of that period would use on normal day-to-day occasions – for his daily practice, for the teaching of pupils, etc., when it would have been out of place to use his ceremonial 'full-dress' silver set. Could not the fact that his pipes were of silver in the age of cane betoken that he may well have been 'no ordinary piper'?

To come next to his articles of personal adornment: the small round beads of lapis-lazuli could have come from the edge of a tunic or similar garment, or from a girdle or belt.[18] Personal attendants on the king, such as the standard-bearer of Ur, wore a tight-fitting skull-cap closely covered with such small lapis-lazuli beads; the thought at once arises that he might have been the king's piper. But this is hardly likely, for the exacting Sumerian religion at this period required that at the death of a king or queen the royal musicians should die also and be buried in the same grave as their royal master or mistress, presumably that they might be at hand to enliven the royal life of the hereafter with their music. In any case, the catalogue describes the head-dress of the standard-bearer as consisting of *thousands* of these small beads, whereas in the case of the piper no such unusually large number is stated; also, the long faceted date-shaped beads of gold and cornelian found in the coffin indicate a different form of head-dress from that of the palace official. They were in fact the common head-dress ornaments of the man of substance and honourable position, and were strung together on a cord or silver chain to wear above a head-cloth, in the manner of the *brim* or *aqayl* of the modern Arab. The small conoid beads of cornelian were used as separators between the longer date-shaped beads. Of such a head ornament Woolley says: 'The richest variety of *brim* as worn by men at court consisted of three very large beads, one gold and two lapis, generally faceted date-shaped, with four cornelian rings between and one either side of the large beads.' Our piper had only two of these date-shaped beads, not three. A third might, of course, have escaped the eye of the searcher. In the official account, the illustrated plates of the book of the Ur discoveries, however, do show that the head-string *could* consist of only two such long beads instead of three. Perhaps whereas three long beads in the head-dress denoted incontrovertibly the upper-class Ur citizen, two might indicate (term beloved of our own Victorian age) 'upper-middle class'! The lower orders of Ur wore beads of ordinary stone, while the poor Sumerian wore no beads at all but just a plain beadless cord to keep his head-cloth in position. The indications would seem to be, from the sumptuary aspect, that the Piper of Ur was not without honour and importance in his own city – possibly by the very virtue of his musical attainments.

The most curious items remaining in the catalogue are the cockle-shells; for these were customarily used by the ladies of Ur as receptacles for their cosmetics. They used them in pairs – one for the container and one for the lid; and the remains of cosmetics, paint or powders now reduced to a hard paste, have actually been found in such shells – as the official account describes them. Such a paste prompts the idea that a pair of these cockleshells could have been useful to a piper for containing his tuning wax.

None of the fabric of the clothes in which the dead were buried survived in the graves of the Ur cemetery. From pictorial sources, however, notably that of the so-called Standard of Ur, and from mouldings or delineations in terra-cotta and carvings in stone, the style of Sumerian dress is known. For the lower part of the body, it consisted of a kilt. This was sometimes of a kind of tufted or tasselled material, either of the fleece of a sheep with the wool gathered into tassels, or having tufts of wool attached to a cloth base – it is not known which. The sheepskin may have been worn towards the inside, i.e. next to the skin, or have been shaved off with only a fringe of wool remaining and showing round the foot. Sometimes the lower edge of the garment was scalloped. The *Encyclopaedia Britannica* adds that the kilt had, in the centre, 'a cod-piece resembling a highlander's sporran'. As regards the upper part of the body, graves have been found in which there is a row of buttons lying in orderly fashion down the front of the body; this seems to indicate a shirt or tunic open at the neck and secured by buttons.[19] Soldiers wore a kind of plaid over their shoulders.

How may we sum up the picture of this the world's first known piper from these rather moving and pathetic 'bits and pieces' of his personal belongings which he took with him to the grave? I think we could say that by all the signs he was a man publicly admired and perhaps loved in life for his music. He was obviously deeply and widely mourned at his death, for his grave contained a greater number of tributes and 'offerings' than any other private burial in the cemetery – that is to say as distinct from the great and fantastic entombments of king or queen with their court, in the royal graves. The Piper of Ur would seem to be a man who had amassed at least a modest fortune, probably from his art; and who from his habiliments was likely to have been accepted at court. The weight of evidence seems to indicate that the playing of the pipes was his profession in life. As we shall see, pipers of the older world *could* amass a fortune from their piping – and could even have a monument erected in their honour as, later, in ancient Greece they erected a statue to Pronomus the Theban piper; and as in modern times they erected a cairn to the MacCrimmons – though none of the MacCrimmons ever made a fortune!

Today the personal possessions of the Piper of Ur are widely scattered. His pipes are in Philadelphia. His beads are in Baghdad. London has his limestone burial bowl. The whereabouts of his tools and his whetstone, his needle and his copper arrowhead are not thought important enough to gain an entry in the catalogue of the official account.

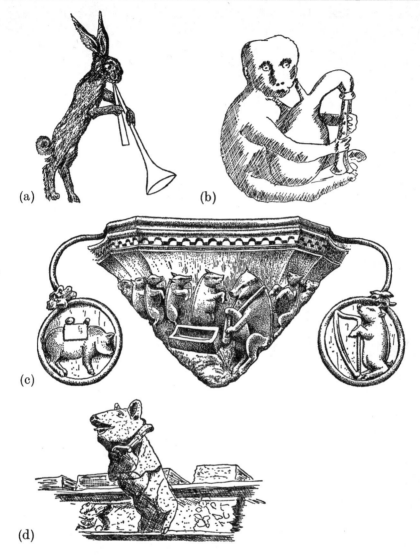

*Figure 7*   Animals playing bagpipes

(a) Hare playing the divergent
    double-pipes of unequal length;
    from A Collection of Prayers.
    Harleian MSS No. 6563 (from
    Dalyell, Plate XXI)

(b) Monkey playing droneless bag-
    pipe ('*chorus*') with double
    chanter. Stone-carving at St
    John's Church, Cirencester (from
    Carter's Specimens)

(c) Wood carving on misericord, of
    pig playing the single-drone
    bagpipe to other pigs dancing;
    choir-stalls, Beverley Minster
    (drawn from photograph)

(d) Pig bagpiper in Melrose Abbey;
    Stone carving; drawn from
    photograph by School of Scottish
    Studies, Edinburgh University.

We do not know the name of the Piper of Ur, the first piper ever discovered, who was born about five thousand years ago. It may lift the heart of the Scot to know that he wore the kilt, with something resembling the sporran, and a plaid when he went into battle; and that, to complete the picture, he sported a feather in his bonnet! (*Ur Excavations*, p. 238.)

### The Ur seal

It has already been assumed as the natural order of things that the single pipe came before the double. Although the earliest actual specimens of the musical pipe ever to be discovered are the silver (double) pipes of Ur, pictorial representations also recovered at Ur show that the single pipe was known and almost certainly in use also by the Sumerians.

According to F. W. Galpin in *The Music of the Sumerians*, Plate 2, such a representation is seen specifically on an engraved seal of lapis lazuli recovered from one of the Dynastic tombs in the cemetery of Ur. The picture on the seal shows a monkey seated under a tree, playing a single pipe to a group of other animals. It thus forms the earliest example of a pictorial fantasy running right through the history of musical instruments, the fantasy of depicting them as being played by animals. For some strange reason, the bagpipe, and its predecessor, the mouth-blown reed-pipe, seem to be the favourite instruments for such zoomorphic conceits. Here, at Ur, we see it in 2800 B.C. or thereabouts.

The real importance for pipe history of the picture on the Ur seal is that it shows the monkey playing with both hands placed on the single pipe; for here we see, in the two forms of the pipe at this very early stage, both (a) the single chanter, fingered with the fingers of both hands, and (b) the two chanters of the divergent pipes, each chanter fingered by the fingers of one hand. This is a fundamental division of types which has persisted right through the five thousand years or so from the days of Ur of the Sumerians to the present day.

F. W. Galpin in *The Music of the Sumerians* regards the single pipe pictured on the seal as slightly earlier in date than the double silver pipes. He tells us that the name of the Sumerian single pipe appears to have been the *na* (or in the later Akkadian culture, the *nabu*). The first of these two names still appears in the Middle Eastern *nay*. From Sumerian records, it appears that the single pipe was sometimes made of copper.

## Egypt: the Lady Maket Pipes

The Piper of Ur remains anonymous. To find the first piper whose name is known, we must go to Illahun in Egypt, where in 1889–90 a set of divergent double-pipes was found beside their owner in a mummy case by Sir

William Flinders Petrie. He describes the find in his book *Ten Years Digging in Egypt*.

> The main prize [i.e. among the finds at Illahun] was a family tomb, probably of the end of the nineteenth or early twentieth dynasty . . . More than a dozen coffins were piled in it, each containing several bodies, all the wrappings of which were reduced to black sooty dust . . . In the richest coffin, the only one containing a name, that of *The Lady Maket*, were two musical reeds [i.e. reed-pipes] carefully slipped into a larger reed for protection; the scale shown by their holes is the major scale.*

This is all he says in this particular account about this important discovery, and for further information we must go to an article on the Pipes in the *Musical Times* of October 1890 by T. Lea Southgate, following their exhibition in London. Southgate writes:

> The lady's name (Maket) was inscribed on her gold scarab brooch, also on a small silver scarab set in a ring, and on another ring, all found within her coffin. It also contained her pipes in their case. The pipes were made out of some thin cane or hollow water reed. One, $17\frac{1}{2}$ inches long, had four finger holes, and the other, of $17\frac{1}{8}$ inches long, had three. The outside measurement is but a quarter of an inch. The fingerholes are not rounded but oval in form and become progressively smaller from the top to the bottom of the pipes. D. J. Blaikley fitted the pipes with single reeds, and after their silence of three thousand years, 'Lady Maket's pipes were played again.'

Miss Kathleen Schlesinger[20] says that Blaikley tried both modern oboe reeds and the stiff *arghul* type of (single up-cut) beating reed. She herself, with a modern replica of the Lady Maket Pipes specially made for her own extensive researches in the subject, says that she got an eight-foot C (i.e. the note C two octaves below middle C) with a straw reed.

Perhaps the most interesting fact that emerges from these accounts is that the first piper in the world's history whose name is known to us was a woman!

The date of the Lady Maket Pipes, as estimated by Flinders Petrie, would seem to be somewhere between 1580 and 1160 B.C., reckoned by the sometimes varying chronology of the dynasties by the Egyptologists. Even the Lady Maket was not the first woman piper, but only the first whose name is known to us. The mummy of a nameless woman, of the period of the late Middle Kingdom, was found by Lord Carnarvon and Howard Carter (the team who later found the famous Tutenkhamun

---

* Petrie gives no musical authority for his statement on the scale, but Miss Kathleen Schlesinger, in *The Greek Aulos*, would appear to confirm it as correct from her experiments with exact models of the twin Lady Maket Pipes.

Tomb) in a rock-hewn tomb of Middle Kingdom period in the necropolis
at Birabi, Egypt, in 1910–11. The lady was the possessor of a whole
caseful of reed-pipes found beside her in the mummy case. These are
described in the account by the two archaeologists,* as: 'Mummy of a
woman covered with a mat with a long pile. On her right side, a wooden
cylinder covered with leather and containing six musical reeds.'

The period allotted to these pipes by the authors of this account, i.e. of
the late Middle Kingdom, would appear by this writer's computation to
be between 2160 and 1580 B.C., say perhaps about 1880 B.C., which would
be about three centuries earlier than the Lady Maket Pipes.

As we may see from this and later chapters, the girl piper of today,
periodically derided by some of our Scottish diehards, is no new
phenomenon!

## The last millennium B.C.

By the beginning of and during the last thousand years before Christ, the
double-chanter pipes were known and played all over the old world of
the Near and Middle East. Of the two varieties, namely the parallel and
the divergent pipes, the latter seem to have been by far the most numerous, and to have eclipsed in popularity the closely bound double chanters
of ancient Egypt. These divergent pipes were similar to the Sumerian
pipes we have been discussing; one of the two pipes generally had three
fingerholes and the other four.

None of the music for these ancient pipes has survived in notation. We
can only surmise from the instruments themselves and from reconstruc-
tions of them what form it took. With the parallel pipes this is easy; the
pipes with the open fingerholes sounded the melody, and the other pipe,
with the holes stopped up with wax, or reduced in number to one in the
initial construction of them, sounded a drone to accompany it. With the
divergent pipes it is not so easy to guess at their form of music. There are
three apparent possibilities: (a) they could have been played in unison;
(b) one of the pipes could have been used as a drone to the melody on the
other as with the parallel pipes; (c) they could have played in two musical
parts. On the face of it, the last seems the most likely. One does not need
three fingerholes (giving a minimum scale of four notes, with many more
notes possible by overblowing) in order to sound a drone, even a variable

---

* Lord Carnarvon and Howard Carter, *Five Years' Exploration at Thebes*. The
measurements of the pipes are: (a) 26·5 cm long 'with four notes'; (b) 36·5 cm
long with three notes; (c) 30·5 cm with two notes; (d) 28 cm with four notes on
one side (three were intentionally blocked up with resinous material and on the
other side there was a hole or note); (e) 25 cm with five notes (a crack mended
with resinous material); (f) 23·15 cm long, with five notes. The reeds average
12 mm in thickness. 'Notes' here means fingerholes as described in the Cairo
Museum Catalogue.

drone; while as to playing the two pipes in unison, this would not be easy because one pipe usually had three fingerholes and the other four, and because the pipes often differed in length.*

From Ur in Sumeria, the divergent double-chanter pipes can be traced under different names right up through Mesopotamia and Arabia to the eastern Mediterranean, to the countries of Israel and Phoenicia; to Troy and sacred Mount Ida and the Hellespont; and finally to those lands and islands near the Hellespont which later were to become the eastern empire of Greece.

The Sumerians seem to have had two different forms of the instrument; the *sem* and the *malilu*. Probably they did not differ so much in essentials as in the material of which they were made. Galpin[21] quotes the ancient Sumerian hymn *ishtar* which mentions a *malilu* made of lapis-lazuli and pearl. The *sem* was made of silver, copper or bronze.[22] Probably however more work-a-day materials such as cane or reed may also have been used.

On the borders of Sumeria were the Akkadians, who had been driven out by them somewhere about the year 4000 B.C. (just about the time of the Flood). The Akkadians had their own names for their pipes, which were also of the divergent type. There was the *halhallatu* and the *sinnitu*.†They also had the *imbubu*, a variety which we find also in Syria as the *abuba* where it was played in the temples by Syrian girls. We shall meet these girls later in Rome as the *ambubaiae*.

The Book of Samuel, in its account of Nebuchadnezzar's orchestra at Babylon during the Captivity, gives us, in its original Aramaic text, what is almost certainly the Babylonian name for the divergent pipes, namely, the *masroqita*.

The country of Elam with its capital of Susa, lying to the east of

* We may reasonably infer that something of the general technique and style of music of the ancient divergent double-pipes may survive in the *launeddas*, the folk instrument of Sardinia. These consist of three pipes (a triple-pipe); one, longer than the others, is a drone, and the other two are chanters, with four fingerholes in each. (The word *launeddas* is the plural, referring to the three pipes of the instrument, and it cannot be used in the singular.)

A bronze figurine of a player of the *launeddas* is to be seen in the Museo Archaeologico di Cagliari in Sardinia; its date has been estimated variously from 900 to 300 B.C. The instrument is said to have been in continuous existence since then. It resembles the ancient divergent pipes, but with the addition of a drone (*tumbu*), which is not variable in pitch. Other resemblances to the ancient double-pipes are that wax is used to tune the pipes (though not to stop one of the pipes down to a drone), and that the continuous unbroken sound is maintained by means of nasal inhalation. The *launeddas* are thought to descend directly from the double-pipes of antiquity, with an added drone.

The music of the two chanters, sounding above the drone, is almost always in two parts, largely of an independent contrapuntal character. See A. F. W. Bentzon, *The Launeddas, a Sardinian Folk Music Instrument*.

† Galpin (*The Music of the Sumerians*, p. 35) suggests, however, that the *sinnitu* may have been a two-stringed lute.

Babylonia, had the double-chanter pipes also, as is known from a carved stone slab of 688–626 B.C. now in the British Museum, of the royal Elamite orchestra of twelve players, one of whom is playing the divergent pipes.

In Asia Minor, at the great festival of Adonis, the wailing of reed-pipes was an essential part of the ritual. Here the god was known as *Abobas*, a name which certainly suggests the pipe-name *imbubu*, mentioned above. In Phoenicia, the god was known as *Gringas*, a name which the Greek writer and musicologist Athenaeus (*c.* A.D. 200), quoting Xenophon and Aristoxenus, gives also to the reed-pipe used at the ceremonies.

Of the Phoenicians and the double-pipes, the Greek geographer Strabo makes the statement that it was soon after the Trojan War and the fall of Troy (? 1194 B.C.) that the Phoenicians began to trade and colonize beyond the Pillars of Hercules, i.e. the Straits of Gibraltar. One of the purposes of their voyages is said to have been to trade in tin with the *Cassiterides*, the tin islands, i.e. the Isles of Scilly off the coast of Cornwall in Britain. If Strabo's account is true (though it may well not be, for he came late on the scene, being born *c.* 64 B.C.), this makes it possible that Phoenician sailors, who doubtless included musicians, could have played the Phoenician double-pipes in the Scilly Isles, and perhaps in Cornwall too, as early as the dawn of the first millennium B.C. This would give the inhabitants there a preview of them a thousand years before they were brought to Britain in substantial numbers by the pipers of the Roman armies. But perhaps this is being over-credulous.

Curt Sachs[23] thinks that it was from the Phoenicians that the Israelites got their double-pipes, which were known in Hebrew as the *halil*, a word apparently having the meaning of being pierced or bored out. (We find an obvious cognate of it in the name *halhallatu* of the Sumerians.) Although the Israelites regarded the Phoenicians as Philistines, it was with the King of Tyre in Phoenicia that King Solomon made a contract at the building of the First Temple to employ Phoenician craftsmen in both wood and metal for the work. Hiram, a master-craftsman of Tyre, was employed by Solomon to make the metalwork of the sanctuary!

In Egypt, pipe history has some important differences. The indigenous form was the parallel double-pipe, which Curt Sachs has said he discerned upon a relief (now in the Cairo Museum) of as early as 2700 B.C., in the Fourth Dynasty.[24] The name of the Egyptian instrument seems to have been the *ma'*, *ma.t* or *met*. A thousand years later, the ancient parallel pipes were to be supplanted by the ubiquitous divergent pipes.* It is thought that they were introduced by invading armies, or as a hopeful tribute to the conqueror in Egypt's victorious wars from the defeated kings, in the form of musicians, dancing girls, etc. Possibly the nomadic Hyksos, early invaders of Egypt, brought the divergent pipes with them.

---

* The ancient parallel pipes does survive as a folk instrument in the modern Egyptian *zumarra*, and in its counterpart with the long drone-pipe, the *arghul*.

It is interesting to observe that the Jewish historian Josephus equates the Hyksos with the Israelites in Egypt, at the time of Moses and Aaron.*

Early writers have been more than generous with stories of the ancient pipes. Herodotus (born 490–480 B.C.), for example, has a score of anecdotes about the pipes and pipers: for instance, about Alyattes (610 B.C.), who in his war against the Milesians, marched to the music of pipes and harps; about the piper recounted by Cyrus who played to the fish in the sea in the hope of piping them ashore; about pipers who led the processions at the festivals of Dionysus and Artemis; about the flayed skin of Marsyas that hung on his tree at Celaenae as the result of his ill-fated piping in competition with Apollo, his empty skin itself presaging in a sort of way the bagpipe yet to be discovered (see pp. 28–9). Xenophon, too, gives us a graphic description of the dancing competitions of Thracians, Ænians and Magnesians in full armour to the music of the pipes, at Paphlagonia in Asia Minor. All help to fill in the picture.

In taking leave of the divergent pipes of ancient Babylonia and Mesopotamia with their different names, we have to admit that knowledge of some of these instruments is still vague. One at least of the instruments named above may have been an end-flute or a wind instrument of the whistle or recorder type, like that most ancient discovery of all, the little three-holed bone whistle of Tepe Gawra; but we can be certain that whatever their names, it was the divergent reed-pipes that were supreme in the ancient world. This was the form of the pipes which was to spread to the Greek empire and colonies in Asia Minor; and from there to Greece itself, where it was to enter upon its golden age.

## Greece

εἷς ἄνεμος, δύο νῆες, ἐρέττουσι δέκα ναῦται
εἷς δὲ κυβερνήτης ἀμφοτέρας ἐλάει.
    (heis anemos, duo nees, erettousi deka nautai;
heis de kubernētes amphoteras elaei.)

One wind, two ships, ten sailors rowing; and one steersman directs both.[25] [Description of the Grecian double-pipes from *Anthologia Palatina*, XIV. 14.]

### The vocabulary

*Aulos*, plural *auloi* (αὐλός, αὐλοί)    The reed-sounded mouth-blown

* Josephus Apion, 1. 14 (Loeb ed., p. 195n); 'Hyksos', *Encyclopaedia Britannica* (14th ed.). This is not now accepted. Modern opinion identifies the Hyksos as semitic invaders and conquerors of Egypt in 1730 B.C. It is thought to have been the Hyksos who raised Joseph of the Old Testament to his administrative post in Egypt. See W. Keller, *The Bible as History*, p. 101.

double-pipes of ancient Greece. These have been almost invariably
mistranslated in English editions of the Greek classics as 'flutes' or
alternatively as the 'double-flute(s)'. Being nearly always played as a
pair, the singular form *aulos* is almost always used to denote the two
pipes, together considered as one musical instrument.

*Auloi elymoi* (αὐλοὶ ἔλυμοι)   A characteristic type of *auloi* consisting of
two pipes of unequal length. These were said to be of Phrygian origin
and were known as 'the Phrygian pipes'. Pipes of equal length were also
used, but there seems to have been no specific Greek term for them.
The Romans called them *tibiae sarranae*. The latter type were said to
have been introduced from Lydia and from Phoenicia and were known
as the Lydian or Phoenician pipes.

*Monaulos* (μόναυλος)   A single pipe; also used, but more rarely
mentioned by the Greek writers than the double-pipes.

*Auletes* (αὐλητής)   A player of the *aulos* – in common English or Scots
parlance, a piper. The word has similarly been almost consistently
mistranslated as 'flute-player'. The pipes of both Greece and Rome
seem to have been played as often by women as men. The usual
English term for the woman piper would be 'girl-piper'. This is usually
mistranslated in the classics (*vide* the comedies of Aristophanes) as
'flute-girl'.

*Kalamos* (κάλαμος)   The water-reed or cane from which the earlier and
simpler *auloi* were made. The cane of the *kalamos* was also used for the
reed, in distinction to the straw reeds of the Egyptians and probably
the Babylonians, Israelites, etc. This is an important point in the
development of the sound-producing element of the pipes, as the change
from straw reed to cane reed must have increased the loudness and
penetrating power of the instrument.

*Glossa* or *glotta* (γλῶσσα or γλῶττά)   Thought to be the word for the
tongue of the reed of the pipes, possibly of the single beating reed.
(Cf. *zeugos*, below.)

*Glottis* (γλωττίς)   The socket or narrow passage in the end of the pipe
into which the reed was fixed.

*Holmos* (ὅλμος)   A kind of hollow pear-shaped bulb of wood which
could be fitted into the top end of the pipe; it lengthened the pipe, thus
lowering the pitch. A second and third bulb could be fitted into the first,
thus adding still further to the length and to the depth of pitch of the
pipe.

*Phorbeia* (φορβειά)   A band of leather or other material which passed
across the mouth and round the cheeks and was fastened at the back
of the head. It was pierced at the front with two holes to allow the
mouthpieces of the two pipes to pass through into the mouth of the
piper. Its exact function is not yet clear (see pp. 29–30).

*Plagiaulos* (πλαγίαυλος)   An *aulos* of which the reed is inserted in a hole in the side of the pipe. The pipe, a single one, was held transversely across the face of the player like a flute. It may have been depictions of this instrument on sarcophagi etc. which gave rise to the ubiquitous and sweeping mistranslation of *aulos* as a flute, and of the *auletai* as *flute players*. It was said to have been a Lydian invention.[26] The British Museum has a statue of Midas of Phrygia playing the *plagiaulos*.

*Zeugos* (ζεῦγος)   The mouthpiece of the *aulos* – possibly containing a double reed, as the word *zeugos* means a pair of like things, which could perhaps refer to the two leaves of the double reed (cf. *zeugites*, p. 204 n = tongue of the musical reed.

### The *aulos*

The literature of both ancient Greece and Rome has many allusions to pipes and pipers. The music of the pipes was one of the facets of everyday life in both. This may surprise many people, even those who have been brought up on the classics. The reason for such ignorance is rather curious; it is that, until very recent years, practically every translator of the Latin and Greek classics into English has misleadingly translated the Greek word *aulos* (plural *auloi*) and its Latin equivalent *tibia* (plural *tibiae*), as *flutes*. Both in fact mean musical pipes sounded by a reed.\* For countless generations of classical scholars this has given a completely false picture.

Nowhere is this more glaringly apparent than in translations of descriptions by Thucydides, Aristotle and others, of the use of the pipes by the Spartans in battle. The image of these tough troops advancing to the attack to the 'tootle' of the flute is very different from that of going in to the 'skirl'† of the pipes – at least to the Scottish reader.

A possible reason for this almost unvarying literary convention, which will be found in edition after edition of the translations of the Greek and Latin writers, is the failure of the Greeks and Romans themselves to provide a name which would clearly differentiate between an instrument played by a reed, and one blown in the manner of a flute.

The true flute, held transversely and cross-blown, did not appear in Grecian or Roman art until very late, and the presumption is that it did not exist in the more ancient days of these cultures. Indeed, Curt Sachs says that while in pre-Christian times Greek and Roman artists have depicted many 'oboes' (see p. 141) they have left no trace of a flute.[27] He dates the first flute depicted in Graeco-Roman antiquity at A.D. 169,

---

\* Curt Sachs amusingly recalls (1940, p. 138) that at school, whenever in the Greek class the word *aulos* occurred, his old teacher never failed to observe that 'the sensitive ears of his beloved Greek heroes [were] so obviously superior to the Wagner-glutted ears of modern college boys [that] a flute, the weakest of instruments, sufficed to inflame their ecstasy and desire for combat'!

† 'Skirl' in pipers' parlance really means a rough, badly produced note!

though he immediately qualifies this with the statement that 'this flute has now been ante-dated by an Etruscan flute' and allots to it the period of the second century B.C.[28]

Perhaps the most inexcusable example of such mistranslation of the word *aulos* as flute, because it is so recent and yet ignores modern musicological knowledge, and also because it occurs in such an important work, is to be seen in the *New English Bible* (New Testament). According to the publication announcement, this was 'translated afresh from the Hebrew and Greek texts and founded on all the resources of modern scholarship'. The New Testament was published in 1961, and appeared afresh in a second edition for the complete *New English Bible* in 1970, for which, to quote the announcement again, 'the translators have renewed their work, and taken account of suggestions and criticisms'. Yet we find the account of the raising of the daughter of Jairus (Matt. 9:18) as follows: 'When Jesus arrived at the president's house and saw *the flute-players* [my italics] and the general commotion, he said, "Be off! The girl is not dead; she is asleep".' The original Greek has αὐλητάς (auletas) i.e. players of the reed-sounded *aulos*, and therefore pipers, not flute-players. The Jerusalem Bible does no better; again the pipers are 'flute-players'. The passage is interesting as showing (allowing for the fumbled translations) that Jesus of Nazareth must have known the sound of the pipes.

Most of the reed-sounded pipes of the ancient world named in the previous section shared this same ambiguity in their nomenclature: there was nothing in their names to indicate that they *were* reed-pipes and not for instance end-blown flutes – the *sem* of the Sumerians, the Assyrian *imbubu*, the Syrian *abub*, and others. All seem to refer to the pipe considered as a tube rather than to the means of sounding it. The Roman name *tibia*, also meaning a shin-bone, denoted the Roman reed-pipes, thus continuing the ambiguity. Indeed the only nations which had names that specified whether a pipe was reed-sounded or flute-blown were the Arabs and Persians of a later date.[29]

Curiously, the same ambiguity persists to the present day in our own naming. The Gaelic word *feadan*, used for the chanter of the Highland bagpipe and in modern convention for the practice-chanter, basically means any pipe-like or funnel-shaped conformation, natural or artificial, through which the wind is free to blow: for instance a narrow gully in the hills, an open drain below a barn or, finally, the chanter itself. Our own familiar term 'the pipes' indeed, when one comes to think of it, has the same ambiguity, and it is only by familiarity and convention that we understand the term as meaning the (bag-blown) reed-pipes.

When we give the Greek *aulos* and Latin *tibia* their proper meaning of *reed-sounded* pipes, we find the whole perspective of the musical scene changes. The cold austere sexless tones of the flute give way to the warm and exciting sound of the pipes. We find it at once possible to identify ourselves with both the sound and the scene. In a subtle way both come into sharper focus and are brought nearer to us across the millennia; and we can begin to see the history of the pipes as one continuous story that stretches across the well-nigh incredible space of nearly five thousand years, from the pipes of Ur to the sound of our own Highland pipes of the present day.

The Greeks had every chance to acquire the reed-pipe early, from Egypt and from Asia Minor. The Early Bronze Age Minoan and Mycenean civilizations, the former stretching back to perhaps 2500 B.C. and the latter to about 1600 B.C., included traders within the Mediterranean and the Black Sea. The products of Crete and the Peloponnese had found their way to Egypt and Asia Minor bringing with them an exchange of culture. These two ancient civilizations came to an abrupt end in 1200 B.C., probably as the result of invasion, and were followed by a historically blank period which archaeology finds it hard to pierce. During this period of several centuries the sea-trade of the former Minoan and Mycenean lands, later to become Greece, seems to have languished and to have given place to the thrusting enterprise of the Phoenicians, who traded both in Grecian seas and much farther afield, as we have seen. In the eighth century B.C., however, Grecian trade began to revive, and in the two succeeding centuries to develop rapidly. From the sixth century B.C. onwards, communication with Egypt grew as Greek mercenaries were employed in large numbers by the Saite kings, and later by Amasis (569–525 B.C.). Doubtless all this brought greater knowledge of Egyptian arts, including their music and instruments.

With the later conquest of Egypt in the fourth century B.C. by Alexander the Great, Egypt came under Greek sway. On the break-up of Alexander's empire, the Macedonian Ptolemy came to the throne of Egypt. The fact is relevant to our subject, for the twelfth king of the Ptolemy dynasty was popularly known as Ptolemy Auletes, which means Ptolemy the Piper, from his liking and playing of the pipes.* By the time of Ptolemy the Piper, however, both Egypt and Greece had passed under the Roman power, and the subject belongs more properly to that period. We must therefore retrace our steps a little.

The ancient Bronze Age Minoan and Mycenean civilizations gave place in due course to the Homeric Age; and this brings us to the first mention of the pipes in Greek literature, namely in the *Iliad* of Homer. Estimates of Homer's date vary from 1159 B.C. (by Philostratus) to 685 B.C. (by Theopompus); which latter date would seem too late in the light of further knowledge. The *Oxford Classical Dictionary* gives his date at before 700 B.C.

---

\* Charles Burney, *A General History of Music*, vol. 1, p. 229, quotes Strabo as saying of Ptolemy Auletes: 'This prince submitted to wear the robe, the buskin, the crown, and even the bandage and veil of a *Tibicen* [piper]'; and adds, 'as may be seen on a beautiful Amethyst in the King of France's possession of inestimable value, which is supposed to have been engraved by command of this prince'.

Here then, in Homer's *Iliad*, we have the first written description of the use of the pipes whether in peace and war, early in the first millennium B.C. It reads as follows: 'When he [Agamemnon] glanced out across the Trojan plain, he was confounded by the innumerable fires burning in front of Ilium, by the music of the flutes and reed-pipes,* and the voices of the troops.'

Though Troy was not itself Phrygian, Homer relates that the Phrygians were allies of the Trojans. Phrygia was the great cradle of the art of piping in classical times; and the Phrygian pipes, the *tibiae impares*, were to become one of the most distinctive and popular of the various types of pipes later to be heard in Rome.

Curiously enough, though Homer mentions the pipes in the *Iliad*, he does not do so in the *Odyssey*. In the latter work, the music, to which there is frequent allusion in Homer's pages, is entirely described as for voice and lyre. This fact, negative though it is, may not be without significance; for the *personae* of the *Odyssey*, gods and humans alike, may be said to be mostly either Greek, or cast in the Grecian mould, in distinction to the Trojans, Phrygians, Carians and other peoples who share the pages of the *Iliad*. This could perhaps mean that, though the pipes were to be heard at Troy, they were not yet used by the Greeks themselves. The traditional date for the fall of Troy is 1184 B.C.† Greek tradition itself held that the reed-pipes had come to them from their Asiatic neighbours.[30]

There was probably little difference between the early forms of the Greek *aulos* and the pipes of the neighbouring countries from which they almost certainly inherited it. They were, to begin with, made from a water-reed as were the Egyptian pipes. Vase decoration of about 600 B.C. onwards shows that the Greek pipes had the same three and four fingerholes as the double-pipes of further antiquity. Throughout the centuries of classical Greece, however, various improvements were introduced. Materials other than the water-reed of the marshes came to be used for the pipes themselves. The Elgin Collection at the British Museum possesses a pair of Greek *auloi* made of sycamore (see p. 206). Kathleen Schlesinger mentions a pair of *auloi-elymoi*‡ made of boxwood and tipped with horn.

The number of fingerholes in the *aulos* was increased progressively to as many as eleven. Because no more than four holes could be fingered by each hand, the extra holes above that number had a device by which they could be covered by movable rings, a more sophisticated equivalent of the ancient piper's stopping of the fingerholes with wax. These rings,

---

* E. V. Rieu, *The Iliad*, ch. 10. Rieu places Homer in the tenth century B.C.; ibid., p. xv.

† Sir W. Smith, 'Troy', *A Smaller Classical Dictionary*. His date is not far different from the date given in *Encyclopaedia Britannica* (14th ed.).

‡ I.e. *auloi* of unequal length, probably the Phrygian type; K. Schlesinger, *The Greek Aulos*, and *Encyclopaedia Britannica*, 11th ed., 'Bagpipes'.

the forerunners of the keys of the wind instrument of today, enabled the same set of pipes to be played in different keys or modes. Two such *auloi* with movable rings are in the British Museum. It is a notable fact that, although vase decoration (which forms a kind of pictorial commentary of its era from 600 B.C. onwards) shows no more than the three or four holes in the two pipes, no actual pipes, either Greek or Roman, have as yet been found with as few as four holes, though quite a number of pipes have been recovered. Vase decoration does show that before the invention of the movable rings it was customary to carry several sets of pipes for the various modes, in a kind of quiver hung over the shoulder by a cord.

The same vase decorations show us how the pipes were held and how the fingers were placed. Sometimes the pipes are shown held horizontally in front of the player, sometimes in a drooping position; sometimes they are held close together in a nearly parallel position so that it becomes easy to mistake them for the parallel pipes (but the Greeks used only the divergent pipes) or widely splayed apart. The Greek writer Aristoxenus of Tarentum, who flourished about 318 B.C., implies that the relative position of the two pipes was changed as a means of raising and lowering the pitch. On the face of it this seems absurd and the action smacks of showmanship rather than technique, but Kathleen Schlesinger, in *The Greek Aulos*, suggests the explanation that by splaying or slewing the pipes outwards as he played, the player shortened the effective playing length of the reed in his mouth and by so doing, raised the pitch from the first to the second harmonic, i.e. a fifth higher. Sachs observes[31] that the bore of these early pipes was narrow enough to exclude the production of the fundamental tone, so that overblowing meant a jump of only a fifth,* as might also this shortening of the tongue of the reed. Another method of altering the pitch or key of the pipe was by adding a kind of bulb-like piece to the end of it to lengthen the pipe. These bulbs surrounded the stalk of the straw reed (one well-known vase illustration actually shows the player in the act of changing bulbs). Whatever the methods of tuning and fingering employed, it is obvious that the technique of the Greek pipes was intricate and sophisticated.

Even more interesting is the glimpse we get for the first time from Greek literature of the method of blowing by nasal inhalation. A detailed description of it comes to us from a later Latin writer, Aulus Gellius, who lived about A.D. 123–65. He is writing about Alcibiades, the Greek states-man and commander-in-chief of all the Athenian sea and land forces in 407 B.C., and says:[32]

> Alcibiades the Athenian, in his boyhood, was being trained in the liberal arts and sciences at the home of his uncle Pericles; and Pericles had ordered Antigenides, a player on the pipes, to be sent for to teach the boy to play on that instrument. But when the

---

* I.e. from the second to the third note of the harmonic series.

pipes were handed to him, and he had put them to his lips and
blown, disgusted at the ugly distortion of his face, he broke them
in two and threw them away. When this matter was noised abroad,
by the universal consent of the Athenians of that time the art of
playing the pipes was given up. This story is told in the twenty-
ninth book of the Commentary of Pamphilas.

It seems to have been only by the genteel amateur that the playing of
the pipes, and of other musical instruments such as the lyre and the
kithara, came, in the end, to be looked upon as an occupation beneath his
dignity. Isobel Henderson, in the *New Oxford History of Music* (vol. 1,
p. 340), observes that the fall of Athens in 404 B.C. marks the point at
which began 'a divorce between the citizen [i.e. the amateur] and the
professional [musician], between theory and practice, *from which Europe
still suffers*'. These last five words, which I have italicized, are a bold
assertion – but they may well be right!*

This distortion of the face by the puffing out of the cheeks in playing
the ancient double-pipes forms the theme of one of the most familiar of
the ancient Greek myths, that of Apollo and Marsyas. The tale is almost
too well known to need retelling, were it not that it is the earliest folktale
of the musical pipes. The story of the Greek pipes would be incomplete
without it.

The tale runs that the goddess Pallas Athena made for herself a double
reed-pipe (and note that the myth particularly specifies a *double*-pipe)[33]
out of a river reed – or as some would have it, the bones of a stag. She
found that she could produce the most beautiful sounds from the pipes.
Most of her fellow deities were utterly charmed with her music; but
Aphrodite and Hera for some strange reason both started to laugh.
Although they tried to hide their laughter behind their hands, Athena
noticed it, and stopped playing. To try to find out what they were laughing
at, she went off by herself to Phrygia† – which of course, she being a
goddess, took only a moment or two. There she hid herself in a wood and
found a pool by a stream where she was able to watch her reflection as she
played. She was quite shattered to see what a sight she looked with her
cheeks puffed out in the act of playing. She threw down her pipes in utter
revulsion and, to give more force to her annoyance, laid a curse on anyone
who should ever take them up again. A satyr by the name of Marsyas
happened to find the pipes, and picking them up he made the experiment
of blowing them. To his astonishment he found that (having been played
by a goddess) they played of themselves the most entrancing music.
Marsyas the satyr was delighted. He attached himself to the train of
Cybele, the 'Great Mother' goddess (who in Roman days became acknow-

* Aristotle makes the unkind remark: 'Professional musicians we speak of as
vulgar people, and indeed we think it is not manly to perform music, except
when drunk, or for fun'; *Politics*, IV. 7.
† Phrygia was acknowledged to be the cradle of the art of piping.

Plate 3  Terracotta figurine of a woman playing the divergent double-pipes. From a Phoenician cemetery at Akhzir near Haifa (8th–6th century B.C.).

Plate 4  Detail from the Ludovisi Throne in Rome. A nude *hetaera*, one of two white marble figures flanking the throne, playing the Greek *aulos* or reed pipes. The Ludovisi Throne dates from the fifth century B.C. It was discovered in 1887 in the vast grounds of a villa which occupied the site of the classical Gardens of Sallust.

ROMA – FLAUTISTA – ARTE GREGA V SEC. a. C.
(MUSEO NAZIONALE ROMANO)

Plate 5  Hellenistic figurine in terracotta from Alexandria, c. last century B.C. This is generally accepted as the earliest representation of the bag principle applied to the blowing of a musical pipe (here probably sounding a drone only). From the volume *Ägypten*, ed Hans Hickmann, 1961, in the series *Musikgeschichte in Bildern*.

*Plate 6*  Greek vase decoration. A male *aulos* player with cheeks distended, wearing the *phorbeia* or cheek strap (Inventory No. E 270).

*Plate 7  Maenad* with *aulos*-playing *Silenus*. Relief from the sarcophagus found at Patras, dated at the first half of the second century A.D. Though the sculpture is Greek, it is very late in period, and the pipes are of the same period and type as the Roman *tibia*, as played at the Festival of Cybele, the left pipe being curved at the end and ending in a saxophone-like bell.

ledged as the patroness of piping), and in Cybele's train Marsyas went around Phrygia playing the pipes, to the delight of the Phrygian peasantry. Soon he began to grow conceited about his playing, and to boast that even Apollo on his lyre could not make better music. Apollo heard of his boast, and was of course furiously angry. He challenged the satyr to a musical contest, the winner to be allowed to do what he liked with the loser. Marsyas accepted the challenge. The Muses were sent for to sit in judgment of the musical merits of the two competitors. The result was a dead heat; the competitors were adjudged equal in their performance. Apollo then suggested that they should play their instruments the wrong way round and that they should sing as they played! – to which Marsyas, to his undoing, agreed; but while it was not unduly difficult for Apollo to play his lyre either upside down or back to front, Marsyas naturally found it impossible either to play the pipes through the wrong end or to sing as he blew them. Marsyas therefore lost the contest. Apollo took his revenge on the presumptuous satyr to the full, in accordance with the terms of the contest that the winner should do as he liked with the loser. He had him skinned alive, and his skin nailed to a tree. The curse of Pallas Athene upon the player of the pipes was fulfilled.

The dénouement of the story, the flaying of Marsyas, does not greatly concern us. What is important is that the myth confirms the method of blowing the double-pipes, as we have already glimpsed in the true incident of Alcibiades; and as the myth must have obviously proceeded from human to fabled use by the 'gods', and not vice versa, it means that the method must have been older than the myth. The Grecian deities of Olympus and Mount Ida date only from the Homeric Age, for there is no trace of them in the previous Minoan and Mycenean cultures; but this method of blowing the pipes obviously goes back long before the Grecian deities, possibly as far back as the Piper of Ur himself – and even he had probably inherited it!

There is no record of the continuity of sound in the twin-pipes being broken for purposes of phrasing, either by stopping the breath stream or by 'tongueing' the reed as with our modern woodwind instruments. The sound of the drone-pipes has almost certainly consisted of a continuous unbroken stream of musical tone from the earliest times to the pipes of the present day. Phrasing and tongueing may of course have been used in the playing of the mouth-blown single pipe without a drone, the *monaulos*, which was also to be heard in Greece. We do not know and have no means of finding out; but it does not in any case concern us here.

The ancient technique of blowing the pipes with puffed out cheeks and by nasal inhalation was aided by the use of the *phorbeia*. Curt Sachs[34] thinks that the purpose of the device was to ensure a steady pressure in the cheeks, and also (in the case of the much more powerful and strident pipes of the Romans) to support the cheeks and alleviate the strain on them. It seems to me just as likely that the real purpose was to hold the pipes in place and prevent them from dropping from the mouth; for when the fingers are raised from all four fingerholes there is nothing to hold the pipe, which will be resting on the thumb only. With the three-holed pipe, the pipe could be gripped between the forefinger and thumb; the vase pictures show clearly that this was done. As a means of maintaining the pressure of the cheeks and not primarily of holding the pipes in place, it would seem that this would only be practically possible if the *phorbeia* had been of elastic material – and of course elastic had not yet been invented.

The pipes were obviously as much a musical instrument for the female player as for the male, as they were in ancient Egypt. They were an inseparable adjunct of the theatre, and in the comedies of Aristophanes, for example, the 'girl' piper was a *sine qua non*. In the Greek theatre, however, female characters were played by male actors – with the slightly paradoxical consequence that the girl-piper (or 'flute-girl' as she is consistently mistranslated in English) was a man or boy dressed in skin-tight costume – padded where required, with, as the introduction to *The Frogs and other Plays* tells us,[35] 'the more interesting anatomical details painted on'. In *The Wasps* of Aristophanes, the girl-piper has an integral part in the play. The old man Procleon, drunk to the point of being past all discretion, abducts the girl-piper Dardanis from a banquet – 'a serious matter, kidnapping girl-pipers!' as the play has it.*

In *The Acharnians* and in *Lysistrata* there arises the shadowy suggestion – one can call it nothing more – that as early as Aristophanes himself, that is, the fourth century B.C., an actual bagpipe, as distinct from the mouth-blown drone-pipe, may have already been invented and in use. This suggestion was first commented on by Kathleen Schlesinger in the eleventh edition of *Encyclopaedia Britannica*. In *Lysistrata* there is an apparent reference to taking a bladder to make the music for a Spartan dance.[36] In *The Acharnians*, Aristophanes pokes fun at the musically snobbish intelligentsia of Boeotia by making a band of 'low' Theban pipers escort a Boeotian merchant all the way from Thebes† to Athens. As they approach the house of Dicaeopolis, he exhorts them with the words: 'You skirlers who have tagged along with me from Thebes, blow up the dog's arse with your pipes of bone!' The musically offended Dicaeopolis appears at the door of his own house with his fingers in his ears to deaden the appalling noise, and exclaims: 'Stop that row and go away from my door, you hornets!' To the Boeotian merchant he demands:

---

* Charles Burney, *A General History of Music*, vol. 1, p. 428, observes; 'The most celebrated female flute-player [i.e. piper] in antiquity was Lamia . . . Her claim to admiration from her personal allurements does not entirely depend upon the fidelity of historians, since an exquisite engraving of her head, upon an Amethyst, with the veil and bandage of her profession, is preserved in the King of France's collection, which in some measure authenticates the account of her beauty.'

† Thebes in Boeotia, Greece, not the ancient Egyptian city of the same name.

'Where have these bumbling Chaeridian wasps flown from?' To which the Boeotian replies with equanimity, 'By Iolaus, they've been yowling at my tail all the way from Thebes'. This somewhat plain-spoken reference to the dog's anatomy might possibly allude to that kind of bagpipe of which the bag is formed from the skin of an animal *au naturel*, of which there are many varieties to be found at the present day.* In most of these animal skin (and animal-resembling) bagpipes, the blow-pipe or insufflation tube generally enters the animal's skin somewhere towards the upper part of the back; but it is not impossible that if such an instrument *was* in existence in Aristophanes' time use might have been made of the natural rear orifice of the animal. If the reference is to be accepted as evidence, it would place the first appearance of the bag-blown pipes at least as early as the latter half of the fourth century B.C., which is several hundred years earlier than the first definite reference to the bagpipe in recorded history.

There is so much of fascination and interest in the history and lore of the pipers and the construction and technique of the pipes of ancient Greece and Rome that one could very easily get bogged down and never reach the avowed target of our saga, the Scottish Highland bagpipe. It is no exaggeration to say that the whole period of the two civilizations of Greece and Rome was a golden age of the art of piping. One is therefore forced to be frugally selective. Two particular features of the Greek story, however, stand out particularly for us because of their associations and resemblances to the Scottish picture.

The first is the use of the pipes in battle by the Spartans, or Lacedaemonians; for here the resemblance to our own use of them is quite astonishing. A description of it is conveniently to be found in the work of Aulus Gellius. He wrote in the second century A.D., but his entertaining work *Noctes Atticae* contains extracts from very much earlier Greek and Latin writers. Gellius says:[37]

> Thucydides, the most authoritative of Greek historians, tells us that the Lacedaemonians, greatest of warriors, made use in battle, not of signals by horns or trumpets, but of the music of the pipes,† certainly not in conformity with any religious usage or from any ceremonial reason, nor yet that their courage might be roused and stimulated, which is the purpose of horns and trumpets; but, on the contrary, that they might be calmer and advance in better order, because the effect of the flute-player's‡ notes is to restrain impetuosity; for they were firmly convinced that in meeting the enemy and beginning battle nothing contributed more to valour

---

* Such as the *zukra* in Tunisia, the *mih* in Croatia, and certain types of Hungarian bagpipe (see Appendix III).
† *Tibiarum*, of the pipes.
‡ *Tibicinis*, player of the *tibia* or reed-pipes.

and confidence than to be soothed by gentler sounds and keep their feelings under control. Accordingly, when the army was drawn up, and began to advance in battle array against the foe, pipers* stationed in the ranks began to play. Thereupon, by this quiet, pleasant, and even solemn prelude, the fierce impetuosity of the soldiers was checked, in conformity with a kind of discipline of military music so to speak, that they might not rush forth in straggling disorder.

But I should like to quote the very words of that outstanding writer [i.e. Thucydides] which have greater distinction and credibility than my own:

'And after this the attack began; the Argives and their allies rushed forward eagerly and in a rage; but the Lacedaemonians advanced slowly to the music of many flute-players† stationed at regular intervals; this not for any reason but in order that they might make the attack while marching together rhythmically, and that their ranks might not be broken, which commonly happens to great armies when they advance to the attack.'

. . . Finally [Gellius continues], Aristotle wrote in his volume of *Problems*, that the custom of the Lacedaemonians which I have mentioned, of entering battle to the music of the flute-players [i.e. pipers], was adopted in order to make the fearlessness and ardour of the soldiers more evident and indubitable. 'For' said he, 'distrust and fear are not at all consistent with an advance of that kind, and such an intrepid and rhythmical advance cannot be made by the faint-hearted and despondent.'

Two excerpts on the same subject from Plutarch's life of Lycurgus, the semi-mythical 'law-giver of Sparta', are worth adding to the picture:

(a) If we will take the pains to consider their [the Spartans'] compositions, some of which were still extant in our days, and the airs on the flute [*aulon*=pipes] to which they marched when going into battle, we shall find that Terpander and Pindar had reason to say that music and valour were allied.

(b) When their army was drawn up in battle array and the enemy near, the king sacrificed a goat, and commanded the soldiers to set their garlands upon their heads, and the pipers to play the tune of the Hymn of Castor,‡ and himself began the paean of

* *Tibicines*, again, pipers.
† The text (here in Greek) has *auleton*, i.e. players of the *aulos* (reed-pipes), i.e. pipers.
‡ Castor was the mythical son of a king of the Spartans. He and his brother Pollux were regarded as 'presidents of the public games, the inventors of the war-dance, and patrons of poets and bards'; E. H. Blakeney, *A Smaller Classical Dictionary*, 1910.

advance. It was at once a magnificent and terrible sight to see them march on to the tune of their flutes [i.e. pipes], without any disorder in their ranks, any discomposure in their minds, or change in their countenance, calmly and cheerfully moving with the music to the deadly fight.[38]

The other particularly interesting feature of ancient Greek piping, because of its familiarity, is the solo-piping contests. These could well be described as '*pìobaireachd* (pibroch) competitions', in the literal meaning of the Gaelic word, similar to those held in Scotland today. The most notable of these took place at Delphi on the slopes, appropriately, of Mount Parnassus, as one of the items of the Pythian Games, traditionally said to have been instituted by Zeus himself. The festival took place every five years. It was held in celebration of the Pythian Apollo, who, according to the ancient myth, slew the Python, a monster serpent which arose from the silt left upon the earth after the Deluge of Deucalion. Deucalion can be said to be the Greek Noah, whose 'ark' came to rest after 'the Flood' upon Mount Parnassus itself.

The pipe music forming the subject of the competitions was known as the *nomos pythicos*, or Pythian Nome (*nomos* or *nome* being a particular musical form). The slaying of the serpent formed the theme of the 'pibroch'. Like its later Scottish *pìobaireachd* counterpart, the *nomos pythicos* was in five movements.* They were as follows:

1 A prelude, *anakrousis*, which gave out the theme (corresponding to the Scottish Gaelic *ùrlar*). This was a general setting of the scene of Apollo's fight with the serpent.
2 The 'first onset of the contest' (*ampeira*).
3 The 'contest' itself (*katakeleusmos*).
4 The triumph following the victory (*iambus* and *dactylus*).
5 The last hissing of the serpent as it expired (*syrinx* or *syringes*).[39]

The *syrinx*, besides being the Greek name of the 'pan-pipes', was also a device on the *aulos* consisting of a 'speaker' hole in the pipe which facilitated the production of the harmonic overtones; and the name would seem to imply that this last movement was the opportunity for a display of playing technique in the higher harmonics of the pipes.

The melody of the theme of the *nomos pythicos* was somewhat dubiously attributed by Strabo to Timosthenes (270 B.C.), an Admiral of the Fleet, serving in Egypt under the second Ptolemy. Besides being a composer, he was also the author or compiler of a book on marine harbours. Commentators, however, have declared Strabo to be mistaken in dating the composition of the theme of the *nomos* as late as Timosthenes, and that it has been more reasonably ascribed by other ancient writers to Sac-

* For the five movements of the Scottish *pìobaireachd* see F. Collinson, *Traditional and National Music of Scotland*, p. 65.

adas, who was himself the winning piper or *auletes* at the Pythian Games three hundred years before Timosthenes, during the fifth century B.C.[40] The names of other winning pipers at these contests at the Pythian Games have been recorded by both Pindar and Pausanias; they include the pipers Pronomos, Timotheus and Ismenias (who is said to have paid a sum equal to £1,000 for his pipes, which he bought at Corinth)[41] and, most celebrated of all the Pythian Games pipers, Midas of Agrigentum, who was twice winner. Pindar wrote special odes to the victors at the various Greek Games, the Pythian, Olympian, Nemean and Isthmian. (These were not confined to the musical competitions, for the Greek games were mainly athletic contests.) Of Midas of Agrigentum, the Pindar Scholia tell us that at one of the piping competitions his reeds broke in the middle of his performance. He whisked the reeds out of the end of the pipes and finished the piece by blowing across the open ends of the pipes, using them as 'end-blown flutes'. Though it seems more like a conjuring trick than a true piping performance, it must have been a tremendous *tour de force* on account of the difficulty, or near impossibility, of blowing two end-flutes at once. However dubious it may have been from the point of view of the ethics and standards of piping, Midas was granted the victory by popular acclaim. He was also the winner of one of the piping competitions at the Panathenaea, held every fourth year in Athens.*

Other famous pipers of ancient Greece were Nicomachos, who is said to have become rich by his playing; Aristomenes; and a woman piper, Lamia (*c.* 360 B.C.), in whose honour a temple was raised in Athens. Pronomos, who developed the key-changing movable rings on the Greek *aulos*, had a statue raised to him by the grateful Thebans. A statue was also raised to the piper Midas of Phrygia (who must have been a different person from Midas of Agrigentum, mentioned above, which is in Sicily).[42]

In taking leave of our Grecian predecessors in the art of piping, we may add as postscript the statement from a lost work of Theophrastus (*c.* 370 B.C.), preserved to us by great fortune by Aulus Gellius in his *Noctes Atticae*, mentioned above. It is of the belief in his time that the sound of the pipes was a cure for rheumatism!

# Rome

### The vocabulary

*Tibia* (shin-bone)   The Roman reed-sounded mouth-blown double-pipes, almost invariably mistranslated in English editions of the classics as 'flutes' or 'the double-flute(s)'.

---

* These musical contests at the pan-Athenian games were said to have been instituted by Pericles in 446 B.C. Before that they had presumably been purely athletic contests.

*Tibiae impares*  The Roman version of the Greek *auloi elymoi*, the double-pipes of unequal length known both in Greece and Rome as the 'Phrygian pipes'. The left-hand pipe, the longer pipe of the two, was curved in shape. The right-hand pipe was straight. The biggest and loudest form of the *tibiae impares* was the *Berecynthian pipes*, an important type. The left-hand pipe of these terminated in a horn bell, not unlike the modern saxophone. The Berecynthian pipes were also known as the *tibia furiosa* or 'mad pipes', from the frenzied orgiastic nature of the dancing in the Berecynthian festival of which they were a feature. They became very popular in Rome.

*Tibiae sarranae*  The double-pipes of equal length, also known as the Lydian or Phoenician pipes, usually smaller than the *tibiae impares*.

*Tibiae duae dextrae*  Or *tibia* consisting of two right-hand pipes, may have been, as the name implies, the two right-hand (straight) pipes taken from the unequal length *tibiae impares*, used as a pair. These were almost certainly longer and probably more powerful than the Lydian pipes.

*Tibia incentiva*  The lower-pitched of a pair of double-pipes.

*Tibicen*  A player of the double-pipes, a piper (male).

*Tibicina*  A female player of the double-pipes, a 'girl-piper'.

*Tibicinium*  A playing on the pipes; piping; a '*pìobaireachd*'.

*Tibiarius*  A pipe maker.

*Capistrum*  A mouth-band; the Roman name of the *phorbeia* of the Greeks (*q.v.*).

*Harundo*  A water-reed; hence, a reed used for a musical pipe, possibly pan-pipes; obviously a Latin version of the plant *arundo donax*, the reed plant from which so many ancient pipes were made (see Appendix II).

*Lingula*  The tongue of the pipe-reed.

*Utricularius*  A bagpiper; also a wine trader (also, the master of a boat for river-ferrying – e.g. troops – floated on inflated bladders or skins).

*Collegium tibicinum*  A guild of pipers (of the mouth-blown pipes).

*Corpus utriculariorum*  A guild of ferry-masters; the term has also been taken to mean a bagpipers' guild, but there is no evidence for this.

*Fistula*  A small pipe; a pitch pipe; possibly a 'recorder' type of pipe.

## Borrowed Greek words

*Ascaules* (rare)  A bagpiper (the word was probably first used in this sense by the Romans).

*Auletes* (*ae*) (m.)  (from the Greek) a piper.

The Romans believed that their pipes and the art of piping had come to them from the Greeks. Ovid in his *Fasti*[43] refers to the art of the pipes as the *ars graia*. If, as seems likely, Ovid is correct, it forges a further link in the chain of development – Sumeria and Egypt; Phrygia, Lydia (Asia Minor) and Phoenicia; Greece; Rome. It seems equally possible, however, that the Roman pipes may have come from the Etruscans, on the doorstep of Rome to the north, who stemmed, according to Herodotus, from Lydia in Asia Minor; or they could have come perhaps from Sicily, which was colonized early by the Phoenicians and later by the Greeks.

It was a well-known tradition, of course, that the Romans were descended from the Trojans through Aeneas, who was one of the defenders of Troy. At the fall of Troy, Aeneas is said by tradition to have escaped and to have fled first to Mount Ida in Phrygia (the cradle of the Phrygian pipes) taking with him from Troy the images of the gods, including, notably, that of Pallas Athene, the 'inventor' of the pipes. Later, Aeneas is said to have crossed the seas, and after his encounter with Dido at Carthage, to have landed at Latium in Italy, the country of the Latini, where he became the ancestral hero of the Romans. If the story were true one could see a direct route for the progress of the pipes on their long journey from Sumeria and Egypt to Rome, by way of the Phrygian pipes and pipers at Troy mentioned by Homer. But it is generally agreed that the story of Aeneas has no historical foundation.

The pipes, however, are mentioned quite early in Roman semi-history and tradition, They appear in the reign of the second (legendary) king of Rome, Numa Pompilius, the successor to Romulus (who was reputed to be the son of the god Mars). Romulus was traditionally said to have founded the city of Rome in the year 753 B.C.; this gives us the period of roughly the late eighth century B.C. for King Numa, if he existed!

Numa is credited by the historian and biographer Plutarch with the founding of the original trade guilds of Rome, of which the Pipers' Guild was given the premier place. It was a guild of practising musicians which became as powerful a body as the Musicians' Union of today; it acquired, through legal backing, a near-monopoly of piping work in Rome, challenged only by the provocative Syrian girl-pipers, the *ambubaiae*, of whom more later. Plutarch recounts that Numa, arranging the people into categories by their arts and trades, instituted the companies of pipers, goldsmiths, carpenters, dyers, shoemakers, tanners, braziers and potters.[44] It is notable, and perhaps indicative of the ubiquitousness of pipers and piping in the life of Rome, that Numa mentions them first in the list of the Guilds. Equally important is the tradition, also recorded by Plutarch, that Numa instituted the presence of a piper at the sacred sacrifice of the Roman religion. It is said that this ordinance was not so much for the sake of the music itself, considered as a part of the ritual, as for the purpose of covering up any extraneous sounds from the mundane street life of the city. Plutarch continues:

In all public processions and solemn prayers, criers were sent ahead, to give notice to the people that they should forbear their work, and rest . . . and that the streets should be free from all noises and cries that accompany manual labour, and that they should be left clear for the sacred solemnity.

As far as Numa is concerned, we are dealing with legend and tradition rather than history; but it does show that the use of the pipes (mouth-blown of course) was a recognized accompaniment to the religious cere-mony of the sacrifice to the gods, which was one of the frequent and customary duties of Roman life; and that it was a custom old enough to be lost in the myths of antiquity even in ancient Rome.

Semi-legendary also were the famous 'Twelve Tables' containing the ancient Roman Laws, in which pipers were said to be specifically men-tioned. The laws were said to have been carved upon twelve tables of wood, and to have been adopted as the original written laws of the Romans, the *ius scriptum*, in 451–450 B.C. The original wording became lost, but Cicero (106–43 B.C.), in *De Legibus*, says 'we learned the Law of the Twelve Tables in our youth as a required formula, though no-one learns it nowadays'.[45] The Law contained a curious proviso regarding pipers: not more than ten of them were to be allowed at a funeral! To quote Cicero again:

There are rules in the Twelve Tables, which were borrowed for the most part from the [Greek] laws of Solon which provide for the limitation of the expense and the mourning at funerals . . . The expense then, is limited to three veils, a purple tunic, and *ten flute-players** . . . At those public games, which are held without chariot races or the contest of body with body, the public pleasure shall be provided for with moderation, by song to the music of harp and pipes (*in cantu fidibus et tibiis*). Next (since the public games are divided between theatre and circus) there shall be, in the circus, contest of body with body, consisting of running, boxing and wrestling; also horse-races, which shall last until a decisive victory is won; the theatre shall be filled with song to the music of harp and pipes, the only limitation being that of moderation, as the law prescribes.[46]

This limitation of the pipers to ten at a funeral led later to one of the most extraordinary and ludicrous events in the history of Rome – a pipers' strike! – probably the earliest organized strike ever recorded. It seems that the law gradually ceased to be observed, and there was a recurrence of the extravagance and licence which it sought to curb. In the year 311 B.C., the *aediles* (lesser magistrates) in Rome decided to enforce the law. The anger amongst the pipers can be imagined, for pipers and funerals, like 'freedom and whisky' as Robert Burns was later to observe,

* The text has *tibicinibus*, i.e. *tibia*-players, i.e. pipers.

seem naturally to 'gang thegither'. Things came to a head when the
*aediles* decided to ban the pipers also from holding their customary
annual gathering at the temple of Jupiter. The pipers went on strike.

It should be explained that most of the pipers were employed by the
state, and had become a necessary part of all kinds of state occasions and
ceremonies. They played at the circus, and at public and private banquets.
They had their part in the 'triumph' bestowed upon a successful general
after a campaign.* The pipers had therefore a considerable weapon in their
hands. Having decided to go on strike, they left the city of Rome in a body
and went off to Tibur, a favourite place of resort some eighteen miles
outside the city.

The absence of the state pipers caused unbelievable chaos in the daily
life of the city. The theatres of the spoken word could not function, for
the *cantica* of the Roman comedy were accompanied throughout by the
pipes;† the circus was without music for the entry of the gladiators;
official and private banquets had to be eaten in empty silence – that is, as
far as background music was concerned; the deceased were carried to
their resting places without the solace to the mourners of the pipe-lament.
Most serious of all, the sacred ceremonies and sacrifices of the Roman
religion could not proceed according to the ancient ordinances of Numa,
with a piper supplying the appropriate background music. After enduring
for some days all the inconveniences of a piperless Rome, the Senate
sent representatives to the local authorities at Tibur to use their influence
with the pipers. But it was to no purpose; the pipers remained 'out'.

Finally one of the more influential of the Tiburtines agreed to try a
ruse. He was a freedman (a former slave) who had acquired wealth;
according to Ovid, he was 'a man worthy of any rank', obviously a natural
tycoon-type of the day. This man threw a party for the pipers at his
country house a short way out of Tibur, and invited them all to come to
the gathering, with their pipes. The party flowed freely with drink (here
Livy is unkind enough to add, in his account of the strike, 'which people
of that profession are generally greedy of') until they got very drunk. At
a given signal, a messenger came to raise the alarm that the authorities
were on their way to break up the party because it was unduly rowdy –
and probably also to arrest some of the noisiest offenders. The pipers, in a
panic, stumbled out of the house and into the wagons which had brought

* If a general had won a victory by force of arms, he entered Rome riding in a
  four-horse chariot and wearing a crown of laurel, heralded by the fanfares of
  trumpets. If the campaign had been brought to a successful issue by persuasion,
  threats or diplomacy, the general entered the city on foot, wearing a crown of
  myrtle, and escorted by a large body of pipers; see Plutarch, *Marcellus* 22,
  trans. Dryden, revised by Clough.
† These pipes of the theatre were the Roman version of the pipes used by the
  competitors at the piping contests at the Pythian Games; Diomedes, quoted by
  A. A. Howard, 'The *aulos* or *tibia*', *Harvard Studies in Classical Philology*,
  vol. 4, p. 40.

them out from Tibur, and which they thought were going to take them back there. They were soon fast asleep from the drink, and the wagons, instead of going back to Tibur, drove them back through the night to Rome – to the Forum itself; and there they found themselves when they had recovered from their stupor in the morning, probably feeling rather sheepish. The populace thronged about them, doubtless making a fuss of them, and succeeded in persuading them to go back to work. The Senate agreed that their festival should be restored to them, and that on three days in every year, in the month of June, the pipers should be allowed to roam through the city in festal garb, 'making music and enjoying the licence that is now customary; and to such as should play the pipes at sacrifices was given the privilege of banqueting in the temple' as Ovid says. The three days were known as the festival of the lesser Quinquatrus which was held yearly thereafter on June 13 (the Ides), 14 and 15.[47]

The strike of the pipers seems to have been one of the sensations of the era, for although it took place in the year 311 B.C. it was still being talked and written about three hundred years later by such writers as Ovid, Livy, Plutarch and Quintilian.[48] The story, besides being amusing, is of interest as showing how completely the music of the pipes permeated the life of the city of Rome. It was so pervasive indeed that there is hardly a Latin writer of the times who does not mention somewhere in his works the instrument or its player, often in the most unexpected context.

Thus we find Varro, 'the most learned of the Romans', a retired naval commander, in his 'Concerning the Things of the Countryside' (*De Re Rustica*), writing,

> 'Grazing and agriculture are different things though akin, just as the right pipe [i.e. of the double-pipes] is different from the left, but still in a way united, inasmuch as the one is the treble, while the other plays the accompaniment of the same air.' 'You may add this,' said I, 'that the shepherd's life is the treble, and the farmer's plays the accompaniment . . . Wherefore the Art of Agriculture *accompanies* the pastoral because it is subordinate, as the left pipe is to the stops* of the right.' 'You and your piping!' retorted Agrius.[49]

In his *Geography* Strabo supplies us with much of our information about the piping competitions at Delphi. The rather ponderous Quintilian, in his complete course of Rhetoric written for the education of Roman youth (from infancy upwards), emphasizes the importance of starting with a good teacher; he draws a simile from a famous piper and teacher of piping, Timotheus, who used to charge a pupil double fees if he had studied the pipes under any other master before coming to him, on the theory that he would have the extra task of eradicating the faults acquired under his previous teacher!

Even Julius Caesar, who was not noticeably musical, recounts that he

* I.e. the fingerholes.

accepted as a favourable omen the apparition of a piper 'of superhuman size and beauty' who appeared to beckon him on at the moment of indecision on the crossing of the river Rubicon, an irrevocable step which must inevitably lead to civil war (and incidentally led to the coining of a phrase).

Other classical writers who have mentioned the pipes include Suetonius, Dio Chrysostom, Martial, Aristotle, Cicero, Juvenal and Aulus Gellius, besides the writers of purely musical treatises.

The pipes used by the Romans were roughly the same as those of Greece. They possessed both the *tibiae impares* (the double-pipes of unequal length, the Greek *auloi elymoi*) and the equal-length *tibiae sarranae*, for which there does not seem to have been a specific Greek name. The main difference seems to have been that the Romans liked their pipes bigger and noisier. One gets the impression that with the Romans the sheer volume of sound had increased immeasurably from the delicate sound of the ancient *aulos* of Greece.

The loudest of all the Roman pipes were the Berecynthian pipes. These were played originally by pipers from Phrygia at the yearly festival of Cybele, surnamed Berecynthia, also known as Rhea, the Great Mother of the gods. The festival was to celebrate an ancient myth, of which the whole theme was the making of a noise! In the myth, the female attendants of Rhea clashed shields and helmets to drown the cries of the new-born baby Zeus. They did this so that his father, the god Kronos, would not hear the infant's cries and devour him as he had devoured all his previous offspring in order to counter a prophecy that his infant son should dethrone him as king of the gods.

This clashing of shields and helmets was metamorphosed at the yearly festival into the banging of drums, the clashing of cymbals, and the strident sounds of the Berecynthian pipes. So wild was the music of the Phrygian pipers that it aroused the worshippers (and often the onlookers too) to orgiastic frenzies in which they cut and lacerated themselves with swords and knives;* some of the neophytes of the priesthood of the cult even castrated themselves publicly!

The cult of Cybele was brought to Rome in 204 B.C. on the direction of the Sibylline Books of prophecy, which were to be consulted in times of national emergency. They were brought there at the outbreak of the Second Punic War. When the war was won (seemingly because of the assistance of the goddess Cybele in accordance with the advice of the Sibyl) it clearly gave licence to the Roman citizen to keep the yearly festival in her honour, with its hysterical outbursts of shrill noisy piping and din and physical excesses. At first Roman citizens themselves were

---

* Curt Sachs, *The History of Musical Instruments*, p. 138, doubtless thinking of the strong stiff cane reeds and saxophone-like horn of the Berecynthian pipes, observes that the sound of the Roman pipes could be as shrill and exciting as the sound of 'their relatives, the bagpipes of modern "Scotch" regiments'.

forbidden to take part in the Berecynthian cult ceremonies; but in time the ban was ignored, and the Berecynthian pipes themselves became a popular musical instrument. Street bands of pipes, drums and cymbals began to be a familiar sight in Rome.*

There must have been as many girl-pipers in Rome as men players, for one finds such writers as Quintilian referring to a piper, as often as not, as 'she', as when he quotes Pythagoras as ordering the piper to change 'her' strain. Martial the poet, in one of his epigrams, writes: 'The drunken piper bursts our ears with her bibulous cheeks; often she uses two pipes at once, often only one'. The latter statement gives us a glimpse of a particular effect in the use of the double-pipes. With one pipe it would be possible to use staccato and clipped phrasing effects, more in the nature of the oboe than of the continuously sounding pipes as generally understood.

Ovid, in a rather fanciful and probably fictitious postscript to his account of the pipers' strike, adds that the person in authority in Rome who had to deal with it thought it expedient to conceal the exact number of pipers who had been brought back in the wagons – probably so the pipers would not know how much the strike had been affected by their return. He ordered that the pipers should be masked and that they should be dressed in long cloaks which should cover them completely. Then he ordered that the girl-pipers, who apparently had had no part in the strike and had stayed in Rome, should dress similarly and mingle with their male confreres to add to the apparent number of strikers who had returned to work – a crude strike-breaking dodge, but one which incidentally shows us the plentiful number of girl-pipers available for the deception. Ovid goes on to say that this dressing-up by both sexes was the origin of the fanciful garb of the pipers thereafter at their own festival of the Lesser Quinquatrus.

The most colourful of Rome's girl-pipers were the famed *ambubaiae*, Syrian girls who lived in the basement of the Roman circus. It was generally understood that they were prepared, whether from inclination or necessity, to augment their income, by a profession even older than piping. Their profession, historically speaking, was an honourable one, for they came of the ancient tradition of the sacred temple prostitutes of the Syrian religious ritual mentioned by Herodotus and others. There was an ordinance (introduced in 115 B.C.) which allowed only Latin pipers to play in Rome. This probably applied chiefly to the appointment of State girl-pipers, for which it would be necessary to satisfy the law's requirements as to nationality; and probably also to fulfil the conditions of entry to the Pipers' Guild, namely that they should be fully professional. If the Syrian country of origin of the girls debarred them from entering Rome as pipers, it might be easier to gain entrance to the Eternal City as members

* Propertius exclaims of the Berecynthian festival, 'Why do some gash their arms with sacred knives, and cut their limbs to the sound of the Phrygian pipes?'; *Elegies*, II, xxii.

of another profession, in which prospective customers were not likely to demand proofs of their nationality, a profession which was under Roman law perfectly legal. They would not be required to satisfy the Pipers' Guild that they were fully professional musicians, for they could easily say that as pipers they were merely enthusiastic amateurs! The *ambubaiae* short-circuited the Pipers' Guild by forming a guild of their own, which the poet Horace dignifies as a 'Collegium' – one presumes, by virtue of their piping hobby rather than of their accredited profession. They would without doubt play upon their own national pipes of Syria, the *tibiae sarranae*, the small pipes of equal length; and the evidence would suggest that they were talented pipers.

In one of his *Satires*[50] Horace mentions the *ambubaiae* in a regretful allusion to the death of a popular singer. He writes, 'The College of Ambubaiae, the drug-pedlars, the beggars, actresses, music-hall comedians and all that clamjamfrey, are grieving and mourning at the passing of the singer Tigellius. He was so generous, they say.'*

Some of the Emperors of Rome played the pipes, or were closely interested in them, from the semi-mythical king Numa, who instituted the pipers' guilds in the seventh century B.C., onwards. They include Verus (co-emperor, A.D. 164–9), Elagabalus (A.D. 218–22), Severus Alexander (A.D. 222–35) and Carinus (A.D. 284–5). The last-named incidentally anticipated by roughly fifteen hundred years Lady Nairne 'wi' her Hundred Pipers an a' an a' ', for he staged a march-past of no less than two hundred pipers at the Roman circus.

The most spectacular imperial player of the pipes (with full lighting effects of Rome in flames) was the Emperor Nero; but as it is with him that the first definite and concrete mention of the actual bagpipe is associated, as distinct from the mouth-blown pipes of the three preceding millennia, he merits fuller consideration a little later (p. 43).

### The invention of the bag

We have already seen shadowy suggestions of a bagpipe centuries before the period at which we have now arrived; first in a representation on a relief from a Hittite palace at Eyuk, of date 1300 B.C., discovered in the first decade of this century by Professor John Garstang;[51] second, in the references by Aristophanes in the fourth or third century B.C. (see p. 30). In both cases the suggested form of the instrument is that of a bag formed by the whole skin of the animal, with chanter and/or drone inserted in it.

---

* Charles Burney, *A General History of Music*, vol. 1, p. 429 and note, writes of the Ambubaiarum Collegia: 'The following of this profession became so numerous and licentious that we find their occupation prohibited in the Theodosian code; however, with little success, for Procopius tells us that in the time of Justinian, the sister of the Empress Theodora, who was a *tibicina* [female piper] appeared on the stage without any other dress than a slight scarf loosely over her.'

In Aristophanes' *The Acharnians* the picture presented is that of a chanter or chanters, and drone. This is suggested by the reference in the play to bumble-bee or hornet pipers. Even if these references are accepted as having a factual basis, the instrument must have been of quite localized use, and probably rustic; for it failed to influence the mainstream of the development of the bagpipe.

More definite evidence turns up in a series of terracotta figurines from Alexandria which have been dated as belonging to the reigns of Ptolemy VIII to Ptolemy X (roughly speaking, the last century B.C.).[52] The best known of these shows a seated man wearing a Syrian or Phrygian conical hat, playing a set of pan-pipes; he is accompanying them by means of a bag under his arm, into which is tied what is obviously a pipe sounding a drone, which he holds loosely in his right hand. There is a scabellum or time-beater under his right foot, and an assistant dwarf clashing a pair of small cymbals. The contribution of the dwarf does not include the playing of the drone, which must therefore be sounded by the player himself by means of the bag under his arm. The figurine suggests that the combination of *syrinx* and bag-blown drone must have been common then. This is confirmed by two other similar figurines which have since come to light; each shows the pan-pipes (*syrinx*) accompanied by a pipe similarly blown by a bag under the arm of the player.

These figurines are the earliest indubitable representations of the bag-pipe principle, though as yet the bag is only used to blow a drone, and not a chanter. This bag-sounded drone must have been a very rudimentary instrument, for there is no apparent means of inflating the bag during performance. The music must therefore have stopped while the deflated bag was blown up again by the player. Astonishingly, what appears to be a representation of this same combination of pan-pipes and bag-blown drone turns up in the form of a crudely carved Roman altar of limestone in Roman Britain (Gloucester) to be presently described.

It was during the reign of the Emperor Nero, in the first century A.D., that we find the first specific mention of the bagpipe by name (in Latin). This was in Nero's oath uttered in the last days of his life, that if the gods would deliver him from the hands of the conspirators who were seeking his death (to bring an unbearable tyranny to an end) he would in return honour the gods with a great musical festival. At this he would himself perform as a *hydraula* (on the water-blown organ), as a *choraula* (on a form of mouth-blown pipes), and as a *utricularius*.*

---

* See Nero in Suetonius' *Lives of the Twelve Caesars*. In *The Traditional and National Music of Scotland* (p. 160) I hazarded a guess that the Emperor Nero's oath to play the pipes in public was an undertaking to do penance for his ill-lived life, and that it could be inferred from this that the bagpiper was held in low regard in ancient Rome. I have since realized, however, that this was far from being the case. The great pipers of Greece and Rome were figures of public adulation, and even had statues erected to them—though they were, it must be remembered, players of the mouth-blown pipes, not the bagpipes.

*Utricularius* is a Latin word primarily connected with a wine-skin or other bag of skin (see p. 35). The essential feature was the bag which could be filled with liquid (wine), or with air. Nero is obviously using the word in connection with an air-filled bag to blow the musical pipes. That he did in fact mean a bagpipe received confirmation from another writer of the same period as Suetonius, Dio Chrysostom, 'the golden-mouthed' (born A.D. 40), in a sarcastic reference to Nero's bagpipe playing (though he prudently doesn't mention the late emperor by name). Dio Chrysostom, who writes in Greek, says:

> That a man will paint better than the painter when himself not a
> painter . . . or that he will sing more musically than the musician
> when unacquainted with the art . . . such is not to be expected.
> And yet a certain king of our time had the ambition to be wise in
> this sort of wisdom . . . not of such things as do not receive
> applause among men, but rather of those things for which it is
> possible to win a crown – I mean singing to the cithara,* reciting
> tragedies, wrestling and taking part in the *pancration*. Besides they
> say that he could paint and fashion statues, and play the pipes,
> both by means of his lips and by tucking a skin beneath his arm-
> pits, and so avoiding the reproach of Athena.[53]

There we have the truth without doubt, that the bagpipe had publicly appeared in Rome. The date was sometime in the second half of the first century A.D. Dio Chrysostom's reference to the player's avoidance of 'the reproach of Athena', that age-old facial contortion of puffing out the cheeks to use them as an air-reservoir, is important, for it shows that the bagpipes in question were not just the pan-pipes accompanied by a rudimentary bag-blown drone, as used in Egypt (which now belonged to the Roman Emperor), but a bag providing the wind for a reed-sounded chanter or (more probably) chanters.

Nero (born A.D. 37) was a complicated personality. Cruel, lecherous and a sexual pervert, as by accounts he was, his viciousness was combined with a passionate aspiration to excel in the arts, particularly in the art of music. He instituted the *Neronia* in Rome, a quinquennial festival of music, athletics and horsemanship, modelled on the great Greek games. He studied both singing and the lyre under the best masters to be had. He entered the musical competitions in singing and lyre playing in Rome. Not content with his triumphs there (which could hardly be other than suspect) he went to Greece (now a conquered country under the political suzerainty of Rome) and contested in the musical competitions there, including the historic Pythian Games, lining up as an ordinary competitor and giving every evidence of real nervousness and even stage fright.† He

---

* A large box-lyre.
† His biographer Suetonius does not record that he also competed in the ancient
  piping competitions, performing the extremely difficult *plobaireachd*-like
  Pythian Nome, a fact which we learn from other authorities.

was also apparently a composer, probably for voice and lyre. He is said by Suetonius to have performed veritable musical marathons such as singing to his own lyre accompaniment the whole of an apparently long work, *The Fall of Ilium*, and the entire 'opera' of *Niobe*, to the crowds at Rome; the latter took so long at one year's *Neronia* that there was no time left for the other competitors to perform! It therefore becomes obvious that there was no question of 'doing penance' in Nero's vow to play the bagpipe, but that he considered it an instrument worthy of his undoubted musical talents.

There can, however, be no doubt that the bagpipe was still a new instrument in Nero's day. Dio Chrysostom (*c.* A.D. 40 to after A.D. 112), though familiar with the life of Rome, cannot even put a name to it, and obviously skates round the necessity of doing so in his satire (*Orat.* lxxi.9). Another writer of the period, the poet Martial (A.D. 40–*c.* 104), solves the difficulty by borrowing a name for the instrument, or rather the player of it, from the Greek, viz. *askaules*.[54] This is our old friend *aulos*, a pipe, plus *askos*, a bag. One musicologist has rather amazingly deduced from this and from the fact that Greece lay to the east of Rome and had colonial settlements in Asia Minor, that the *askaulos*, the bagpipe, must have come from the East, which is about as irrational as we ourselves saying the same of the telegraph and the telephone and other such Greek-derived names!

In dating the appearance of the bagpipes in Rome at somewhere between A.D. 54 and 68, the years of Nero's reign, one should for the sake of completeness mention one literary reference which, thought by some to refer to the bagpipe, could put such a dating out of court. This is in a poem attributed to Virgil; and Virgil died in 19 B.C., over half a century before Nero was born. The reference is, however, so doubtful that it can hardly be accepted as evidence. The poem begins:*

Copa Surisca, caput Graeca redimita mitella,
    Crispum sub crotalo docta movere latus,
Ebria famosa saltat lasciva taberna,
    Ad cubitum raucos excutiens calamos.
Quid iuvat aestivo defessum pulvere abisse
    Quam potius bibulo decubuisse toro?
Sunt topia et kalybae, cyathi, rosa, tibia, chordae,
    Et triclia umbrosis frigida harundinibus,
En et Maenalio quae garrit dulce sub antro,
    Rustica pastoris fistula in more sonat.

Syrisca the inn-keeper, her head bound with Greek kerchief,
    trained as she is to move her swaying limbs to the sound of her

---

* Virgil, *Minor Poems*. Short's *Latin Dictionary* defines *excutio* (line 4) as 'to shake out, as of the arm in hurling or swimming', which does not at all seem to suggest exerting steady pressure on a bag under the arm.

castanets,* within her smoky tavern, tipsily dances in wanton wise,
shaking against her elbow her noisy reeds. What boots it to stay
outside when aweary with the summer's dust, rather than to recline
on the thirsty couch of grass? There are garden nooks and arbours,
mixing-cups, roses, pipes, lyres and cool bowers with shady canes.
Lo! too, the pipe, which twitters sweetly within a Maenalian grotto,
sounds its rustic strain in shepherd fashion.

Syrisca is stated to be dancing to the sound of her own castanets, so
she could not have been fingering the chanter of a bagpipe at the same
time. 'Shaking her noisy reeds with her elbow' probably means no more
than it literally says: she is shaking pieces of reed or cane strung together
perhaps as dress ornaments, to make them rattle, in her pseudo-exotic
dancing. One has seen such an act a thousand times at fair-booths and
cheap cabaret turns. The poet says that the music of the *tibia* (mouth-
blown pipes) and *chordae* (lyre or harp) was going on *inside the tavern as
well*; and it is doubtful how the classical *tibia* would have sounded in
concert with a half-drunken dancer attempting to play both castanets and
bagpipe at once!

It is not difficult to guess how and from whence the bag idea may have
come to Rome; for we have seen that it had been known in Egypt for a
hundred years at least as a bag-blown drone accompanying the *syrinx* –
and Egypt now belonged by conquest to the Roman emperor.

It is probable that the early Roman bagpipe as played by Nero, the
*tibia utricularis*, was simply an adaptation of the bag principle to the
Roman *tibia*, the divergent mouth-blown pipes. This would, of course,
take the form of a bagpipe with *two* chanters, each covered by the fingers
of one hand. Such a bagpipe is, in fact, still in use in Italy today under the
name of the *zampogna* (see Appendix III).†

It is not unreasonable to suppose that the *zampogna* may well be the
direct descendant of Nero's *tibia utricularis*. There is said to have been a
carving of such a bagpipe on a marble relief on an archway in medieval
Rome over the gateway of the palace of the Prince of Santa Croce, near
the church of San Carlo ad Catinarios. This is described by a Veronese
writer, Francesco Bianchini in 1742, who gives what purports to be a

* A note in the Loeb translation, says, 'The castanets were made of pieces of
  reed or wood.' It seems doubtful to me that castanets would be played by
  shaking them against the elbow – if that is the meaning of the passage.
† Baines, *Bagpipes*, p. 100, tells us that a player of the instrument in Palermo
  named the two pipes of the *zampogna*, *canto* (right-hand chanter) and *trombone*
  (left-hand chanter, in the sense of 'large trumpet'). The name conveys a perfect
  picture of the left-hand pipe of the Roman Berecynthian pipes, with its bell-
  shaped end.
     A curious and perhaps wildly imaginative conception of the bagpipe as
  divergent double-pipes blown with a bag is to be seen in the painting by the
  sixteenth-century artist Gaudenzio Ferrari, at Santuario Saronno in Italy; but
  this is too late to be accepted as historical evidence.

drawing of it. Unfortunately the instrument is drawn from such an angle that only one chanter is visible. The drawing is far from conclusive, and the period of the archway and its carvings has not so far been ascertainable. Probably the story is best ignored. A reproduction of Bianchini's drawing is given in Stainer's *Music of the Bible* (p. 122). Grattan Flood[55] suggests that the carving represents a Celt playing on the Irish war-pipes!

To many of the Roman pipers of the old school, the introduction of the bag-blown instrument must have seemed a retrograde step, for it scrapped at one stroke many of the patiently acquired methods of playing of the past thousand years. This applied particularly to the use of the harmonic overtones as a normal part of the technique; for while it is possible to get the occasional high note on the bagpipe by the abnormal method known as 'pinching' (stopping the fingerhole with the fingernail and putting additional pressure on the bag) the use of notes beyond the basic compass of the fingerholes is strictly speaking foreign to the technique of the bagpipe. The denial of the use of the harmonic overtones must have drastically curtailed the compass of the new instrument compared with the old; for the compass of the *aulos* and *tibia* with their harmonics has been stated by Aristoxenus to have been two octaves and a fifth. Proclus,[56] in his commentary to Plato's *Alcibiades*, says that from each hole of the pipe at least three tones could be produced (i.e. the basic note as fingered, plus two harmonics above).

## Roman Britain

At the time Nero was hysterically offering to play the bagpipe in the circus at Rome, A.D. 68, something a great deal more important was going on: the Roman invasion of Britain. It had been in fact going on for some twenty-five years, having been embarked upon by Nero's predecessor, Claudius, in A.D. 43,* when Nero himself was a boy of six.

It may be reasonably expected that the Romans would have brought their musical instruments with them to Britain, if not in the early years of military conquest of the island, at least in the 360-odd years of occupation that followed. Sooner or later, these would be manufactured in Britain itself, either by the Romans or by the Gaulish craftsmen they brought over and employed.

There is ample evidence that they did so. The double-pipes were in ancient Britain before the Romans came, pictorially at least, through the coinage: a bronze coin of the reign of Tasciovanus (*c.* 20 B.C.), one of the kings of ancient Britain, shows on its reverse the double-pipes being

---

* For our purpose we may discount Julius Caesar's two short incursions into Britain in 55 and 54 B.C., which were little more than reconnaissances in force followed by complete withdrawal.

played by a centaur.* In Roman Britain carvings of the double-pipes may be seen on the Roman stone found at Bridgeness in East Lothian, now in the National Museum of Antiquities of Scotland in Edinburgh, and on a stone slab in the museum at Corbridge. Pictures of them are to be found on Roman mosaics at Keynsham in Somerset, at Sherborne in Dorset, and on a cup from Hockwood, Norfolk. They appear amongst the engravings on two of the dishes of the Mildenhall Treasure from Suffolk, discovered in 1946. There is, too, the charming little figure of the girl-piper found at Silchester in 1961, which, as might be expected, has been entitled 'The Flute Girl'.† On the single-pipe which the girl holds are to be seen projecting 'stops' similar to those fitted to the more advanced models of the *aulos* and the *tibia* to operate the metal bands which opened or covered extra fingerholes. The instrument could in this instance be a true flute, for the 'flute-girl' is holding it transversely across her body, as if about to raise it to her mouth to play it as a flute is played; but then the *plagiaulos* was also held in a similar way.

Most interesting from our point of view of all the finds of representations of musical instruments in Roman Britain, is a little stone figure, now in Gloucester Museum, which may possibly represent the god Atys, nude except for a Phrygian cap, playing the pan-pipes and accompanying them with a bag-blown drone, the bag of which he holds under his left arm. The figure, 14 in high, is carved in the round upon a Roman altar of limestone. It was discovered in 1962, and was identified as of the god Atys by Professor J. M. C. Toynbee.[57] It is strikingly similar to the *syrinx* and drone of the Alexandrian terra-cotta figurines already described.[58]

Atys, in Greek myth, was the lover of the Phrygian goddess Cybele, in whose honour was held annually in Rome the wild festival which was accompanied by the noise of the pipes, drums, and cymbals. So this little stone figure found at Gloucester may be not only the earliest representation by many centuries of a bagpipe in Britain, but a link with the earliest history and mythology of the pipes.

Other carvings and mosaics in Roman Britain depicting the *syrinx* have been found in Norfolk, Suffolk, at Welshpool in Montgomeryshire, but none with the suggestion of an accompanying drone. In the Leicester Museum the pan-pipes appear as being played by a kilted man!

---

* See R. P. Mack, *The Coinage of Ancient Britain*, London, 1953, p. 67. Tasciovanus was one of the successors to Cassivellaunus who opposed Julius Caesar in Britain in 54 B.C.; see J. M. C. Toynbee, *Art in Britain under the Romans*, p. 25. He probably reigned somewhere between 20 B.C. and A.D. 5. The motif of a female centaur playing the double-pipes is also to be seen in the Roman sculpture of the altar of (?) Amemptus; see Mrs Arthur Strong, *Roman Sculpture*, London, 1907. Her book contains several illustrations of players of the double-pipes depicted on Roman sculpture, all shown playing the instrument with cheeks distended for nasal inhalation.

† Reproduced under this title in *Studio*, July 1961. The figurine is now in Reading Museum. See Plate 8.

Some of these various representations, including those of the lyre and *kithara*, may of course be regarded as classical motifs, belonging, even in those days, to the far past and so separated by centuries from the daily life of the Romans living in Britain during the occupation. Such, certainly, would be the motifs of Apollo playing his lyre, or sometimes the larger instrument of the same type, the *kithara*;* there are at least nine examples of this in England, one of them as far north as Carlisle (on a bowl at Tullie House Museum). Such also would be the carving on a slab at Corbridge, of the satyr Marsyas playing his double-pipes in competition with Apollo with his lyre. Other such classical motifs are of maenads or satyrs playing the *syrinx*, tambourine, cymbals, or the double-pipes themselves, examples of which are to be found scattered throughout England.

The only form of musical pipes depicted in Roman Britain, with the exception of the rudimentary bag-blown drone played by the god Atys of the little altar at Gloucester, are the mouth-blown pipes. In every instance these are the double-pipes, except for the single example of the Silchester 'flute-girl'. Presuming that an instrument popular in Rome would also be popular with Romans in Britain, whether military or civilian, one would expect that Nero's bagpipe would have found its way over. The remarkable fact, however, is that after the reign of Nero, the instrument is never mentioned again by any writer of the classical Roman period.[59] Dio Cassius, who takes Roman history up to A.D. 229, writes in Greek, and always uses the word *aulos* for the pipes; and as we know the *aulos* was mouth-blown.

Dio Cassius, incidentally, makes interesting mention of the pipes at the flight of Cleopatra and her ships from the great sea-battle of Actium, with her lover Antony deserting the battle in its midst to follow her. On her arrival back in Egypt, Cleopatra wished to deceive her subjects into thinking that she and Antony had gained the victory, and gave orders for songs of triumph to be sung and for the pipes to be played, as her ships approached the harbour.[60]

Following Dio Cassius comes the *Historia Augusta*. This continues the story of Rome, and therefore of Britain, to the year A.D. 285. The *Augustan History* gives us a glimpse of the music-loving Roman emperors. Some of these played the pipes; others, like Carinus of the two hundred pipers before mentioned, were content to be patrons. The *Augustan History* is written in Latin; but where the pipes are mentioned, it is the old Greek name *aulos* that is used. Sometimes the player is referred to as *pythaules*; but the term would seem to be loosely and inaccurately used in the context of the later classical Roman period, for *pythaules* was the term used of the player at the Pythian Games at Delphi in Greece.

Nowhere does the writer of the *Augustan History* mention the bagpipe.

* For a description of these two instruments and their differences see Sachs, op. cit., pp. 130–1.

It is difficult to know what to make of this. Does it mean that the bag-blown version of the double-pipes disappeared from use, possibly for centuries, by the Romans after a brief spell of popularity in Nero's time? Did it ever appear at all in Britain in the hands of the Romans?

There have been several false clues which have led antiquarians to believe quite firmly that it did so appear in Britain. There are for instance a number of references in Latin inscriptions, though not in Britain, to the *collegium utriculariorum* and the *Utriculariorum Corpus*, which have been eagerly translated by antiquaries as meaning colleges of piping and as the Corporation of Pipers. Some of these references come from the scenes of the Danube campaigns, in which levies from southern Scotland took part under Roman leadership as auxiliaries of the legions, and it would be nice to think that the Scots had their colleges of piping on the banks of the Danube in Roman days! Unfortunately, the word *utricul-arius*, as has been said (p. 50), ordinarily means the master of a ferry-boat, consisting of a raft or other form of vessel floating on inflated skins. As the names of the individual *utricularii* which have come down to us are all of men from the vicinity of the great rivers of the Roman campaigns, the Danube or the rivers of the south of France,* it is more likely that the term *utricularii* refers to ferrymen and not bagpipers. There was un-doubtedly a *Collegium* or guild of pipers in Rome; but this was the *Collegium Tibicinum*; and the *tibicen*, with his feminine counterpart the *tibicina*, was the player of the mouth-blown pipes, usually the double-pipes.

Students of bagpipe history were long misled by a seemingly conclusive piece of evidence that the Romans brought the bagpipes to Britain. This was the astonishing find of a small brass figure of a bagpiper found at the Roman embarkation camp of Richborough in Kent. The antiquarian Edward King, writing in his *Munimenta Antiqua* (p. 20), describes how his friend the archaeologist and historian of Sandwich, Kent, William Boys, was digging under the foundations of the *sacellum*, the chapel for the reception of the Roman standards, about the year 1790. He came across a little bronze or brass figure of a bagpiper. The platform of the *sacellum* under which he found it was of concrete five feet thick and Edward King describes how Boys 'mined underneath' this solid mass for eleven feet. King reports:

> In digging under all these foundations to make these various
> discoveries, was found, at the bottom of all (and therefore plainly
> in a place where it must have been lost and buried *before the works
> were first begun*) [King's italics] a little bronze figure of a Roman
> soldier, playing upon a pair of bagpipes. This great curiosity was
> given to me by my friend Mr. Boys, and is now in my possession.
> . . . It most clearly ascertains [i.e. indicates], from the place it was

* I am indebted to Professor J. M. C. Toynbee for pointing out this fact.

found, and the time it must have been lost, the use and existence of this instrument among the Romans, on their very first arrival in this island. It [the brass figure] seems to have been part of the *Ephippia*, or horse trappings, of some Roman knight, and to have been designed to be suspended before the breast of the horse, hung on by leathern thongs passing through the two cavities behind the pipe; and secured, at bottom, by another thong, beneath the feet, which part is now broken off.

The whole equipment of the figure is most curious – the precise form of the bag and pipes, and the manner of holding and managing them; the helmet; the purse or ancient scrip on one side, and the short Roman sword or dagger on the other; and the coat and belt – And the whole is a proof that the bagpipe was virtually no Scotch, but a Roman instrument.

With the mention of this circumstance therefore, we will finish the description of this ancient and interesting fortress;* only just observing at the same time, that a similar little bronze was found on the outside of the walls, and that other bronze figures have also been found there, particularly a figure of Mercury; and a vast quantity of Roman coins, of such kinds as might be expected in a camp.

On the face of it, this evidence seemed unassailable; and it was strengthened rather than weakened by the finding of a similar figure at Glanton, Northumberland. Glanton lies some thirty miles to the north of Hadrian's Wall, but is quite near enough to have lain within the orbit of normal Roman military reconnaissance and activity, particularly of the mounted troops. Nevertheless, the first doubts of the Roman provenance of the little bronze bagpiper were cast shortly afterwards in an account of the Glanton find by a Northumbrian antiquarian David Dixon in 1895, in his book on Whittingham Vale. Dixon says (p. 234), 'A curious relic – a brass repoussé knife handle representing a bagpiper – was found at Glanton a few years ago and is now in the possession of Mr. Bolam, Ravensdowne, Berwick-upon-Tweed.' Bolam had evidently dated the find as being fifteenth-century work, for Dixon continues:

In a letter to Mr. Bolam, the Baron de Cosson thus describes it:— The figure of the piper is most curious. I find it difficult to offer any definite opinion with respect to its date, but my own impression is that it belongs rather to the sixteenth than to the fifteenth century. It is certainly a knife handle; and in the South Kensington Museum there is a complete knife with a handle much of the same general form, but with – if I remember rightly – a grotesque animal's head in the place of the piper.

* I.e. the fortified Roman camp at Richborough.

The little brass piper next appears in a find at Whitby Abbey, which is
described with an illustration in *The History of Cleveland* (*Yorkshire*),
by J. C. Atkinson (p. 143). The illustration is described as 'a wood-cut of
piper knife-handle attached to knife'. It was found in an ancient kitchen
midden along with other objects at Whitby Abbey, which was built in the
eleventh century. This and other finds are listed as 'knife hafts, coins etc;
also a bone and ivory comb inscribed with a runic legend. The wood-cut
shows clearly that the bagpiper forms the handle of the knife to which it
is attached. The knife is enclosed in its sheath, which shows very clearly
a pattern of repoussé work.'

The sequel comes in an illustration in *Knives and Forks* (Fig. 54) by
Charles Bailey, Keeper of the Department of Metal-work at the Victoria

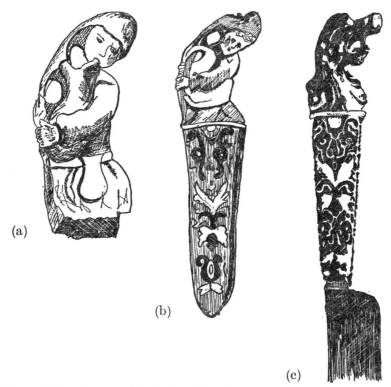

(a)

(b)

(c)

*Figure 8*  Bagpipers and knife-handle in brass

(a) The brass bagpiper found at
Roman fort, Richborough, Kent;
from King's *Munimenta Antiqua*

(b) Knife with bagpiper handle, in
its sheath of brass repoussé work,
found at Whitby Abbey (from
Atkinson, *The History of
Cleveland, Yorkshire*)

(c) Knife with griffin's head at
Victoria and Albert Museum,
London; enamelled brass repoussé
English seventeenth-century
work. The motifs on the handle
are closely similar to those of
Figure 8b.

and Albert Museum. This shows a knife with handle of enamelled brass repoussé work which does not include, it is true, a bagpiper but a griffin's head; the pattern of the enamelled work, however, is closely similar in motif to that of the bagpiper knife-handle found at Whitby Abbey; the bagpiper forming the handle of the Whitby Abbey knife is in its turn practically identical with the bagpiper found at Richborough. Finally the design on the sheath of the Whitby Abbey find is similar in motif to that of the handle of the knife in the Victoria and Albert Museum; and this is classed by Charles Bailey as seventeenth-century (? English) work. It has been subsequently amplified elsewhere as 'English work of the seventeenth century, though of a type often described as Flemish'.*

So dies the myth of the little Roman bagpiper, for almost 150 years accepted as unquestionable evidence of the use of the bagpipe by the Roman soldiers in Britain. In spite of all the conscientiousness and care exercised by the excavator of Richborough Fort, Mr William Boys, it becomes clear that the bronze figure must somehow have fallen into his 'dig' from a higher, more modern layer.

Another apparently convincing clue of Roman use of the pipes in Britain has suffered the same fate. This is the so-called Stanwix Stone, which is said to have stood for long during the latter part of the eighteenth century and much of the nineteenth outside an inn at Stanwix near Carlisle.† Stanwix was one of the stations of Hadrian's Wall. Many Roman altars and other carved Roman stones of the local red sandstone have been found there, so that it is not surprising that the figure of a bagpiper carved in the same local red sandstone should at first be accepted as Roman, even by knowledgeable antiquarians. Collingwood Bruce, in *Handbook of the Roman Wall* (p. 225), notes it thus:

> The figure of a piper now in the Carlisle Museum was found at Stanwix. Hutton‡ thus notices it – 'I observed a stone in the street [i.e. in Stanwix] converted into a horse-block three steps high, with the figure of a man in a recess eighteen inches in height, in a Roman dress, and in great preservation. I wondered the boys had not pelted him out of the world.'

F. Haverfield[61] describes the stone as follows:

> [A] Block of red sandstone measuring 34 inches in height, 36 inches in depth and fifteen inches in width. On one side is a recess, and in it the figure of a bagpiper in relief, about 20 inches high. This stone was first noticed by Hutchinson in the last [i.e. eighteenth]

* Information from William A. Cocks, F.S.A.Scot.
† Information from the curator of the Tullie House Museum, Carlisle, Mr Robert Hogg.
‡ William Hutton, a noted antiquary; see Haverfield's account below.

century; he describes it as being 'upon a door in Stanwyx'. It was
next noticed by William Hutton, who walked the Wall in 1802;
he describes it as 'a stone in the street converted into a horse
block'. Subsequently it was lost, but was found again in 1878 and
added to the Museum in 1884. It has always been traditionally
accepted as a Roman bagpiper, but the costume of the piper
suggests a much more modern origin.

Later authorities, in cataloguing the Roman stones from Hadrian's
Wall now at Tullie House, have more positively refuted the Roman origin
of the Stone; and it is not now included among the accredited Roman finds
at the Museum; indeed it is not now even considered to merit a place
under cover in the Museum itself, but is relegated to the grounds, and
stands at the gate. Far from being in a state of 'great preservation' as
William Hutton found it, it is now so weathered that it is difficult to
discern the bagpipe at all. This seems a pity, for even a false clue is sometimes worth preserving in order that future historians may evaluate it
for themselves.

Finally we must discuss the attitudes of writers on the Scottish bagpipe
to the question of whether the bag was known in Roman Britain. W. L.
Manson in *The Highland Bagpipe* attributes to the Greek writer on music,
Aristides Quintilianus (probably third century A.D.), the statement that
'the bagpipe was known in the Scottish Highlands in his day' and adds,
'this however may be set aside as a reference of no value, seeing that the
Highlands was then an unknown world to the Greeks'. The statement is
ill considered. Aristides lived centuries after Greece became a Roman
province, and well after the commencement of the Roman invasion of
Britain. As an informed writer he would certainly know as much about
Scotland, i.e. Caledonia, as did the Roman historians and chroniclers of
the invasion, some of whom were Greek and wrote their account in the
Greek language. Aristides does not mention Scotland. What he does say
is that 'those practising warlike dances are of passionate disposition, and
rush headlong to the combat – such as the Thracians and the whole Celtic
nation'.[62] As the Celts were spread from the fringes of Asia in the east to
Ireland in the West, Aristides' statement can hardly be taken as referring
specifically to the Scottish Highlands; neither does he anywhere make
any mention of the bagpipes. We read in Xenophon's *Anabasis* that the
Thracians danced in full armour to 'the music of the pipes'; and from
other classical references it appears that the music of the pipes was always
popular to dance to; but the pipes mentioned or implied by all such
classical writers were of the mouth-blown variety.

Grattan Flood also refers in *The Story of the Bagpipe* to this interpretation of Aristides by Scottish writers and adds a nationalistic contribution
with the remark that the passage 'can only apply to the Celts of Ireland'.

Manson[63] seems also to be mistaken in his description of the Roman

legionary 'distance slab' found at Bridgeness, Bo'ness, on the Firth of
Forth. He says,

> About 1870 a stone was dug up from the ground near Bo'ness, on
> which was sculptured a party of Roman soldiers on the march.
> They were dressed in short kilts, and one was playing the bagpipe.
> The instrument was very similar to those of the present day except
> that the drones were shorter.

The facts are that the Romans depicted on the stone are taking part in
a sacrificial ceremony at an altar within the portals of a small temple.
Except for the boy acolyte, who wears a short garment (and possibly also
the player of the pipes, the length of whose garb is hidden in the picture), the figures taking part are not wearing military garb (certainly not
kilts!), but the robes appropriate to the ceremonial. The pipes, which
ritual and custom required at the ceremony of sacrifice, are the mouth-
blown double-pipes, the Roman *tibia*. They do not in the least resemble
the bagpipes of any nation; and to say that 'the drones are shorter' is
therefore sheer nonsense. A panel at the left-hand end of the stone
depicts natives being ridden down by a cavalryman.

It is obvious that Manson could not have seen the stone; we can only
conclude that he received a garbled description of it at second or third
hand.

I have also seen a letter in a piping journal, from a piper in Western
Canada, which he wrote, one may add in extenuation, on the basis of
mere recollection, which reads: 'Quintilianus – I think Marcus Fabius –
saw among prisoners marching through Rome "a wild Caledonian with
his bagpipes".' I would be most glad to be proved wrong, but in a careful
search of the works of Quintilianus I have found no such passage.

With all our apparent clues one by one discredited, we are left uncertain
as to whether the true bagpipe as we know it was ever seen in Britain in
the hands of a Roman piper. There is no representation of it of Roman
date to be found anywhere in Britain, either in stone-carving, pottery
decoration, terra-cotta, coinage design or mosaic decoration, in all of
which, forms of art depictions of the mouth-blown double-pipes are to be
seen. There are no references to it in Latin or Greek literature during the
period of the Roman occupation, beyond those regarding Nero's proposed
performance on it. All we can say is that the principle of the bag was
established in a rudimentary form in Alexandria in the last century B.C.,
as we know from the Alexandrian figurine; that the same crude form of it
was apparently carved in stone by a Roman or Roman-employed sculptor
at Gloucester, some time, probably rather early, during the Roman
occupation; and that it is said to have been a popular instrument in Rome
itself during the first century A.D. We can only surmise that any musical
instrument popular in Rome, and so easily carried about, was more than

likely to have made its appearance somewhere in Britain during the 350 years of the Roman presence there.

The bagpipe apparently never had any official status as an instrument of the Roman army, whose military instruments were the trumpet (*tuba*, *lituus*) and horn (*cornu*, *buccina*). The sixth-century Latin historian, Procopius, in his history of the wars, *De Bello Gothico* (VI, xxiii, 19–23), refers to the sound issuing from 'leather and very thin wood'; this has sometimes been mistakenly thought to refer to the use of the bagpipe as a military musical instrument in the field. A careful perusal of the whole passage, however, makes it obvious that the instrument referred to is a light cavalry trumpet, which was seemingly so made, i.e. of wood covered with leather.

The Roman general Belisarius, to whom Procopius was secretary, was having much trouble in trying to recall his troops by shouted commands, which could not be heard above the noise of battle. The result was that they were repeatedly ambushed and cut off by the enemy, who drowned the sound of the Roman commands to return by clashing their weapons on their shields. Procopius pointed out to the general that in the noise of combat the human voice was useless for giving clear commands. He advised the use of the trumpet, but observed that the soldiers could not differentiate between signals for attack and retreat when they were sounded on the same type of trumpet.* He therefore recommended the use of the cavalry trumpet as a signal to attack, and of the infantry trumpet to sound the retreat; for, he says, the troops cannot fail to differentiate between the two, because the sound of the first issues from leather and thin wood, and the other from thick brass. Belisarius agreed, and told Procopius that the signal to retire would accordingly be sounded on the infantry trumpet. There is plainly no reference here to a bagpipe.

Though there is no mention of the bagpipe being used as a military instrument, it may well have been used by the Roman soldier as a means of pleasure and relaxation in his off-duty hours. One has to emphasize, however, that there is no evidence of it, either in writings, carvings or archaeological remains in Britain. Roman musical pipes, both of bone and of wood, have been found in Britain, notably in London, and are now in the London and Guildhall Museums;[64] but there is nothing to show that these were anything else than the divergent, mouth-blown double-pipes, the *tibia*.

## Scotland

It has been a comparatively simple and straightforward task to trace the route of the pipes (i.e. the mouth-blown pipes) from Babylonia and from ancient Egypt through Asia Minor to Greece, from Greece to Rome, from

---

* In the light of the various bugle calls of later military practice, this seems a strange pronouncement.

Rome to Britain, and, by the hands of the soldiers of the 2nd Augustan Legion of the Roman army, up the length of Britain, to Bo'ness on the southern shore of the Firth of Forth in Scotland. But here the trail peters out. To establish a link between the Roman double-pipes on the south shore of the Firth of Forth and the ancestor of the Scottish Highland bagpipe a comparatively few miles further north is extremely difficult, if not impossible.

There can be little doubt that the Highlanders (in those days the Caledonians) must have known all about the Roman *tibia* during the occupation of the rest of Britain. It is true that the inhabitants of Caledonia were the implacable enemies of the invading Romans. Four times during the Roman occupation of Britain, the fortified lines of Hadrian's and the Antonine Walls were completely overrun and destroyed by the Caledonians, in their major efforts to drive the Romans from the country. Between these military disasters to the Romans, however, the frontier was stabilized for spans of nearly a hundred years at a time. During these periods there existed peaceful commerce between the Romans and the natives of Britain, and between the physically divided populations of the Britons living on either side of the fortified frontier. There were two specially constructed customs gates constructed in Hadrian's Wall in Northumberland, at Housesteads and at Portgate, where civilians were allowed to enter and cross into the other territory for the purpose of peaceful trading. The civilian settlements or *vici* (singular, *vicus*) sprang up near the main Roman military stations, at Carlisle for instance, and at Housesteads; and in Scotland itself at Trimontium near Melrose, the latter *vicus* still seemingly existing as the village of Newstead.

The sounds of the double-pipes must have been heard everywhere throughout Roman-occupied Britain; for the pipes were obligatory at the religious sacrifice, at least of any sacrifice of an official nature, which would include those held by the army at 'church parades'. Indeed, Cicero had stated in the time of Julius Caesar that without the customary music (always of the pipes, but sometimes augmented by the lyre or *kithara*) the proceedings of the sacred ritual were vitiated.

The Roman soldier prayed often to his gods for victory or preservation in battle; and wherever there was a military altar there would be a military piper to play before it. Nearly a hundred such military altars have been found in the vicinity of Hadrian's Wall alone. (One wonders if the Northumbrian love of the pipes could be a distant legacy of those days of the Roman pipers, so long to be heard across the breadth of this part of the country!) Twenty more altars have been discovered at the Antonine Wall in Scotland, stretching across the narrow waist between the Firths of Forth and Clyde.

In addition, the Roman defensive system based on the Antonine Wall had its outliers in the advanced fortified posts at Inchtuthil, some fifteen miles north of the River Tay; at Fendoch in the mouth of the Sma' Glen;

at Dalginross near Comrie, and at Bochastle near Callander, all in Perthshire. There was also the advanced marching camp, not yet located, from which the great Battle of Mons Graupius was fought. At all those places the sound of the Roman pipes must have been wafted to curious and perhaps not altogether unappreciative ears across the fortified lines. There could be no question of their being inaudible at the distance ensured by the fortifications; for as Curt Sachs has observed,[65] the sound of the ancient Greek and Roman pipes, from the power that must have been required to blow them, 'could be as shrill and exciting as the sound of their relatives, the bagpipes of modern Scottish Regiments' – and the sound of the great Highland war-pipe has been said to be audible seven miles away.

Nevertheless we must be careful to remember that the double-pipes were not a military instrument in the true sense of the term, though they were played at the religious observances of the soldiers. Neither were they solely a musical adjunct of religion, forbidden to be played at other times. They provided the music, as at Rome itself, for the theatre, the circus, and other, sometimes licentious, secular occasions.

It was in the civilian settlements of the *vici*, however, near the Roman military base camps in southern Scotland and in the north of England, that the opportunity of hearing, seeing, studying and learning the Roman pipes, if the natives of Scotland had been so disposed, must have occurred in plenty; and they could easily have learned how to make and play them if they had wished. There was plenty of fraternization between the Roman soldiers and the natives of Britain of both sexes when the two nations were not actually engaged in warfare. The Roman soldier could and did serve in the army for as long as twenty years, and often lived during the whole of his service in the same part of the country. Until the third and fourth centuries of the occupation, they were not allowed to marry formally the native women; but girlfriends were always connived at by the rulers of Roman Britain, and many life-long and faithful associations were so formed. In a diploma of Roman citizenship found at Chesters, on Hadrian's Wall, bestowed upon the 'foreign' (i.e. non-Roman) troops of the Wall for faithful service, the right is given of lawful marriage to the 'wives' they had acquired, or 'with those they may afterwards take, provided one at a time.' Later, the Roman soldiery in Britain were allowed not only to marry their long-term girlfriends, but to lease small areas of land on their discharge or retirement, on condition that their sons served in the Roman army; and the civilian settlements, the *vici*, became the permanent homes of the wives and families of the Roman soldiers and of the retired veterans (as well as sheltering the itinerant traders and official travellers).

There was considerable interchange of goods between the two cultures. Such manufactured goods as Roman pottery were eagerly sought after by the natives of Britain, and found their way as far beyond the occupied areas as the Outer Isles. The Roman coinage circulated freely and widely, both directly from the hands of the Roman military establishment and in the ordinary course of commerce.[66] Probably, as far as the pipers and the otherwise musically inclined of both nations were concerned, tunes and tricks of musical technique formed an acceptable form of currency, as they do among pipers to the present day.

Yet, strange to say, there is no evidence that the double-pipes of the Romans ever caught on among the Caledonians of the north, though the gift of music and a natural love of it has always been one of the characteristics of the Celt. The well-defined trail of the divergent mouth-blown pipes which can be traced unbroken from ancient Babylonia comes to a sudden stop at the Romano-British frontier. How can one explain it? Could it be that they had pipes of their own of a different species already, and had no desire to change?

*Indigenous pipes?*

Did the Caledonians, the Highlanders, in the days before the bag made its appearance, have a species of mouth-blown pipes different from that used throughout most of the rest of the European world? To consider this question fully, we must recapitulate briefly the history of the reed-pipes as we have been able so far to elucidate it. It will be remembered that during the third millennium B.C. two main species of double reed-pipes emerged. In one, the species typified by the silver pipes of Ur, two separate pipes were held divergently in the form of a V with the apex of the V in the mouth. One pipe was held in each hand. In the other, the species typified by the indigenous pipes of ancient Egypt, two single pipes were bound closely together. The player fingered the two parallel pipes as one, playing a single, unaccompanied melody, *with both hands on the chanter*. A further development of this latter species was the use of wax to stop all the fingerholes of one pipe, except the lowest. The drone was thus discovered. Soon the drone-pipe was deliberately constructed with only the one hole; and very much later, its length was extended, so as to produce a truly bass note. The bag, of course, had still to come.

These were the two main types of double-pipes of the pre-bag era, the *divergent* and the *parallel* pipes. The general characteristics of the two species, divergent or parallel, two-part harmony or single melody with or without drone, continued their independent existence in bagpipe form.

We may now ask ourselves: did the Scottish Highland bagpipes have their origin in the divergent double-pipes of the Roman legions, or could they have sprung, at however great a remove, from the ancient Egyptian parallel pipes? (We may discount the single chanter of the Ur seal because it is not typical of the pipes of that part of the world, i.e. Babylonia and Mesopotamia.)

It seems likely that the Scottish (and English) bagpipes must somehow have stemmed from the Egyptian model, and have arrived in Britain before the Romans; for, although they had every chance of acquiring the Roman pipes, with which they must have been perfectly familiar, the peoples of both the occupied and unoccupied territories of Britain seem to have totally rejected them. Certainly it is the Egyptian parallel pipes, with their drone, that resemble more closely the Highland pipes towards which we are working our way. The question therefore arises, how did the two-handed chanter and drone arrive in Britain, and in Scotland in particular?

Several explanations are possible. First, of course, such an inherently simple instrument could have been invented independently by the folk of the Scottish Highlands, extremely musical as they have always been, in pre-Roman times. It is not impossible indeed that even the bag component could have been discovered by the ingenious Highlander and applied independently of the discoveries of other countries. This of course can only be the purest speculation, for which there is no actual evidence.

The second possibility is that the two-handed chanter and drone might have come to Scotland, either directly or indirectly from Egypt (or elsewhere in the Middle East), by one of the very early Mediterranean migrations. The history of the reed-pipes covers such a vast period, reaching back to the third millennium B.C., that there was plenty of time for such a thing to happen. Megalithic immigrations, those of the folk of the stone circles, and the gigantic stone *menhirs* and the 'chambered cairns', are said to have reached Scotland from the Mediterranean by way of the west coast between 2000 and 3000 B.C., which fits the time factor very nicely. Alternatively, such immigrants, bringing with them the pipes in their Egyptian form, could have come over, at a further remove, from Ireland. The early civilizations of Ireland had close affinities, ethnological and cultural, with those of Spain. A race of Iberian stock as a component of the ancient peoples of Ireland and Scotland is a fact of commonplace knowledge.* The term 'Mediterranean race', however, does not necessarily denote direct contact with Egypt; so we are still left with a large gap in the jig-saw puzzle.

A further possibility is that the two-handed chanter and drone may have infiltrated across the land-mass of Europe, rather than via the Mediterranean sea.

The parallel pipes of bone found in an Avar grave mentioned by Baines may be an important link in the chain.† One of these had five

---

* 'The few human bones found in Irish Bronze Age sites indicate that the population of Ireland during the period belonged to the Mediterranean race – a relatively short dolichocephalic (long-headed) and dark-complexioned people to be seen today in their fullest purity in Spain'; 'Ireland', *Encyclopaedia Britannica* (14th ed.).

† *Bagpipes*, pp. 51–3. Listed by Denis Barthe ('Die avarische Doppelschalmei von Janoshida', *Archaeologica Hungaria*, xiv, Budapest, 1934) as seventh or eighth century A.D., but in Baines's opinion similar to bone pipes of the Scythians of about six centuries before (quoting Pollux, *Onomasticon*, iv, 74).

*Plate 8* The Silchester 'flute-girl'.
Discovered at Silchester in 1961.
$4\frac{1}{4}$ in. high. The instrument is
probably a reed-pipe with the reed
inserted in the side of the pipe.
Professor J. M. C. Toynbee describes
it as 'a single pipe with projecting
stops.' She notes 'a conspicuous
blend of classical and Celtic elements'
in the figurine, and adds, 'The
drapery would seem to be intended
to represent a Greek *peplos*; but its
stylized, vertical folds . . . are
typically Romano-British.' Cf. her
*Art in Britain under the Romans*,
p. 121.

*Plate 9* Pictish slab (c. tenth century)
recently discovered at Lethendy Tower,
Perthshire, where it was built into a
stair. The musician on the right is
playing on the triple pipe. The only
other known example of the triple pipe
in the British Isles is on St
Muiredeach's Cross at Monasterboice in
Ireland, which is also of tenth century
date. There is a plaster cast of this
cross, showing the triple pipe, at the
Victoria and Albert Museum, London.

*Plate 10*  Bagpipe with single drone carved on a stone frieze in Roslin Chapel, Midlothian.

The chapel was built in 1441, but the drone of the bagpipe had already made its appearance in Britain nearly a century before.

fingerholes (requiring both hands on the chanter) while the other has two; this suggests a variable drone. The pipes had originally been bound together.

There were several later immigrations into Scotland, including that of the Celts in *c*. 500–400 B.C. There does not seem to have been any very direct contact between the Celts and Egypt; but there were Celts in Asia Minor, namely in Galatia. The peoples of Asia Minor however, as we have seen, seem to have favoured the divergent pipes, which almost certainly reached them from Babylonia.

Finally it is conceivable that, though the Roman legions themselves apparently did not possess this form of the instrument, some of the auxiliary units of the Roman army, the *alae* (cavalry wings) and the foreign cohorts, might well have brought the two-handed chanter from their own countries. These non-Roman 'foreign' contingents came from all over Europe, as far as the fringes of Asia Minor, and from North Africa. There was stationed at Ribchester in Lancashire an *ala* of Sarmatians from the borders of Scythia, beyond the river Don in Russia; and a battalion of Syrian archers at Carvoran on the Wall; there were three cohorts of Thracians from the Balkans, of which the second cohort actually served in Scotland. A cohort of Tungri was stationed at Housesteads; a cohort of Batavians at Carrawburgh; one of Astures from Northern Spain at Greatchesters, and other cohorts of Hispani besides. By the agency of traders and other permitted travellers, perhaps even through occasional visits of relatives of the British wives of the retired Roman veterans, there would be no difficulty in acquiring the knowledge of any exotic musical instrument that came into the country with these 'foreign' Roman auxiliaries, by the peoples of unconquered Caledonia in the north, beyond the Roman walls.

## The hornpipe

In the ancient Scottish chronicles there are stories by Andrew of Wyntoun and John of Fordun concerning the founder of the Scottish nation. It is said that one, Gedeyl-Glays, came from Scythia somewhere north of the Black Sea and that he received the hand of the daughter of the ruling Pharaoh of Egypt, the Princess Scota, as reward for his help against the vexatious Israelites within the Egyptian borders. One of his sons was said to have been among the Egyptians drowned in the waters of the Red Sea after the Israelites had got across. In the Egyptians' hostility to all immigrants after the Israelite incident (or probably rather, the Hyksos invasions of Egypt) Gedeyl-Glays was politely asked to quit the country. He and his Egyptian wife, the Princess Scota, settled in Spain, where eventually he died; his son by Scota, Hyber, went to Ireland and colonized it under the name of Hibernia. From there the children of Scota, by then known as the Scots, migrated in their turn across the short sea passage to Dalriada, on the mainland of the country to become known as Scotland (bringing with them their ancient Stone of Destiny).

If these tales had been true, we would have the perfect explanation of how the two-handed chanter and drone came to Scotland from ancient Egypt; for the amusing thing is that the time-schedule fits closely. Gedeyl-Glays and Scota left Egypt not long, comparatively speaking, after the new-fangled divergent pipes were introduced into Egypt from the east, to compete with the indigenous two-handed parallel pipes of the Old Kingdom (see p. 20). Curt Sachs dates the introduction of these divergent pipes into Egypt at about 1500 B.C.[67] The date of the Exodus of the Israelites from Egypt (and therefore of Gedeyl-Glays of the story) has been put by scholars at about 1300 B.C.,[68] which is possibly near enough to fit.

Unfortunately, the story of Gedeyl-Glays and the Princess Scota must be dismissed as a complete fable. But it is not impossible that the ancient Chronicles have as their basis the folk-memory or tradition of an east-west migration, into which this colourful though purely imaginary history of the Scottish race had been embroidered. Martin Martin,writing in the late seventeenth century of Fionn and Ossian and their band of hero-warriors (now recognized to be legendary), states that tradition had it in the Hebrides in his day that they had come to Ireland from Spain. The Irish, too, had their own migratory traditions of the 'Milesians' – migrant invaders from the eastern Mediterranean.

Beneath all the overlay of legendary fabled traditions, there seems the reasonable possibility of factual basis, however slight, far removed and twisted. There do seem to have been migrations, whether of peoples or of ideas and skills, from the eastern to the western Mediterranean, both Celtic and pre-Celtic – or as we might say, both Bronze Age and Iron Age, some of which reached Britain and Ireland via Spain and Brittany. It is fully possible that the Welsh *pibgorn*, with its Scottish counterpart the Stock and Horn (in use as a folk instrument in Scotland up to the days of Robert Burns) and the English version of the same instrument, the hornpipe, could have been so brought from the east.

The modern generic name for all three of these instruments is the hornpipe. It is an ancient instrument, widely distributed, both in its single-pipe and parallel double-pipe (drone) form; it is, in fact, a two-handed chanter. It derives its name from the fact that it terminates in an animal horn. Though the larger forms of such a horn may give some added acoustical effect to the instrument, many hornpipes, as Baines points out, have a horn too small for it to make much, if any, difference to the sound. It has been suggested that the horn feature may have come about in ancient times through a cult significance rather than an acoustical one.

Some hornpipes have the reed covered with a cap of horn as in the Welsh *pibgorn*, or of wood as in the Scottish example (like the modern practice chanter). Most have the single beating-reed of the clarinet type, as distinct from the double reed of the oboe.

Historically, the important feature of the Welsh *pibgorn* is the curious, characteristically serrated ornamentation of the horn-bell. In this it bears an astonishing similarity to examples of the same type of instrument found in the Greek archipelago and further east.

Hornpipes range in their distribution from the Atlantic coast of Europe to the Urals and to India.[69] The characteristic serration of the bell is found in a number of countries stretching from Syria* to Wales. The hornpipe exists in its unornamented form in many other countries, filling in the geographical gaps.

Not all of these are single-pipes. In a number of countries, hornpipes have two bores within their single tubes; there are also double hornpipes, i.e. two pipes attached to each other. In both cases, the basic plan is the same as with the ancient parallel pipes of Egypt. The fingerholes correspond in both bores (or both pipes) so that each pair of holes is covered by the same finger. In some, however, one of the bores, or pipes, has only one, or perhaps only two, fingerholes; it sounds a constant or a variable drone to the melody of the other pipe, as with the ancient Egyptian prototype.

This feature of the hornpipe is of crucial importance in the evolution and history of the bagpipe: as we said earlier, the bag is only an addition to an existing instrument. As far as the bagpipe with the two-handed chanter and drone is concerned, it is to be found in many countries of the world to the present day simply as the application of the bag principle to the indigenous hornpipe.

The hornpipe, as has been said, is an ancient instrument. It is not possible to date the period of its migration from its home of origin in the east to its arrival in the west.† Baines suggests that the hornpipe might have originated with some megalithic cult,[70] and observes that this would place its arrival in Britain as early as around 2000 B.C.‡

* And even from Ceylon according to A. H. Frere in a letter to W. Blandford, 17 December 1929. Frere was Honorary Custodian of the Musical Instrument Museum, Royal College of Music, London, a meticulous and painstaking organologist.

† Henry Balfour, 'The old British "pibcorn" or "hornpipe" and its affinities', *Journal of the Anthropological Institute*, vol. 20 (1890), reached the conclusion that the hornpipe came to Britain with the Celtic migrations; this would still have been some four to six centuries or so before the Romans, though not before the supposed trading voyages to the Scilly Isles mentioned by Strabo. Baines's dating of the arrival of the hornpipe in Britain as early as 2000 B.C. seems just as likely.

‡ A. H. Frere to W. Blandford, 17 December 1929: 'I have reason to believe that the pibgorn family, ranging from Anglesey to Ceylon, is intimately connected with the builders of the megalithic monuments; for they are characteristic instruments wherever such monuments exist, and nowhere else.' He made the same statement in correspondence with the Custodian of the Museum at Canterbury, apropos the Basque hornpipe, the *alboka*, in 1934. But two archaeologists have doubted Frere's theory that there is a direct affinity between the *pibgorn* and the megalithic builders.

The hornpipe has, in fact, two possible cult attributes: the horns; and the serration of the horn-rims at the lower end of the instrument. The latter, because of the 'halo' of facets of light glinting around the rim from the serrations, presents a kind of 'eye-motif' or 'sun-motif', a symbol found in prehistory. The Basque variety of hornpipe, the *alboka*, has an additional possible cult attribute in the purely decorative feature of a 'wheel-motif' of wood attached to the underside of the instrument. (The wheel was an adjunct to fire- and sun-worship, but is probably later than the sun- or eye-motif.)[71] It is possibly significant that in some specimens of the *alboka* the rim of this segment of a wheel is also serrated. The wheel-motif has obviously no effect on the sound of the instrument.*

Unfortunately archaeology is silent upon the subject; no actual specimens of the parallel pipes with horn-bell terminations, or remains of them, have been found in prehistory or antiquity† (though there are plenty of examples of the divergent double-pipes). This could simply mean that the materials of which the hornpipe is made, wood and horn, have not withstood the disintegrating process of time, as the Egyptian hornless pipes have done. Nevertheless, it makes a vital gap in the evidence.

If, however, the instrument is as ancient as has been suggested, there must have been both time and opportunity for a hornpipe with a two-handed chanter to have reached Britain and to have become firmly established there long before the Romans came, with their divergent double-pipes. Perhaps this was the indigenous form of pipe that with-stood and survived the competition of the Roman pipes. Certainly if the megalithic theory of origin were correct, it would be convenient to pipe-history!

In conclusion, as the Highlanders did not adopt the double-pipes of the Romans, we are brought back again to the theory that they already had pipes of their own, and that these pipes were either invented by the Highlanders themselves or were brought by one of the migrations, possibly far back in time, in the form of the Egyptian parallel pipes, or the hornpipe.

* Baines (*Bagpipes*, p. 31) gives a fascinating map showing the present distribu-tion of the various species of hornpipes. One species forms a line from the western shore of the Caspian Sea, through Phoenicia and southern Greece to Scotland; another extends from Syria through Egypt, North Africa and Morocco to Wales. Other species are strung across Europe.

† But see J. M. Coles, 'Irish Bronze Age horns and their relations with northern Europe', *Proceedings of the Prehistoric Society*, n.s., vol. 29, for the suggestion that the Celts had bronze reed-pipe horns of the *pibgorn* type.

# Chapter two

# Britain after the Romans

## The Roman legacy

The Roman occupation of Britain, which began in A.D. 43 under Claudius, may be said to have come to an end in the year 410 with the withdrawal of the Roman military forces garrisoning the country for urgent use nearer home. The occupation had lasted for the impressive interval of just over 360 years. One cannot tell to what extent or how long the memory and knowledge of their music, and particularly of their divergent double-pipes, remained after they had gone.

It can hardly be said that the Romans 'departed' in the complete sense of the word, for as we have seen, by the year 410 many generations of retired veterans, both of the legions and of the foreign auxiliaries, had married British wives and settled permanently at such centres as London, Bath, Catterick, Carlisle, or in the smaller *vici* near their place of military service.[1] Latterly, soldiers for the Roman armies had been recruited, apparently as volunteers, among the natives of Britain, both north and south of the Wall. Some of the more musically gifted of these recruits may well have become pipers. Among the retired veteran pipers, there must have been many willing and eager to hand on their art to the younger generations in Britain, their own children amongst them.

How long such traditions lasted we cannot tell. That the divergent double-pipes were being played both in England and on the Continent by itinerant minstrels and 'joculators' as late as the tenth century, seems to be evident from drawings and illuminations in tenth-century manuscripts,* though one cannot always be sure that the illustrators were working from the contemporary scene and not just copying from earlier manuscripts. It is also impossible to say whether any such playing had remained as an unbroken tradition from the Romans, or whether it was re-imported by minstrels, who were to a certain extent cosmopolitan

---

* Notably at the British Museum (Cotton MS. Cleopatra C viii; Harleian MS. no. 603); at Paris (Bibl. Nat. Lat. 6); at Rome (Vatican Pal. Lat. 39). Buhle, *Die musikalischen Instrumente in den Miniaturen des frühen Mittelalters*, Leipzig, 1903, ch. I, 'Die Blasinstrumente', gives other references. A number of these are reproduced by Joseph Strutt in *Sports and Pastimes of the People of England.*

*Figure 9*  Figures playing divergent double-pipes

(a)  From 'Anglo-Saxon Gleeman's Bear Dance'; tenth century; British Museum manuscript, reproduced in Strutt, *Sports and Pastimes*

(b)  After twelfth-century manuscript (Rom. Vatican Pal. lat. 39)

(a)                              (b)

in their comings and goings from the Continent. Whatever the truth of the matter, we continue to find drawings or illuminations of pipers playing the erstwhile Roman double-pipes. Such drawings continue into the fourteenth century as in the Luttrell Psalter. Later representation is supplemented in sculpture. Here we begin to find the double-pipes portrayed both as reed-pipes and as recorders; the latter are identifiable by their fipple-hole, as in the sixteenth-century example at Cirencester Church.

We should perhaps mention here a curious development that appears in the tenth century, in the form of a triple-pipe. A representation of it is to be seen on the face of St Muiredeach's Cross at Monasterboice in Ireland (early tenth century). Another has been recently discovered on a 'Pictish' slab, probably of the tenth century, at Lethendy Tower in Perthshire.*

These are of great interest. It seems that at least one, if not two, of the three pipes must necessarily have sounded a drone, for it would hardly be practical to finger three chanters all playing melodic parts. If this is so, it anticipates the date for the appearance of the drone in Britain by about four centuries; for the accredited appearance of the drone as a development from the previous droneless bagpipe was in the early fourteenth century.

There is a fine plaster cast of the Monasterboice Cross in the Victoria and Albert Museum, London, which shows the triple-pipe clearly. The chanter (apparently the left pipe of the three) seems to be a two-handed one, and it looks as if both the other pipes may have been drones. The

* Cf. Greenhill and Fisher's article on the Lethendy Slab which is to appear in *Proceedings of the Society of Antiquaries of Scotland*, vol. 104, 1974–5.

fingering of the other example, on the Lethendy slab, is not conclusive, though the triple form of the pipe appears clearly in the carving.

From the topographical location of these triple-pipes, one in Scotland and one in Ireland,* one is tempted to wonder if the instrument could have been a Celtic one, unrelated to the more common double-pipes. The triple-pipe, as we have said (see p. 19n.), is to be found at the present day in the form of the *launeddas*, in Sardinia; it has often been classified as a modern instrument, but a votive bronze was found in Sardinia of date between eighth and sixth century B.C. depicting the instrument.† The date is roughly right (though perhaps a little early) for the Celtic migrations; but there seems to be no mention of a Celtic invasion of Sardinia. Whether the triple-pipe is of Celtic or older provenance must await more expert pronouncement. One cannot find suggestions of the triple-pipe in the stages of an east-west migration as one can the hornpipe and *pibgorn*.

A further example of the triple-pipe is to be seen in an illuminated manuscript psalter in Glasgow University. The instrument has been wrongly named as pan-pipes.[2] The psalter is thought to be of English (Yorkshire) provenance from the late twelfth century, by which time the image of the triple-pipe could have been copied by successive monkish copyists.

# Ireland

Before we discuss the pipes in Ireland, we should mention the curious tradition in Irish Celtic folktale, of the vocal droning sound known as the *dord fian*, ascribed to the ancient hero-warriors Fionn and Ossian and their followers.

Gerard Murphy, in his notes to the collection of Celtic folktales known as the *Duanaire Finn* (see p. 70), describes this as a kind of humming noise made with the lips drawn together. It must have originated before the advent of Fionn himself, for it was said to have been made by nine men together, until Fionn's time, when the number was increased to thirty-one or, according to another version, fifty men – all making this humming or droning in concert.[3]

The *dord fian* was apparently used as a kind of gathering or assembly call by the *Fian*. It is mentioned frequently in the folktales, in such lines as 'The note of a bell have I heard in Druim Deirg where the Fian were wont to hunt; [but] more sweet to me, when our hosts [the Fian] had

---

* There is possibly also a second one in Ireland, at Clonmacnoise, see Baines, *Bagpipes*, p. 59.

† See Sybille von Cles-Reden, *The Realm of the Great Goddess: the story of the megalith builders*, 1961, p. 149. She describes the bronze as 'an ithyphallic hermaphrodite playing a pipe with three tubes, of the kind that still survives in the south of the island and is known as the *Launeddas*'.

come, was the Dord Fian gathering them.' Another line runs 'When Fionn took his seat on a hill, the Dord Fian would be faultlessly sounded.' In another passage Fionn, in danger, urges his companions to die nobly, sounding the Dord Fian. Again, 'Fiachna and Inse, sent by Oisin for news, hear the Dord Fian'.

One cannot guess if the *dord fian* had any basis in fact. Other Celtic musical traditions such as that of the *suantarghleas*, music which had the power of sending its hearers into a deep sleep, plainly belong to the realm of fancy.

The Irish scholar Eugene O'Curry mentions the *crónan* as a sort of humming or 'vocal purring'* in chorus accompanying a folksong or dirge. One cannot say if this *crónan* had any affinity with the *dord fian* of the folktales or not; but it does seem as if the vocal drone may sometimes have been used as an accompaniment to a sung melody. Whether the Irish vocal drone or *crónan* came before the pipes, or whether it stemmed from them, it would seem that the musical device of the drone, vocal or instrumental, was an ancient Irish tradition.

It is from Ireland, which never suffered Roman invasion, that the first clear references in these islands to native pipes and pipers appear, and are to be found in the Brehon Laws. These were the ancient Laws of Ireland, of which the earliest parts are traditionally ascribed to King Cormac Mac Art, who died in A.D. 266.[4]

Presumably at first the Laws were unwritten. Later, they were written down in the two ancient books, the *Senchus Mór* (Great Book of the Old Laws) and the *Book of Acaill*. In the (ancient) introduction to the *Senchus Mór*, an account is given of its original compilation:[5] In A.D. 438, a collection of the pagan laws (of Ireland) was made at the request of Saint Patrick; and Laegaire, King of Ireland, appointed a committee of nine learned and eminent persons, including himself and St Patrick, to revise them. At the end of three years, these nine produced a new code, from which everything that clashed with the Christian doctrine had been carefully excluded. Necessarily excluded therefore would be any reference to the use of music by voice or instruments in the pagan pre-Christian rituals of older Irish religions.† This new code was known as the *Senchus Mór*.

The actual book left by St Patrick has long been lost.[6] Copies made on vellum are dated at from the eighth to the tenth century.[7] These are now preserved in Trinity College, Dublin, the Royal Irish Academy, Dublin, the British Museum and elsewhere. They are described as being difficult

---

* O'Curry, op. cit. See his reference on p. 130 to musicians, i.e. purrers (*cronainaig*) and p. 246.

† This seems to be the first instance of the stultifying influence of the Church on the ancient native folklore; it was to reach its peak in Scotland in the infamous destruction of pipes, fiddles and harps in the nineteenth century described by Alexander Carmichael in *Carmina Gadelica*, Edinburgh, 1928, vol. 1, p. xxx.

to decipher, consisting as they do of the original text, widely spaced, with commentaries written between the lines in a smaller hand where there is room.

The vital reference to pipers occurs in a passage laying down the order of precedence at the king's court.[8] First there are the king's four body-guards:

> a front man, a rere man and two sides men. . . . It is they that are proper to be in the southern part of the house to attend on him going out of the house, and from without into the house. The companies [the King's visitors] are behind these. Poets are behind these; harpers (crutti) behind them. Pipers (cuslennaig),* horn-blowers and jugglers are placed in the south-east part. In the other side of the house is his [the King's] champion's seat. A man of deeds is placed to guard the door. His spear is placed in front of each of the last two perpetually against the confusion of the ale-house.† The chief's 'saer'-tenants are placed behind these. These are the parties who are companions of the chief. Hostages are placed behind these, judges behind them. His [the king's] wife, or his judge is placed behind these; the King behind these. Unredeemed pledges (hostages) in locks (locked chains) are placed on the east side of the champion's seat.

The commentary on the transcription notes after the word 'jugglers': 'Musicians and sportmakers in general, viz., equestrians and chariot-drivers, pilots and conjurors . . . and all in like manner'. Also on the transcription is a note to the commentary: 'Musicians, i.e. purrers (cronainaig); sportmakers, i.e. pipers (fedanaig).‡

St Patrick himself may be said to form a link between the two piping traditions, Roman and native. He was born in Wales during the Roman occupation, i.e. about A.D. 389. At the age of sixteen he was seized by a band of Irish raiders, probably acting under the orders of the Irish king Niall Noigiallach ('Niall of the Nine Hostages'). St Patrick in his auto-biographical 'Confession' tells us that his boyhood years were lived in a

---

* The commentary on the vellum translates the word 'cuslennaig' as 'flute-players'. This is presumably wrong; the flute was never a national instrument in Ireland in the historic sense, though it has become popular in modern times.

† P. W. Joyce, *A Smaller Social History of Ancient Ireland*, pp. 348 ff, 502, states that the ancient Irish were very careful that there should be no quarrelling or fighting or unseemly disturbance, from drunkenness or any other cause, at the formal *dals* or *aenachs* or meetings.

‡ In *The Gaelic Dictionaries* 'feadan' is given as 'a crevice, natural or otherwise, through which the wind blows' hence, the chanter of a bagpipe'. '*Cuisle*' is given as 'a vein, a blood-vessel, an artery' hence, a pipe'. '*Cuisleanach*' is given as 'a piper, one who plays on a reed'.

state of paganism, 'being ignorant of the true God',[9] until his capture and subsequent escape to Gaul, his religious studies at Auxerre, his ordination and his return to his life's mission to Ireland in A.D. 432.

Doubtless as a boy living in Wales under the Roman occupation he must many times have heard the sound of the Roman pipes. When he and his colleagues mentioned pipers in the Brehon Law governing the entourage of a king, he must have been aware from personal knowledge of any differences that existed between the pipes of Ireland and the Roman pipes of his boyhood.

There is no pictorial representation or literary description of the pipes of Ireland at that date. They would then almost certainly be mouth-blown (probably by nasal inhalation) and not bagpipes.

Grattan Flood[10] gives a steady trickle of references from Irish literature and historical account – enough to show that pipes and pipers did undoubtedly exist there at an early period. He cites a seventh-century tale describing the king's palace of Da Derg, *Bruidhaen da Derga*[11] with an account of the persons who came to pay homage to King Conaire the Great. Among them were 'nine pipers from the fairy hills of Bregia [in County Neath]'. That they were probably 'fairy pipers' does not of course lessen the importance of the reference to the instrument at that date. In the tale, the set of pipes is called *tinne*, one of the meanings of which the Gaelic dictionary gives as 'a piece of a column' which one supposes might be applied to the straight tube of the pipe. Flood also gives a tenth-century reference to keeners (professional mourners) at the death of Donnchadh, King of Ossory, in the year 975; their keening is accompanied by 'cymbals and pipes played harmoniously'. He quotes an Irish manuscript of the eleventh century which refers to the minstrel Donnbo as 'the best minstrel in Ireland at pipes, trumpets and harps' (see also O'Curry, pp. 309–12).

A striking mention of the pipes occurs in Ossianic tales. This is to be found in the *Duanaire Finn*, a collection of tales of the *Fian* written down by a captain in O'Neill's Irish regiment in Spanish service in Flanders in 1622 for his friend Captain Sorley MacDonnell, also an officer in the Spanish army in the Netherlands. The sentence in question runs, 'In the spike of Goll, son of Morna's helmet (well did he endure) was a piper playing his good pipe in the battle.' This reference is thought to be a late addition to the tales, which go back in oral tradition to at least the ninth century. It could mean that the status of the piper had risen through the intervening centuries, in Ireland at least, to the point where Goll, the great chief and opponent of Fionn, could be represented as making him the crowning motif of his headpiece. The tales of Ossian were of course common to Scotland and Ireland.

In the history of the *Teach Miodhchuarta*, preserved in two ancient vellum manuscripts, one the book of Glendalough (twelfth century) and the other the *Leabhar Buidhe* or Yellow Book of Lecain, there is an ancient poem:[12]

In The house of Temur,
Engraver and Skilful Rath builder,
Shield maker and vigorous soldier,
In the King's house used to drink beer;
It was their lawful privilege,
Druid, chess players and arch buffoon,
Pipers and tricky jugglers,
The Colptha for their share of meat, in truth,
When they come into the King's house.

The poem is illustrated on the vellum by a ground-plan of the principal compartments of the King's house at Tara, with the names of the several ranks, professions and trades which were privileged to sit in them. It also gives the order in which they were located and the names of the different portions of the meat to which each was entitled; two cows, two *tinnes* (?) and two pigs was the quantity for dinner:

Time for us to describe
What lawful share, what distinction
Is due to each degree. . . .
Before the many,
The harpers with music,
The trumpeters and the cook,
Let us place in their order. . . .
Good pipers,* chess players,
In the eastern aurraidin†
A proper colptha is given for their skill
– – is put on their dish.

It will be noted that the pipers were given as their portion of the cooked meat (i.e. the pig) the *colptha* or calf of the leg. The harpers got the pig's shoulder.

It may be of interest to quote here the late-seventeenth-century writer Martin Martin[13] on this subject of the distribution of such portions of meat by a Highland chief to his various henchmen:

Before money became current, the chieftains in the Isles bestowed the cow's head, feet, and all the entrails upon their dependents; such as the physicians, orator, poet, bard, musicians, etc., and the same was divided thus; the smith had the head, the piper had the &c. [*sic*] And it may not be unworthy of remark to this day, namely that when a farmer kills a beef or pig, it is customary to send the head to the smith, whose kitchen often presents the spectacle of from fifty to one hundred heads obtained in this manner.

* Cuslennaig.
† Divisions of the hall.

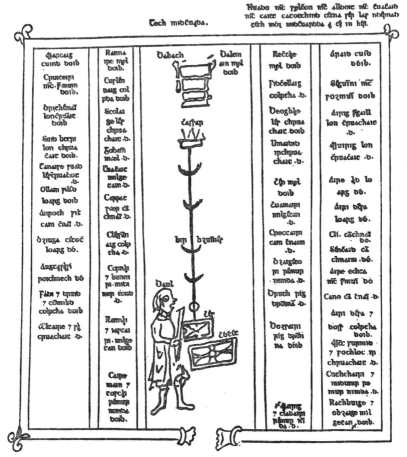

*Figure 10* The seating plan of the Feast of Tara from the book of Glendalough (*for key see opposite*). From George Petrie, *Antiquities of Tara Hill*

In the *Book of Leinster* (twelfth century) there is a poem on the ancient Irish *Fair of Carman*, containing the verse:

> Pipai,* fidli, fir ceangail,
> cnamfhir ocus cuslennaig,
> sluag etig engach egair,
> beccaig ocus buridaig.

> [Pipes, fiddles, gleemen,
> bones-players and pipers;
> a crowd hideous, noisy, profane,
> shriekers and shouters.]

* This seems to be one of the earliest examples of the use of the word '*pipe*' (from Latin) for the musical instrument. It is stated in Short's *Latin Dictionary* to be late Latin, and is never used in this sense by the classical writers.

*External Division (left)*

1 Horsemen
2 Harpers
3 Brehons
4 Professors of literature
5 Tanist-professors
6 Ollave-poets
7 *Anroth*-poets
8 *Briuga cetoch*
9 *Augtarsairsi*
10 Augurs and druids and *commilid*
11 Housebuilders and carpenters

*External Division (right)*

12 Charioteers
13 Huntsmen
14 *Airig forgaill*
15 *Muirig*
16 *Aire aird*
17 *Aire desa*
18 *Cli*
19 *Historian*
20 *Aire-echta*
21 *Cano*
22 *Aire desa* and doss

*Internal Division (left)*

27 Distributors
28 Pipers (Cuislennaig)
29 *Scolaige*
30 Smiths
31 Shield-makers
32 Chariot-makers
33 Jugglers
34 Trumpeters and footmen
35 Distributors and fishermen
36 Shoemakers and *toscairi*

*Internal Division (right)*

37 Herdsmen
38 Chess-players
39 Drink-bearers
40 Braziers
42 Mariners
43 *Creccairi*
44 *Braigetori*
45 King's fools
46 King's door-keepers

The following are the names in the
*Central Division* of the House reading
within the frame from top to bottom

47 Vat
48 Cup-bearers
49 Flame [of the lamp]
50 Spit
51 Waiter
52 Thigh [the piece of meat which the
   waiter is roasting]
53 Flame [of the fire]

*Note:* Petrie leaves a number of the Irish terms untranslated, which are therefore
here set down as they are.

O'Curry gives a complete translation of this poem from the Irish Gaelic in
79 quatrains (op. cit., vol. 3, pp. 529ff).

Similar references to the existence and use of the pipes in Ireland
continue through the thirteenth century, with Geoffrey the Piper (1206)
and William the Piper (1256).[14] Throughout the fourteenth century too,
the story continues with Irish soldiers with their pipers at the Battle of
Crecy in 1346; with penalties laid down in the infamous Statute of Kilkenny
(1366) against the receiving or entertaining of pipers as potential spies;
and with an entry in the Patent Rolls of 1375, specially exempting a
piper from the provisions of the Statute, in licensing Donal O'Moghan, an
Irish piper, to live within the English 'pale'.[15]

Estimated at fourteenth or fifteenth century also is the Irish version
of the thirteenth-century *chanson de geste*, *Fierbras*, in which we find the
following:[16]

*Ocus adubairt Sortibrandus: 'A tiagerna sinnter adhurca ocus piba
agaibh do tinol bur slua(i)gh, ocus dentar innsaight mór libh maille
reighthibh ocus re ginntlighechta ete do trasgairt in tuir.'*

[And Sortibrand said: 'Let horns and pipes be sounded by you,
to muster your hosts and let a great attack be made by you,
together with battering-rams and other contrivances, to lay low
the tower.']*

Further records of similar character carry the evidence of Irish pipers
into the fifteenth and sixteenth centuries, and so into the general corpus
of bagpipe history.

## Wales

Similar evidence exists for the existence of the pipes in Wales in the
centuries following Roman rule. In a mythological poem attributed to the
sixth-century poet Taliesin occur the lines:[17]

Wyf bard ac wyf telynawr    [I am a bard and I am a harper,
Wyf pipyd ac wyf crythawr,   I am a piper and I am a crowther.]

The date ascribed to the manuscript in which the poem is found is the
latter part of the thirteenth century.

The ancient laws of Wales also give us a glimpse of pipers. These were
codified, probably as in Ireland, from oral tradition, by Hywel Dda
(Howell the Good) king of west Wales, about A.D. 942 or 943. The north
Wales version of the laws, or Venedotian Code, of which the main source
is the 'Black Book of Chirk' of about 1200, has a passage which may be
translated,

> Every chief of song whom the lord shall invest with office is to be
> provided with an instrument; to wit, a harp to one, a crowd to
> another and pipes to a third;[18] to each according to his usage; and
> when they die they are to leave them to the king.

This would seem to relate to the early *eisteddfod*.

The Welsh books *Brut y Tywysogion* and *Brut y Season* describe, as the
first *eisteddfod* of which there is unquestionable record, a feast held at
Christmas 1176 by Lord Rhys (Rhys ap Gruffydd): 'And then the Lord
Rhys held a special feast in the Castle of Aberteifi: and he instituted two
contests, one between the bards and the poets, and the other between
the harpers, crowthers and pipers *(telynoryon a chrythoryon a phibydyon)*.'

Flood, it might be added, gives an earlier date for the first *eisteddfod*,

---

* Ed. and trans. Whitley Stokes, *Revue Celtique*, XIX, pp. 154–5 (1898). Maigne
d'Arnis, *Dictionary of Medieval Latin*, gives 1357 as the earliest known example
of *'pipa'* with the meaning *'cornemuse'* (bagpipe). This passage suggests that
they were then acquainted with the idea of the pipes (or shawm) as a war
instrument.'

but quotes no authority for his statement that 'Welsh critical writers cannot assign an earlier date for an Eisteddfod than the middle of the seventh century.' He also relates that King Griffith of North Wales (Gruffydd ab Kynan), at an *eisteddfod* at Caerways in 1100, gave a prize of a silver pipe for the best piper.*

I. C. Peate, in his 'Welsh musical instruments',[19] mentions Iolo Godi (fourteenth century) in a reference to his *chevi-benigl a chod* (pipe and bag). He also refers to 'the most amusing and detailed description by Lewis Glyn Cothe (fifteenth century) . . . where the noise of the heron-voiced bagpipe is likened to the howling of a sad, hoarse bitch imprisoned in a chest'.

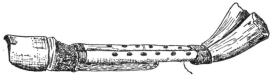

*Figure 11*   The Welsh double pibgorn or hornpipe
National Museum of Wales

G. Hartwell Jones in *Celtic Britain and the Pilgrim* quotes a Codex of Pope Calixtus II dated 1140 in the archives of Santiago Cathedral in Spain which mentions Welsh pilgrims singing to the accompaniment of the lyre, timbrel and flute; others to the British and Welsh harp and *crwth*. One wonders if the word flute may not be one more example of its use to denote a reed-pipe.

An object which could be of prime importance concerning the Welsh pipes is a double hornpipe or *pibgorn* in the National Museum of Wales at Cardiff, described by Dr Iorworth Peate. This has twin pipes of cane with six fingerholes in each, corresponding in position. The pipes lie closely parallel, and are waxed together in a wooden bed or yoke. The pipes, having six fingerholes, together form a double two-handed chanter. Each pipe terminates in a cow-horn which is bound to the pipe with black twine. The yoke has provision, in the form of a groove cut around it, for tying it into a bag.

This could be the very missing link we are seeking – a *pibgorn* or horn-pipe, native to these islands, which resembles the parallel pipes of ancient Egypt (though with the additional feature of the cow-horn terminals) of a type come from the east at some far-off period of history (see pp. 63–4). It is not too much to say that this unique specimen *could* contain the whole history of the development of the bagpipe in these islands. Though this specimen does not possess a drone, it would be easy to make one by the age-old method of stopping all but one of the fingerholes in one of the pipes with wax or resin. The vital point is, as Baines observes,[20] whether

* This seems extremely doubtful; Gwynn Williams makes no mention of it in his
  *Welsh National Music and Dance.*   Grattan Flood here uses the word *bagpipe* (!)

or not 'this Arab-looking double pibcorn', as he describes it, is indeed
Welsh. Peate states that it came from a cottage in north Wales and that
on the mouthpiece it bears the inscribed date 1701. If indeed it is Welsh,
then, to quote Baines further, 'it is not only the only surviving Welsh
bagpipe, but a specimen of unique importance in bagpipe history and
typology'.

Baines also adds a small drawing from a sixteenth-century Welsh
manuscript in the British Museum[21] of two such pipes, but without horn-
bells, attached to a bag; and a sketch from the same manuscript of a
bagpipe which appears to have a chanter and a separate single drone.

The manuscript being of the sixteenth century, however, is of the period
when the two-drone bagpipe as well as the single-drone one had already
appeared in England and probably in Scotland too. Nevertheless we know
so little about the Welsh bagpipes that all information or illustration from
early contemporary sources is important.

### Conclusion

We may now consider the position of the pipes, still mouth-blown, in all
four countries of the British Isles during the first millenium A.D. We have
shown that in Ireland and Wales the pipes existed from a very early date.
In Scotland, we have the Lethendy slab (c. tenth century) with its triple-
pipe; and the possible evidence of the frustratingly weathered carvings on
St Martin's Cross on Iona, also tenth century, of a group of musicians, one
of whom *may* be playing a mouth-blown pipe (to whose music another
figure may even be dancing!). A harp or curved *crowd* or *crwth* may be
distinctly discerned among the group. The latter were instruments of
which we find mention in plenty in the heroic folktales of both countries:
the tales of Cú Chulainn and those of Ossian and the Fian.

We have as yet no definite mention of indigenous pipes in England. The
hornpipe, which is of the same genus as the Welsh *pibgorn*, is mentioned
later in Cornwall (notably in the thirteenth century); in Lancashire,
Nottinghamshire and Derbyshire, and in Lowland Scotland (though not
until the eighteenth century). We cannot assign a probable date for its
early appearance in those parts of Britain except by analogy with the
undoubtedly early Welsh *pibgorn* discussed above.

Though we have no record of indigenous pipes in England in the first
millennium, that is not to say that they did not exist. Here again we can
only deduce by analogy.

# The bag (the *chorus*)

So far we have been careful to refer to the instrument in Britain simply
as 'the pipes' and not as the bagpipes; for our contention is, as we stated

*Plate 11* Detail from the Luttrell Psalter, c. 1330.
This is one of the earliest depictions in manuscript of the bagpipe with the single drone.

*Plate 12*  The miller in *The Canterbury Tales* of Chaucer (1340?–1400). One of the earliest references to the bagpipe in English literature is contained in the 'Prologue' (see p. 86).

at the beginning of our story, that the bag was an addition to an existing instrument; and there can be little doubt that in the early musical history of Scotland, Ireland, Wales and England, the pipes must almost certainly have been mouth-blown – probably with the ancient technique of nasal inhalation. This method had travelled with the mouth-blown pipes wherever they had penetrated. Some Scottish pipers are known to use the method at the present day with their practice chanter, by which they are able to play a whole long tune without a break. I have heard a Scottish piper play each long movement of a *piobaireachd* on the practice chanter in this manner.

We have now arrived at the most difficult period of bagpipe history. Literary references and iconography have carried us to the tenth century and a little later and, so far as we can see, we are still dealing with the mouth-blown pipes. We have seen no mention of bagpipes since the Roman emperor Nero's histrionics of the first century A.D.

One possible theory is that during the centuries immediately following the birth of Christ the principle of the bagpipe became lost. A number of experts have come to the same conclusion. Curt Sachs tells us that 'the first medieval mention of bagpipes is in a spurious letter of St Jerome to Dardanus, which can be traced back to the ninth century';[22] and Baines confirms this[23] by saying that 'for the resumption of bagpipe history [i.e. since Nero as quoted by Suetonius] Sach's statement, made nearly twenty years ago, remains valid.'

The alleged letter of St Jerome, which may be read in modern reprint,[24] says (in translation), 'At the synagogue in ancient times, there was a *chorus*; a simple skin with two brazen pipes; and by breathing through the first one, the second pipe emits the sound.'[25]

We shall hear more of this instrument, the *chorus*: but to deal first with the alleged letter, it may be said that expert opinion is that no instrument of such description was ever used in the synagogue in the days of St Jerome or earlier. Sachs declares indeed that 'no such bagpipe-like instrument ever existed in Israel in Biblical times' – in spite of the claims of numerous Biblical commentators that the *sumphonia* of Nebuchad-nezzar's orchestra was a bagpipe, a claim which Sachs demolishes convincingly also. Sachs avers that the letter is a forgery which can be traced to the ninth century, and his opinion has been generally adopted, as Baines indicates.

Although we must regard the St Jerome letter as a forgery, it can be regarded as a fraud which has become respectable with age; for the ninth century, which is now thought to be its date, is still early enough to constitute a useful historical landmark in pipe-history. Such an instrument as the letter describes, though it may be disallowed as of the period of St Jerome (c. 340–420), must certainly have existed in the ninth century, for the writer (i.e. the forger) could hardly have evolved a fictitious instru-

T.B.—7

ment out of his own consciousness. It does also introduce us to an important new word in bagpipe history, the *chorus*, meaning a bagpipe with a chanter and blowpipe only, without any drone.* We know that from the moment of its appearance, any early writer who uses the word *chorus* in the context of musical wind-instruments means a bagpipe, and not a pipe blown by the mouth.

At this point one must observe that one piece of evidence earlier than the ninth century seems to exist for the bagpipe after its long hiatus. This is in the form of a carved figure among a large number of sculptures upon an archway at Tack-i-Bostan, near Kermanshah in Persia.† The arch, one of two, and its sculptures, is said to have been erected during the lifetime of the Persian monarch Khosroo Purviz (Khosroo the Conqueror). Near the top of the arch is carved a band of four musicians, one of whom is playing what is undoubtedly a bagpipe type of instrument. The bag is a large one and is held in front of the player, a characteristic position which has been noted elsewhere in the east and occurs in Elizabethan pictures of the playing of the Irish war-pipe, and in the paintings of Pieter Breughel the Elder.[26] No chanter is visible, and it is possibly simply a drone-instrument accompanying the other instruments, like the drone accompanying the pan-pipes in Hellenic Alexandria, or the modern Indian bag-blown drones, the *s'ruti upanga*, and the *mashak*.[27] The other instruments depicted on the arch in concert with the bag-drone are a shawm, pan-pipes, and another instrument too defaced in the carving to be identifiable.[28] Khosroo Purviz lived in A.D. 590–628. The sculpture would seem to be the earliest representation of the bagpipe since the Roman period. But even at the date of the Tack-i-Bostan sculpture, there is a long stretch, about five and a half centuries, without any evidence of the existence of the bagpipe; the likely explanation seems to be, as we have suggested, that it had dropped out of use, and been forgotten, and had to be re-invented.

Illustrations of the *chorus* exist in two woodcuts taken from a ninth-century manuscript from the Benedictine monastery of St Blaise in the Black Forest.‡ One of these shows the instrument as a bladder with an

---

* In *Old English Instruments of Music*, p. 56, F. W. Galpin suggests that the word 'chorus' may be cognate with the Welsh 'crwth', derived from the old Irish 'crot, cruit', and that it was a stringed instrument; but this in no way tallies with the use of the word in the period, and we may proceed on the generally accepted meaning of the word pending further evidence.

† See A. Upham Pope, *A Survey of Persian Art*, vol. 4, Pl. 163b.

‡ Gerbert, *De Cantu et Musica Sacra*. Martin von Hornau Gerbert was an ordained priest at St Blaise in 1744. A fire at the monastery in 1768 destroyed all the manuscripts on which his book was based, and presumably this manuscript was among those lost. The woodcuts, which have been reproduced in almost every book on the bagpipe, are presumably from Gerbert's work. Cf. article on Gerbert in *Grove's Dictionary of Music and Musicians*.

insufflation tube issuing from one side and a chanter from the other. The
chanter terminates in the carving of an animal's head, characteristic of
the instrument of the period. In the other woodcut the bag is formed by
the whole skin of an animal. The blowpipe enters the skin at the back of
the lower neck, and the chanter issues from the animal's mouth. This
chanter also terminates in the carved representation of an animal, thus
duplicating the animal's head motif in the single instrument.

*Figure 12*    Drawings of two woodcuts from the St Blaise manuscript

Such animal-headed chanters and bags are to be seen in other contemporary pictures of the droneless bagpipe or *chorus*, as in a thirteenth-
century manuscript miniature in the Leipzig Staatsbibliothek[29] where
both bag and chanter terminate in an animal's head; and in the Biblio-
thèque Nationale, Paris,[30] where the bag is animal-headed but the chanter
is of plain conical shape.

These are all examples drawn from the Continent; but at least three
English illustrations of the droneless bagpipe or *chorus* may be cited:
first, in a fourteenth-century Bodleian manuscript[31] which shows a
bagpiper and a regal player playing together. The regal was a small
portable organ, the medieval equivalent in a sense of the piano-accordion.[32]
In this example the bagpipe has apparently no insufflation tube, though
one cannot be certain of this from the drawing, which is entitled 'A Fool's
Dance'. Second, 'A Remarkable Dance', a Royal Library thirteenth-
century manuscript[33] which shows a young woman balancing herself
upon the shoulders of a bagpiper. The bag of the instrument, though not
the chanter, terminates in an animal's head. Third, 'Stilt Dancing' from
a thirteenth-century manuscript[34] in which a man is depicted playing the

bagpipe while perched upon a high pair of stilts. The chanter of his bagpipe terminates in the animal's head motif.

All these bagpipes, in the sense that they consist of a bag, a chanter, and (except in the case of the first example) an insufflation tube, but without any drone may be seen as illustrations of English examples of the *chorus*.

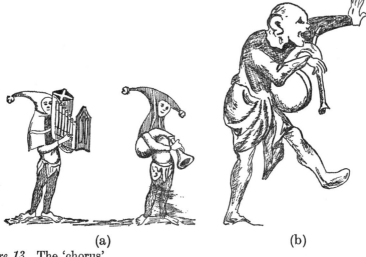

(a)                                                    (b)

*Figure 13*   The 'chorus'

(a) The 'chorus' or drone-less bag-          (b) 'Chorus' early fourteenth century,
    pipe and *regal*; from *Fool's*                  from British Museum manuscript
    *Dance*; Bodleian No. 964 as                    2B, vii, f. 197.
    reproduced in Strutt *Sports and*
    *Pastimes* (fourteenth century)

A carving in stone of a droneless bagpipe is also reported from a church in Hull (see p. 84).[35]

Other writers besides Gerbert of St Blaise have described the *chorus* in the same sense, notably Welefridus Strabo,[36] a Benedictine monk, in the ninth century and Nicholas de Lyranus or Lyra,[37] a Franciscan monk, in the fourteenth. Whether such writers described the instrument from personal observation or whether they were merely copying the supposed letter of St Jerome, one cannot tell.

Before we discuss the earliest use of the word *chorus* in this sense in Britain in the twelfth century, one should mention that some scholars believe that they see an eleventh-century reference to the bagpipe in *The Exeter Book* (*Codex Exonienses*).[38] This is one of the treasures of Anglo-Saxon poetry. It was presented to Exeter Cathedral by Leofric, Bishop of Exeter 1050–71, and is still in the Cathedral library. Besides the poems, it contains a number of riddles. Riddle no. 31 describes its subject as 'A strange thing singing in a house. It has feet and hands like those of a bird, though it cannot fly or walk. Its nose points downward. It has in its foot the gift of beautiful melody. It is trapped out with decoration. It waits at the feast until the moment arrives for it to display its art.' The riddle ends with the usual challenge to put a name to 'the creature'.

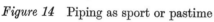

(a)                                           (b)

*Figure 14*   Piping as sport or pastime

(a) A young woman balances upon the shoulders of a bagpiper with drone-less bagpipe; from a thirteenth-century British Museum manuscript, Royal Lib. 14.E.iii as reproduced in Strutt *Sports and Pastimes*

(b) A man playing the drone-less bagpipe while standing on stilts; from a thirteenth-century British Museum manuscript Royal Lib. 14.b.v.; as reproduced in Strutt *Sports and Pastimes*

It may be noticed that both the bagpipes have a chanter stock carved in the shape of a head, that of (b) being an animal's

    Scholars are not all agreed on the riddle's solution, one proposing a fiddle and another an organistrum or mechanically-bowed hurdy-gurdy. If the riddle does intend the bagpipe as its solution, it provides evidence for the existence of the instrument in England in the eleventh century.
    Riddle no. 69 in *The Exeter Book* describes 'a creature' which 'sings through its sides; its neck is crooked and cunningly fashioned; upon its shoulder-blades it has two sharp shoulders.' The accepted solution is *a shepherd's pipe*. If this is correct, it gives the earliest date for the first

literary allusion to the hornpipe, stock and horn, *pibgorn* series of instruments.

The first clear reference in Britain to the actual word *chorus*, meaning a bagpipe, is by the twelfth-century Welsh monk and archdeacon of Brecknock, Giraldus Cambrensis. It is worth giving his words in the original Latin:[39] 'Hibernia quidem duobus tantum utitur at delectatur instrumentis cythera salicet at tympano; Scotia tribus, cythera, tympano, at choro; Gwallia vero cythera, tibiis at [*sic*] choro.' This means 'Ireland uses and delights in only two instruments, namely the harp and the tympanum; Scotland uses three, the harp, the tympanum* and the *chorus* (bagpipe); Wales uses the harp, *tibia* and *chorus*.'

Giraldus is inaccurate in omitting the pipes (at least in their mouth-blown form) from the Irish list, though he mentions the *tibia* as well as the *chorus* for Wales. The omission is strange, because he gives such a detailed account of the Irish musicians, the harpers, in his writings. The important point is that here at last is a mention of the bagpipe in these islands. Grattan Flood gives a reference to the 'bagpipe' (*sic*) contemporary with that of Giraldus by John Brompton, Abbot of Jervaulx Abbey in Yorkshire, writing in 1170.[40] Brompton writes in Latin as Giraldus does, and doubtless he also uses the word *chorus*. (I have not been able to find the passage in Brompton's considerable tome.)

The reference (see p. 80) to the *chorus* by Nicholas of Lyra (fourteenth century) is of particular interest because it connects in a curious way with the bagpipe in Britain. After describing the *chorus* in words similar to the alleged description of it by St Jerome, he adds, 'in French, the *chorus* is called a *chevrette* (*vocatur Gallice chevrette*)'. A local form of the word, *cabrette*, still prevails as a bagpipe name in southern France.[41] *Chevrette* means a small she-goat, a doe, a roe-deer. Dauney pertinently asks,[42] 'was its skin used in making the bag of the bagpipe?'

Curiously we are given the direct answer to Dauney's question in an entry in the Wardrobe Account[43] of the reign of Edward II of England in 1307, which is in fact contemporary with this Nicholas of Lyra. This records two payments to Janino Chevretter, i.e. player on the *chevrette*. It can hardly be doubted that he was a bagpiper. If we accept this as correct, this Janino or John is the earliest bagpiper to be mentioned by name in Britain. Another piper, Ralph of Breadsall, Derbyshire, finds mention in this same year, 1307.[44]

For the next mention of the *chorus* we must go to the fifteenth-century Walter Bower's *Scotichronicon*, a continuation of John of Fordun's *Chronica Gentis Scotorum*, for a description of the musical accomplishments of King James I of Scotland (reigned 1424–37). He is described by

---

* The word tympanum (tympano, tiompan) is thought to refer to a stringed instrument like the psaltery or dulcimer (a plucked or struck zither). See 'tympano', *Grove's Dictionary of Music and Musicians*; H. Farmer, *A History of Music in Scotland*, p. 26; O'Curry, op. cit., vol. 3, p. 238.

*Figure 15*   Single-drone bagpipes

(a)  Melrose Abbey; buttress ornamentation at south-east corner
of the abbey exterior; probably
fourteenth century; from a
photograph by the School of
Scottish Studies

(b)  Bench-end, Honington, Suffolk;
fourteenth century

(c)  Finchingfield Church, Essex;
fourteenth century

(d)  Beverley Minster; one of the
stone carvings in the north aisle
of the nave representing the
Guild of Musicians

(e)  From an illustration in the
Gorleston Psalter, *c.* 1330;
(British Museum); F. W. Galpin
says in his *Old English Instruments of Music* (4th edition,
London 1965, p. 132) that this is
one of the earliest depictions in
manuscript of the bagpipe with
a drone which he has noticed.

Bower, who writes in Latin, as performing 'in tympano et choro, in psalterio et organo, tibia et lyra, tuba et fistula',[45] which Dauney (p. 97) translates as 'the tabour,* the bagpipe, the psaltery, the organ, the flute,† the harp, the trumpet and the small shepherd's (single) pipe'.‡

Henry Farmer sees a representation of the *chorus* among the instruments carved on St Martin's Cross at Iona, and gives an 'interpreted' drawing of it in his *History of Music in Scotland*; but the interpretation is very doubtful indeed.[46] I believe that the carving in question, if it is a pipe, is a mouth-blown pipe – possibly even a parallel double-pipe.

The Piper's Stone at Ford Church, Northumberland (thirteenth century), recently removed from the churchyard to the floor of the church itself, shows what may have been just such a droneless bagpipe. The stone is incomplete, and shows only the bag and the chanter; but presumably the missing portion showed the blow-pipe. There is no evidence of its ever having had a drone, though with an incomplete carving one cannot be sure. We are on safer ground, however, with the carving in a church at Hull, mentioned earlier (p. 80),[47] probably of the fourteenth century, which also shows a bagpipe, here palpably without a drone.

It was not long before the droneless bagpipe, the *chorus*, began to yield to the process of evolution; succeeding representations of the instrument, both in stone church-sculpture and in wood-carving, show a drone. We see it in Scotland in the two carvings at Melrose Abbey, in the Piper's Stone, Skirling, Peeblesshire (? from Skirling Castle, built *c.* 1315) and in Roslin Chapel, Midlothian; in England at the church of St James, Norwich; on the gnome-like figure of the piper at the fourteenth-century church of Finchingfield, Essex; at St John's, Cirencester; in the wooden misereres of Boston parish church; and in the crosier presented to Winchester School by William of Wykeham in 1403. Some of these are early fifteenth century; most are fourteenth century, and it is there that we may place the first appearance of the single-drone bagpipe.

Most of these carvings portray the single chanter, fingered by both hands; but some, as at St Mary's Church, Warwick; East Harling Church, Norfolk; St Mary's Church, Shrewsbury; Altarnun Church, Cornwall; and a notable example at Hexham Abbey, have two divergent chanters, one held and fingered with each hand. Such motifs cannot be taken as a direct legacy of the Roman occupation. As Baines observes,[48] they are probably the work of Italian masons brought to England, to whom the double chanter was the more familiar form.

The motif of the animal pipe player, which we first met in the engraving

* Almost certainly a misinterpretation; cf. Farmer, *A History of Music in Scotland*, p. 26.
† Bower probably misused *tibia* for flute, so Dauney's translation is probably right here. It is hardly likely that King James played upon the Roman *tibia*!
‡ Baines, *Musical Instruments through the Ages*, p. 228, gives it as his opinion that the fistula was an instrument of the recorder type.

(a)                              (b)                                    (c)

*Figure 16*   Double-chanter bagpipes

(a) Bench-end, Altarnun, Cornwall; sixteenth century

(b) Bench-end, Davidstowe, Cornwall; sixteenth century

(c) Priory Church, Great Malvern, Worcestershire; detail from memorial window, sixteenth century; this is one of the many 'angel-pipers' decorating churches and chapels throughout England —and one at Roslin in southern Scotland—without an example of which no book on the bagpipe would be complete. These ethereal players of the bagpipe mostly favour the instrument with single chanter, as on the crosier of William of Wykeham in New College Oxford (fifteenth century), at Exeter Cathedral, York Minster, and many churches all over England; but there is an identical angel-figure to the above with similar *double*-chanter bagpipe, in St Mary's Church, Warwick, as reproduced by Baines, *Bagpipes* (p. 102)

on the seal from ancient Ur, has always been popular, both in carvings and in pictures. In European church architecture from about the thirteenth century onwards we find carvings of animals playing the bagpipes. A good example of animals playing the double-chanter bagpipe is to be seen at Ripon Cathedral. Dalyell, in the illustrations to his *Musical Memoirs*, gives other examples of animals playing both single- and double-chanter bagpipes. Unfortunately he does not always give exact place references. His named examples include Melrose Abbey (a pig playing a single-chanter bagpipe) and Westminster Abbey (a monkey-like animal also playing a single-chanter bagpipe). Illustrations from an illuminated Book of Prayers in the British Museum, quoted by Dalyell, include an interesting picture of a hare playing two unequal-length mouth-blown pipes, of which the left pipe, the longer of the two, has a trombone-like bell, suggestive of the ancient Phrygian pipes. Such illuminations, however, were often copied from earlier manuscripts, and one has to allow for the inaccuracies and fanciful alterations and additions typical of medieval copyists.

By the fourteenth and fifteenth centuries, the bagpipe with its chanter and single drone must undoubtedly have become a familiar sight and sound throughout Ireland, England and Scotland.

## The literary references

During the fourteenth and fifteenth centuries the first literary references to the bagpipes appear, as distinct from the Latin historico-topographical writings of Giraldus and John of Brompton. The best known of these is undoubtedly that of Chaucer (1340?–1400)[49] in the *Canterbury Tales*. The passage occurs in the 'Prologue', where Chaucer describes each pilgrim separately. He concludes his description of the 'stout carle', the Miller, and commences the movement of his cavalcade with the lines

> A baggepipe well cowde he blowe and sowne [sound],
> And therewith he brought us out of town.

There is an interesting sidelight on the use of the bagpipe by Chaucer's and similar bands of pilgrims in a passage from a state trial[50] shortly after Chaucer's death, in the reign of Henry IV (1399–1413):

> I say to thee that it is right well done that Pilgremys have with them both Singers and also Pipers, that when one of them that goeth barefoot striketh his toe upon a stone, and hurteth him sore and maketh him to bleed, it is well done that he or his fellow begin then with a Song, or else take out of his bosom a *Baggepype* for to drive away with such mirthe the hurt of his fellow.

A possibly earlier reference is to be found in Langland's *Piers Plowman*, thought to have been written between 1360 and 1369. Langland is disclaiming any personal musical accomplishments:[51]

> Ich can nat tabre, ne trompe, ne telle faire gestes,
> Ne fithelyn, at festes, ne harpen;
> Japen ne jagelyn, ne gentilliche pipe;
> Nother sailen ne sautrien, ne singe with the giterne.

> [I cannot play the drum or the trumpet, or tell pretty stories,
> Or fiddle at feasts, or play the harp,
> Or jape or do juggling, or gently play the pipe,
> Or sailen (?) or play the psaltery, or sing with the gittern.]

It is perhaps significant that piping is described by this fourteenth-century poet as an art which can be performed *gentilliche* (gently) when we think of the loud and strident tone of the Scottish Highland bagpipe of today. The English bagpipe seems to have gained its popularity as a small-toned peaceful instrument of the countryside, rather than a clangorous accompaniment of the battlefield, though we are presently to chronicle some examples of its battle use by the English also.

Two allusions to the bagpipe occur in the poem attributed to King James I of Scotland (1424–37), *Peblis to the Play*.[52] These are in stanza V:

> The bagpipe blew and thai out threw,
> Out of the town's untold.

> [They came out of the town in untold numbers at the sound of the bagpipe.]

And in stanza XX:

> With that, Will Swane came sueitand out
>     Ane meikle miller man;
> 'Gif I sall dance, have done, lat se,
>     Blaw up the bagpipe than,
> The schamon's [salmon's] dance* I mon begin.'

Another late fourteenth- or early fifteenth-century allusion to the instrument may be found in the last verse of William Dunbar's 'Testament of Mr Andrew Kennedy':[53]

> I will nae Priests for me shall sing,
>     *Dies illa, dies irae,*
> Nor zit [yet] nae Bells for me to ring,
>     *Sicut semper solet fieri,*
> Bot [only, but only] a Bag-pyp to play a Spring
>     *Et unum* Ale-wyfe *ante me*
> Instead of Torches for to bring,
>     *Quatuor lagunas cervisiae. . . .*

The anonymous fifteenth-century Scots poem of *Cockelbie's Sow* has the lines, 'Clarus the lang clype/Playit on a bag pype.'[54]

# The public records from 1350

We may now begin to look in the public records for the main contribution to the story. The first use of the word 'piper' in the Scottish Records is

---

\* A high-leaping dance; it appears to have been one of the favourite dances on Peebles Green.

in the Accounts of the Great Chamberlain of Scotland for 1362, in the reign of David II, son of Robert the Bruce. There, a payment to *piparijs* of forty shillings may be seen.[55]

If, however, we accept, as seems justified, the *chevrette* as being the bagpipe, then the payment by Edward II of England (the Bannockburn Edward) to Janino Chevretter in 1307 anticipates this by fifty-five years.[56] Earlier still, there is mention of a Scots musician, John of King-horn, referred to in the records as *fistulari regis*, in 1303–4. This could mean at that date a player of either a shawm, a recorder or a bagpipe. If the latter was his instrument, then the honours for the first mention of a bagpiper must remain with Scotland. 'Honours' is perhaps hardly the appropriate word in this particular case, for the record is of payment to the said John of Kinghorn by Edward I of England for entertaining him while he was wintering in Scotland; and one cannot accord much honour to a man for piping to the invader of his country. But, to quote Henry Farmer, *'force majeur* and the prospect of "siller" are sovereign per-suaders!'.[57]

It is almost certain, however, that for nearly a century before this, the term *piper* was concealed under the general term of *minstrel*, whether it denoted a bagpiper or a player of the shawm. In England, under their various titles of *minestrel, joculator regis, jongleur, jugleur* and others, minstrels can be traced back to the Domesday Book (1085–6).[58] Though they were originally singers to the harp, the minstrels learnt to play various other musical instruments as these appeared and came into use. As the bagpipe is mentioned as a popular instrument by Giraldus Cam-brensis in the twelfth century, we may assume that it found its way into the hands of the minstrels of that period. Other instruments of the time, which one may presume the minstrels also used, were the *harpe, lute, fethill, rybybe, horne, trompe, gittern, crowd* and *tabour*. The minstrels of the Court, referred to in the official records, were normally under the supervision and direction of the King's Harper,[59] he being the player of the most ancient, and therefore senior, musical instrument of the group.

We find an oblique twelfth-century mention of the minstrels of David I of Scotland (1124–53) as jugglers and dancers at the Battle of the Standard, fought over the possession of the Scottish king's lands in Northumberland and Cumberland in 1138. This is said to occur in the account in Latin by the contemporary historian Aethelred ar Ailred, abbot of Rievaulx.[60]

Henry Farmer mentions records of payment to the King's minstrels in the reign of Alexander III, while on his ill-omened visit to the Court of Edward I at Westminster in 1278 to do homage for his lands in England – not, as he emphatically declared, for his Scottish kingdom (for, said he, *'To that* none has a right save God alone!').

Edward I had his own minstrels, who would almost certainly include pipers. If these travelled with his armies, as one may suppose, the possi-bility emerges that when Edward, 'Hammer of the Scots', carried off the

Crowning Stone of the Scottish Kings from Scone in 1296 (or, as has been credibly suggested, a piece of the local red sandstone hastily substituted for it by the Abbot of Scone) it could well have been to the musical accompaniment of the English pipes that it made its way southwards.

So we come to the reign of Robert the Bruce. History (as distinct from tradition) (see pp. 132–4) is silent about the presence of the Scottish pipes upon the field of Bannockburn, and mentions only trumpets and horns at the battle. As we may see from the foregoing pages however, it is not improbable that the sound of the pipes could have risen from either side. It is even quite possible that Edward II's minstrel already mentioned, Janino Chevretter, was present with his *chevrette* at the battle.

Of the years remaining to Robert the Bruce after he had won independence for Scotland, we are told of disbursement by him to his Scottish minstrels at the Christmas festivities in 1328, while at the nuptials of his son, later David II, in the same year, the Scots minstrels received in all £66 odd.

Mention has already been made of the reference to the word *piparijs* in the accounts of the Great Chamberlains of Scotland during David II's reign. We cannot, however, yet be quite certain that *piparijs* means bagpipers; it could have meant players of the mouth-blown shawm.

Ritson[61] gives an account of the Battle of Halidon Hill, fought in 1333 in the reign of Edward III, at which the English pipes are said to have been heard on the field. The account, attributed by Ritson to 'an old chronicler', says, 'The Englisshe mynstralis blewe hir trumpes and hir pipes, and hidously astrede the Scottis.' This confirms that the minstrels included pipers, but whether bagpipers or shawm-players we are again unable to say.

As will be shown, this use of the word 'minstrel' to include or even specifically to mean 'piper', persisted into the sixteenth century and later, particularly of the 'toun minstrel' or town piper, a term common in Scotland. By that time, however, 'piper' definitely meant 'bagpiper'.

For some time longer we have to accept the ambiguity of the word 'piper', or to find the instrument and its player concealed in the term minstrel. Thus we are told that the court minstrels of Robert II (1371–90), successor to David II, were received at the Spanish court.[62] In England, according to Grattan Flood, a Roll of Accounts for 1360–1 states that Edward III had five pipers in his 'King's Band of Music', of which the names are given: Hankin, Fitzlibekin, Herniken, Oyle, William Harding, and Gerard. Though Flood would seem here to be justified in his use of the word 'pipers', he is incautious in his use in early references of the terms 'bagpiper', *'pìob mhór'*, and 'piper'. Thus he mentions pipers in the reign of Edward I,\* whereas the terms actually used in the records of Edward's reign are those for minstrel, such as *jongleur, joculator regis*, etc.

Grattan Flood's most misleading statement of all is his reference to the

\* Earlier still, Flood, p. 30, refers to a bagpipe competition, see p. 75, above.

Irish manuscript known as the *Dinnseanchus*. He classifies this as 'an Irish topographical history in the British Museum dated 1300 which describes the Irish kerne who accompanied King Edward [I] to Calais in 1297'. He adds also that 'In this manuscript there is an illuminated initial letter with the quaint device of a pig playing with all-becoming gravity on a set of bagpipes'.

The *Dinnseanchus* or *Dindshenchas* is an Irish collection of legends connected with the origin of place names, and has nothing to do with Edward I of England. As regards the manuscript with the illuminated initial letter, the Royal Irish Academy has informed me that the date for the manuscript in their catalogue of Irish manuscripts[63] is '(?) 16th century'. The Academy adds that a previous *incorrect* dating of the manuscript (done in 1814 by Charles O'Connor in *Rerum Hibernicarnum Scriptores*) may have misled Flood to date it at 1300. Furthermore, the bagpipe of the illuminated initial letter has distinctly got two drones; and authorities (including Flood himself, p. 48) are generally agreed that the second drone to the bagpipes did not begin to make its appearance until early in the sixteenth century (see p. 87).

The first indubitable use of the word bagpipe in the public records occurs in the Wardrobe Accounts of the eighth year of Edward III of England, 1334.[64] The entry states that a licence was granted to Barbor the Bagpiper to visit the schools for minstrels in parts beyond the seas; and a similar licence was granted to Morlan the Bagpiper, with forty shillings for his expenses. The English word *bagpiper*, in the contracted form and spelling of the period, *baggepip*, occurs in the midst of the Latin text of the account entry as follows:

> *Morlano, Baggepip licencd . . . Scolas menistralis in partibus tran mare.*

The stroke through the last letter in *baggepip* denotes the word bagpiper. The entry for Morlan is a line or two lower down the same page of the account book, and is in similar form.

In the account book of Eleanor, Edward III's sister, occurs a similar entry, with the English word 'bagpiper' appearing in the midst of the Latin text. Incidentally, in the apparent lack of a Latin word for bagpiper, it would appear that the old term *chorus* had by then dropped out of use – except for its unexpected appearance in a treatise on the French bagpipe, the *musette*.[65]

As these entries regarding English 'bagpipers' are earlier than the reference in 1362 to the payment to *piparijs* by David II of Scotland, it is reasonable to suppose that David's *piparijs* were bagpipers also.

During the reign of Edward III's son, Richard II, John of Gaunt established in 1381 the Court of Minstrels at Tutbury in Staffordshire; we may assume that at this Court of Minstrels piping had its place. The Court was presided over by a King of Minstrels, elected yearly with a pomp and ceremony akin to that of the Mastersingers of Nuremburg in Germany. Though the object of the Court's institution was a purely musical one, the festivities at Tutbury descended through the centuries following, into the barbarous annual bull-baiting or 'bull-running'. Here the bagpipe definitely took a major part, as the lines from a ballad, 'Robin Hood and Clorinda the Queen of Tutbury Feast', spoken by the King of the Minstrels, will show:

> This Battle* was fought near Tutbury Town,
> When the bagpipes baited the bull;
> I'm King of the Fidlers, and swear 'tis the truth,
> And call him that doubts it a gull![66]

Henry IV (1399–1413) was apparently no great friend of piping and minstrelsy – at least not of the minstrels of Wales. In 1402, the third year of his reign, a statute was passed for their suppression. This Act, in Norman French, inveighs against the mischief being wrought in the inciting of the Welsh people to insurrection by 'Westours, Rhymours, Minstralx et autres Vagabonds'.[67]

The term 'vagabonds' in respect of musicians and others of the artistic professions is one we are to meet often in the succeeding ages for the purpose of condemnation and attempted suppression of them.

Henry V, the victor of Agincourt, served his minstrels better than his father had done. When he was preparing for his voyage to France in 1415, he engaged eighteen minstrels to follow him to Guyenne at a wage of 12d a day.[68] Although on the night preceding the battle he 'gave the order for silence, which was afterwards strictly observed',[69] Monstrelet, the French chronicler, speaks of the English camp resounding with the national music. By this time the bagpipe, as we have seen from the records of Edward III (three reigns previous), had become one of the accepted instruments of music of minstrelsy; thus it is highly probable that the strains of the bagpipe were heard in the camp at Agincourt. Whether these could be described as martial strains or not, however, we have no means of knowing, only that it was national music.

Henry VI (1422–61), who succeeded Henry V, continued to nourish the good cause of minstrelsy; and so, probably, of piping. At the annual feast of the fraternity of the Holie Crosse at Abington, twelve priests each received the princely sum of 4d for singing a dirge; and twelve minstrels, who seemed to command a higher fee, were rewarded with 2s 4d each, with diet and feed for their horses.[70] Some of these minstrels, the 'Liber Niger Domus Regis' tells us, came from Maydenhithe (Maidenhead).[71] Henry VI was himself a composer. Two pieces of church music, a Gloria and a Sanctus for three voices, are attributed to him.

Here, chronologically, we must cross the border into Scotland again to mention the Scots King, James I (1424–37), for James was a player of the

* i.e. of the baiting of the bull.

bagpipes himself – the first monarch of either country of whom such an accomplishment is recorded.

We have already noted that the poem attributed to James, *Peblis to the Play*, mentions the bagpipe (see p. 87). On the evening of the fateful night of 20 February 1437, in the hours before the King was to fall by the hands of the ruthless band of assassins who forced their way into Black-friars' Convent where he was staying (Perth Castle being under repair), the contemporary account tells us that he had 'passed his tyme yn redying of romans, in synging and pypynge, in harpying, and in other honest solaces of grete pleasance and disport'.

James II (1437–60), successor to James I, was unfriendly to the wan-dering minstrels (doubtless including pipers), who had come to be looked upon as a social and political menace; and in 1449 he passed an Act for their suppression.[72]

James III (1460–88) went to the opposite extreme, and was evidently a lover of the arts. He made court favourites of his musicians, architects and followers of similar professions. He instituted the Scottish Chapel Royal, which he intended to be a college of music.[73] He retained in Scotland a celebrated Cambridge musician, Dr William Rogers, and knighted him. Among the group also were William Cochrane, his favourite architect, and Torphichen, his dancing master.

Unfortunately these favourites of the king got on the wrong side of the nobles, who grew to detest them as 'the king's fiddlers and bricklayers'. In the summer of 1482 James demanded help from the nobles to repel an English invasion; they made it a condition, before they would take the field, that he should surrender his favourites to their discretion. Peremp-torily, James refused; whereupon they broke into the royal quarters at Lauder, seized the unfortunate artists, and hanged the lot over Lauder Bridge.

Crossing the border again, we come to Edward IV of England (1461–83). In the Liber Niger Domus Regis we find an account of the household establishment of Edward IV which shows that that king's minstrels included pipers, though the term almost certainly still included players of the mouth-blown shawm, as well as of the bagpipe. This account may be conveniently read in the musical histories of Charles Burney and Sir John Hawkins. To quote from the latter[74] Edward IV had:

> Minstrelles thirteene, whereof one is virger, which directecth them all festyvall dayes in their stationes of blowings and pypings, to such offices as the officers might be warned, to prepare for the king's meats and soupers; to be more redyere in all services and due tyme; and all these syting in the hall together, whereof some be trompets, some with the shalmes and smalle pypes, and some are strange mene coming to this court at fyve feastes of the year. . . . Aulso having into court, servants to bear their trompets, pypes

and other instruments, and torche for wintere nights whilest they blow to suppore [supper] of the chaundry.

Perhaps we may see in these servants the early English counterpart of the Scottish Highland piper's *gillie phìobair* or piper's attendant, whose duty it was to carry his master's pipes.

The account is of interest also for its description of the *wayte* (wait) or musical watchman whose duty it was to make his rounds sounding his pipe, at stated times during the night. The *wayte* was the forerunner of the town waits and town pipers, and the mention of the latter in town and burgh records carries the history of the pipes along still further. Hawkins describes this official as 'a wayte, that nightely from Mychelmas to Shreve Thorsdaye *pipethe watch* within this court fowere tymes; in the somere nightes iij tymes, and make the Bon Gayte at every chambre, doare, and offyce, as well for feare of pykeres and pillers. He eatethe in the halle with [the] mynstrelles.'[75]

After Edward IV of England we come next in time to a name notable in bagpipe history, that of James IV of Scotland (1488–1513), the king who was to perish in the flower of his manhood at Flodden.

For James IV's reign, we have what may be considered the first really informative references to the bagpipe in the official records in the *Accounts of the Lord High Treasurers of Scotland*.[76] In the second year of James's reign we find the entry, often quoted, of English pipers, paid for playing to the king of Scotland at the gates of Edinburgh Castle. The year is 1489, and it reads: 'ITEM. To Inglis pyparis that com to the castel yet [gate] and playit to the king, viii £, viii s.'

James was evidently fond of the sound of the English pipes, for the accounts show that the English pipers returned two years later, in 1491: 'Aug. 21, ITEM: to iiij Inglis pyparis, viii unicorns.'* In 1497 occurs an entry figuring the famous cannon at Edinburgh Castle, 'Mons Meg', here referred to simply as 'Mons': 'July 21, ITEM: to the menstrallis that playit before Mons doun the gate, xiiij s.' There can be little doubt that here the menstrallis would be bagpipers. It was not the first time 'Mons Meg' had been moved 'doun the gate', for she had been similarly transported by teams of oxen in 1489 for the siege of Duchal, the castle of Lord Lyle in Renfrewshire; though we do not hear of any musical accompaniment on the earlier occasion.

Following numerous similar entries of payments to *menstralles*, including pipers, we find in 1503 an important reference, because it is the first to make mention of the 'toun' or 'commoun' piper: 'Oct. 6, ITEM: to the commoun piparis of Aberdene, xxviij s.' Also under October of the same year we find a similar payment: 'ITEM: to the commoun piparis of Edinburgh, xxviij s.'

In 1505 we have the interesting reference to 'the drone' with its apparent

* A unicorn was a piece of gold worth 18*s* Scots.

T.B.—8

meaning of a musical instrument in itself, in the entry, 'ITEM: to the tua piparis of Edinburgh, the franch quissalar, the Inglis piper with *the drone*, ilk man, ix s.' In the same year there is reference to Nicolas Gray who also played 'on the drone'; and in 1507 a similar reference to 'Jamie who played on the drone'.

By 1507 we are only six years away from the fateful year of Flodden; it is significant that after 1507 we find no more mention of 'Inglis piparys'. By then, James was grimly prepared to content himself with Scots musicians, augmented by Italians (trumpeters) and by 'Franche men' of the Auld Alliance.

In the year of Flodden itself, 1513, James marched to the Scottish border for the battle on 22 August. Characteristic of the canny Scot, he paid his debts to the musicians of the court before he set out. On 6 August, some sixteen days before he went to meet his fate, we find in his accounts the entry, pathetic in its later overtones: 'Aug. 6, ITEM: to the Italiane mentralis, for thame and the franche tabernis [i.e. drummers], fidlaris, organeris, trumpettis, extending to the nowmer [number] of xj. personis, to every ane of thame iiij.£. vij.s. vj.d., for their termis wagis of lamis [Lammas] last bypast, xlviij.£. ij.s. vj.d.'

At Flodden itself, tradition has it that Hastie, the town piper of Jedburgh, probably with other Scots pipers, played his pipes upon the battlefield. He would almost certainly be in that wing of the Scots army commanded by the Earl of Home, who brought back his Borderers safely under cover of darkness, the night following the battle. Hastie thus survived the battle, and tradition has it that he lived to leave his pipes to be handed down through succeeding generations of the Hastie family. They were shown to John Leyden in the late eighteenth century by the living member of the family.[77]

The English contemporaries of James IV were Henry VII* and Henry VIII. Henry VII was a generous patron to his musicians. To some he gave annuities and to others gifts.[78] His privy purse expenses, quoted by Chappell over thirteen years, show many payments to musicians – flute players, harpers, choristers, 'fidelers', dancers, organ-players, luters; also contributions to children and '*maydens* for May-games' and for '*morris daunces*'. The entries which Chappell quotes from the royal accounts do not actually include bagpipers, but he follows up with the words,

> There is also a great variety of payments to the musicians of different towns, as – the 'Waytes' of Dover, Canterbury, Dartford, Coventry and Northampton; the minstrels of Sandwich, the shams [i.e. shawms] of Maidstone; to bagpipers, the king's piper

* Chappell, *Popular Music of the Olden Time*, p. 48, says, 'little occurs about music during the short reigns [before that of Henry VIII] of Edward V and Richard III, whose years of accession amounted together to no more than two [1483–5].'

[repeatedly]; to the piper at Huntingdon etc.; to harpers (some of whom were Welsh).

For further details of such payments, Chappell refers the reader to the publication *Excerpta Historica* (1833)[79] where he says the compiler declares:

> To judge from the long catalogue of musicians and musical
> instruments, flutes, recorders, trumpets, sackbuts, harps, shalmes,
> bagpipes, organs, and 'round organs' clavicords, lutes, horns,
> pipers, fiddlers, and dancers, Henry's love of music must have been
> great; which is further established by the fact that every town he
> entered, as well as on board the ship which conveyed him to
> Calais, he was attended by minstrels and waits.

Henry VIII (1509–47) is also an important monarch in bagpipe history. He was an accomplished musician and composer. Being the younger of two brothers and therefore not expected to accede to the throne, he was intended by his father for the Church, with a remote view to attaining to the archbishopric of Canterbury. Music therefore formed a necessary and special part of his education.[80]

Despatches written by ambassadors have described his musical abilities. Pasqualigo, the Venetian ambassador who had formerly served in the same capacity at the courts of Spain, Portugal, Hungary and France, wrote of him: 'He speaks French, English and Latin and a little Italian, plays well on the lute and virginals, sings from book at sight, draws the bow with greater ability and strength than any man in England and jousts marvellously. Believe me, he is in every respect a most accomplished prince.' Holinshed tells us[81] that 'he exercised himselfe dailie in shooting, singing, dansing, wressling, casting the barre, plaieing at the recorders, flute, virginals, in setting of songs and making of ballades.' Joint despatches to the Doge of Venice by his three ambassadors at the English court, including Pasqualigo, go further in saying that 'he plays almost on every instrument, and composes fairly'. Hawkins, in his *General History . . . of Music*, prints a Latin motet by Henry VIII for three voices. An anthem, earlier mistakenly attributed to William Mundy, has since been proved to be the composition of the English king. The ballad 'Pastime with good companye', the 'King's Ballad', for three voices, is by him. A manuscript in the British Museum[82] contains five four-part songs, twelve three-part songs, fourteen pieces for three viols, and one piece for four viols, which are all credibly attributed to Henry.

Most interesting to us here, however, is the fact that, in an inventory which lists the musical instruments (some three hundred, large and small) belonging to the English king at the time of his death in 1547,[83] there appear five sets of bagpipes. One of these, described as 'A Baggepipe with pipes of Ivorie, the bagge covered with purple vellat', was in the collection

*Figure 17*    Engraving on the bard of silvered armour belonging to Henry VIII
(1509–47)

at the Palace of Westminster. The other four, also listed as 'bagge pipes
with pipes of Iverie', were at Hampton Court.

    If we accept literally the wording of the despatch of the Venetian
ambassadors at the English court to the Doge of Venice, that he 'plays
almost on every instrument', it is possible that Henry VIII, to however
limited an extent, was a piper, as was James I of Scotland a century
before him. He had on the horse bard of his silvered armour the engraving
of a bagpipe. This is now to be seen in the National Armoury at the
Tower of London.

We have now traced the emergence and progress of the bagpipe in ·Britain
from the first mention of the crude *chorus* to the point where it had
become a musical instrument worthy of being played by the king himself.
We have heard of it chiefly as an instrument of the court minstrels. That
is not to say, however, that the bagpipe was not as much an instrument of

the ordinary folk as of the court (see e.g. Fig. 18): the countryman could make a bagpipe for himself more easily than many of the musical instruments of the time. But the existing records in which the bagpipe is mentioned are simply more concerned with the court than with the ordinary life of the countryside.

*Figure 18*  Detail from Hogarth's picture 'Southwark Fair' (1733), showing bagpiper with single-chanter two-drone English bagpipe of the period. Note typical bell-ends to the pipes

# 1500 — 1800

**The Scottish town pipers**

> 'The auld loveable use.'
> (from town laws regarding the town piper)

Towards the end of the fifteenth century we find, particularly in Scotland, the emergence of the *toun* piper or *toun* minstrel, who was a public servant of the town or burgh. In England the same duty was undertaken by the town waits,[84] but these usually consisted of a band of from four to six players. The chief instruments were usually *hautboys* (Fr. *hautbois*) or shawms. In Scotland the town minstrels frequently consisted only of a bagpiper and a drummer. Reference has already been made (see p. 93) to the first recorded mention of the town pipers, viz. the 'common piparis' of 'Aberdene' and Edinburgh. We now go on to trace the growth and ramification of these throughout the country, to the point where they were to be found in almost every town and burgh in Scotland big or small, in the Lowlands at least. It was the start of a growth in use and popularity of the instrument that was to lead eventually to the bagpipes becoming Scotland's national instrument; though one must add that this was to be quite as much on account of the fine music that was to be composed for it.

The town and burgh pipers of Scotland, largely a Lowland institution, were mostly maintained out of the public funds. In the earlier days of their existence however they were maintained by a compulsory levy on private citizens of substance. In Edinburgh in 1487 for instance, the Town Council ordered that the town's three pipers should be provided with their sustenance and their livery by a charge on private persons of means, which worked out at 3d per piper yearly.[85] Refusal to pay was met with a fine of 9d.

At Dundee the town piper was paid twelve pennies yearly by each householder in the town. Many of the town pipers wore the town's distinctive livery. The piper of Dalkeith, old Geordie Syme ('a famous piper in his time'), was allowed, besides a small wage, a suit of clothes: this consisted of a long yellow coat lined with red, red plush breeches, white stockings and shoes with buckles. Neil Blane, the town piper of the unnamed locality portrayed by Sir Walter Scott in *Old Mortality*, had a salary of five marks and a new livery coat of the town's colours yearly. A mark or *merk* was worth 13s 4d Scots, or $13\frac{1}{3}d$ sterling.

The chief duty of the town or burgh piper was to play through the streets of the town once in the early morning to usher in the day and awaken the townsfolk for their day's work, and again in the evening. People went to work early in those days. In Dundee, Jedburgh and Lanark the piper's round started by official edict at 4 a.m. (under penalty of forfeit of his wages and eight days' imprisonment!). At Perth and Dalkeith it was 5 a.m. The evening round varied from 6 p.m. at Lanark,[86] and 7 p.m. at Perth to 8 p.m. at Dalkeith and Jedburgh.

Other duties of the 'commoun piper' were to play at the 'Riding of the Marches' or boundaries of the burgh,[87] as shown by the entry of payment to Johne Watsone the town piper of Lanark in 1566–7 of vjs viijd for the *landmuris*; to play his pipes at the town's horse races and fairs; and, according to Sir Walter Scott in *Old Mortality*, to play in the day of the election of magistrates. The piper was also in evidence at bridals and in the harvest field; but whether these occasions were officially required of him or whether they were in the nature of perquisites is not recorded.

Not all the Scottish towns were favourably disposed to the idea of the town piper, and those that were, sometimes changed their minds. Until 1630 Aberdeen had its piper, but in that year it was decided to dispense with his services – not, be it said, because of cost, but rather for reasons of culture. To quote the burgh records:

> The Magistrates discharge the common piper of all going through the town at nycht, or in the morning, in tyme coming, with his pype – it being an incivill forme to be usit within sic a famous burghe, and being often found fault with, als weill by sundrie nichtbouris of the toune as by strangers.

One wonders if already the bagpipes were beginning to be thought of as a Highland instrument, with that slight disdain of things Highland which at one period was inclined to be shown by the Lowland towns, including those of the East coast fringe, of which Aberdeen was one. It was an attitude which was to earn a sharp lesson at the hands of the Highlanders under Montrose, at Tippermuir, Aberdeen itself, Aldearn, Alford, Kilsyth and Dundee.

On the other hand, Manson tells us that the death of the last of the town pipers of the Highland city of Perth in the beginning of the nineteenth century (for Perth had a town piper as late as 1831) was much regretted, 'the music having an effect in the morning inexpressibly soothing and delightful'.[88]

Of the city of Edinburgh, it would seem to be a question of expense rather than musical appreciation which influenced the magistrates concerning the institution of town piper. For a time shortly before 1660 the office of piper seems to have lapsed there, and the city made do with a drummer. In that year, however, they added a piper, John Johnstone, to the strength again, 'to accompany the town's drummer throw the town morning and evening', paying him his salary and livery as in former years. During his term of office, however, Piper Johnstone had the temerity to ask for a free house – at which the magistrates promptly decided that his services could be dispensed with!

The free house was, in fact, a customary perquisite of the town piper, as at Jedburgh, where the 'Piper's House' stands to this day.* In some burghs a small allotment of land was provided for the piper's use, which was known as the Piper's Croft.

Sir Walter Scott, in a footnote to his observations on the town pipers of the Borders, says, 'It is certain that until a very late period, there was one [i.e. a piper] attached to each Border Town of note, and whose office was often hereditary.' In *Old Mortality* he lists the emoluments of the town piper as:

> The Piper's Croft, as it is still called [the novel was written in 1816] a field of about an acre in extent, five merks, and a new livery coat of the town's colours, yearly; some hopes of a dollar upon the day of the election of magistrates, providing the Provost were able and willing to afford such a gratuity; and the privilege of paying, at all the respectable houses in the neighbourhood, an annual visit at spring-time to rejoice their hearts with his music, and to beg from each a modicum of seedcorn.

One could say that in their morning and evening piping, the town pipers of Scotland were the direct descendants, in a more democratic form, of the older 'Waits of the Royal Household'. Their duties are well described by the Reverend James Mackenzie in his *History of Scotland*:[8]

* It is in Duck Row at the foot of Jedburgh Canongate. It was occupied by the Hastie family, who claimed to have held the office of town piper since the battle of Flodden.

We have minstrels who hold a life appointment in the service of the burgh; their instruments are bagpipes, to be sure.* Evening and morning and at other times needful the pipers march through the town to refresh the lieges with *Broken Bones at Luncarty, Port Lennox, Jockie and Sandy, St Johnstone's Hunt's up,* and the like inspiring strains. The law of the burgh requires that the pipers 'sall have their daily wages and meat of the neighbours of this guid toon circularly, conform to *the auld loveable use*'. Some of the burghers are so lamentably void of taste that they count the music dear and grudge the piper his 'reasonable diet circularly'. Some even refuse to entertain the piper when it comes to their turn, and get fined for their pains.

It is significant that here again the historian refers to the town pipers as minstrels, a term which continues the tradition that goes back to the days following the Norman invasion, and invests the piper with the dignity of a very ancient office. So we find the term minstrel used time and again of the burgh piper in the old records, as for instance in the extract from the *Records of the Royal Burgh of Lanark*[90] for 1566: 'John Watsone, toun menstral, to gang throw the toun with the syws† morne and evening, and quhen it is weit, that the swyche may nocht gang, that the said Jhone sall gang himself throw with the pyp morne and evening.' Similarly, the Minutes of the Town Council of Glasgow of 3 April 1675 record that John McClaine was appointed as 'common piper and minstrel'.[91]

The following are some of the Scots towns and burghs which are mentioned in various sources as having their common piper and 'menstral'. It is necessarily far from complete, and could be supplemented by a search of the records of the Scottish burghs: Edinburgh, Glasgow, Aberdeen, Perth, Dumfries, Dalkeith, Dumbarton, Bridgeton (one of whose town pipers, William Gunn, published a book of pipe-music in the nineteenth century), Biggar, Keith, Glenluce, Falkirk, Lanark, Linlithgow (whose town piper of 1707 was excommunicated for immorality), Peebles, Galashiels, Dundee, Jedburgh and Kilbarchan. One of the town pipers of Kilbarchan was the famous Habbie Simson – a local worthy who lived during the seventeenth century; at his death was written the well-known serio-comic poem, 'The Life and Death of the Piper of Kilbarchan'[92] or, to give the poem its full title,

* Not invariably; in 1594, Aberdeen's town minstrel Johnne Cowper was employed to play the 'almany *quhissel*' (i.e. the fife), *Aberdeen Town Council Register*, 24 November 1574. Cf. James Maidment, *Analecta Scotica* (Edinburgh, 1834–7), vol. 2, p. 325. The town of Linlithgow still has, or had till recently, a fife-player and drummer.

† The swyche (swasche, swesche, swys) was the deep tenor drum carried by the town's drummer. Farmer, *A History of Music in Scotland*, pp. 95, 148, says it was introduced in the reign of James V (1513–42). Here 'swys' means the drummer; he would not take the drum out in wet weather for fear of damage to the drum heads.

The Epitaph of Habbie Simson,
Who on his drone bore bony flags;
He made his Cheeks as red as Crimson,
And babbed* when he blew the bags.

It was composed by Robert Sempill or Semple (*c*. 1595–*c*. 1668) of Beltrees
which is three and a half miles from Kilbarchan. The poem is too long to
quote in its entirety, but the following stanzas will give an idea of its
style and contents:

Kilbarchan now may say, 'alas!'
For she hath lost her Game and Grace
Both 'Trixie' and 'The Maiden Trace'†
    But what remead?
For no man can supply his place–
    Hab Simson's dead.

Now who shall play 'The day it daws'?
Or 'Hunt up', when the Cock he craws?
Or who can for the Kirk – town – cause,
    Stand us in stead?
On Bagpipes now no Body blaws,
    Fen Habbie's dead.

At Clark-plays when he wont to come;
His Pipe played trimly to the Drum,
Like Bikes of Bees he gart it Bum
    And tun'd his Reed.
Now all our Pipers may sing dumb
    Fen Habbie's dead.

And at Horse Races many a day,
Before the Black, the Brown, the Gray,
He gart his Pipe when he did play,
    Baith Skirl and Skreed,
Now all such Pastime's quite away,
    Fen Habbie's dead.

Alas! for him my Heart is sair,
For of his Springs, I gat a skair,

---

* 'Bab' is an old Scots term meaning to 'dance or bob'. John Leyden, in his
  Introduction to *The Complaynt of Scotland*, says that among the Border pipers,
  who used the bellows-blown pipes (as possibly Habbie Simson did also), 'the
  perfection of their art was supposed to consist in being able to sing, dance, and
  play upon the bagpipes at the same time.'
† Two bagpipe airs of the period.

At every Play, Race, Feast and Fair,
  But Guile or Greed,
We need not look for Pyping mair,
  Fen Habbie's dead.

In writing the poem of Habbie Simson, the author stumbled on a verse-metre which was to make this epitaph, in the words of David Daiches,[93] 'perhaps the most influential poem in the whole of Scots literature, imitated by Allan Ramsay, Fergusson, and Burns, and called by Ramsay, "Standard Habbie" [metre].'

Such fame did Habbie Simson acquire through the popularity of Robert Sempill's poem – rather more, one suspects, than through his piping – that in 1822, which must have been nearly two hundred years after his death, a statue of him was placed in a niche of the steeple of Kilbarchan church, where it is still to be seen.

Another story is the true tale of the town piper of Innerleithen who undertook, for a wager, to play his pipes all the way up the long climbing road over the Moorfoot Hills from Innerleithen to Heriot (the road incidentally near which the author of this book has his home). It was a hot summer day, and the task proved too much for him. Just over the crest of the pass he collapsed and fell dead. He was buried at the side of the road where he fell. A flat upright dressed stone with a cross painted on its face and the words 'Piper's grave' marks the spot.

### The Kirk

Towards the end of the sixteenth century in Scotland we see a new factor affecting the progress of the bagpipes, as it did that of other musical instruments and music-making. This was the heavy hand of the Reformed Kirk. Up to the Reformation, the bagpipe had been looked upon kindly by the Church, and even used, like the organ, as an adjunct to Christian worship. In 1536 for instance, the bagpipe is mentioned as being played during church service in Edinburgh, under the older religion.[94] It is even stated that in some of the small churches where an organ could not be thought of, a bagpipe furnished the music.[95] This could conceivably be true in England, where they used small bands of wind instruments in many of the village churches instead of an organ; but Henry Farmer, who is the authority, makes no mention of such use of the bagpipe in church in Scotland as a regular practice. Indeed, the restrictions of pitch and compass of the instrument make its use in church hardly practicable.

By 1556, however, religious troubles were coming to the boil in Scotland. In June of that year riot broke out among the populace of Edinburgh against the carrying of the image of St Giles in procession through the streets by the adherents of the Roman Catholic church. The image was seized, and, in the words of John Knox, 'first drowned in the North Loch

[and] afterwards burnt'; another image, which Knox described as 'a marmoset idol' (a small grotesque image), was borrowed from the Grey Friars and fast fixed upon a barroe, called their 'fertour' (a portable shrine or reliquary). 'There assembled priests, friars, canons and rotten Papists, with tabors and trumpets, banners and bagpipes.'[96]

By the later years of the century the Kirk was firmly in control, and able to vent its displeasure on all who offended it, including players of the bagpipe whose strains assailed their ears at the wrong time and place. We find in the Kirk Sessions Registers, all over the country, records of unfortunate pipers being 'comperit', 'summondit', 'admoneist', 'delated' (or 'accusit'), 'ordainit to forbear', 'inhibit', 'requirit to find caution', 'continewit' (condemned to languish in the jail or in the church steeple) and even 'banest' (banished) for playing their pipes 'out of turn'. In 1597 the Kirk Session of St Andrews records that three pipers were ordered to abstain from playing in the streets after supper or during the night; and in addition they were admonished to keep the Sabbath holy, and to attend the sermon on the Sabbath and on Wednesday. At Stirling in the same year the Privy Council received a complaint against William Stewart for bringing into the kirk-yard 'two or three pipers, thereby tempting a number of people to dance there in tyme of prayers'. Similar admonitions are recorded all over the country. The Kirk Session Register of Holyrood House records that the minister found two women of his congregation *full** on a week-day, and dancing with 'pypers' playing to them. At Coldingham in Berwickshire, a party of youths were brought before the Presbytery for allowing their revels on a Saturday night to continue after twelve of the clock had ushered in the Sabbath, and for carrying their piper through the streets of Coldingham in the early hours of Sunday morning.

The Water of Leith on the north side of Edinburgh seems to have had particularly troublesome pipers, especially at sermon time on the Sabbath; time and time again we read of pipers at the Water of Leith admonished for playing the bagpipe on Sunday, or for playing for the lasses to dance to their music. George Bennet, James Brakenrig, Thomas Cairns, William Aiken and Richard Watsone were all pipers of the Water of Leith who fell foul of the Kirk for playing their pipes 'in tyme of sermon upoun the Lord his Sabbath'.

It was perhaps reasonable enough for the times that the Kirk should take action against the playing of the pipes on the Sabbath, particularly when it occurred in open competition with the minister in his preaching of the sermon; but the Kirk was particularly savage against any kind of merriment during Christmas or Yule tide to the accompaniment of the pipes. The Records of Elgin are significant in showing a number of instances of this. A resident in the burgh of Elgin in 1593, who rejoiced in the unlikely name of Tiberius Winchester, was 'compeirit' for 'gysing

* *Scoticè, fou'.*

through the toun on December 27 [note the date] accompanied by a piper'. Five days before Christmas of 1599, the Kirk Session of Elgin issued the edict that:[97]

> all profain pastime [is] inhibited to be used by any persons within the burgh or college, and specially futballing through the toun, snaw-balling, singing of carrellis or uther prophane sangis, guysing, pyping, violing and dancing. . . . All women and lassis forbidden to haunt or resort there under the pains of public repentance, at the leist during this tyme quhilk is superstitiouslie keepitt fra the 25th day of December to the last day of Januar nixt thereafter, quhilk ordinance the minister sall intimat furth out of the pulpitt.

But the practice evidently continued, for twenty years later we still find it stated that during the Christmas season 'the lasses had committed ane offense in dansing with ane pyper in Johne Hamiltoune's house'; and the elders of the Kirk were required to see that 'the actes were observed against dancing and *auld rites* at the festuall dayis callit Yooll'.* Finally, in 1601, at Elgin also, Alexander Thome was not only cautioned for piping on the night of 24 June to the dancing of Agnes Pyerie, but he was ordered by the Kirk Session to marry the girl in the morning!

Later on, we were to see bagpipe history take a more sinister turn in the association of the pipes with the devil, both by the Church and the Law, in the witch trials that were to bring so many unfortunate women to the stake and the fire, and to besmirch the record of seventeenth-century Scotland. A typical example was the record of a group of women burnt for sorcery at Borrowstounness (Bo'ness) in 1679 on being convicted of 'meeting Satan and other witches at the croce of Murestane above Kinneil, where they all danced, and the Devill acted as piper'. Marian McNeill in *The Silver Bough* (vol. 1, pp. 143, 144) says that the witches' coven had its devil or 'officer', its Ring-Leader (leader of the Ring Dance), its Piper and its Maiden, the last two being peculiar to Scotland. At a witch trial at Tranent, East Lothian, in 1659, 'Douglas was the pyper'. At Kirkliston in 1655, William Barton's wife stated in evidence that 'One night, going to a dancing upon [the] Pentland Hills he [the devil] went before us in the likeness of a rough tanny-dog . . . playing on a pair of pipes'. The official evidence continues: 'The Spring he played (*says she*) was, the silly bit Chiken, gar cast it a pickle and it will grow meikle . . . . *She was burnt with her husband*' (see George Sinclair, *Satan's Invisible World Discovered*, Edinburgh, 1685, reprinted 1871, pp. 160–4).

The picture of the devil playing the bagpipes for the witches' dance was put to superb use by Robert Burns in 'Tam o' Shanter' – the place, Kirk-Alloway; the hour, midnight:

* The point here is of course that the Reformed Kirk considered Yule to be a purely popish festival.

There sat Auld Nick, in shape o' beast,
A tousie tyke, black, grim and large,
To gie them music was his charge:
He screw'd the pipes and gart them skirl,
Till roof and rafters a' did dirl

The bagpipes were now indeed in bad repute with the Kirk!

### The great pipe

An interesting feature of these Kirk Session Registers is the occasional
reference to the 'gryit' or 'grytt' (great) pipe; for this provides our first
glimpse of the Great Highland bagpipe in the records. For instance, in
Elgin in 1592, James Roy, pyper, was:

> accusit for ganging through the toun playing of his gryit pyipe in
> the nycht season . . . and lykwayes for playing this last Sonday
> upoun his gryit pyip at efternone in tyme of preaching . . . and
> thairfor thai [i.e. the Kirk Session] appoint him to stand in the
> hairclayth on Sonday nixt and mak his repentance publiclie and
> that he remain in the steeple till he find caution to do the same.

Similarly, in 1600, John Lay, pyper, was 'inhibitt to pas throch the toun
or yit playe besyd the toun on a *grytt pipe* under the paynes of baneisment
furth of the perroche [parish]'.

The point is of some interest as implying the existence of a smaller
instrument also. There was of course the Lowland bagpipe (which from
the early eighteenth century was blown by bellows). It may have possessed
a gentler tone than the mouth-blown pipes: but one instinctively associates
the Lowland pipe with the southern part of Scotland, e.g. as at Dalkeith,
rather than the northern territories of the country from which these
records come. The term 'great pipe' is a literal translation of the Gaelic
'*pìob mhór*', the complementary term being *pìob bheag* (small pipe). We
find both terms in a Gaelic *waulking* song (i.e. a Hebridean work song for
the shrinking of cloth), of which the date is probably early seventeenth
or late sixteenth century, from the mention in the song of 'Donald Gorm',[98]
who died in 1617 (cf. Campbell and Collinson, p. 68, l. 288).

Ruidhleadh mu seach air àn ùrlar,
Le pìob mhór nam feadan dùmhail,
Le pìob bheag nam feadan siùbhlach.

[Reels in turn upon the floor,
With the great pipes of bulky chanters,
And the little pipes of swift-playing chanter.]

In another version of the same story (K. C. Craig, *Orain Luaidh*, Glasgow,

1949, p. 94) the critical reference may be translated: 'a reel . . . to the small pipes of quick chanters, to the great pipes of bulky drone-tops'. (See also Margaret Fay Shaw, *Folksongs and Folklore of South Uist*, London, 1955, pp. 251–2.)

It must be emphasized of course that few, if any, of such summonses and 'compeirings' by the Kirk Sessions such as those quoted above refer to the official town or burgh pipers, for they were under the direct authority of the magistrates and bailies, who could punish their offending burgh servants with such severity as the case might require. Neither should the frequency of such misdemeanours by the ordinary 'private' piper be taken as a tendency of pipers as a class to transgress, but rather as an indication of the growing popularity of the bagpipes in Scottish life. By the time of which we are writing, the bagpipes were well on their way towards becoming, if they had not already become, the acknowledged national musical instrument of Scotland.

## The bagpipe in rural life

In England in the sixteenth century we find the bagpipe becoming an accepted part of both rural and urban life, though perhaps it was more popular in the country than in the town. We hear of it everywhere throughout the English countryside. It becomes part of the life of the village green, of the May-day festivals, of the fair, of the wedding ceremony. This is clear from the ever-increasing references in the literature of the time. The place of the bagpipe among the other musical instruments of the period cannot be better illustrated than in the *Poly-Olbion* of the Warwickshire poet Michael Drayton (1563–1631). This is a long topographical poem written between 1613 and 1622, describing the beauties of the English landscape and the life of the people as the poet saw it at that period. Drayton travelled the length and breadth of England to acquire the necessary knowledge to write it. It is worth quoting the whole passage:

> The English, that repined to be delay'd so long,
> All quickly at the hint, as with one free consent,
> Struck up at once and sung, each to the instrument
> (Of sundry sorts that were, as the musician likes),
> On which the practic'd hand with perfect'st fing'ring strikes,
> Whereby their height of skill might liveliest be exprest.
> The trembling Lute some touch, some strain the Viol best,
> In sets that there were seen, the music wondrous choice,
> Some, likewise, there affect the Gamba with the voice,
> To shew that England could variety afford.
> Some that delight to touch the sterner wiry chord,
> The Cithren, the Pandore, and the Theorbo strike:

The Gittern and the Kit, the wandring fiddlers like.
So were there some again, in this their learned strife,
Loud instruments that lov'd the Cornet and the Fife,
The Hoboy, Sackbut deep, Recorder and the Flute;
E'en from the shrillest Shawm unto the Cornamute.
Some blow the Bagpipe up, that plays the Country-Round;
The Tabor and the Pipe some take delight to sound.

'The Sundry Musiques of England'[99]

For a reference to the bagpipe at the May-day festival, we have the Devonshire poet, William Browne (1591–1643) in his *Britannia's Pastorals*:

As I have seen the Lady of the May
Sit in an arbour, . . .
Built by a May-pole, where the jocund swains
Dance with the maidens to the bagpipe strains.

An anonymous book of 1609 with the lengthy title of *Old Meg of Herefordshire for a Mayd Marian, and Hereford towne for a Morris-dance; or twelve Morris-dancers in Herefordshire of 1200 years old*, contains the lines 'Middlesex men for tricks above ground; Essex men for the Hey; Lancashire for Hornpipes; Worcestershire for bagpipes; but Herefordshire for a Morris-dance, puts down not only all Kent, but very near (if one had line enough to measure it) three quarters of Christendom.'

The Lancashire hornpipe, mentioned above, was the county's favourite dance, which took its name from the instrument on which it was played; we have already described it as a mouth-blown reed-pipe, terminating in the horn of an ox, sheep or goat (see pp. 62–4). According to Chappell, the music of the hornpipe existed in more than one form, some pieces being called jig-hornpipes or hornpipe-jigs, and others bagpipe-hornpipes. Of Lancashire and the bagpipe we quote again from Drayton,

So blyth and bonny now the lads and lasses are,
And ever as anon the bagpipe up doth blow,
Cast in a gallant Round, about the hearth they goe,
And at each pause they kisse: was never seene such rule,
In any place but heere, at Boon-fire, or at Yeule;
And every village smokes at Wakes with lusty cheere,
Then, Hey, they cry, for Lun, and Hey for Lancashire.

Drayton mentions other counties for their bagpipes, such as,

Beane-belly Lestershire, her attribute doth heare,
And bells and bagpipes next, belong to Lincolnshire.

and of the Lincolnshire bagpipe also, in another song of Drayton's about the river Wytham, in Lincolnshire. It is the river that speaks:

Thou, Wytham, mine own town, first watered with my source,
As to the eastern sea I hasten on my course,
Who sees so pleasant plains, or knows of fairer scene?
Whose swains in shepherd's gray, and girls in Lincoln green,
Whilst some the rings of bells, and some the bagpipes ply,
Dance many a merry Round, and many a Hydegy.

Shakespeare's Falstaff speaks of the Lincolnshire bagpipe in a passage from *Henry IV*, I.ii:

FALSTAFF    'S blood, I am as melancholy as a gib cat or a lugged
            bear.
PRINCE      Or an old lion, or a lover's lute.
FALSTAFF    Yea, or the drone of a Lincolnshire bagpipe.

The Lincolnshire bagpipe appears also in a prose work of the Elizabethan dramatist Robert Armin (1588–1612), *A Nest of Ninnies*:

At a Christmas time, when great logs furnish the hall fire . . . and
indeed all revelling is regarded . . . amongst all the pleasures
provided, a noise of minstrels and a Lincolnshire bagpipe was
prepared; the minstrels for the great chamber, the bagpipe for the
hall; the minstrels to serve up the knight's meat and the bagpipe for
the common dancing.

Among the ballad titles in Robert Laneham's *Letters from Kenilworth* (1575)[100] describing the ballad collection of Captain Cox, mason of Coventry, is 'The Sweet Ballade of the Lincolnshire Bagpipes'.

The above reference to the bagpipe as a musical instrument appropriate to the Christmas season calls to mind the old song, though it is of somewhat later date, 'The Queen's Old Courtier', in the verse[101]

With an old fashion when Christmas was come,
To call in his neighbours with bagpipe and drum,
And good cheer enough to furnish every old room,
And old liquor able to make a cat speak and a man dumb.
     Like an old courtier of the Queen's
     And the Queen's old courtier.

Shakespeare has other telling references to bagpipes and bagpipers. He closes *Much Ado about Nothing* with the lines:

MESSENGER    My lord, your brother John is ta'en in flight,
             And brought with armed men back to Messina.

BENEDICK     Think not on him till tomorrow: I'll devise thee brave
             punishments for him.

                                                *Strike up pipers*

For a picture of the bagpipe at the English fair, we have the ballad of 'Bartholomew's Fair', beginning:

Adzooks she went the other day to London town,
In Smithfield such grazing, such thrusting and squeezing
A city of wood, some folks do call it Bartledom Fair . . .
Where trumpets and bagpipes, fiddlers were all at work,
And the cooks sang – Here's your delicate pig and pork.[102]

At weddings the bagpipe was a favourite instrument on both sides of the
Border. John Brand, in his *Popular Antiquities*, quotes from Veronis,
*Hunting of Purgatory* (1561):[103]

I know a priest – this is a true tale that I tell you and no lye –
which, when any of his friends should be maryed, would take his
*backe-pype*, and so fetch them to Church, playing sweetlye afore
them; and then would he lay his instrument handsomely upon the
aultore, till he had maryed them, and sayd masse; which thyng
being done, he would gentylle bring them home again with back-
pype.

Dalyell contributes the observation 'In England, and I believe, in
Scotland also, the piper at a wedding has always a piece of the bride's
garter tyed about his pipes.'[104] In Scotland, however, the bigotries of the
Kirk of the period eventually caught up with these innocent frolics; and
we find from the Kirk Session Registers of Perth and Stirling of 1592 and
1648 respectively that no 'pypers' were henceforth to be allowed at
wedding festivities.

The strains of the bagpipe were called upon to lighten the tasks of the
harvest field. Chappell quotes a foreign observer in the reign of James I
(of Great Britain and Ireland) who relates that he saw 'In England, the
country people bringing home, in a cart from the harvest field, a figure
made of corn, round which men and women were promiscuously singing,
preceded by a piper and a drum'.[105] At the time of the sheepshearing,
Henry Best of Elmsworth, *Yorkshire: Rural Economy in 1641*,[106] has an
entry: 'At my Lord Finche's custom at Walton for Clipping, the bagpiper
was paid 6d for playing to the clippers all the day.' A less pleasing example
of the piper in the harvest field is given by Robert Surtees in his *History
of Durham*, of a court trial in which a man had made forcible entry into a
woman's field of ripe grain at Birtley, mowed and carried away her crop,
while his piper played from the top of the loaded wagon as the corn was
being cut.[107]

To complete these activities of the bagpiper, we may cite Surtees again,
who tells us that it was not unusual to beguile labourers at tasks other
than those of the harvest field with the strains of the instrument. He quotes
the parish registers of Gateshead for 1633 for the entries, 'To workmen,
for making the streets even, at the King's coming, 18s.4d., and paid the
piper for playing to the menders of the highways five several days, 3s.4d.'[108]

### The tunes

What of the bagpipe tunes of these days? In England, the bagpipe was
the instrument of the country dance, of the round, the hornpipe and all
such lively dance measures. William Chappell[109] gives the titles of a few
of the pipe tunes of the sixteenth and seventeenth centuries popular in
England. One of these is 'Dance after my pipe', or 'The shaking of the
Sheets', mentioned under its first title by Ben Jonson in *Every Man out
of his Humour*, and under the second in an old song, the words of which
give us the name of another bagpipe tune:

> The piper he struck up,
> And merrily he did play –
> The Shaking of the Sheets,
> And eke The Irish Hay.

Other tunes specifically mentioned as being for the bagpipe in the plays
of the period, given by Chappell, are 'The Catching of Quails' (to be found
in *The Dancing Master*), 'Sellinger's Round' and 'Hankin Booby'. In
*Love's Welcome at Welbeck*, Ben Jonson gives a song to a hornpipe tune
which is to be accompanied on the bagpipe.[110] Among English song airs
mentioned by Chappell as played on the bagpipe are 'Who liveth so merry
in all this land', and 'By the Border's side as I did pass'; the latter, as its
name indicates, is a Border tune, but probably from the English side of
the Border.

E. W. Naylor, in *An Elizabethan Virginal Book* (i.e. the Fitzwilliam
Virginal Book), cites a number of old English tunes of the thirteenth to
sixteenth centuries (pp. 141–8), including 'Sumer is icumen in', 'Goe from
my window, go', 'John come kiss me now', in which the underlying
harmony 'implies a variable drone as in a bagpipe'. The variable drone,
however, though it is to be found today in several Continental bagpipe
species, has never been known in the British bagpipe (except, in a sense,
by the use of the 'regulators' on the Irish *uilleann* pipes, which are outside
our purview).

A drone which is required to be varied in the course of a tune must of
course be under the control of the fingers (which have primarily to finger
the melody chanter). This is possible in the double-hornpipe or double-
recorder; in this both pipes lie under the fingers side by side, and the
fingerholes of one are reduced in number to the bottom two, or perhaps
three. This pipe will then sound the drone, variable in pitch according to
which of the fingerholes are stopped.

These airs may well have originated or been adapted as tunes for the
double-hornpipe or double-recorder rather than for the bagpipe. If they
were indeed for the bagpipe, they must indicate a corner of bagpipe
history in England of which we know nothing.[111]

In Ireland we find, for the bagpipe, the tune known variously as '*The fada*', '*The faddy*', or '*Rinnce Fada*'* (a 'long dance') which Flood says is 'generally tripped to the accompaniment of a bagpipe'; also the tunes of '*An Cnotadh Ban*' or 'The White Cockade', 'Lament for Owen Roe', 'Miles the Slasher', 'MacAlistrum's March', etc.

For Lowland Scots bagpipe tunes we find two airs, 'The Day it Dawes' and 'Into June', as part of the recognized repertoire of the Lowland town pipers. Other Lowland Scots tunes mentioned as pipe tunes are 'Pitt on your shirt on Monday', the older sett of 'The Flowers of the Forest', the 'Ring Dance', mentioned above, given by Leyden and 'Soor Plooms of Galashiels' (1700).

Probably many of the favourite song airs of the late sixteenth and early seventeenth century were played on the pipes, either by adapting the tune to bring it within the compass of the instrument where necessary, or by extending the upward compass by the method known as 'pinching'. This is a necessary technique in playing, for example, 'Soor Plooms of Galashiels', an acknowledged Border pipe tune. Other such song tunes include 'The Soutars of Selkirk', 'Andro and his Cutty Gun', 'Where will my guidman lie', 'Dumbarton's Drums', 'The Captain's Lady', 'Alas that I cam o'er the Muir', 'Katie Bairdie', 'Bessie's Haggies', 'Lang Kale in Aberdene', etc.

## The second drone

Of the instrument itself, the most notable event of the sixteenth century was the addition of the second drone. It is not possible to say with absolute certainty when this appeared in Britain. Pictures of Scottish and English sixteenth-century bagpipes are rare. Contemporary stone-carvings of the two-drone bagpipe of the period immediately following its introduction seem to be non-existent. On the Continent, pictures are more plentiful. Albrecht Dürer (1471–1528) provides us with several, of which the earliest and best known is '*Der Dudelsachpfeifer*' (1574), now in Vienna. This is sometimes known as the 'Irish bagpiper', and the instrument depicted, to be the ancient Irish *piob mhór* or great Irish war-pipe. How Dürer came across his model of the Irish piper is not known. There were said to be Irish *kerne* with the army of Henry VIII, who was on the Continent at this time, and it was possibly one of their pipers whom Dürer came across and used for his model.

An informative, if rather gruesome, set of illustrations of the two-drone pipes of this same period is found on the common theme of the time, The Dance of Death, in which the figure of Death, generally in the form

* John Leyden gives the dance and its tune as the '*Rinceadh-fada*', Rinkey, or 'field dance of the Irish' performed in circles and probably similar to the 'Scottish Ring-dance'. Introduction to *The Complaynt of Scotland*, p. 131.

of a skeleton, is often portrayed as playing the bagpipes. Hans Holbein the Younger (1497–1543) made a whole series of woodcuts on this theme. In these, the bagpipe is standardized throughout the series: it has two drones of equal length issuing from adjacent but separate stocks, the drones having bell-shaped ends. There is a cruder woodcut of the period on the same theme, certainly not by Holbein, in which the skeleton figure of Death dances beside an hour-glass; it is reproduced by both Flood and Manson. Here the drones, one of which is shorter than the other, terminate in bobbin-shaped ends more after the Scottish than the English fashion.

### England: the last act

Let us now follow out to its conclusion the last act of the play in England: a conclusion which was to leave the Scottish bagpipe, and eventually only the Scottish *Highland* bagpipe, as the sole survivor of its kind among the four nations of Britain, except for the sturdy little Northumbrian pipes, and their cousins of the bellows, the *uilleann* pipes of Ireland. In England, it was the end of an evenly matched progress that had gone on for some six centuries in at least three of the countries of these islands, Scotland, England and Ireland; for Wales had dropped out of the contest earlier.

We left the English bagpipe in court life in the time of its hey-day, the days of Henry VIII, whose reign lasted until nearly the mid-sixteenth century. It was to continue for some time yet, both as a musical instrument enjoying official status at the royal court, and, as we have seen, as one belonging to the folk.

For the record of the bagpipe's continued existence at court we now have the aid of H. C. Lafontaine's useful work, *The King's Music*, with its lists of court musicians drawn from the Record Office and from the Lord Chamberlains' accounts. It shows that Edward VI, whose brief reign of six years followed that of Henry VIII, had his court 'bagge piper', Richard Woodwarde, whose name appears in the Account of Liveries at the Coronation of Edward VI.

Richard Woodwarde's name appears also nine years later (1555) in the reign of Mary Tudor. Here he is described not as a bagpiper but simply as another musician. This is to be found in a list of some thirty-six court musicians, all of whose musical instruments, except that of Richard Woodwarde and five others, are specified by name, e.g. 'sackebutts', 'flewtes', 'violons', 'vialls', 'dromslaeds' (drummers), 'harpers' and 'lewters'.

It is curious that the bagpipe should not be included by name in the list. One wonders if, by this time, it was thought of, for some strange reason, as an instrument 'not quite nice'; for although the presumptive evidence (through the continued appearance of the name of Richard Woodwarde in the lists of court musicians) is that the bagpipe was still played at court, it is never again mentioned by name in the royal lists, except for an isolated appearance a hundred years later.

In the list for 1556, a year later than the instance above, we find the name of Richard Woodwarde again, coupled with that of Richard Pyke, both described as musicians, among pages of other lists in which the court musicians are listed according to their instruments. For the next two years, to 1568, these two 'musicians' are bracketed together, until, in 1569, Richard Pyke drops out, and his partner Richard Woodwarde is left with his nameless instrument, among a long list of other court musicians playing sackbuts, trumpets, flutes, fifes and viols. We know that Richard Woodwarde was a bagpiper, and we may reasonably surmise that Richard Pyke was one also. We may assume therefore that both Mary Tudor and her successor Queen Elizabeth had two bagpipers among her musicians.

Yet another bagpiping Richard, Richard Edward, 'Bage piper', appears in the Accounts of Liveries dated 1547–8. This, however, is in the reign of Edward VI, among the Accounts of Liveries for the Household at the burial of his father, Henry VIII.

The instrument makes one more appearance almost a hundred years later, in the reign of Charles II, among the musical instruments of 'His Majesty's Chappell Royall' in London. The player was William Tollett, who was appointed in 1663–4 as 'bag-piper in ordinary' to Charles II. The king had had good opportunity of hearing the pipes, and of acquiring a love for them, for he was crowned, not at Westminster, but (despite Cromwell) at Scone, and eighty Scots pipers are said to have played at his coronation. More than that, he had heard the great Patrick Mór MacCrimmon play. By one account this was said to be at Torwood near Stirling, where, in July 1651, the Royalist army assembled to try conclusions with Cromwell and Lambert – though other accounts give the occasion as on the field of the Battle of Worcester, a month later.

Whether Charles's William Tollett was a player of the Scots or English bagpipes is not known. Tollett is not a particularly Scots name. Charles I was said to have a liking for the Lancashire pipes.[112]

Tollett was the last of the official English pipers of the Royal Household in London. After the announcement of this appointment his name does not appear again. Even he must be accounted an anachronism. The long continuous line of English court bagpipers which began in the reign of Edward III in 1334 with Barbor the Bagpiper and his colleague Morlan petered out in the reign of Queen Elizabeth in 1569 with Richard Woodwarde, over two centuries later.

Although the bagpipe disappeared from the royal court, it was to enjoy a century more both as an English folk instrument and as a military one. In Ben Jonson's *Irish Masque*, performed in 1613, we are told that six men danced to the bagpipe; and Ben Jonson makes reference to the instrument in his plays.

There is a remarkable piece of sculpture called 'The Bagpipe Boy' by Caius Gabriel Cibber (1630–1700), the father of Colley Cibber, the English actor. The seated boy plays a typical bagpipe of the English pattern, but with three drones, issuing independently from the bag like a Scots Highland bagpipe. This seems to be the only representation in sculpture of an English mouth-blown bagpipe with three drones (see p. 189).

William Hogarth, the artist (1697–1764), includes the bagpipes in several of his pictures of English life, notably in his picture 'The Beggars' Opera', done some time between 1728 and 1732; in 'Southwark Fair' (1733) and in his 'Election Entertainment' (1755–8). Hogarth's bagpipes are all of similar pattern, namely with two drones having bell-shaped ends.

In the well-known children's song, probably of the eighteenth century, 'Old King Cole', the king calls for his pipers three; and these arriving on the scene, the song continues:

> Tootle, tootle too, tootle too, went the pipers,
> Twang, twang a-twang, twang-a-twang, went the harpers,
> Tweedle, tweedle dee, tweedle dee, went the fiddlers,
>         And so merry we'll all be.

In 1702 we find an antiquary and topographer, Ralph Thoresby, writing from the midst of the guild pageantry at Preston, Lancashire: 'got little rest, the music and Lancashire bagpipes having continued the whole night';[113] while as late as 1732 Dalyell notes that there was recorded, also at Preston, 'a very merry wedding' at which there were seven bagpipers.[114]

By this time, however, the English bagpipe, except in Northumberland, was declining in popularity. By the end of the century it had disappeared altogether. As *envoi*, we may quote a mid-seventeenth-century song, which shows the contrast between the pastoral English bagpipe and the war-like Highland *pìob mhór*. It is the period of the glamourization of the English shepherd and shepherdess:[115]

> The life of a shepherd is void of all care,
>     With his bag and his bottle he maketh good fare;
> He hath yon green meadow to walk in at will-a,
>     With a pair of fine bagpipes upon a green hill-a;
> Tringdilla, tringdilla, tring down-a-down dilla.

## Ireland: the *pìob mhór*

In the sixteenth century we have our first pictorial representations of the Irish war-pipe or *pìob mhór*. The best known is to be found in John Derricke's *The Image of Ireland*, written in 1578 and published three years later. The book is dedicated to Sir Philip Sidney – he who found his heart moved by 'the old song of Percie and Douglas more than by a trumpet'. (He does not say what he thought of the sound of the pipes.) Sir Philip Sidney lived in the reigns of Elizabeth and James I.

Derricke's poem is illustrated by a woodcut of the Irish *pìob mhór*. It shows this to have been a large instrument, taller than its player, with two drones and a chanter, all three very long. The drones are of unequal length. The bag is held in front of the player, and it is difficult to see how he exerted the pressure necessary to create that loudness and shrillness of the *píob mhór* which is said to have been audible at a distance of several miles. The chanter appears in the picture to be almost as long as the player's legs, and, allowing for exaggeration in the drawing, must have been fully two feet long. The fingerholes appear to be correspondingly widely spaced, and the player's fingers are widely stretched to cover them.

Another woodcut, of rather clumsy execution, now at the British Museum, depicts the Irish pipes at the Battle of Ballyshannon in 1595. Crude though these two drawings are, they are valuable as being among the very few contemporary pictures of the Irish *píob mhór*. An actual specimen* of the Irish *píob mhór* used to be among the exhibits at the Musée de Cluny, Paris. This was said to have been played at the Battle of Fontenoy in 1745 by one of the pipers of the Irish Brigade who fought on the side of the French against the English troops. A recent writer, describing them, says that the chanter had very large holes that would take a stout finger to cover, and that the present-day chanter looks miniature in comparison.[116]

The musician Galilei, father of the astronomer, in his *Dialogue* published in Florence in 1581, says of the Irish and their *píob mhór*, 'To its sound, this unconquered, fierce and warlike people march their armies and encourage one another to feats of valour. With it also, they accompany their dead to the grave, making such mournful sounds as almost to force the bystander to weep.'[117]

We see many glimpses of the Irish *píob mhór* throughout the history of the next couple of centuries. At the Battle of the Boyne, in 1690, we find a clash between the sound of the Irish and the Scottish Highland pipes, for the Scots and Irish fought on opposite sides. What a grand noise *that* must have been. At Cremona, in 1702, the *píob mhór* of the Irish Brigade

---

* It seems, most regrettably, to have been lost. Alexander MacAuley, in a letter to me in 1969, says: 'The curator of the Musée de Cluny showed me a book of specimen items in the Musée made in 1902, that proved the Irish *píob mhór* were here. They were shown on a colour plate, very faded, with a pale green bag-cover. Of the two short drones, one had a split. . . . According to the curator they had been removed from view years before, either into storage or disposed of.' They were almost certainly the only specimens in existence of the ancient Irish war-pipe.

    Alexander MacAuley later sent me a sketch he had made in 1936 of the Irish *píob mhór* at the Musée de Cluny. This shows that the two drones issue from the same stock. The pipes of the drones curve outwards from each other as they leave the stock, the two drones taking the shape of an elongated letter U. One pipe is slightly shorter than the other (cf. Baines's remarks on comparative drone lengths, *Bagpipes*, p. 119). Mr MacAuley suggests that the pipes were bent to a curve, after being bored out, by methods of applied heat known to workers in wood.

was heard in battle against the Germans, when they played an old Irish Gaelic air which afterwards was called 'The Battle of Cremona'. At the Battle of Fontenoy in 1745 when, again, the Irish Brigade was fighting against the English troops on the side of the French, they played the tunes 'St Patrick's Day in the Morning', 'White Cockade', and the renamed 'The Battle of Cremona'.

## Surviving bagpipes

### Ireland: the *uilleann* pipes

This was the last time the Irish *píob mhór* was heard in battle. For nearly two centuries a rival bagpipe to the *píob mhór* had been gradually coming into favour in Ireland and was eventually to replace it. This was the *uilleann* pipes, the bag of which was filled with a bellows. The bellows was held under the opposite arm to that of the bag; the pipes were laid across the knees of the player, who was seated. *Uilleann* is Gaelic for 'elbow'; it was thought that the pipes were so called because the bellows is strapped to the right elbow. The distinguished writer on Irish folk music, Dr Donal O'Sullivan, however, disallows this explanation.[118]

The *uilleann* pipes made their appearance in the last decade of the sixteenth century.* They were on the scene early enough to catch the ear of William Shakespeare, writing *The Merchant of Venice* between 1594 and 1598. He wrote the name of the pipes phonetically, but not accurately so, for he called them woollen pipes ('woollen' is, of course, very near to *uilleann* in sound). By doing so, he perpetrated a classical absurdity for all time, and one that has given rise to considerable puzzlement. The passage, in *The Merchant of Venice*, iv.i, has been skated over by most of the writers on the bagpipe of a more reticent age. It is Shylock who speaks:

> Some men there are, love not a gaping pig;
> Some, that are mad if they behold a cat;
> And others, when the bagpipe sings i' the nose,
> Cannot contain their urine; for affection,
> Mistress of passion, sways it to the mood
> Of what it likes or loathes. Now for your answer.
> As there is no firm reason to be rendered,
> Why he cannot abide a gaping pig;
> Why he, a harmless necessary cat;
> Why he, a woollen bagpipe; but of force
> Must yield to such inevitable shame
> As to offend, himself being offended.

* Flood, *The Story of the Bagpipe*, p. 95, gives 1588 as the year in which the *uilleann* pipes 'came into vogue' in Ireland.

Shakespeare's name for the instrument, the woollen bagpipe, did not 'stick' and we find it nowhere else. The name *uilleann* did give place to a further corruption, and one quite as meaningless, in the term *union* pipes, a name by which until more recent times they have become generally known. The spread of general musical knowledge, and a growing familiarity with the instrument through radio and television, has, however, caused it largely to revert to the former name of *uilleann* pipes.

The *uilleann* pipes have soft reeds and a sweet tone, in complete contrast to the harsh clangour of the *píob mhór*. They are primarily a chamber instrument, and were certainly never meant for the battlefield. All through the seventeenth century and most of the eighteenth, they gained in popularity at the expense of the old national war-pipes, until finally towards the end of the eighteenth century, the *píob mhór* went out of use.

A revival of the Irish *píob mhór* took place about the beginning of the present century, chiefly through the efforts of a small band of enthusiasts that included Lord Castledown, Sean Leslie and a Belfast man, Francis Joseph Biggar. One of the versions that was popular in this revival was a slightly altered form of the *píob mhór* called the 'Brian Boru' pipes, invented by Pipe-major H. Starck. These had three drones of different lengths all emerging from one stock, and a chanter with a complete chromatic scale. This was, however, a *revival*, and as such it cannot properly enter into our story.

So we may take our leave of the Irish pipes and press on to the Northumbrian pipes, which with the Scottish Highland pipes remain the sole survivors of the considerable family of bagpipes.

## Northumbria

It may seem paradoxical, after having brought the history of the English bagpipe to a conclusion, to follow with an account of the Northumbrian bagpipe. The fact is, however, that the Northumbrian instrument seems to have been imported from France, out of line with the development and final decline of the English bagpipe *per se*; and indeed, far from being in decline, it continues to develop healthily to the present day.

There was an ancient bagpipe once in use in Northumberland which could be described as part of the true general bagpipe tradition and history of these islands. Like the rest of its English brethren it has become extinct. This is the Northumbrian 'war-pipe'. As far as is known, no specimen of it has survived.[119] That is a pity, for a genuine specimen could have provided an important link with the Scottish Highland bagpipe, of which the genealogy, in spite of continuous and diligent research by its devotees, is still vague and uncertain. All we know about the Northumbrian war-pipe is that it was mouth blown,* and had either a single bass

* Here 'mouth-blown' refers to the method of filling the bag.

drone or two tenor drones, after the fashion of the true English bagpipe as well as of the general type used on the Continent. William Cocks, who wrote the article on bagpipes in the fifth edition of *Grove's Dictionary of Music*, says there that the ancient war-pipe of Northumberland 'was probably identical with the old Scottish Highland pipe'.

One should here correct a statement by the authors of *Northumbrian Minstrelsy*, J. Collingwood Bruce and John Stokoe; they write: 'Two species of bagpipes have been in use in Northumberland – the large pipes and the small. The large pipes differed in nothing from the Highland bagpipes, and they were used in the early part of this century [nineteenth] by the piper who was attached to the Northumberland Militia.' As far as can be ascertained, however, the old mouth-blown pipes went out of use before this period. The pipes used by the Northumberland Militia at that date were the half-long pipes, which were bellows-blown.[120]

Three other types of bagpipe are known in Northumberland besides the extinct war-pipe. These are, the half-long pipes, the shuttle pipes, and the small-pipes. These are all bellows-blown, and it is appropriate first to examine the history of the use of the bellows as part of the instrument.

*The bellows*

The earliest known mention of the bellows-blown bagpipe is in the *Syntagma musicum\** of Michael Praetorius (1571–1620). This is written mostly in Latin, but with frequent interpolations in German. The volume concerned (one of four), the *Organographia*, dealing with bagpipes and other wind instruments, was published in 1618. It contains the earliest known illustration of a bellows-blown bagpipe; and Praetorius states that the instrument is of French origin. The illustration is that of the type of bagpipe known later as the musette.

C. E. Borjon, describing the instrument in his *Traité de la musette* published in 1672, says that the bellows had been in use then for some forty or fifty years; but this is evidently an underestimate, for it dates the introduction of the bellows between 1622 and 1632, i.e. at least four years later than the year in which the illustration of it had already appeared in Praetorius.

The mouth-blown English bagpipe was in use until the middle of the eighteenth century (see the illustrations of it in Hogarth's picture 'The Election Entertainment' of 1755). This is over a hundred years after the introduction of the bellows on the Continent. It is therefore apparent that the bellows of the Northumbrian pipes was not a development from the English mouth-blown bagpipe, but an intrusion from an outside source; for by 1755 the Northumbrian bagpipe was a fully developed instrument.[121]

---

\* The earliest known work on musical instruments, Sebastian Virdung's *Musica Getutscht*, published at Basle in 1511, mentions only the mouth-filled bagpipe, the *cornemuse à bouche*.

No writers have attempted to give a date for the introduction of the bellows into Britain, but Edward Ledwich in *The Antiquities of Ireland* (Dublin, 1790) says that at the close of the sixteenth century considerable improvements were made to the Irish bagpipe, namely by taking the pipes from the mouth and causing the bag to be filled by a small pair of bellows. Grattan Flood gives the date of the invention of the Irish *uilleann* (bellows-blown) pipes at about 1588. (Shakespeare makes his reference to them in 1594.) It is therefore reasonable to suppose that the bellows bagpipe was known at least in Ireland some time before its mention and illustration by Praetorius in 1618; and a fairly safe estimate for this would be the latter part of the sixteenth century.

The first evidence for the bellows-blown bagpipe in England (i.e. Northumberland) is a set with musette-type shuttle drones mentioned by William Cocks,[122] bearing the inscription of a deed of gift of 1695.* Thus the bellows are mentioned earlier in the Irish *uilleann* pipes than in the Northumberland ones, but expert opinion seems to be that the bellows was imported first into England in the latter part of the sixteenth century, and exported from there to Ireland.

The earliest form of drone in the Northumberland bellows-blown bag-pipe was the shuttle or barrel drone, which was the type of drone used in the French musette as mentioned by Borjon in his treatise. This shuttle or barrel consisted of a cylinder of wood about six or seven inches in length and about one-and-a-half inches in diameter. The shuttle is pierced lengthwise with a number of narrow bores which are connected in series by end-pieces of U shape; and those form the requisite length of bore, extending backwards and forwards inside the shuttle, for the right pitch of the drone. The bore of the drone terminates in an open groove down the outside of the cylinder; it can be tuned by lengthening or shortening it with a movable slide or covering. The drones are sounded by double reeds of the oboe type.†

There can be little doubt that the shuttle pipe of Northumberland was based upon the musette of France. The shuttle and bellows were both completely typical of the French instrument. During the early years of its introduction into Northumberland, the bellows was carried into Ireland also.

## The chanter

The original shuttle pipe of Northumberland was a small-pipe, i.e. a

---

* They are described and illustrated in the *Newcastle Weekly Chronicle Supplement*, 27 January 1894. The inscription reads: 'The gift of Simon Robertson to Salathiel Humphries 1695.'

† Lyndesay G. Langwill, author of *The Bassoon*, London, 1965, sent me the following note: 'precisely the same composite bore in a cylinder of wood is that of the *rackett* or "sausage" bassoon. The German name is derived from *rauke* = crooked. The *musette* drone may have evolved from the *rackett*.'

miniature pipe, with an open-ended chanter. It was not conical in bore
as are the Scots chanters and as were those of the rest of the land, but
cylindrical both in bore and in its external shape. It had seven fingerholes
(later increased to eight) and a thumbhole. Specimens exist dating back to
as early as 1700. Sometime during the eighteenth century, probably early
rather than late, the chanter was closed at the end. This means that when
all the holes are stopped, the chanter ceases to sound. This is the fundamental difference between the modern Northumberland pipes and the
Scottish, and between them and most of the bagpipes of other countries:
whereas in the Scottish pipes the sound is continuous, in the Northumberland species it is not. It is thus possible to cease the sound at the end
of a phrase, to repeat a note with a separate attack between the note and
its repetition and, most characteristic of the technique of the instrument,
to play notes staccato. None of these effects is possible with the continuously sounding chanter of the Scottish and other bagpipes. A note can
only be 'repeated' on the Scottish chanter by means of an intermediate
'cut' or 'grace-note' called a warbler.

The system of fingering the closed chanter, by raising and lowering one
finger at a time before the succeeding finger is raised, is remarkably
similar to the system of fingering the French musette.[123] This could be
further evidence of the hereditary relationship between the two. In the
Scottish Highland bagpipe several of the holes of the chanter are normally
uncovered at the same time, as they almost certainly were in the old
Lowland pipe.

The eight holes of the old open-ended Northumberland chanter (seven
fingerholes and a thumbhole at the back) correspond to the eight holes
of the scale of G major, that is, from the second bottom line of the treble
stave to the octave above; and when all the holes were stopped, the full
length of the pipe sounded the F sharp below the keynote, making nine
notes in all.[124] The closing of the ends of the chanter robbed it of the
lower F sharp, the note resulting from the full length of the open pipe.

Keys were later added to the Northumbrian chanter. These were four
in number to begin with: they extended the lower compass of the fingered
scale downwards from G by three notes, F sharp, E and D; and also gave
the additional note A above the top G of the old keyless chanter. More
keys were added later, to give still more notes below and above the
fingered chanter scale, and to give chromatic notes between the fingered
ones. The modern Northumberland chanter may have as many as seventeen keys giving a fully chromatic scale from low B natural below the
treble stave to B natural above the treble stave, that is, a compass of two
octaves.[125] Curiously enough, whereas most instruments of the kind have
risen in pitch over the years, or rather the centuries, the G, the keynote
of the Northumbrian chanter, is now actually below modern pitch, being
somewhere between our F and F sharp. The bore of the modern Northumberland chanter is cylindrical.

## The drones

It is in the drones of the Northumberland pipes, rather than in the chanter, that an interesting relationship appears between the pipes of the three countries, England (Northumberland), Ireland (the Uilleann pipes), and Lowland Scotland. All three share the use of the bellows, and the drones, instead of emerging from the bag through separate stocks, spring from a common stock. The sequence of this development in the three countries is significant. The use of a common stock was once thought to be a characteristic of the old Irish *píob mhór*, but the evidence is not conclusive. The only existing specimen of the instrument is now lost; there is a sixteenth-century woodcut in Derricke's *Image of Ireland*, but in it the stock is partly obscured by the piper's head. The Dürer engraving of a bagpiper, *Der Dudelsackpfeifer* (dated 1514, now at Vienna), would seem to be the one referred to by Flood as that of an Irish bagpiper and his pipe, that of the Irish *píob mhór*. This, however, can only be a matter of surmise, for Dürer himself is silent on the subject.* Here again the drone pattern is inconclusive, with the evidence of the picture not seeming to tip the scale in favour of separate drones. In the drawing of the Battle of Ballyshannon made by a soldier in the field, two separate drones are distinctly visible. Finally, in the drawing of a pig playing the bagpipes, from an Irish manuscript of probably the sixteenth century, two drones distinctly issue separately. It may be presumed that the instrument was drawn from an actual bagpipe or the recollection of one (but see later note from Alexander MacAuley, p. 115).

From Ireland, the use of the bellows and the single common stock for the drones in the *uilleann* pipes seems to have travelled next to Lowland Scotland, to appear in the Lowland or Border bagpipe. This bagpipe had three drones; all, as has been said above, emerged from the same stock. They were similar in pitch to the drones of the Highland pipes, i.e. two tenor drones sounded A, the top line of the bass stave, and a bass drone sounded the A an octave below.

In the meantime the shuttle drones of the early small Northumbrian instrument, seemingly borrowed from the French musette, were not fully satisfactory. The many bends of the bore within the shuttle demanded strong wind pressure to blow them. So also did the drone reeds, which were of the double, oboe variety. Across the border in Scotland the remedy, as in the Border pipes, appeared ready to hand. The shuttle was scrapped altogether, and straight pipes were used for the small-pipe drones; in addition, the 'oboe' reeds were replaced by single beating reeds of the clarinet type which are easier to blow. Reeds of this type are used in the drones of the Highland bagpipe.

* Such a bagpipe is also to be seen in an engraving, dated 1535, entitled 'A German Shepherd'; it is reproduced by Dalyell, *Musical Memoirs of Scotland*, plate XII, and copied by Flood, *The Story of the Bagpipe*, pp. 75, 77.

It was from these small-pipes that the larger 'half-long pipes' of Northumberland, already mentioned, would seem to have developed; these were a larger and more powerful instrument for marching and general out-door purposes than the chamber-sized small-pipes. The 'half-long' pipes have all the essential features of the small-pipes on a larger scale – the bellows, the chanter, and the three drones issuing from one stock, sounding an octave tonic with the fifth in between. The drones of the half-long pipes rest on the shoulder, whereas those of the small-pipes rest on the arm. The half-long pipes have been revived in Northumberland for the use of Scout troops, etc.

So we have the interesting historical sequence that the bellows, almost certainly introduced from France first into Northumberland, found their way into Ireland for the *uilleann* or union pipes; and from thence to Lowland Scotland. The drones, on the other hand, issuing from a common stock, travelled from Ireland (in the Uilleann pipes) to Lowland Scotland, and from there to Northumberland, to replace the not wholly satisfactory shuttle drone.

This can best be shown in tabular form:

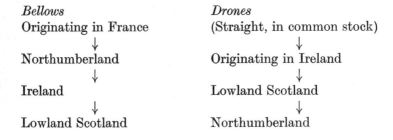

| *Bellows* | *Drones* |
|---|---|
| Originating in France | (Straight, in common stock) |
| ↓ | ↓ |
| Northumberland | Originating in Ireland |
| ↓ | ↓ |
| Ireland | Lowland Scotland |
| ↓ | ↓ |
| Lowland Scotland | Northumberland |

We have now mentioned all four types of the Northumbrian pipes: the ancient mouth-blown war-pipes, now extinct; the large 'half-long' bellows-blown pipes; the shuttle small-pipes; and the modern small-pipes. All three latter types are bellows-blown. To complete the picture, it is necessary to make a few more observations about the last of these, the small-pipes.

The chanter of the Northumbrian small-pipes, as has already been stated, is of cylindrical shape, both internally (the bore) and externally. The drones were at first three in number; they sounded the keynote in octaves, with the fifth sounding in between. (This is the case both in the small-pipes and in the half-long pipes.) They were therefore of three different lengths. Later, additional drones were added to the small-pipes. Four drones became the more usual number to begin with, but these were increased subsequently to five or even six. Usually only three of these were used at one time, playing the keynote and fifth, according to the key of the music. Stops were inserted into the open ends of the drones to silence those that were out of harmony with the key being played.

## The Scottish small-pipes

Another member of this interrelated bagpipe group must be mentioned here, although it particularly concerns Scotland. This is the miniature version of the Lowland pipes, the Scottish small-pipes. These have a set of bellows, an open-ended chanter of nine notes (seven fingerholes and a thumbhole) and three drones in one stock. The drones may be tuned to an octave tonic as in the Lowland and Highland Scottish pipes. The alternative tuning is unique in the history of the Scottish bagpipe: the drone harmony may be the octave tonic with the fifth between, as in the Northumbrian instrument. But whereas the tonic of both the Scottish Highland and Lowland pipes may be reckoned as A natural, the tonic of the Scottish small-pipes is the same pitch as in the Northumbrian; that is, it is the written note G natural, sounding somewhere between F natural and F sharp.

The Scottish small-pipes are the same size as the Northumbrian small-pipes, and may be easily mistaken for them. The bore of both Scottish and Northumbrian small-pipes is cylindrical, but the exterior of the Scottish small chanter tapers from the foot upwards, like the present-day chanter of the Highland pipes. The Scottish small-pipe chanter is open-ended; but then, so were the earlier Northumbrian small-pipe chanters, so this is not a decisive means of identification. One must also take into account occasional amateur interference with the true design, such as the drilling out of the end of a closed chanter to convert it to an open one.* William Cocks tells me in a letter:

> A pretty good guide as to whether or not a set of small-pipes is Scottish [or Northumbrian] is to be found in the mounting of the drone-slides. Scottish are of ivory or horn, whereas Northumbrian are invariably of metal. This also applies to the stocks. A decorative feature which is found only on Scottish examples is that of 'combing' with groups of fine lines.

In addition to the bellows-blown Scottish small-pipes as described above, there has also existed at one time a mouth-blown form of Scottish small-pipe. Joseph MacDonald, writing in 1760, says in *A Compleat Theory of the Scots Highland Bagpipe*:

> Though the Reels and Jigs peculiar to the Pipe are in large companies as at Weddings etc., played to good effect on the greater Pipe, yet they have besides, thro' the Highlands in general, a smaller Bagpipe, Compleat, the same in form and apparatus with

---

* Askew, 'The origins of the Northumbrian bagpipe', *Archaeologia Aeliana*, 4th series, vol. 9 (1932), further observes that 'even the scale given by the Lowland chanter cannot be cited as evidence one way or the other [i.e. for distinguishing the Scottish from the Northumbrian small-pipes] as by the use of different reeds it can be made to produce either the scale of G or A.'

the greater, differing only in size, and used for Dancing Music alone, altho' all other Music peculiar to the instrument may be played on it as truly, though not so grandly, as on the large Pipe.

As I wrote in an earlier book:[126]

> In a catalogue of prices in the early editions of J. & R. Glen's musical publication *Collection for the Great Highland Bagpipe* (first published in 1870) three different sizes or types of bagpipes are listed: the Great Highland or military bagpipes; half-size or reel bagpipes, blown with mouth or bellows; miniature or chamber bagpipes, blown with mouth or bellows. In a still earlier price-list by Alexander Glen in 1860, all these types appear; in addition there is the Lovat reel pipe, also blown either by mouth or bellows, which seems to have been an intermediate size between the half-size or reel pipe and the miniature or chamber bagpipes. A specimen of the miniature or chamber bagpipes, mouth-blown, may be seen in the Royal Scottish Museum in Chambers Street, Edinburgh. Half-size pipes of the same pitch as the full-size Great Highland bagpipe, but of smaller diameter and with softer reeds, are still occasionally manufactured; but, of course, these do not come truly under the classification of 'small-pipes'.

The Scottish small-pipes, though they seem to have been more plentiful in past times, are now extreme rarities. Askew states[127] that only three examples are known to him. One of these bears the inscription, '1st. Highland Battn. Jan. 4, 1757. Hon. Coll. Mongtomery.' The Hon. Archibald Montgomerie, afterwards the Earl of Eglinton, raised the 77th Regiment (Montgomery's Highlanders). His commission as colonel was dated 4 January 1757, as inscribed on the small-pipes. The regiment is stated to have had thirty pipers and drummers.[128] Why a Highland regiment should possess small-pipes as distinct from the time-honoured *piob mhór,* the great Highland war-pipe, is a mystery. It is interesting that the date 1757 should accord so closely with Joseph MacDonald's mention of the small instrument in 1760. This is after Culloden, when the bagpipe was proscribed in the Highlands as 'an instrument of war', and such miniature pipes being exempt, may have come into use; but proscription or fear of proscription of the pipes did not exist in a Highland regiment raised by government sanction for the war against the French in North America.

# Chapter three

# The Great Highland bagpipe

## The early pipes

Tha biadh is ceòl an seo, mar thubhairt am madadh-ruadh, 's e ruith air falbh leis a' phìob.
[There's meat and music here,
As the fox said as he ran off with the bagpipe.]

The Great Scottish Highland bagpipe is the major survivor of the family of bagpipes that have appeared in the British Isles since the *chorus* in the twelfth century. Here we enter the realm of tradition as much as of verifiable history; for one must depend on both for a succinct and credible account of Scotland's national instrument. In compensation, however, the Highland memory is a long one, and in the main, surprisingly accurate, as I can vouch for in my researches in other categories of Gaelic music. Moreover tradition concerning the Highland bagpipe can often be buttressed by verifiable facts; and so it is from a mixture of both, in the typical Gaelic way of things, that we must proceed.

There is no reason why we may not suppose that the bagpipe went through the same stages of development in the Highlands of Scotland as in the other areas of the British Isles. Even going back to the period of the Romans, there can be little doubt, as has been said, that the Highlander knew quite well what was happening on the other side of the Wall, in music as in everything else. The Highlander, or perhaps we should here revert to the term Celt, has always been possessed of a healthy inquisitiveness and curiosity – a fact first noted by Julius Caesar.* The Highland chiefs were educated, travelled and well-informed men. They had taken part in the political councils of the Kingdom of the Scots, at Perth, Scone and Edinburgh, since the end of the first millennium A.D. The chief travelled when away from home with an entourage or 'tail' which included in these early days a minstrel or minstrels as well as his bodyguard. Doubtless the chief's minstrel kept both his musically keen ears and his

---

* 'A people who call themselves Celts, though we call them Gauls', Caesar, *The Conquest of Gaul*, I, i; IV, i (Penguin ed. especially p. 110 regarding their inquisitiveness!).

eyes open in everything that pertained to music – and a good deal else besides. There would hardly be a self-respecting musician of the chief's household in the twelfth century who had not heard of the new *pìob*, the *chorus*, consisting of a *feadan* or hornpipe-type chanter fitted with a bag or skin and a blow-pipe, and a couple of hundred years later in the fourteenth century, a drone. The *ersche clareschaw* (Gaelic *clàrsach* player) who played at the command of James I surely made it his business to stroll up the Royal Mile to Edinburgh Castle and listen to the 'Englis pyparis' playing at the Castle 'yet' (gate). Thus it is highly probable that the bagpipe, from a very short time after its first appearance in rudimentary form in Britain, would be known and played in the Highlands. In these earlier times it was probably the same gentle-toned instrument that was played elsewhere in the islands, with such local differences and variations from the *pibgorns*, and *hornpipes* of the rest of Britain, as the Gaelic *feadan* (now fitted with a bag) possessed.

## Battle instruments

The bagpipe in Scotland was probably, to begin with, an instrument of peace rather than war; for in the earlier days of the country's history, the instruments of war were the trumpet and horn. Barbour in *The Bruce* describes the use of both these as a means of misleading the enemy in a campaign. The occasion of which he writes was a raid into England by the Scots in 1327 by Sir James Douglas and Sir Thomas Randolph, in the last years of King Robert the Bruce (died 1329) and the first year of the reign of Edward III in England. The passage is important enough to quote in full:[1]

| | |
|---|---|
| 'That we planely on hand sall ta | 'That we shall plainly undertake |
| To giff thaim opynly battaill: | To give them battle openly, |
| Bot at this tyme thair thoucht sall faill. | But at this time this expectation will be disappointed. |
| For we to morne her, all the day | For we tomorrow, here, all the day |
| Sall mak als mery as we may: | Shall make as merry as we may: |
| And mak ws boune agayn the nycht; | And make ourselves ready for the night; |
| And then ger mak our fyris lycht; | And then light our [camp] fires, |
| And blaw our hornys, and mak far, | And blow our horns, and make good cheer, |
| As all the warld our awne war, | As if the world belonged to us, |
| Quhill that the nycht weill fallin be. | Until darkness has fallen entirely. |
| And than, with all our harnays, we | And then with all our harness, we |

| | |
|---|---|
| Sall tak our way hamwart in hy. | Shall take our way homeward in haste. |
| And we sall gyit be graithly Quhill we be out off thair daunger, That lyis now enclossyt her. | And we shall be guided directly Until we are beyond their power, Who are now lying here surrounded. |
| Than sall we all be at our will. | Then shall we all be where we want to be. |
| And thai sall thaim trumpyt ill, Fra thai wyt weill we be away.' | And they shall give up, as being shamefully deceived, When they realize that we are gone.' |
| To this haly assentyt thai; And maid thaim gud cher all that nycht, Quhill on the morn that day was lycht. Apon the morne, all priuely Thai tursyt harnays, and maid redy; Swa that, or ewyn, all boun war thai. And their fayis, that agane thaim lay, Gert haiff thair men, that thar war ded, In cartis, till ane haly sted. All that day carriand thai war, | To this they wholly assented; And made good cheer all that night, Until the light of day next morning. In the morning, all secretly They packed up their equipment and made ready; So that, by evening, they were completely prepared. And their foes, who were camped in the neighbourhood, Caused their dead to be taken away, In carts, to a church-yard. All that day they were carrying them away, |
| With cartis, men that slayn war thar. That thai war fele mycht men well se, That in carying sa lang suld be. | With carts, men that were slain there. That they were many, one may well see, Because it required so long to take them away. |
| The ostis baith that day wer In pess: and quhen the nycht was ner, The Scottis folk, that liand war In till the park, maid fest and far; And blew hornys; and fyris maid, And gert mak thaim (bathe) brycht and braid; | Both the hosts that day were In peace; and when the night was near, The Scots folk that were lying Within the park, made feast and merriment; And blew horns, and made fires, And made them both bright and broad; |

| | |
|---|---|
| Swa at that nycht thair fyris war mar, | So that that night their fires were more [to be seen], |
| Than ony tyme befor thai war. | Than at any time before. |
| And quhen the nycht wer fallyn weill, | And when the night was well fallen, |
| With all the harnayis ilka dele, | With all the equipment, every part of it, |
| All priuely thai raid thair way. | All secretly they rode away. |
| Sone in a moss entryt ar thai, | Soon in a marsh they are entered, |
| That had wele two myle lang of braid. | That was fully two miles in breadth. |
| Out our that moss on fute thai yeid: | Across that marsh on foot they went; |
| And in thier hand their horss leid thai. | And led their horses by hand, |
| And it was rycht a noyus way: | And it was very troublesome going: |
| And nocht for thi all that thai wer | But nevertheless the entire body of them |
| Come weill out our it, hale and fer; | Came well out over it safe and sound; |
| And tynt bot litill off thair ger. | And lost but little of their gear. |

The incident is confirmed by Froissart in chapter 18 of his *Chronicles*, in the following account of the same campaign:

The Scots, seeing the English thus take up their quarters, ordered part of the army to remain where the battalions had been drawn up; and the remainder retired to their huts, where they made marvellously great fires, and, about midnight such a blasting and noise with their horns, that it seemed as if all the great devils from hell had been come there. Thus were they lodged this night, which was the night of the feast of St. Peter, the beginning of August 1327, until the next day, when the lords heard mass: afterwards, everyone armed himself, and the battalions were formed as on the preceding day. When the Scots saw this, they came and lodged themselves on the same ground they had done before; and the two armies remained thus drawn up until noon, when the Scots made no movement to come towards the English, nor did these on their part make any advances, for they dared not to attempt it with so great disadvantage. Several companions passed the river on horseback, as did some of the foot, to skirmish with the Scots, who also quitted their battalions to meet them, and many on each side were killed, wounded, and taken prisoners. In the afternoon

the lords ordered every one to retire to their quarters, as it seemed
to them that they were drawn up to no purpose; in this manner
they remained for three days. The Scots, on their side, never
quitted the mountain; but there were continued skirmishings on
both sides, and many were killed and taken prisoners; in the
evening they made large fires, and great noises with their horns
and with shouting.

Again Froissart, describing the Battle of Otterburn (the 'Chevy Chase'
of the ballad) in 1388, in the reign of Robert II, Bruce's grandson, notes
this same use of horns in the battlefield:

The barons and knights of Scotland . . . [had] formed themselves
into a strong body, and had fortified their camp in such a manner
that it could be entered by only one pass. . . . When this was done,
they ordered their minstrels to play as merrily as they could. The
Scots have a custom, when assembled in arms, for those who are
on foot to be well dressed, each having a large horn slung round
his neck, in the manner of hunters, and when they blow all together,
the horns being of different sizes, the noise is so great it may be
heard four miles off, to the great dismay of their enemies and their
own delight. The Scots commanders ordered this sort of music
now to be played.

It is a pity that Froissart does not relate what instrument the Scots
minstrels played so merrily! Was it the bagpipes?

It is certainly possible, chronologically speaking, that the minstrels
with the Scots army possessed a bagpipe or two, at least in the second of
these two campaigns, the Battle of Otterburn (1388). There is official
mention of pipers, though admittedly not bagpipers, in the Scottish
Exchequer Rolls for 1377 – eleven years before Otterburn. On the English
side, in 1334 Edward III had sent 'Barbor the bagpiper' overseas to
perfect his technique – more than fifty years before the Battle of Otterburn.

Of the Battle of Halidon Hill (1333) Ritson quotes an old chronicler
(unnamed) who recounted that 'The Englisshe mynstralis blewe hir trumpes
and hir pipes, and hidously astrede the Scottis' (see p. 89). In spite of
this 'old chronicler's' tale (if he really existed) the probability, as already
mentioned, is that the bagpipe of the day was a gentle-toned instrument,
which had not yet become the loud, clanging great pipe of the battlefield
or acquired battle-status. If the minstrel or minstrels blew their pipes
during the military adventures mentioned above, their sound must have
been completely drowned by the din of the horns, of which, Froissart tells
us, every foot-soldier carried one.[2] It is doubtful if even the modern
Highland *pìob mhór* could be heard above the din of several thousand men
all blowing horns at the top of their bent at the same moment!

## The harp

Before the war-pipes made their appearance in the Highlands, the instrument for stimulating the courage of those about to engage in battle was
the harp, used as an accompaniment to the *brosnachadh*, or incitement to
battle. This was sung or chanted by the official bard. The earliest allusion
to this military 'pep-talk' was the famous rallying speech of the leader of
the Caledonians, Calgacus, before the Battle of Mons Graupius in A.D. 82,
ending with the famous bitter words concerning the Roman invaders:
'They create a desolation and call it peace!' (solitudinem faciunt, pacem
appellant!).

Tacitus tells us that this forerunner of the Highland *brosnachadh* on the
eve of the battle of Mons Graupius was received 'with enthusiastic singing,
and confused applause'.[3]

The last time we hear of the *brosnachadh* being sung is before the Battle
of Harlaw in 1411; it was composed by the last of the hereditary bards,
Lachlan Mór MacVurich. Thereafter it seems, before and during battle,
the voice with its harp accompaniment gave place to the sound of the
war-pipes – the *pìob mhór*.

The harp was not supplanted altogether as an instrument of war for
some time, however. We find it still being carried on a military campaign
at the Battle of Balrinnes (1594), also known variously as the Battle of
Glenlivet, of Glen Rinnes and of Strathnavon. It was fought between
Argyll, holder of the king's commission (James VI), and the Catholic earls
of Huntly and Errol. Argyll was thirsting to avenge the killing of his
brother-in-law, the 'Bonny Earl of Moray'.*

According to one account,[4] Argyll, besides taking trumpets, drums and
the bagpipe, took with him his harper. He also had in his train a spae-wife
or witch, for the purpose of divining where his enemies had hidden their
goods and treasure. The spae-wife delivered herself of the prophecy that
on the morrow after the battle, 'Argyll's harp would be played in Buchan
[Errol's home ground]' and that 'the bagpipe should sound in Strathbogie
[the seat of the earl of Huntly]'. The prophecy turned out to be true, but
not quite in the way Argyll interpreted it; for it was Errol and Huntly,
and not Argyll, who called the tune; the harp, bagpipe, spae-wife and all,
fell into their hands as the victors.

* Dr J. L. Campbell of Canna sent me the following note: 'The situation was
  much more complicated than a matter of personal vengeance. See Sheriff
  J. R. N. MacPhail, "Papers relating to the Murder of the Laird of Calder" in
  *Highland Papers*, I, 143 (Scottish History Society). Of Moray's murder Sheriff
  MacPhail writes that "its causes and its consequences are of greater consequence
  than the incident itself, and, as might have been expected, are proportionately
  unknown". Sheriff MacPhail's Introductory Note to these papers is very
  important and interesting. The murder of Campbell of Calder was connected
  with that of the Earl of Moray, and the King's Chancellor was involved in both
  of them as were Campbell of Ardkinglass and Campbell of Lochnell in the case
  of Calder's.'

There is a ballad of the Battle of Balrinnes; it is interesting because it is the only ballad in Lowland Scots to make specific mention of the bagpipes in battle. It was first printed in 1681 in Edinburgh, and was almost certainly of later composition than the period of the battle itself. A Latin manuscript in the National Library of Scotland gives what is probably an account nearer in period and more authoritative in detail, and it states all the salient points of the story, i.e. the bagpipe,* the harp and the spae-wife.

The mention in the account of trumpets and drums in the Highland army is interesting for, if it is true, it ties up with the earlier accounts of the music of the battlefield by Barbour and Froissart (see pp. 126–9).

A much later reference to the harp and its role in Highland life *vis-à-vis* the bagpipe occurs in Mrs Ann Grant of Laggan's *Essays on the Superstitions of the Highlanders of Scotland.*[5] She says:

> The Harp was . . . the national music of the highlands; of which their songs, adages, and legends of all kinds, afford sufficient proof.
>
> During the cruel wars between king's men and queen's men,† in the minority of James VI, the unity of the clans was in a great measure broken.
>
> A sanguinary spirit was introduced, and the sweet sounds drawn by love and fancy, or by grief or tenderness, from the trembling strings of the *clàrsach*, gave way to the ruder strains of martial music, which the bagpipe was so much better suited to convey.
>
> Still this did not supply the place of that instrument, so dear to bards and heroes, the use of which was in some degree continued, till the sanguinary conflicts, in the time of the civil wars, destroyed, for a season, all the functions of music, but those of summoning the tribes to war, animating the battle, and bewailing its victims.
>
> For these purposes, the harsh and bold, or querulous and mournful strains of the pipe, were best adapted.

Alexander MacDonald in his poem in praise of the pipes (cf. p. 138) disparages the music of the harp as:

*Ciuil bhochd, mosgaideach phrámhail*
  *Air son shean daoine is nionag*
(Poor, dull, sleepy tunes for old men and girls)

James VI, born 19 June 1566, was proclaimed King of Scotland in the following year, on the enforced pseudo-abdication of Mary Queen of Scots. His minority may be said to have extended till 1583, while a long series of

* *'Tibiam utricularum maximam'*, i.e. the great bagpipe.
† I.e. the factions supporting the regents of James VI (and later James himself) and Mary Queen of Scots.

regents and others wielded the state power, until at the age of eighteen he shook off the shackles and assumed the royal power.

Mrs Grant obviously believed that it was during the second half of the sixteenth century that the war-pipe replaced the harp as the most popular and widely used musical instrument of the Highlands. This is understandable, for the sixteenth century, considered as a whole, was the period when the attempts to restore the Lordship of the Isles, and the religious conflicts of the time, both seem to have produced a break in popular Highland tradition.

## *The* pìob mhór

One can readily see how the voice and harp would have given way to the *pìob mhór* in battle. The thin sound, in the open air, of the voice of the bard, and the feeble tone of the little Celtic harp, could obviously be heard by only a few of the assembled host nearest to the bard – probably only the captains. One can imagine an army gathered in the cheerless dawn, stamping their feet with both impatience and cold, while the bard drooled on inaudibly and interminably, his unheard exhortation punctuated with an occasional chord on the harp; while impatient warriors growled for action.

The change to the exhilarating clangour of the pipes must have been electrifying, if such an anachronism be permissible. It was a sound to stir the blood before the battle began, and to sustain the spirits of the warriors in the midst of it – as the Greeks, described by Thucydides, had discovered nearly two thousand years before.

It is impossible to say exactly when the Scottish pipes – which we must now understand to mean the Great Highland bagpipe – were first used in battle. There is a tradition of the Clan Menzies that they had their pipes with them at Bannockburn (1314). A set of bagpipes with a chanter, blow-pipe and single drone, known as the Menzies Bannockburn pipes, were preserved in the family of Menzies of Menzies. They are said to have belonged to the MacIntyres who were hereditary pipers to the Menzies, and who themselves put great value on them 'from their having been in the family for several hundred years'. These pipes are described in detail by D. P. Menzies,[6] who says of their tone, on hearing them played, that 'it was somewhat loud and harsh. From their having only one drone, the air or melody is heard more distinctly than in the modern bagpipe.'

There is no chronological reason against such a bagpipe having been in existence at the date of Bannockburn; but there is nothing to go on except tradition. This tradition was gathered, according to D. P. Menzies, from 'an old pupil of the MacIntyres, Alexander Menzies of Aberfeldy'. This set of bagpipes is referred to by MacIntyre North in his *Book of the True Highlanders* (with an illustration of them) as 'the remains of the oldest known bagpipes'. The chanter, of characteristically tapering bore, ends in a trumpet-shaped bell measuring two inches in external diameter, with three turned lines on its bottom surface. In addition to the usual finger-holes there are two extra holes on each side of the chanter near the foot. By tradition, these extra holes were bored on the advice of a fairy, who predicted that with them the chanter would produce music 'the like of which had never been heard before', and which 'would strike fear into the hearts of the enemy'.* The blow-pipe, oddly, is square, but graduates into the round at the blowing end. Of the single drone, only the top half is original.

The single-drone bagpipe, as has already been stated, is to be seen in an illustration in the Gorleston Psalter as early as 1306, and there is no reason to suppose that it may not have reached Scotland at much the same period. 1306 is eight years before the date of the Battle of Bannockburn.

The bag and bag-sockets of the Bannockburn pipes are modern replace-ments. These replacements, to quote again from D. P. Menzies's descrip-tion, were carried out by Pipe-major Duncan MacDonald of Aberfeldy, who, on completing them, 'played a selection of Highland tunes'. To get them to sound, the wormholes had to be filled up; 'after much trouble and care, he was successful in restoring them to a playing condition'. Their tone is said to be somewhat loud and harsh (which does not bear out the descrip-tion of bagpipes of that period – but doubtless much depends on the type of reed used).

The following note is added to the description, from Pipe-major MacDonald, obtained from an 'old pupil of the MacIntyres':

> I have interviewed Alexander Menzies, Aberfeldy, with regard to the old relics of bagpipes, said to have belonged to the MacIntyres, hereditary pipers to the Menzies of Menzies. Alexander Menzies, now over eighty years of age, lived in the next house to the MacIntyres in Rannoch, from 1820 to 1840, and was a pupil learning pipe-music with them. He well remembers seeing the pieces of the old bagpipes with the MacIntyres, who put great value on them, from their having been in their family for several hundred years.

These MacIntyres who taught Alexander Menzies lived at Rannoch in later times. They seem to have been sent from time to time to the MacCrim-mons at Dunvegan for tuition.

According to D. P. Menzies's account, Donald Bane MacIntyre, piper to the chief of Menzies, and possessor in his turn of the Bannockburn pipes, died during the chieftainship of Sir Neil, sixth Baronet of Menzies. Donald Bane left two sons, one of whom, Robert MacIntyre, had earlier become

---

* Seton Gordon, *Highways and Byways in the West Highlands,* p. 166, gives another tradition. He says that it was the Clan MacDonald and not Menzies before whom the pipes were played at Bannockburn.

piper to Robertson MacDonald, chieftain of Clan Donald.* Robert, being the elder son, inherited the Bannockburn pipes. When the chief of Clan Donald died, Robert MacIntyre emigrated to America (in 1790) but left the Bannockburn pipes with the MacDonalds of Loch Moidart (Kinloch-moidart), in whose family they remained for several generations.†

This is probably why they are frequently called the MacDonald pipes; there is a story that they were played before the MacDonalds, and not the Menzies, at Bannockburn.[7] There can be little doubt that the 'Menzies' and 'MacDonald' pipes are one and the same, for they are described by Seton Gordon as consisting of a chanter, drone-top, and four-sided blow-pipe. The chanter, like the Menzies chanter, has the extra hole or holes near the foot. It is not known if these pipes still exist.

Another famous set of bagpipes, which bears the date 1409 in Roman numerals, known as the Glen pipes, has been described by Robert Glen in an article written in 1879[8]:

> The writer of this possesses a set of bagpipes bearing the date 1409. This instrument has only two small drones and chanter . . . The two drones are inserted in one stock or joint, that holds them to the bag, which is formed of a forked branch of a tree, the fork giving the drones the proper spread for the shoulder. Carved on the stock are the date MCCCCIX and the letters R. McD. along with a representation of a lymphad or galley, such as is seen on the sculptured crosses of the West Highlands. On the reverse side is to be seen a triple floriated knot, and on the upper parts of the fork are two carved bands of interlaced work near to the metal ferrules. The lower joint of one of the drones is ornamented in the centre with a carved band in the same style; the corresponding joint of the other drone is not original.
>
> The head-piece of both drones at the top are cup-shaped, and have each three bands of interlaced work, two on the joint, and one near the ferrule at the head.
>
> The chanter at the head, and at the lower or bell end, is finely

---

* Dr J. L. Campbell of Canna observes: ' "Robertson MacDonald" is hardly correctly described as "chieftain of Clan Donald"; still less so as "chief of Clan Donald". There is no one recognized chief of Clan Donald – the heads of the various main branches take it in turn. The family involved is the MacDonalds of Kinlochmoidart.'

† Dr Campbell adds the following note: 'The story is at odds with the chronology given by the *Clan Donald*, [A. and A. MacDonald, *The History of Clan Donald*, 1904, vol. 3, p. 301]. Margarita MacDonald, born in 1773, succeeded her brother Donald who died unmarried in 1804. In 1799 she married Lt-Col. David Robertson who added the name MacDonald to his own when his wife succeeded to the estate in 1804. His eldest son succeeded as MacDonald of Kinloch-moidart in 1844 on his mother's death. If Robert MacIntyre emigrated to America in 1790, he could not have been piper to Lt-Col. Robertson who only married Margarita in 1799'.

ornamented in harmony with the carving on the other parts, and is also studded with nails round the edge of the bell. It has been repaired with two brass bands and the same number of string ligatures.

The blow-pipe is quite modern, the original having been lost. The ferrules are of bronze, and are highly ornamented in the Celtic style. Four of them have been wanting, and replaced by brass ones.

The wood of which these pipes are made is to all appearances that of the thorn, and in respect of measurement they are much the same as those of the present day. The bag and cover are matters of no importance, as those articles soon wear out and must be renewed. The instrument on the whole has an aged and battered appearance, and the finger-holes on the chanter are very much worn.*

This set of pipes was long accepted as a genuine bagpipe relic of the early fifteenth century, bearing as it does a date that carries us back to two years before the Battle of Harlaw. Modern research, however, no longer accepts them as being of the period of the date carved upon them. Both the style of ornament and the lettering indicate a much more recent origin.† For long exhibited at the National Museum of Antiquities of Scotland in Edinburgh, they have for some years been withdrawn as not antique; though they may still be seen on request.

A set of bagpipes similar to the Glen pipes described above is said to have been formerly in the ownership of J. McIndewar of Walker-on-Tyne,[9] and to have been examined by William Cocks; but its present whereabouts is not known. This might be thought at first sight to favour the genuineness of the Glen pipes. That this is not necessarily so may be adduced from the parallel case of the Celtic harp or *clàrsach*; several specimens of this, similar in appearance and shape, were formerly thought to have been antiques, but they have since been adjudged to be of fairly modern manufacture.

There is an early mention of the Great Highland bagpipe at the Battle of the North Inch of Perth between the clans Quhele and Chattan in 1396, where sixty Highlanders, thirty from each clan, fought to the death in the presence of the king, Robert III. The causes of the fight are obscure. Andrew Lang, the Scottish historian, thinks that they may have fought about lands in Lochaber.

Here we enter upon the realms of folktale and of the romantic novel,

---

* The pipes are said to have been discovered by a Glasgow antique dealer, from whom they came into the hands of Robert Glen. See 'Notices of pipers', *Piping Times*, vol. 22, no. 12 (September 1970).

† Information given to me personally by Dr Kenneth Steer, Secretary, the Royal Commission on the Ancient and Historical Monuments of Scotland. Dr Steer is to publish his conclusions on the Glen bagpipes in his forthcoming book on *The Late Medieval West Highland Carvings*.

namely *The Fair Maid of Perth* by Sir Walter Scott. Concerning the Battle,
Sir Walter writes (ch. 34, p. 658):

> The pipers on both sides blew their charge, and the combatants
> again mingled in battle, not indeed with the same strength, but
> with unabated inveteracy. They were joined by those whose duty it
> was to have remained neuter, but who now found themselves
> unable to do so. The two old champions who bore the standards
> had gradually advanced from the extremity of the lists, and now
> approached close to the immediate scene of action. When they
> beheld the carnage more nearly, they were mutually impelled by
> the desire to revenge their brethren, or not to survive them. They
> attacked each other furiously with the lances to which the standards
> were attached, closed after exchanging several deadly thrusts,
> then grappled in close strife, still holding their banners, until at
> length, in the eagerness of their conflict, they fell together into the
> Tay, and were found drowned after the combat, closely locked in
> each other's arms. The fury of battle, the frenzy of rage and
> despair, infected next the minstrels. The two pipers, who, during
> the conflict, had done their utmost to keep up the spirits of their
> brethren, now saw the dispute well-nigh terminated for want of
> men to support it. They threw down their instruments, rushed
> desperately upon each other with their daggers, and each being
> more intent on despatching his opponent than in defending himself,
> the piper of Clan Quhele was almost instantly slain, and he of Clan
> Chattan mortally wounded. The last, nevertheless, again grasped
> his instrument, and the pibroch of the clan yet poured its expiring
> notes over the Clan Chattan, while the dying minstrel had breath
> to inspire it. The instrument which he used, or at least that part of
> it called the chanter, is preserved in the family of a Highland chief
> to this day, and is much honoured, under the name of the *Federan
> Dhu* [*sic*], or Black Chanter.

In a footnote, Scott adds.

> The present Cluny MacPherson, chief of his clan, is in possession of
> this ancient trophy of their presence at the North Inch. Another
> account of it is given by a tradition, which says that an aerial
> minstrel appeared over the heads of the Clan Chattan, and having
> played some wild strains, let the instrument drop from his hand.
> Being made of glass, it was broken by the fall, excepting only the
> chanter, which, as usual, was of *lignum vitae*. The MacPherson
> piper secured this enchanted pipe, and the possession of it is still
> considered as insuring the prosperity of the clan.

The chanter has a crack in it, which is said to have been caused by its
fall from the heavens.

The weak point in this story is that of the chanter being 'as usual of *lignum vitae*'; for this wood is of the tree *Guaiacum officinale*, which is a native of the West Indies and the north coast of South America (see Appendix I, p. 211). It is a wood of great hardness, density and durability and, because of the diagonal and oblique arrangement of the successive layers of its fibres, it cannot be split. If the Black Chanter is indeed made of this wood, it cannot have been used at the Battle of the North Inch, for the fight took place in the year 1396; *Lignum vitae* was first introduced into Europe by the Spaniards in 1508.[10] Furthermore, one of the features by which the Black Chanter is known is that it has a split in it. This is referred to in a letter from Ewan MacPherson of Cluny in 1821, to Archibald Fraser of Abertarff, his cousin, acknowledging the safe return of the chanter after it had been for some time in the hands of Grant of Glenmoriston.[11] In it he says, 'We are quite convinced of its being the true Chaunter owing to the split up the middle which has been handed down as one of its marks'.

It is difficult to separate facts from folklore about whether the *feadan dubh* or other bagpipes were actually played at the Battle of the North Inch. There is no reference to either pipes or pipers by any of the ancient chroniclers, one of whom, Andrew of Wyntoun, was contemporary with the period of the battle. His account of it is only 28 lines long, and makes no mention of any form of music.[12] Boece, writing in Latin in the fifteenth century, as translated by Bellenden, states that the two clans 'at sound of trumpet, ruschit togidder'. No mention of bagpipes here![13]

The *feadan dubh* or Black Chanter now reposes, after its many adventures (including its sale by auction among the contents of Cluny Castle in 1943, and a subsequent interlude in the strong-room of a Glasgow Bank), at the Clan MacPherson Museum at Creag Dubh, Newtonmore. It bears the inscription, "*'S fhad o chualas, 'S buan a mhaireas 's mor ad.*' (Tentative translation: 'Heard long since; ever will endure; great its good fortune'.)*

We come now, in chronological sequence, to the Battle of Harlaw (1411). Highland tradition has it that both the harp and the bagpipes were played at this battle. James Mackenzie in his *History of Scotland* (London, 1861) tells us that at Harlaw, 'the Highland host came down with pibrochs deafening to hear'; but his history, written for young people in popular story-book style, can hardly be considered sufficient historical evidence, and he quotes no authority for his statement.

There is a piece of bagpipe music called 'The Battle of Harlaw', first printed in Daniel Dow's *Ancient Scots Music*,† which bears the description of a *pibroch*. As it stands, the tune will hardly survive the test of *pìobaireachd* requirements; yet, played at the proper *adagio* tempo of the *pìobaireachd urlar* or 'ground' there is a faint suggestion, in the melodic progressions and repetitions, of the sound of *pìobaireachd*. One must, of

---

* The last word, '*ad*', makes the final phrase untranslatable. William Matheson, Celtic Department, University of Edinburgh, suggests '*àdh*', which would give the translation above.
† Undated. Glen, *Early Scottish Melodies*, p. 218, says *c.* 1775.

course, allow for incorrect notation. The tune also appears in James Johnson's *Scots Musical Museum*.[14] John Glen[15] points out that Johnson, in taking the melody from Dow, has altered the second strain. Flood observes that 'it is safe to say that the pipe melody of *The Battle of Harlaw* does not bear the marks of fifteenth-century work; indeed it has all the characteristics of a seventeenth-century tune.'[16]

There also exists the comparatively well-known ballad, 'The Battle of Harlaw', which appears with its tune in the *Scots Musical Museum*. The tune bears some basic resemblance to the *pibroch* given in the notes to that work by William Stenhouse, and they both obviously stem from the same melodic roots.* Whatever the age of the ballad, which purports to describe the actual battle, it makes no mention whatever of the bagpipes, though it does of trumpets and drums in the hands of the Lowland forces opposing the Highlanders. In one of the three versions of the ballad published by F. J. Child,[17] collected from traditional sources in the early nineteenth century, there appears the line '*Wi*' *a dree dree dradie drumtie dree.*' This seems to suggest the sound of the pipes – it is not far removed from *canntaireachd*, the pipers' sol-fa, and could well pass for a popular imitation of it; but this is no evidence that the pipes were present at the battle. Possibly William Dauney gets as near the truth as anyone when he says that 'either it [the bagpipes] had not been used on that occasion or its martial character had not at that time been fully established.'[18]

There is one circumstance above all else which may point to the probability that it was about the time of the Battle of Harlaw that the Highland bagpipe graduated from a domestic instrument to an instrument of battle. This was the sudden and otherwise inexplicable outburst of professional jealousy against the piper and his instrument by the bard whose duty it was with voice and harp to inspire the Highland host with war-like fervour before the battle.

This was manifested specifically in the biting satire, still extant, by the same bard, Lachlan Mór MacVurich, who composed the *brosnachadh* before Harlaw (see p. 130).[19] This satire, scornfully descriptive of the bagpipe and its genealogy, refers to the *pìob gleadhair* (pipes of clamour) as 'the two sweethearts of the black fiend – a noise fit to arouse the imps'. As J. F. Campbell of Islay remarked, it is 'as bitter and coarse as anything in Dunbar's Daunce'.[20]†

After the Battle of Harlaw, allusions to the Highland bagpipe and its use in battle, though sparse, began to appear both in tradition and in

---

* The tune of the 'Ballad of Harlaw', recorded a year or two ago from the Scots traditional singer Jeannie Robertson by the School of Scottish Studies has, upon examination, the same melodic characteristics as the *pibroch*, although these are not apparent on first hearing.

† Equally of course there are many later Gaelic poems in praise of the pipes, as for instance Alexander MacDonald's famous poem in praise of the *pìob mhór* of MacCrimmon (cf. W. J. Watson, *Bardachd Ghaidhlig*, Stirling, 1932, p. 104). For titles of other similar poems by other poets, cf. ibid., p. 288, notes, 2786.

written accounts. The earliest of these, and it is only tradition, is of the first Battle of Inverlochy (1431), twenty years after Harlaw. This was not the classic outflanking victory of Montrose at Inverlochy, which took place in February 1645, but a less important engagement at which Donald Balloch, cousin to Alexander, Lord of the Isles, defeated the king's forces under the Earls of Mar and Caithness.

Little is known of the details of the battle, but there are no less than two *pìobaireachd* to commemorate it. One is 'Black Donald Balloch of the Isles' March to the First Battle of Inverlochy 1427'. (This is the '*Pìobaireachd Dhomhnuill Duibh*', well known through Sir Walter Scott's setting of words to it as 'The Pibroch of Donald Dhu'.* The other is '*Ceann na Drochaid Mhoridh or Moire*' ('The End of the Great Bridge'), 'Composed in the midst of the Battle at Inverlochy 1427 wherein Donald Balloch, of the Isles, was victorious over the Royal Forces'. The date 1427 is incorrect in the title of both *pìobaireachd*, and should be 1431 as stated above.

The existence of a *pìobaireachd* bearing the name of a particular event does not necessarily mean that it was composed contemporarily with it, though tradition does tell of *pìobaireachd* being extemporized on occasion, notably '*Thug mi pòg do lamh an Righ*' ('I got a kiss of the King's hand') (see pp. 153–4), by Patrick Mór MacCrimmon, and 'In Praise of the Rainbow', attributed to Iain Dall Mackay. But several things militate against the truth of the tradition that 'Black Donald's March' was contemporary, or even concerned, with the First Battle of Inverlochy. First, the tune has also been known by two other names. Joseph MacDonald in his *Compleat Theory* . . . calls the tune 'The Maclean's Gathering'; Alexander Campbell, who noted the tune from the playing of Iain Dubh MacCrimmon (the last of the piping MacCrimmons) in 1815 and took it to Sir Walter Scott, calls it, presumably at the instance of MacCrimmon himself, 'The Cameron's Gathering'. Second, as R. C. L. Lorimer notes on the sleeve of his *pìobaireachd* recordings,† in the *sung* version of the *pìobaireachd* by Calum Johnston (Barra), the singer uses the words '*Pìob agus bratach air faich Inbhir Lochaidh*', i.e. 'pipe and banner at the gathering place [of the Camerons] at Inverlochy'. It appears likely that Inverlochy is here not connected with the battle, but with the Castle of Inverlochy as the trysting or gathering place of the Camerons.

Of the other bagpipe piece said to be connected with Inverlochy and indeed 'composed in the midst of the Battle', '*Ceann na Drochaid Mhoridh*', David Glen in his *Collection of Ancient Pìobaireachd* says in a footnote

* In correct terms '*dhu*' should read '*duibh*'.

† *Pibroch 1*, Waverley ZLP 2034, recorded in association with the British Council. Mr Lorimer states that Black Donald (Donald Dubh) was not Donald Balloch of the *pìobaireachd* title, but a younger man who became chief of the Camerons later, some years after the battle. Donald Dubh was also the name of a young man born about 1485, a son, possibly illegitimate, of Angus Og, the bastard son of John, Earl of Ross and Lord of the Isles. See Andrew Lang, *A History of Scotland*, vol. 1, pp. 483, 507.

(Part V, p. 127) that 'this tune bears the alternative title of "Clan Cameron's Gathering Tune" '. This certainly lends colour to the probability that, as suggested, these two *piobaireachd* are only associated with Inverlochy as the gathering place of the Camerons.

Evidence that the Highland bagpipe was played at this first Battle of Inverlochy in 1431 thus depends on tradition as it did for the Battle of Harlaw in 1411; and tradition seems to be shakily founded in either case. One can only say that, by the known chronology of the history of the instrument, it was not impossible for the bagpipe to be present here, any more than at Bannockburn.

The first written evidence of the use of the bagpipe by the Highlander as a battle instrument is in an account of the mid-sixteenth-century Scottish wars written by a French military officer, Beague, in 1549. It is called *L'Histoire de la guerre d'Ecosse* and was published in Paris in 1556. 1549 was the period following the disastrous Battle of Pinkie (1547) and the 'rough wooing' by the Earl of Hertford, who burnt the Abbeys of Jedburgh, Kelso, Coldingham, Melrose, and Dryburgh, in his efforts to force the Scots to agree to the betrothal of the infant princess Mary, the future Queen of Scots, to Edward, the son of Henry VIII.

The Battle of Pinkie was fought on 9 September 1547. French fleets had been arriving off the coast of Scotland at the entreaties of the Queen Mother, Mary of Guise, at intervals since 1545; and in 1548 a French land force of 6,000 men arrived in the Firth of Forth. Doubtless Beague was a member of one of those contingents. He states that 'fourteen or fifteen thousand Scots, including the savages accompanying the Earl of Argyll arrived . . . and while the French prepared for combat [i.e. with the English invaders] the wild Scots encouraged themselves to arms by the sound of their bagpipes.'

Here then, in the year 1549, we have the first eye-witness account of the use of the Great Highland bagpipe in battle – from a Frenchman! His words are: *'Les Eccossois sauvages se provocquoyent aux armes par les sons de leurs cornemeuses.'*

The use of the Highland bagpipe in battle is confirmed by a Scots writer, George Buchanan, writing in Latin, about the year 1581. In his *Rerum Scoticarum Historia*,[21] he says, speaking of the Highlanders, 'Instead of the trumpet, they use the bagpipe.' His text uses for bagpipe our old friend *tibia utricularis* (*'Loco tubae, tibia utuntur utriculari'*).

Buchanan's reference is very similar to a later one by an anonymous writer of a manuscript work in English, 'The Isles of Scotland in General; Certain Matters Concerning the Realme of Scotland as they were A.D. 1597'. This manuscript appears to have been lost, but John Monipennie,[22] writing in 1612, gives the relevant quotation:*

* See also Alexander Campbell, *A Journey from Edinburgh through Parts of North Britain*, Edinburgh, 1810, pp. 175–7.

*Plate 13* Detail from the Leschman Chantry in Hexham Abbey, Northumberland. Bagpipe with double chanter (c. 1480-91).

*Plate 14* Misericord in King Henry VII's Chapel, Westminster Abbey.
A group of monkeys with a bear playing the bagpipe. The Chapel dates from 1503. The stalls are of various periods.

*Plate 15*   Initial letter from an Irish manuscript depicting a pig playing the bagpipe. The manuscript is a copy of the Irish topographical history, the *Dinnseanchus* or *Dindsenchas* (Stowe, D 11, 2 fol. 34). Thought to be sixteenth-century. See p. 90.

*Plate 16*   Carved wooden figure of a bagpiper on the gable of the Pipers' House at Jedburgh, formerly occupied by the Jedburgh town-pipers. The pipes in the carving represent the Scottish Lowland or Border pipes, having the drones laid along the left arm. The bagpipe here is mouth-blown, not blown by a bellows, which suggests that it is of early date.

Their armour wherewith they cover their bodies in time of war is
an iron bonnet and an 'habbergion' side, almost to their heels.
Their weapons against their enemies are bows and arrows. . . .
Some of them fight with broadswords and axes; in place of a drum
they use a bagpipe.

The next reference to the Highland bagpipe would seem to be in a
'religious' poem said to be written in 1598 in celebration, of all things, of the
defeat of the Spanish Armada! The author was Alexander Hume, minister
of Logie (probably in Fife, though possibly the parish of that name near
Stirling). The poem, described by Manson[23] rather cryptically as 'an
unpublished poem' from the Bannatyne manuscript, is nevertheless
printed in full by John Leyden in his introduction to *The Complaynt of
Scotland*. As it is important in bagpipe history it is worth giving a little
more of the poem than the two lines usually quoted. The title given by
Leyden is 'The Triumph of the Lord after the maner of Men'. Incidentally,
nowhere in the poem is the Spanish Armada mentioned, although the poem
is about a naval battle. The date, roughly speaking, makes the connection
possible, for the defeat of the Spanish Armada occurred in 1588, ten years
before the writing of the poem. The relevant allusion is in the first stanza:

Richt as the prynce of daye beginnes to spring,
And larkes aloft melodiouslie to sing,
Bring furthe all kynde of instruments of were [war],
To gang befoir, and mak ane noyce cleir; [noise clear]
Gar trumpetis sounde the awfull battellis blast,
On dreadfull drummes gar stryke alarum fast;
Mak showting shalmes, and piercing phipheris [pipers] shrill,
Cleene cleave the clouds, and peirce the hiest hill;
Caus michtelie the weirlie nottis [warlike notes] breike,
On hieland pipes, Scottes and Hybernicke;
Let heir be shraichs [shrieks] of deadlie clarions
And syne let of ane volie of cannouns.

The important point is the differentiation by the author of the Highland
pipes from the Scottish (presumably the Lowland) pipes and the presence
also of the 'Hybernicke' or Irish pipes. Quite evidently, all three were
known to the minister in 1598.

## The MacCrimmons

'Simple pipers have been sires of kings' (Hamilton of Bangour,
unpublished poems)

The most important event of the sixteenth century in the history of the

Highland bagpipe was the appearance on the scene of the MacCrimmons, for they changed the whole face of the art of piping. This they did both by their music and by their masterly playing of the instrument; they raised the status of the pipes from that of a rustic instrument mostly used for the playing of short airs and dance tunes, to one possessing its own extended art-form, that of *pìobaireachd*. In this they bequeathed to Scotland and to the world in the course of over two hundred years a legacy of great music that belongs to the pipes alone – a legacy which will certainly endure through the centuries to come.

The MacCrimmons were, as most people will know, the famed hereditary pipers to the Clan MacLeod. Most of them served the chief of the clan at Dunvegan Castle in the Isle of Skye; but we also find them attached to other branches of the clan, namely to the MacLeods at Glenelg* on the mainland, and to the MacLeods of Gesto in Skye.

The early history and genealogy of the MacCrimmons is shadowy and inconclusive. So many traditions exist regarding their origin, few if any of them verifiable, that one is left little better informed than before. These traditions give the ultimate origin of the MacCrimmons variously as from the Norse invaders of Ireland; from Scotland itself; from Italy. It has been said that they sprang from the Druids; or from the bards, because of the name relationship of *Criomthan*† with the ancient High Kings of Ireland – a name shared with Saint Columba; and, because of a similar name relationship, with a famed Norse protector called Rumun.

MacCrimmons as a clan are known to have inhabited the southern part of Harris in the late twelfth and early thirteenth centuries. Their territory was invaded and the clan conquered by Paul Balkeson, a 'Sheriff' of Skye, said to be of Norse extraction; his overlord was the King of Man, who was in turn vassal to the King of Norway.

Paul Balkeson is said to have named Leod, founder of the clan MacLeod (the son of Olave the Black and grandson of the King of Man), as his heir; thus the MacLeods would early have possessed feudal superiority over the MacCrimmons as a clan. A number of the MacLeods, and probably the MacCrimmons along with them, settled in the twelfth century in Ireland, on the lands of the O'Donnells. Later, in the sixteenth century, Rory Mór MacLeod, the great fifteenth chief of the clan MacLeod, went to fight for the O'Donnells in Ireland in 1595 under the celebrated Red Hugh O'Donnell, at the rising of the Ulster clans against English rule.[24]

On returning from Ireland Rory Mór MacLeod is said to have brought back with him a piper called Iain Odhar MacCrimmon, who in this

---

* Glenelg belonged to the MacLeods of Harris (often called 'of Dunvegan') at this time.
† Pronounced 'Crìman' (Creeman). Frequent references to the Irish kings of this name appear in O'Curry, op. cit., vol. 3, *index nominum*.

tradition is said to be the son of Red Hugh O'Donnell's piper Donald MacCrimmon. This Iain Odhar became the founder of the Scottish piping MacCrimmons. Most traditions give the son of Iain Odhar as Donald Mór MacCrimmon, who is the first known composer, and possibly the deviser, of *pìobaireachd*. Another tradition gives Donald Mór as the *grandson* of Iain Odhar, his father being a somewhat nebulous Padruig (Patrick) Donn (dark) MacCrimmon.

Others do not accept the story of Iain Odhar having come from Ireland, and give him a Scottish parent, *Fionnlagh a' Bhreacain Bhàin*, or *Fionnlagh na Plaide Bàine*, i.e. Finlay of the White Plaid. Finlay was known as a warrior rather than as a piper,[25] and tales of his prowess are told to this day.

Another tradition has it that the first piping MacCrimmon (unnamed) was the illegitimate son of the eighth chief of MacLeod, Alasdair Crotach (i.e. hump-backed) (died 1547);[26] and several authorities state that it was this chief who gave the MacCrimmons the lands of Galtrigal in Skye. They lived at Galtrigal before they received from The MacLeods their holding at Boreraig,* on which they established their far-famed College of Piping.[27]

If there were any truth in this tradition that Alasdair Crotach established the MacCrimmons as his hereditary pipers, this would of course rule out the story of Rory Mór, the fifteenth chief, having brought them over from Ireland.

## The Cremona tradition

A stranger and completely different tradition is that a chief of MacLeod, returning from the Crusades by way of Italy, brought back a musician from Cremona to be his piper. From the name of the musician's birthplace he was surnamed Cremoneh;† this later, in the Scottish Gaelic fashion, became MacCrimmon. There is perhaps a little colour for this tradition in that the famous Fairy Flag of Dunvegan has been pronounced by experts to be of Syrian origin,[28] and may possibly have been brought back from the Crusades.‡

The account of the MacCrimmons which might have been the most interesting of all, and which was apparently believed by the MacCrimmons

* Also often spelt Borreraig, e.g. J. G. Bartholomew (ed.), *Survey Gazetteer of the British Isles*, London, 1904.
† If he had lived in Cremona he might be called in Gaelic, '*An Cremonach*'. Dr J. L. Campbell of Canna cites to me the case of a man in Barra in 1937 who had spent much time in Canna and in consequence was nicknamed '*An Canach*'. He adds that there are other instances.
‡ Seton Gordon, *The Charm of Skye*, p. 109, says that the Crusade in question was in the reign of King Alexander of Scotland, but does not say which. There were Crusades during the reigns of all three Alexanders.

themselves, was unfortunately said to be suppressed through clerical bigotry. This was in a book, *The History of the MacCrimmons and the Great Pipe*, written by Captain Neil MacLeod of Gesto in 1826. Gesto, who was a great lover and student of *pìobaireachd*, was a friend of the last of the MacCrimmon pipers, Iain Dubh MacCrimmon, and it was doubtless from him that he got his account. Unfortunately his book contained material which was, for some reason, said to be unacceptable to the clergy, and it was withdrawn. The story goes that only two copies were saved from destruction, both of which were carried to Australia – one by Captain MacLeod's son Norman (died 1847) and the other by Simon Fraser, a descendant of the hereditary pipers to the Frasers of Lovat. (Simon Fraser's son, also named Simon Fraser, died as recently as 1934.) Fraser's copy of Gesto's book was said to have been accidentally destroyed; the other, belonging to Norman MacLeod, was said in 1936 to be in Canada,[29] its exact whereabouts unknown.

With the suppression of Gesto's book, which could have been so valuable to the history not only of the MacCrimmons but of Highland music and piping in general, we are dependent on such scraps of tradition regarding its contents as may have been handed down by hearsay from those who claim to have seen it, or to have information about it. The book is said to have contained a complete and comprehensive account of the MacCrimmon pipers and also of their vocables and scales, some of the details of which were said never to have been fully disclosed by the MacCrimmons even to their most favoured pupils. Unless the alleged remaining copy, said to have been carried to Canada, should ever turn up, all this is for ever denied to us.

The book is reputed to have told a very curious and seemingly circumstantial story regarding the 'Cremona tradition' of the MacCrimmons, received direct by Gesto from Iain Dubh MacCrimmon. This gave as their founder a priest of Cremona named Guiseppe Bruno, the son of whom, Petrus or Patrick Bruno, born at Cremona in 1475, is said to have emigrated to Ulster, Northern Ireland, in 1510. He himself assumed the name of Cremon. In Ireland, he married the daughter of a piping family and changed his name further, in order to come into line with clan tradition, to MacCrimmon.

This Petrus Bruno is said to have had three sons, one of whom was Finlay of the Plaid, already mentioned, the father or grandfather of Iain Odhar MacCrimmon. The name Odhar means dun-coloured. The authors of the MacCrimmon pamphlet[30] pose the interesting question of whether Iain Odhar's distinctive colour of skin may not have been an inheritance from his Italian father.

Thomas Pearston, in a series of articles on the subject in the *Piping Times*,[31] recounts a curious statement, said to have appeared in Gesto's book, that the well-known *pìobaireachd*, 'Lament for the Laird of Anapool', thought to have been composed by a MacCrimmon, had

## Fionnlagh a'Breacain Bhàin
### (Finlay of the White Plaid)

Said to have come from Ireland in the early sixteenth century and to have been the son of Red Hugh O'Donnell's piper. The same is said, however, of his son, Iain Odhar. He is said to have been granted the lands of Galtrigal, near Dunvegan, by MacLeod, in the early sixteenth century.[32]

## Iain Odhar
### (Iain of the dun-coloured skin – Sallow John)

Said to have been hereditary piper to Alasdair Crotach MacLeod during the first half of the sixteenth century. Some authorities consider him to be the Irish piper mentioned above.

## Padruig (Patrick) Donn

Doubtful, nebulous; but said by some authorities to have been hereditary piper to MacLeod in the latter half of the sixteenth century.[33]

### Patrick Caog

('Squinting Peter')[34]

### Donald Mór

born c. 1570.
Hereditary piper to MacLeod from c. 1620. Taught by his father, but supplemented his studies in Ireland.

### Patrick Mór

born c. 1595.
Hereditary piper to MacLeod c. 1640–70.

### Patrick Og

born c. 1645.
Hereditary piper to MacLeod 1670–1730.

### Malcolm

born c. 1704.
Hereditary piper to MacLeod, 1730–60.

### Donald Bàn

born c. 1710.
Killed at Rout of Moy, 1746.

### Iain Dubh

born 1731.
Nominally hereditary piper to MacLeod, 1760–70. Died 1822.

### Donald Ruadh

born 1743.
Intermittently and nominally hereditary piper to MacLeod from 1795. Died 1825.[35]

*Figure 19*  The MacCrimmon family tree

appeared in the book as 'Lament for Giordano Bruno on being burned to death in Rome'.*

Frankly, of course, in the absence of Gesto's suppressed book (if it ever really existed), one cannot accord the Cremona–Bruno story more than extremely doubtful hearsay value, though the contributory evidence is curious and interesting. Even if the book did turn up, the story is still dependent on the accuracy of the family history as transmitted by the MacCrimmons over the space of more than three hundred years, commencing in 1510, and as finally handed on to MacLeod of Gesto by Iain Dubh MacCrimmon in the nineteenth century.

In final judgment it must be fairly stated that the 'Cremona tradition' regarding the MacCrimmons has been rejected in its entirety by modern students of MacCrimmon history.

With so many conflicting accounts of the origin of the MacCrimmons, one can only give a consensus of opinion regarding the earlier members of the family. From Donald Mór onwards, son or grandson of Iain Odhar whichever he was, we are on firmer ground. On page 145 then is the generally accepted family tree of the piping MacCrimmons.

### Pìobaireachd

The chief interest of the MacCrimmons as far as the story of the pipes is concerned lies not so much in their origin as in the fact that they are generally thought to have been the inventors of *pìobaireachd*, or *ceòl mór*, the 'great music' of the pipes. This belief is expressed by one of the great authorities on *pìobaireachd*, the late Archibald Campbell of Kilberry, in his *Kilberry Book of Ceòl Mór*, where he writes (p. 16):

> It is difficult to resist the conclusion that the MacCrimmons were responsible for the form of *Pìobaireachd* which has come down to us, and that they evolved it as that particular combination of sounds most effective in bringing out the best of which the Highland pipe of their day was capable. The process was probably gradual. Possibly some of the irregular, or of the non-Taorluath-Crunluath tunes,† which we have, may mark early steps in that process.
>
> The further theory is propounded that we have few, if any,

* Giordano Bruno (c. 1548–1600) was a famous Italian philosopher who travelled widely through Europe and published many books on religious philosophy. He visited England in 1583. He did not, however, bear any known relationship to the alleged Cremona family of Bruno mentioned above; neither is he known to have been interested in music. The *Encyclopedia Britannica* describes 'Giordano Bruno' as *an atheistical writer*—he was expelled from Geneva as such by the Calvinists. He was obviously a stormy petrel in the sixteenth-century politico-religious scene. He was condemned for heresy by the Inquisition, and burned to death in Rome in 1600.

† I.e. tunes without the characteristic movements known by these names.

*pìobaireachd* much older than A.D. 1600. We have no firm tradition of any MacCrimmon composer earlier than Donald Mór (1570–1640). There is no lament extant for any historical personage earlier or much earlier than that date. We have laments for Queen Anne, and for the Viscount of Dundee, but neither salutes nor laments for William Wallace or for Robert the Bruce. Nor have we any orthodox *pìobaireachd* commemorating any earlier event which we can say with certainty was contemporary with that event.*

If we accept that Donald Mór MacCrimmon was the inventor or originator of *pìobaireachd*, we must also take cognizance of and find some explanation for the fact that there do exist some half dozen or more *pìobaireachd* which commemorate events before the time of Donald Mór. The general belief is that Donald Mór was born about 1570; and this gives us a date of, say, 1590 (when Donald Mór was twenty years of age) as the year round about which *pìobaireachd* began to make its appearance.

There are, however, some half dozen events enshrined in *pìobaireachd* which occurred before 1590. These include: The Battle of Harlaw, 1411 (of which, as already stated, there is a rudimentary and doubtful *pìobaireachd*);[36] The Battle of the North Inch of Perth, 1396 (to which it has been said the *pìobaireachd* of 'The Desperate Battle' refers);[37] 'Black Donald's March to the Isles, 1427;[38] 'The Great Bridge, 1427[39] (both of these are concerned with the first Battle of Inverlochy); 'MacRae's March', 1491[40] and the 'Battle of the Park', 1491[41] (possibly different names for the same battle); 'Hector MacLean's Warning', 1579;[42] 'MacIntosh's Lament', 1526;[43] the 'Battle of Waternish', c. 1578.[44]

There are two possible explanations for these 'pre-MacCrimmon' *pìobaireachd*. One is that a pipe tune of simple, 'pre-*pìobaireachd*' form (which is to say non-*pìobaireachd* form) was composed contemporarily, or nearly so, with the event, and that later hands must have put it into *pìobaireachd* form, with the addition of *taorluath, crunluath*, etc., movements. The other is simply that the *pìobaireachd* concerned was composed at a much later date than the event it commemorates, when *pìobaireachd* form had become understood. The 'Battle of Waternish', 1580, is something of a special case, for it very nearly comes into the period of the acknowledged MacCrimmon composers; but Donald Mór MacCrimmon could have been only about ten years old when the battle was fought, which is hardly old enough to have composed the *pìobaireachd*. I was told by Pipe-major William MacLean of a tradition that 'The Battle of Waternish' was composed by Finlay of the White Plaid, who was the

---

\* We have few, very few, songs that are earlier than 1600 either, except for the Ossianic ballads. The upheavals in the Highlands and Islands that followed the end of the Lordship of the Isles and the abortive attempts to restore it, and the religious conflicts of the sixteenth century seem to have produced a definite break in popular oral tradition. See Collinson, *The Traditional and National Music of Scotland*, p. 50.

grandfather, or perhaps great-grandfather, of Donald Mór. Even if such
a tradition is true, however, the 'Battle of Waternish' could still have been
a pre-*piobaireachd* piece of music which has been put into shape by a later
MacCrimmon; or, of course, it may simply have been composed by one
of the later acknowledged *piobaireachd* composers to celebrate the battle,
which was, for the MacLeods, a fierce and memorable victory of revenge
against the MacDonalds of Clanranald.

To understand the amazing increase in musical status which the
*piobaireachd* conferred on the Scottish Highland bagpipe, one has only to
look at the kind of music which the bagpipe was accustomed to play in
Britain before it arrived. We have already given a list of some of the
acknowledged pipe-tunes of the sixteenth and seventeenth centuries in
England, Ireland, and Lowland Scotland. For the bagpipe tunes of the
Highlands of Scotland we are somewhat handicapped by the lack of
written mention of tune-names of the period. A number of the Highland
airs preserved by Patrick MacDonald of Kilmore, in the first collection of
its kind, are within the compass of the bagpipe; and although his collection
was not published until 1781, some of the airs it contains may well go
back to the seventeenth century – for Highland memory is long.

Such then was the kind of musical fare the bagpipe provided before the
days of *piobaireachd* – concise dance tunes or song airs. These, of course,
continued to be played on the instrument after the invention of *piobaireachd*,
though not by the masters of *piobaireachd* themselves, who were very
strict on that point.

With the advent of the new art-form of *piobaireachd*, we find ourselves
in another musical world where the bagpipe is concerned. No longer are
we bound within the confines of a tune which, however much the piper
may repeat its various internal sections, remains, *in fine*, a more or less
symmetrical piece of minor character. The form of *piobaireachd* is that of
an air or ground (Gaelic, *ùrlar*) followed by a number of variations, some
of them of a particular stereotyped character that belongs to *piobaireachd*
alone. The air itself is *adagio* in tempo. It possesses a breadth of archi-
tectural line which is quite unlike even the most dignified slow song-air;
the Highland bagpipe is capable of rising to it with a nobility which few
can have expected.

After the *ùrlar*, which may be followed by a variation or two of normal
type, come the characteristic *piobaireachd* ornamentations of the air.
First there is the *siubhal** which selects from the notes of the melody of
the ground or *ùrlar* the theme notes which are to form the melodic basis

* The word '*siubhal*' is here used with the general meaning that Angus MacKay
  gives it in *A Collection of Ancient Piobaireachd*, p. iii, i.e. its dictionary meaning
  of 'moving, travelling, progress, the quicker part of a tune in pipe music'. There
  are two different movements possessing this characteristic and purpose: *siubhal*
  proper, which in modern terms consists of a two-note rising figure, low A, followed
  by the theme note; and *dithis*, a two-note falling figure, the theme note followed
  usually by low A, or sometimes by low G.

of the whole of the rest of the *pìobaireachd*. It also breaks up each of the long notes of the *adagio* into figures of two shorter notes, and establishes in this movement a quicker tempo than that of the *adagio*.

After the *siubhal* come the *taorluath* (pronounced 'tòrlu') and *crunluath* (pronounced 'crùllu') movements, each more complicated than the one before it; and these may have their 'doublings'.\* This is not the place for a close analysis of *pìobaireachd* and *pìobaireachd* movements, which may be found elsewhere.[45] Suffice it to say that in the *taorluath*, the theme note, as already selected in the *siubhal*, is followed by a chain of four rapid grace notes; while in the *crunluath* the chain is extended from four to seven notes.

A further floriation of both *taorluath* and *crunluath* may be added in the *taorluath a mach* and *crunluath a mach*, in the last of which the grace-note chain is extended to nine notes following the theme note. The *pìobaireachd* is brought to an end by a repetition or return to the ground or *ùrlar* in simple form, with which it commenced.

This is *pìobaireachd* in its barest possible outline. There is practically no rule of *pìobaireachd* construction for which there is not an exception in an actual *pìobaireachd*. The main thing is that with the invention of *pìobaireachd*, the music of the bagpipe moved out of the sphere of the simple air or dance-tune into that of extended music.

The remarkable thing is that there seems to have been no rudimentary, development stage in *pìobaireachd*. The earliest known *pìobaireachd* are said to be those by Donald Mór MacCrimmon. These are thought to include 'MacLeod's Salute', 'MacLeod's Controversy', 'MacDonald's Salute', 'A Fiery Revenge for Patrick Caogach' ('Squinting Peter', his brother) or 'Squinting Peter's Flame of Wrath', 'The Earl of Ross's March', and 'Donald Dughail Mackay's Lament'. The earliest of these probably date from about 1601. Although they are simple in form as *pìobaireachd* go, they are fully developed and show complete mastery of the medium; there are no signs of groping after a medium not yet properly understood, even though 'A Fiery Revenge for Patrick Caogach' has neither regular *siubhal* nor *taorluath*.

The question arises, where and how did the MacCrimmons get the *pìobaireachd* form? That it sprang into being fully fashioned suggests that the form must have existed ready to hand in another species of music. It did not come in pipe-music form from Ireland or from any other country (Cremona included), for *pìobaireachd* is unique to the Highlands of Scotland.

In attempting to solve the question, one must realize that the creation and subsequent flourishing of *pìobaireachd* depended on two equally

---

\* There is not a great deal of difference between a 'movement' and its 'doubling'. In the latter the cadences or rest-points of the melody at the end of each phrase are filled in with ornamentation similar to the ornamentation of the rest of the movement.

important factors: the existence of a piper who had the necessary genius to apply the form, if it existed in any other medium, to his own instrument; and a patron who was willing to listen to it. Here it was a literal case of 'he who pays the piper calls the tune', and it must be admitted that to one who does not go to some trouble to find out and understand something of what it is about, *pìobaireachd*, with its seemingly endless repetitions, can be the most boring music on earth. For the MacCrimmons, the necessary patron was the chief of MacLeod. In the time of Donald Mór MacCrimmon, who may have composed the first *pìobaireachd*, it was the great Highland chief Rory Mór MacLeod, who was not the kind of man to suffer boredom gladly.

It looks therefore as if the form must have been as familiar to the patron as to the piper – as if it may have existed already in some other musical medium to which he was used, and which he could accept with interest.

There was such music. It was the music of the harp, a music which must certainly have been heard in the hall at Dunvegan quite a few centuries before *pìobaireachd*. There are tombstones in the Highlands of Scotland with carvings of the harp on them of the ninth and tenth century – at Dupplin, at Nigg, Auldbar, Keills and Iona.

The ancient harp music of Scotland, Ireland and Wales must have been every bit as advanced and as complicated as *pìobaireachd*. It possessed an intricacy remarked upon as early as the twelfth century by Giraldus Cambrensis (see p. 82). We may read what he says of it in his *Topography of Ireland*:

> The cultivation of instrumental music by this people [i.e. of Ireland] I find worthy of commendation; in this, their skill is beyond all comparison, superior to that of any nation I have ever seen; for their music is not slow and solemn, as in the instrumental music of Britain, to which we are accustomed; but the sounds are rapid and articulate, yet at the same time, sweet and pleasing.
>
> It is wonderful how, in spite of the great speed of the fingers, the musical proportions are faultlessly preserved throughout, in the midst of the most intricate arrangement of notes and complicated modulations; and how, amid a velocity of notes so pleasing, a regularity so diversified, a concord so discordant, the melody is preserved harmonious and perfect by the faultlessness of their art. . . . They glide so subtly from one mode to another, and the grace-notes sport so freely and with such abandon and bewitching charm around the steady heavier tone of the theme! – The perfection of their art appears to lie in their accomplishing all this with the greatest seeming ease, and without the least appearance of effort.
>
> Hence it happens that the very things that afford unspeakable delight to the minds of those who have a fine perception and can penetrate carefully to the secrets of the art, bore rather than delight

those who have no such perception – who look without seeing, and hear without being able to understand. When the audience is unsympathetic, they [the harpers] succeed only in causing boredom with what appears to be but confused and disordered noise.

In the opinion of many, however, Scotland has by now not only caught up on her Instructor [i.e. Ireland] but already far outdistances and excels her in musical skill. Therefore people now look to that country as to the fountain of the art.[46]

Quite a lot of the above remarks, written in the twelfth century of the harp, would seem to apply equally to the as yet undiscovered art of *pìobaireachd* – even to its power to bore rather than delight those who 'cannot penetrate to the secrets of the art'!

Patrick MacDonald, in his *Collection of Highland Vocal Airs*, published in 1784 (which was only some thirty to fifty years after the harp disappeared from use in Scotland), says that by then 'The harp had ceased to be the favourite instrument for upwards of a century; the encouragement of the people having been transferred to the bagpipe' (Preface, p. 3). 'Upwards of a century' before MacDonald wrote takes us back to the second half of the seventeenth century, to the very zenith of the creative period of the MacCrimmons, the days of Patrick Og MacCrimmon, who flourished *c.* 1643–1730; and of the famous College of Piping of the MacCrimmons at Boreraig, when, however, the harp music was apparently still to be heard in Scotland.*

Donald Mór MacCrimmon, thought to be the inventor of *pìobaireachd*, had every chance of being familiar with the harp music and its musical forms, and of adapting these forms to the bagpipe; for his chief, Rory Mór MacLeod, is said to have possessed 'harper, bard, piper and fool' in his establishment.†

Unfortunately no authentic specimens of the ancient harp music of Scotland survive, except two pieces claimed to be remembered by Angus Fraser, the son of Simon Fraser of Knockie, the compiler of *Airs and*

* Dr J. L. Campbell of Canna sends me the following note: 'Patrick MacDonald's remark that the harp had ceased to be a favourite instrument for upwards of a century must be qualified. Around 1700, the Rev. David Kirkwood wrote or copied an account of the customs of the Highlands of which a copy made by Edward Lluyd exists in the Bodleian Library at Oxford. Kirkwood wrote: "Music. The Greatest Music is Harp, Pipe, Viol, & Trump [i.e. Jew's harp] most part of yᵉ Gentry play on yᵉ Harp. Pipers are held in great Request, so that they are train'd up at yᵉ Expense of Grandees & have a Portion of Land assignd & are design'd such a man's Piper".' Dr Campbell suggests that Patrick MacDonald may have meant only that the harp had lost popularity among the common people.

† This often quoted statement occurs in a note to the Dissertation (said to be by John Ramsay of Ochertyre) 'Of the Influence of Poetry and Music upon the Highlanders' following the Preface to Patrick MacDonald's *Collection of Highland Vocal Airs*. (See William Matheson, *The Blind Harper*, Edinburgh, 1970, p. xxxi.)

*Melodies Peculiar to the Highlands of Scotland* – and their authenticity is not unassailable. In Simon Fraser's second volume of *Airs and Melodies* there are a number of what purport to be specimens of the ancient Scottish harp music. These are pieces consisting of a ground and variations, some of which bear names similar to those of movements in *pìobaireachd*. These names include *ùrlar*, *crunlù fosgailt*, *singling* and *doubling*. A further resemblance to *pìobaireachd* form is that the *ùrlar* is directed, as formerly in *pìobaireachd*, to be repeated after the variation preceding the *crunlù* and also after the *crunlù* itself.

Edward Bunting, in *The Ancient Music of Ireland*, sets down a number of terms, gleaned at first hand from the old Irish harpers of his day, which include some familiar, or formerly familiar, in *pìobaireachd*, including *siubhal*, *canntaireachd*, *barluadh* and *barluadh fosgailte*.*

It is not impossible that we may see in the figuration of *pìobaireachd* itself some internal evidence of the transference of the ancient music of the *clàrsach* or harp to the medium of the bagpipe. *Pìobaireachd* is probably the only sophisticated music in existence in which the decoration may come *after*, and not before, the principal or theme note. There is no inherent reason to be found for this in the technique of the pipe-chanter; the entire compass of the nine notes of the instrument lies conveniently under the fingers, and it is just as easy to light securely on the theme note at the end of a decorative chain of grace-notes as at the commencement of it (see p. 163).

On the contrary, on the harp there could be good reason for playing the theme note first and the decoration after it, rather than *vice versa*; for it is obviously easier to strike the theme note with certainty and accuracy if it is played at the beginning of a rapid decorative arpeggio rather than at the end of it. Also, if the same note as the theme note has already been played in a preliminary decorative sequence, the theme note itself has then to be played on an already vibrating string, when it is always difficult to avoid a certain amount of jarring of the sound.

The longer *pìobaireachd* figurations might, indeed, be said to be the bagpipe's own form of arpeggio. It seems not impossible that the earliest experiments in *pìobaireachd* may have been actual transliterations of harp pieces on the bagpipe. In one well-known *pìobaireachd*, 'Lament for the Harp Tree', there is indeed some evidence that it may have existed primarily as a harp piece by MacLeod's famous harper, Rory Dall Morison, under the title of 'Lament for the [lost] Harp Key'.†

Rory Dall was harper to the MacLeods of Dunvegan in the time of the

* The last two are quoted by Joseph MacDonald in *A Compleat Theory of the Highland Bagpipe*; they are now obsolete. Cf. his p. 1, 'The original terms of art belonging to the bagpipe'.

† See Collinson, *The Traditional and National Music of Scotland*, pp. 236, 245; Matheson, *The Blind Harper*, pp. 154–7. Dr J. L. Campbell of Canna says (personal communication), 'Rory Dall's song on the loss of his harp key is a *double entendre* from beginning to end'.

eighteenth chief, Iain Breac (1664–93); this was also the time of the last years of Patrick Mór MacCrimmon, and of the hey-day of Patrick Og. This is quite late for the use of harp music as material for *pìobaireachd*, but perhaps not too late for the playing of a current harp tune, probably a favourite at Dunvegan, on the pipes. The MacCrimmons, as did all the great *pìobaireachd* composers, considered it beneath their dignity to play light music (*ceòl eutrom*); but if Rory Dall had developed his song air on the loss of his harp key into a fully extended *ùrlar* and variations for the harp, with *singlings, doublings, crunlù* and the accustomed return of the *ùrlar* at conventional points in the piece, it could be no debasement of the MacCrimmon's art to adapt it for his own instrument.

There is another *pìobaireachd* which might also have originated as a harp piece, though solely on account of its early reputed date, 1562,[47] before the time of Donald Mór MacCrimmon, the supposed inventor of *pìobaireachd*. It is 'MacIntosh's Lament'. There are also various nameless *pìobaireachd* all traces of the origin of which are lost. Perhaps one or two of these could have started life as harp tunes?

To sum up: we have no firm and incontrovertible proof that the *pìobaireachd* form was borrowed from the harp music. We can only form our own conclusions as to whether the evidence afforded by Patrick Mac-Donald, by Simon Fraser, by Edward Bunting in Ireland, and perhaps even by Giraldus Cambrensis in his writings on the harp music and harpers of both countries, is strong enough to justify such a deduction. On the face of it, it does seem likely, to say the least, because of the maturity of form of the earliest authentic examples of *pìobaireachd*, that the existing form must have been borrowed from somewhere. What could be more likely than that it was borrowed from the music of the harpers, music on which the early MacCrimmons and everyone else at Dunvegan must have been nurtured, and which progressively waned as *pìobaireachd* waxed, and finally disappeared.

*Note on the* Pìobaireachd, *'I got a kiss of the King's hand', usually attributed to Patrick Mór MacCrimmon (c. 1595–c. 1670), hereditary piper to MacLeod, c. 1640–70*

The following passage from the Wardlaw manuscript[48] is a famous one in Scottish bagpipe history. The occasion was the gathering near Stirling in May 1651 of the Scottish army, Highland and Lowland, of Charles II, with its pipers and trumpeters. The army was later to march south to fight for the king at the disastrous Battle of Worcester in September of that year, from which a large number of them were not to return.

> In the close of April the Aird regiment, Frasers, 400, marched through Inverness, and without rant or vanity, as pretty men as went from the North, and could compeat *ceteris paribus* with so

many of a clan in the King's army, and traveling through Badenoch, through Appin [Atholl?] came to Stirling the beginning of May, and haveing veteran officers, they were exercised once a day, traind enugh ere they came at the Kings camp. Never was Prince more taken up with an army as our King was, especially with the Scotch Highlanders, whom he tearmed the flour of his forces, and still sounded their praise in every society, especially before the generall officers, which bred no small gum and emulation among the Lowlanders, judgeing themselves the farr finer men. There was great competition betuixt the trumpets in the army: one Axell, the Earl of Hoomes [Home's] trumpeter, carried it by the Kings own decision! The next was anent the pipers; but the Earle of Sutherlands domestick carried it of all the camp, for non contended with him. All the pipers in the army gave John Macgurmen [MacCrimmon(?)] the van, and acknowledged him for their patron in chiefe. It was pretty in a morning [the King] in parad viewing the regiments and bragads. He saw no less then [sic] 80 pipers in a crould bare-headed, and John Mcgyurmen in the midle covered. He asked What society that was? It was told his Majesty: Sir, yow are our King, and yonder old man in the midle is the Prince of Pipers. He cald him by name, and, comeing to the King, kneeling, his Majesty reacht him his hand to kiss; and instantly played an extemporanian part Fuoris Póóge i spoge i Rhi [Fuaras pòg o spòg an Righ], I got a Kiss of the King's hand; of which he and they were all vain.

It must be added that pipers are in considerable disagreement as to whether the John Macgurmen of the manuscript was in fact a MacCrimmon.[49]

## MacCrimmon piper contemporaries

We know that other Highland clans must have had their own pipers from an early date. When in 1587 the Clanranalds of South Uist burnt Trumpan Church and the MacLeods attending the church service within, tradition has it that Clanranald's piper played triumphantly outside the church as the flames engulfed their victims.

The MacLeods were swift to take revenge on the Clanranalds for this massacre at the Battle of Waternish, when they caught the latter on their way home and slaughtered them after a fierce fight. The MacLeods nearly lost, but they summoned supernatural aid by waving the Fairy Flag of Dunvegan; whereupon their forces magically seemed to double in the eyes of the enemy, and they won the day. The Clanranalds were slaughtered to a man; and the MacLeods buried them by tumbling a dry-stone dyke over their corpses. From this last detail, the battle became known as the Battle of the Spoilt Dyke.

The *pìobaireachd* commemorating the event is however better known as the 'Battle of Waternish'. It could hardly have been a true *pìobaireachd* that the Clanranald piper played outside Trumpan Church: at that date, 1587, the form, even if it had already been established by the MacCrimmons, could hardly have become common property for other clan pipers so soon. This is not to say, of course, that the Clanranald piper at Trumpan may not have played some form of extended, possibly repetitive strain of melody.

Once invented, the art of *pìobaireachd* probably spread quickly, for there are few things in the Highlands of Scotland which can be kept secret for long. The MacCrimmons were in fact willing, apparently from the first, to take pupils in piping, though they are said to have withheld some of the secrets of their art for themselves alone, particularly as regards *pìobaireachd* composition.

The hereditary pipers of the MacDonalds of Sleat* were the MacArthurs, who learned the art of *pìobaireachd* from the MacCrimmons.† According to Angus MacKay,[50] Charles MacArthur, the best known of them, was sent by Sir Alexander MacDonald of Sleat (for by then the MacDonalds were on friendly terms again with the MacLeods) to study under Patrick Og MacCrimmon at Boreraig, where he remained for eleven years. This was in the late seventeenth or early eighteenth century. The MacArthurs opened their own College of Piping at Peingown, near Kilmuir, in Skye, and it may well have been modelled in its lay-out and organization on the MacCrimmon's College. It is not known when the MacArthur College was started. Pennant, who visited MacArthur (whom he names only as 'MacDonald's piper') in 1772, gives an interesting picture of his establishment:[51]

> Take a repast at the house of Sir Alexander Mac-donald's piper, who, according to ancient custom, by virtue of his office, holds his lands free. His dwelling, like many others in this country, consists of several apartments; the first for his cattle during winter, the second is his hall, the third for the reception of strangers, and the fourth for the lodging of his family; all the rooms within one another.

Other clans had their hereditary pipers also, and most of them were sent to the MacCrimmon's College for tuition. This might be for anything up to a period of twelve years, though probably at spaced intervals. The recognized term of tuition was seven years.

The MacIntyres, pipers to the chief of Clan Menzies, who were the proud

---

* The Clanranalds of South Uist were also MacDonalds, a branch of the Clan Donald.

† They are said to have come from Islay; information from William Matheson, Department of Celtic Languages, University of Edinburgh.

possessors of the precious single-drone Bannockburn pipes mentioned before, came from Rannoch in West Perthshire.

The MacLeans of Coll, one of whom is so vividly portrayed by Boswell in *Tour to the Hebrides*, had for their pipers, the Rankines, who were themselves a branch of the Clan MacLean.[52]

Other clan pipers were the MacKays, pipers to the MacKenzies of Gairloch; and the MacKays of Raasay, pipers to the MacLeods of Raasay; the Campbells, pipers to the Campbells of Mochaster, the MacEacherns of Islay; and the Frasers, pipers to the Frasers of Lovat. One of these Fraser pipers, David Fraser, is of interest as being the subject of an indenture between Simon Fraser, Lord Fraser of Lovat (the Simon Fraser of the '45) and himself whereby Lord Fraser undertakes to send him to the Isle of Skye 'to be perfected as a Highland Pyper' by Malcolm MacCrimmon.[53] It is dated 1743.

Of interest too are the *Clann an Sgeulaiche*, or 'Clan of the Story-teller' who lived in Glenlyon in Perthshire, pipers to the chiefs of Clan MacGregor. One of them, Duncan Mór MacGregor, may possibly have been the composer of the 'Rout of Glenfruin' (1602). Another of the *Clann an Sgeulaiche*, John MacGregor, became personal piper to Charles Edward Stuart (Bonny Prince Charlie) in the 1745 rising. After Culloden, where he was wounded, he became piper to Campbell of Glenlyon.[54]

We also glimpse many anonymous clan pipers through the *pìobaireachd* they composed. There is the piper of Campbell of Glenorchy who composed '*Bodach nam Briogais*' (The Carles with the Breeks) to celebrate the winning of a fight between the Campbells and the Sinclairs, in which the latter were routed. The piper to the MacDonalds of Glencoe too has left his record of the Massacre of Glencoe in 1692, in a *pìobaireachd* of that name. There are the various gathering *Pìobaireachd* of the clans, all of which betoken the existence of a clan piper. These include 'The Grant's Gathering', (*Craigellachie*), 'The MacDougal's Gathering', 'The Mac-Farlanes' Gathering' ('*Togail nam Bó*'), the Sutherland's and the Cameron's Gatherings, the Gathering of Clan Chattan. Joseph MacDonald in his *Treatise* observes that 'Every Chief had a gathering [tune] for his name', which implies that the chief must have had a piper to sound it.

Other *pìobaireachd* with clan associations are 'The MacKays' Banner', 'MacIntosh's Lament', 'MacNeill of Barra's March' (and Lament), 'Struan Robertson's Salute', 'The Sinclairs' March', 'The Gordons' Salute', and others.

It is impossible to say when the Highland clans first began to include the piper as a member of the chief's establishment. There is, as has been said, a tradition that the piper to the Clan Menzies, one of the MacIntyres of Rannoch, played at the muster of the clan at Castle Menzies for their march to Torwood to join the Scottish army at the Battle of Bannockburn in 1314. It is not in the least improbable.

The first mention of a clan piper in official records is hopelessly late to

*Plate 17    Der Dudelsackpfeifer* (the bagpiper).
Engraving by Albrecht Dürer, dated 1514. Grattan Flood is of the opinion
that Dürer's model for the picture may have been an Irish piper on service on
the Continent with the forces of Henry VIII at Tournay in the early sixteenth
century, and that the bagpipe may be the Irish *píob mhór*. This seems pure
speculation.

*Plate 18*　An Irish piper at the head of a group of Irish Kerne.
Woodcut from John Derricke's *The Image of Ireland* (see p. 114).

be of value in the history of the Highland pipes. It is of Robert MacLure, piper to the Buchanans, a Stirlingshire clan, and is to be found in the Kirk Session Register of Stirling for the year 1604.

## Canntaireachd

### Origins

> Like a herald of old, or a bard, or a piper, I can stand here on a green knoll, in a yellow fog, out of the field of the fray, and incite people to battle with *The Mustering of the Clans*, in the old forgotten language of MacCrimmon, piper to MacLeod of Dunvegan; of MacArthur, piper to the Lord of the Isles; . . . and of John Campbell, the Lorn piper, who taught me fifty years ago how to rouse men with strange words out of the Isles –
>
> > *Hiodroho hodroho, haninen hìechin,*
> > *Hodraha hodroho, hodroho hachin,*
> > *Hiodroho hodroho, haninen hìechin,*
> > *Hodraha hodraha, hodraha hodraha,*
> > *Hodraha hodraha, hodraha hachin.*
> >
> > etc.
>
> This is the commencement of the MacCrimmon *canntaireachd* of *Cogadh no Sìth* (War or Peace – The Gathering of the Clans).[55]

Mention has been made in these pages of *canntaireachd*, 'the pipers' sol-fa',* the series of vocables which enable the piper to sing the music of *pìobaireachd* in order to teach his pupil. These vocables also can be written as in the excerpt above, thus making a species of notation by which *pìobaireachd* may be preserved in writing. It forms the most ancient system of notation of the Highland pipes.

*Canntaireachd* is generally thought to have been invented by the MacCrimmons. No date can be assigned to its first use; its origin is shrouded in misty tradition, some of which is almost certainly pure fairy-tale. The lost *Book of the MacCrimmons* by Captain Neil MacLeod of Gesto is said to have given three versions of its origin, all of which we must presume came to him from Iain Dubh MacCrimmon.

One version attributes it to the Italian eleventh-century Benedictine monk and writer on music, Guido d'Arezzo, who is generally credited with being the originator of the solmization syllables, *ut, re, mi, fa, sol, la,* for the notes of the hexachord[56] (an idea that came originally from Greece). Guido took these symbols from the initial syllables of the phrases of a hymn to St John the Baptist. His idea is said to have reached the monasteries in Ireland, from whence it passed to the Irish bards, and

---

* The original meaning of *canntaireachd* as given in the Gaelic dictionaries is 'chanting, singing, warbling'.

T.B.—12

from them to the Irish pipers; and one tradition has it, as has been said, that the MacCrimmons were of their number.

Another story is that *canntaireachd* was invented by Petrus Bruno, the legendary ancestor of the MacCrimmons according to the 'Cremona tradition'. Petrus Bruno was said to have derived it from an ancient secret biblical code founded in the Book of Genesis.[57]

A third suggestion is that the system was brought from Italy by Patrick Og MacCrimmon in the seventeenth century, after visiting that country, probably as a member of his chief's (MacLeod's) 'tail'.

Whatever the truth, *canntaireachd* is generally believed to have been initially the private system of the MacCrimmons, until other piping schools borrowed the idea. Many of the secrets of the MacCrimmon system are said to have been withheld by them from their pupils, and reserved for their own use – and probably also for the enhancement of the *mystique* surrounding their name. Certainly there is a noted lack of unanimity concerning the details of the MacCrimmon system of *canntaireachd* among those who have written about it. Several elucidations of it exist, including one recorded for me by a 'great-great-grand-pupil' of one of the two last 'hereditary pipers' of the MacCrimmon family, the late Pipe-major William MacLean, Kilcreggan; but they are all slightly different.

### Sources

The very existence of *canntaireachd* long remained unknown and unsuspected by musicians or musical authorities outside the close circle of the pipers themselves. General Dalyell in his *Musical Memoirs* relates an incident at a *pìobaireachd* competition in 1816,* which would be comic did it not show the pathetic ignorance of the inner secrets of piping displayed even by the judges of piping at the great competitions of *pìobaireachd* playing in the nineteenth century.

In 1816 one of the competitors, John Campbell, brought for the inspection of the judges, to quote General Dalyell,

> a folio volume in manuscript, said to contain numerous
> compositions; but the contents merely resembling a written
> narrative, in an unknown language, nor bearing any resemblance
> to Gaelic, they proved utterly unintelligible. Amidst many
> conjectures relative both to the subject and the language, nobody
> adventured so far as to guess at either *airs* or *piobrachs*. However
> Murdoch Maclean, a pipe-maker from Glasgow, offered to decipher
> the mysterious manuscript, so as to interpret the true meaning;
> but from these contrasted views sometimes opposing the most

---

* Dalyell gives 1818 as the date but this appears to be wrong. See J. P. Grant, 'Canntaireachd' in *The Pipes of War*, Glasgow, 1920, p. 179n.

reasonable projects, his proposal received no encouragement, and the owner refused to part with the volume, which gave me much regret.

This is probably the earliest authentic reference in print to *canntaireachd*.[58]

The manuscript collection in this strange language proved to be one of three such volumes belonging to the father (grandfather?) of the competitor, Colin Campbell, piper to Campbell of Corwhin. The second and third volumes came to light as late as 1909, when they were acquired by John Bartholomew of Glenorchard.[59] They are now deposited in the National Library of Scotland. Donald Campbell, the father of the original owner of the manuscript, was a pupil of Patrick Og MacCrimmon.[60]

J. F. Campbell of Islay, the celebrated folklorist quoted above, wrote a monograph on *canntaireachd* in 1880. He had an old family servant, whom he calls John Piper, from whom he got his information about piping. Campbell writes, 'I have often seen my nurse, John Piper, reading and practising music from an old paper manuscript, and silently fingering tunes.' According to the late Colonel J. P. Grant of Rothiemurchus, this 'John Piper' was the same John Campbell who possessed the three manuscript volumes of the Colin Campbell *canntaireachd*, and who belonged to the Campbell pipers in Corwhin. Although this John Piper himself possessed the knowledge of *canntaireachd* and could read it and play *pìobaireachd* from it, he proved unfortunately to be incapable of communicating this knowledge. Campbell gives a comic account of his efforts to get 'John Piper' to explain even the single phrase *hi-ri-ri*. To all his questions John Piper could only play a phrase of three notes on his chanter and say, *'that's "hi-ri-ri"'*; and in the end the great folklorist and skilled interrogator of traditional informants found himself completely stumped by his own Highlander servant, and was left no wiser than before.

He did however extract from him the valuable information that there were three different systems of *canntaireachd*: the MacCrimmon, MacArthur, and Nether Lorn. Although Colin Campbell, the owner of the manuscript described by General Dalyell, was a pupil of Patrick Og MacCrimmon, his manuscript is written in the Nether Lorn *canntaireachd*. The two volumes still existing contain some 168 tunes, of which over 60 are not to be found elsewhere.[61]

It seems that even by the time the two books were recovered in 1909, the secrets of *canntaireachd* were as little understood as they had been in 1814, and had to be rediscovered. (J. P. Grant observes that from the manuscript 'it was not hard to reconstruct the system'.)[62]

There is a certain amount of mystery about this, for the older pipers, up to within the past thirty to forty years or so, both learned their art and transmitted it to their pupils by *canntaireachd* only, and not by staff notation. William MacLean told me that he himself was taught entirely by means of *canntaireachd* by his teacher Calum MacPherson, Badenoch ('*Calum Pìobaire*'), and that he never saw a single piece of pipe-music in staff notation all the years of his pupilage. It seems strange that its secrets should have remained a closed book for so long.

Captain Neil MacLeod of Gesto published in Edinburgh in 1828 a collection of *pìobaireachd* notated in the MacCrimmon *canntaireachd* called *A Collection of Twenty Pìobaireachd or Pipe tunes . . .*

A number of *pìobaireachd* were noted down from one of the later MacCrimmons by Simon Fraser, mentioned before, who emigrated to Australia, and who was said to be the possessor of one of the two copies of Gesto's suppressed book on the MacCrimmons. Fraser's mother was a grand-daughter of Charles MacArthur, hereditary piper to the MacDonalds of Sleat. He himself was a descendant of the Frasers who were hereditary pipers to the Frasers, Lords of Lovat. He gives a version of the MacCrimmon system of *canntaireachd* which is different in the sound of the vocables from that published in Gesto's *Collection of Twenty Pìo-baireachd.*[63] A typed copy of Simon Fraser's notation of *pìobaireachd* in *canntaireachd* was brought to this country from Australia by a friend of Fraser's, a piper in the army during the last war, and this came into possession of Pipe-major William Gray of Dumbarton. I was shown these by Mr Gray at his home in the 1950s.

The available sources for the MacCrimmon *canntaireachd* vocables known to me are: (1) from Gesto's *Twenty Pìobaireachd*; (2) from Simon Fraser as published by G. F. Ross; (3) from Angus MacPherson, son of *Calum Pìobaire*, in a letter to me; (4) from a recording by William MacLean, pupil of '*Calum Pìobaire*'. As they all differ, there would be no useful purpose served in setting them down here.

Colonel J. P. Grant, in a letter to me, wrote that the MacCrimmon *canntaireachd*, as used by the few pipers who learned by this system, 'was, as we can now see, completely garbled, and if written down, was incapable of proper interpretation by any third person, unless that person already knew the tune'. He further observes in his article in *The Pipes of War* (p. 180), that, 'among the older-fashioned pipers in Scotland, even just before the [1914–18] war, one constantly heard syllables (*hodroho*, *hiodro*, etc., etc.) being used, generally at haphazard, seldom in their correct place'. He adds, 'The astounding thing is that even fragments of a notation, the system of which had been out of use for so long, should have survived to this day.'

Nevertheless, I can vouch for the fact that there was no hesitancy in the use of the MacCrimmon *canntaireachd* by pipers of my acquaintance. Different authorities or tradition-bearers may have had different versions of the MacCrimmon *canntaireachd*, but they seem to have used them consistently. Perhaps the fact of the matter is that the MacCrimmons never intended their *canntaireachd* to be as rigidly standard and inflexible a system as people have tended to believe, and that, along its broad lines, there was always a certain amount of improvisation and variation. Different pupils, becoming teachers in their turn, probably tended to develop their own idiosyncrasies in the use of it. After all, there is hardly a teacher or conductor of instrumental music anywhere who does not invent his own vocables on occasion, to demonstrate a tricky piece of rhythm, phrasing, or melodic sequence.

Because of this difficulty to reduce what is known of the MacCrimmon *canntaireachd* to a logical and fully understood system, the Nether Lorn system has been adopted for modern use by the Pìobaireachd Society in their published volumes of *pìobaireachd*. The reader is referred to them for exposition of it for modern practical use. The Nether Lorn closely resembles the MacCrimmon system, however, and has almost certainly developed from it.

## *Form*

The purpose of all the systems of *canntaireachd* is obviously the same. (1) They indicate the pitch of the basic notes of the tune (the theme-notes); this requires a series of vocables to stand for the nine notes of the bagpipe scale. (2) They indicate grace-notes or groups of grace-notes coming *before* the theme-note. (3) They indicate the *pìobaireachd* figurations of stereotyped chains of grace-notes coming *after* the theme-note.

The raw material or 'theme-notes' of the tune as in (1) above are, broadly speaking, indicated by vowel sounds; grace-notes which come before the theme note as in (2) are indicated by a consonant or consonants before the vowel sound; while the *pìobaireachd* figurations, coming after the theme-note as in (3) are expressed by extra syllables coming after the vowel sound.

The vowel sounds expressing the nine notes of the chanter scale in the Nether Lord *canntaireachd* are:

| LOW G | LOW A | B | 'C'* | D | E | F* | G | A |
|---|---|---|---|---|---|---|---|---|
| EM | EN | O | O or HO | A,DA or BA | E or DE | VE,DHE or HE | DI, VI or HI | I |
| as in | as in | as in | as in | as in | as in | as in | as in | as in |
| 'hem' | 'hen' | 'blow' | 'blow' | 'far' | 'say' or 'hay' | 'say' or 'hay' | 'see' | 'see' |

written or sung symbols

* Though the notes C and F are nearer in pitch to C sharp and F sharp, they are always called by their letter names, and pipers never use the word 'sharp'.

Single grace-notes coming before the theme-note are mostly expressed by prefixing a consonant such as *h*, *ch*, *t*, *d*, or *b* before the vowel. Here are a few examples showing a grace-note on high G, D and E respectively, prefixing various notes of the scale:

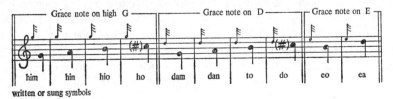

Groups of grace-notes coming before the theme-notes (known as *throws* or *grips*) are expressed by syllables or combinations of consonants prefixed to the vowel sounds expressing the notes of the chanter:

The actual *pìobaireachd* figurations (or '*pìobaireachd* notes' as the older pipers have been heard to call them), are chains of grace-notes coming *after* the theme-notes. These figurations are played so rapidly that they result in a sort of ripple of sound, of which the constituent notes are too rapid for an untrained ear to recognize individually. They are expressed in *canntaireachd* by conventional vocable syllables coming after the vowel sound or consonant-and-vowel sound as already shown above. There are various patterns of *pìobaireachd* 'notes', each of which has its special name.

The *leumluath*. This consists of a pattern of four grace-notes following the theme-note. The pattern ends on the note E. It is expressed by the vocable *bare* (with the *e* pronounced) added to the consonant-and-vowel sound expressing the (embellished) theme-note, thus:

The *taorluath*. This is a five-note 'ripple' following the embellished theme-note. It ends on the note A, and is expressed in *canntaireachd* by the syllables *darid*:

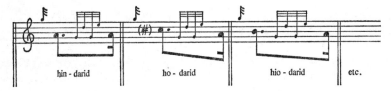

The *crunluath*, or 'crowning movement,* of the *pìobaireachd*. This is a figuration consisting of a 'ripple' of eight notes following the theme-note, and ending, like the *leumluath*, on E. It is expressed by the vocable *bandre*:[64]

It may be noticed that the four-note, five-note and eight-note 'ripples' of the *leumluath*, *taorluath* and *crunluath* are expressed in *canntaireachd* by vocables of no more than two syllables. It is sometimes erroneously said that a piper can sing by means of *canntaireachd* the most complicated *pìobaireachd* rhythms down to the last grace-note of the *crunluath*. This is only true in the sense that what the piper sings is a series of concise conventional symbols which stand for figurations containing a great many more notes in actual performance than are contained in the symbols themselves. In the longer figurations in fact, *canntaireachd* becomes, if the expression be not too mixed, a kind of 'vocal shorthand'.

Even in the Nether Lord *canntaireachd*, which was presumably devised as a regularization of, and an improvement on, the MacCrimmon system, there is much that is ambiguous and capable of being misinterpreted. For example, the notes B and C on the chanter are both expressed by the same vowel *o* (though this *o* could represent two different sounds, as in 'go' and 'for'). The vocables for the notes E and F both have the same *e* sound as in 'stay'; while those of the high G and the high A have the same vowel *i* (pronounced *ee*).[65] As the piping pupil was taught entirely by ear, this would not matter as much as it might appear; for, after the teacher had sung the phrase, to whatever vocable sounds he may have used, the pupil had only to play the tune on his practice chanter as he heard it.

This points to the fact that *canntaireachd* was primarily a vehicle for singing the tune. Only as a secondary purpose would it be used as an aid to memory. It was not meant as a means of playing 'from the score' a *pìobaireachd* which one did not already know; this confirms J. P. Grant's observation to me that the MacCrimmon *canntaireachd* could not be properly interpreted unless the piper already knew the tune. It certainly could not be used as a means of learning how to play *pìobaireachd* without the aid of a teacher, any more than can *pìobaireachd* be properly interpreted from staff notation alone.

Of the three systems of *canntaireachd* enumerated by 'John Piper', the Highland servant of J. F. Campbell of Islay, that of the MacArthurs remains to be discussed. Little exists beyond stray references.[66]

---

* 'Crowning movement' is not a strictly accurate translation of '*crunluath*', but it is a common rendering and a vivid one.

This very ambiguity of *canntaireachd*, and the incapability of staff notation to clarify the rhythm and expression of the music when it came to be used, has certainly helped to foster and safeguard the *mystique* surrounding *pìobaireachd* and the 'secret brotherhood' of its initiates. Perhaps this *mystique* may have had something to do with the survival of the Highland bagpipe over its less-enduring brethren in the rest of Britain (saving always the flourishing piping art in Northumbria).

## The Highland companies before Culloden

Pipers in Scottish armies had existed long before the '45 and the Disarming Act; but these were few, and their status was unofficial, or at best but semi-official.

Thus, in the vague military adventures of Charles I in France in 1627 the king, by way of ensuring a Scottish contribution to his campaign, commissioned MacNaughton of Dunderawe to raise and transport to France 200 bowmen. With them this contingent had a piper, Allester Caddel, who gained commendation from MacNaughton in his report to the Earl of Morton for the way he had kept up the courage and spirits of the company with his piping on their way over to France, when their ship had encountered a French warship, which gave chase. MacNaughton writes from Falmouth, where presumably his ship had taken refuge; and in a postscript he adds, 'My L. – As for newis from our selfis, our bagg pypperis and Marlit [chequered, i.e. tartan] Plaidis serwitt us in guid wise in the pursuit of [by] ane man of war that hetlie followit us.'[67] It is interesting to note that this contingent had both a piper and a harper; the latter was 'Harie m'gra' [Harry MacGraw] harper frae Larg'. One wonders if pipe and harp music were sufficiently alike at that date for piper and harper to swap tunes!

Pipers are also mentioned in Charles I's troubled reign as being present with the Scottish armies of the Covenant under Leslie and Montrose, then both on the same side opposing him. With the Covenanting army also was the Earl of Lothian, who wrote from Newcastle in the summer of 1640: 'We are sadder and graver than ordinary soldiers, only we are well provided of pipers.'[68]

Five years later, when Montrose had changed sides and become 'the King's Lieutenant', he almost certainly had pipers in his mixed force of Highlanders and Lowland gentry,[69] as had his own lieutenant, Sir Alexander MacDonald, 'Colkitto'. Montrose won a victory at Inverlochy on 2 February 1645, by the classical outflanking march of all time; he doubled back across the mountain passes in the depths of winter from Killcumin (now Fort Augustus), to debouch upon Argyll and his Campbells in flank at Inverlochy. John Buchan in *Montrose* says of this (although it may be a justifiable literary touch rather than verified fact) that, as

Montrose's army came down the hillside in the dawn upon Argyll's flank, there arose, besides the trumpets of Montrose sounding the salute reserved for the royal standard, 'the fierce Cameron pibroch, "Sons of dogs, come and I will give you flesh."'

In celebration of the victory, it is likely to have been one of Montrose's pipers who composed the well-known *piobaireachd* on the battle, 'Ceann na Drochaid Big' (The Head of the Little Bridge).

At Montrose's defeat at Philiphaugh in September 1645, it was a Highlander in his army who showed the typical bravery of the piper by playing his pipes on a small mound by the river Ettrick to rally his fellow Highlanders, who had been disastrously taken by surprise, with the tune of 'Whurry Whigs Awa' Man!' until a bullet from one of Leslie's men found its mark, and he fell mortally wounded into the river, there to drown, at a spot known to this day as the Piper's Pool.*

Similar examples of pipers with the Scots armies of the period are numerous. There was the piper with Claverhouse's army at the Battle of Bothwell Bridge, who emulated his compatriot at Philiphaugh in almost exactly similar circumstances, playing the tune 'Awa Whigs Awa''† by the banks of the Clyde to encourage his comrades who were storming the bridge; he finally fell into the river to his death, hit by a Whig ball.

At the Haughs of Cromdale two years later, a piper in the routed Jacobite army under the inept General Buchan performed the same brave act: badly wounded, he climbed on to a rock, where he continued to play until he expired. In his memory the rock is still named *Clach a Phìobair*, the Piper's Stone.

### The Black Watch

The first military companies raised among the Highlanders officially had no pipers, but only drummers, on their strength. Later to become *Am Freiceadan Dubh*, the Black Watch, these were formed at the instance of Charles II, who in 1677 commissioned the Earl of Athole to raise a company of Highlanders 'to be a constant guard for securing the peace of the Highlands'.[70] Their chief activities were envisaged as being no more than to restrain cattle thieves and blackmailers who demanded 'protection dues'.[71]

The number of companies was successively increased from one in 1677 to five in 1691. Two years after that they were transferred to the payroll of the regular regiments. In 1739, six years before the rising of 1745, they

---

* The song air 'Whurry Whigs Awa' Man!' was appropriate more for its title than because it was suitable for the pipes. It exceeds the compass of the chanter, and has much repetition of the same note, uncharacteristic of the technique of the instrument. It is to be found in James Hogg, *Jacobite Relics*, vol. 2, p. 63.

† Not the same tune as that at Philiphaugh. See ibid., vol. 1, p. 76.

were embodied as a regiment of the line, the 43rd (later the 42nd) under
the Earl of Crawford. Until then they had worn the clan tartans of their
individual captains; but about this time, when Lord Crawford took
command, they adopted the dark tartan, generally accepted to have
been the Campbell tartan, by which they earned their name of *Dubh* or
Black.

The government chose the year 1743, of all times, when Scotland was
on the boil with plots for a Jacobite rising, to send the Black Watch,
contrary to the understood terms of its recruitment, for service on the
Continent, where they fought at Fontenoy (1745) and elsewhere. They
were consequently out of the country when Prince Charles landed in
Scotland. They were hurriedly brought back and arrived in England in
October, by which time the Jacobite victory of Prestonpans had been
fought and won.

As has been said, the original companies had no official provision for
pipers, but as they were recruited from Frasers, Grants, Munros, Finlays,
Athole Stewarts and Campbells from Breadalbane, it would be remarkable
if among them there were not men who could and did play the pipes.

The first government forces among the Highlanders which had official
pipers seem to have been the independent companies raised under government authority by Duncan Forbes, Laird of Culloden and Lord President
of the Court of Session, in September 1745. Forbes was authorized to raise
twenty companies, though in the press of events and the time available
he succeeded in raising only eighteen; each company consisted of a
hundred men with a piper and a drummer.

It may be noted that by the time Forbes began to raise the independent
companies, in September 1745, the rising had been in progress for three
months; for Prince Charles had landed in Moidart on 25 July. Prince
Charles's army, which was well organized into regiments and was not the
'Highland rabble' it has often been called, had a magnificent group of
pipers, which included all the clan pipers of those chiefs who were 'out'
for the Prince.

## The Jacobite risings

> 'Twelve Highlanders and a bagpipe make a rebellion.'
> (Sir Walter Scott)*

The middle of the eighteenth century brought a crisis in the history of the
Scottish Highland bagpipe – a crisis that might well have ended its

---

* According to Dr J. C. Corson, Honorary Librarian to Abbotsford, the proverb
  was sent by Scott to J. W. Croker in 1829, when the latter was planning his
  edition of Boswell's *Life of Johnson* (published 1831). The proverb does not
  appear in published correspondence.

existence as the national instrument. This was the change in the old Highland way of life after Culloden, and the effects of the Disarming Act which followed the collapse of the rising.

Each of the two major Jacobite risings of 1715 and 1745 had inspired distinctive contributions to the repertory of *pìobaireachd*. The '15 called forth 'The Battle of Sheriffmuir', 'MacDonald's of Clanranald's Gathering to Sheriffmuir', 'The Prince's Salute', 'The Menzies Salute'; and as a nostalgic aftermath, 'The Earl of Seaforth's Salute', composed by Seaforth's piper during the Earl's subsequent exile.

It is also traditionally said to have given rise to the *pìobaireachd* by Patrick Og MacCrimmon, 'Too Long in This Condition', although this has also been accredited to Patrick Mór MacCrimmon, following the Battle of Worcester in 1651. The Battle of Sheriffmuir gave 'The Sherramuir March' its name. This was an already existing tune identified with the Stewart clan as their march tune; and though the name came with the battle, the tune itself is said to have been played at Pinkie (1547), at Inverlochy (1645) and, later, at Prestonpans (1745).

The very moment of Prince Charles's landing in Moidart, before the 1745 rising, inspired the *pìobaireachd* 'My King has Landed at Moidart'. This was said to have been composed on the occasion by John MacIntyre,* one of the piping family of MacIntyres from Rannoch.

It also gave us, in its deeply, almost unbearably nostalgic aftermath, 'Prince Charles' Lament', a *pìobaireachd* composed by Captain Malcolm MacLeod of Raasay, who held a commission in the Prince's army. In the aftermath also was composed 'Lord Lovat's Lament', by Ewen MacGregor, one of the pipers of the *Clann an Sgeulaiche*.†

The importance of bagpipers in the Jacobite army during the '45 rising can be seen in the following descriptions from the Woodhouselee manuscript, an interesting contemporary account:[72]

#### THE HIGHLANDERS' ADVANCE ON EDINBURGH

The Highlanders had all the advantages and there leaders all the inteligence they cowld desire and on they came with there bagpipes and plaids, rusty rapiers, matchlokcs, and fyerlocks, and tag rag and bob taile was there (p. 20).

#### AT EDINBURGH CROSS

All these mountan officers with there troupes in rank and fyle

---

\* The *pìobaireachd* would have had to be extemporized rather than composed. That this took place on the actual day of Charles's landing has been disputed.

† Archibald Campbell, '. . . *the Clann an Sgeulaiche*', *Piping Times*, vol. 2, part 10 (1950). But he later attributes this *pìobaireachd* to the pupil of Ewen MacGregor, David Fraser. Both were pipers to Simon Lord Lovat (of the '45) (and see Appendix II).

marched from the Parliament Closs down to surrownd the Cross,
and with there bagpipes and loosie crew they maid a large circle
from the end of the Luickenboths to half way below the Cross to
the Cowrt of Gaird. (p. 26) . . . the pipes plaid pibrowghs when
they were making ther circle thus they stood rownd 5 or six men
deep (ibid.).

### THE MANIFESTO OF JAMES VIII AT EDINBURGH CROSS

Chalmers the herald pronunced all this manifesto and declaration
with ane awdable strong voice. I cowld hear at my distance
distinctly, and many much further, for there was profownd silence
after all these military dismissed with bagpipes playing and a
fashon of streamers over ther showlders and the chime of bells
from the High Church steaple gave musicall tunes all the whill
(p. 29).

### AFTER PRESTONPANS

The Prince lay at Pinkey House on Saturday night, and came to
the Palice on Sabath evening with bagpips playing, and the body
of the armie remained at Dudeston. (p. 39).
This citie has answered the demand for 1000 tents. I saw parte go
in cartes for Dudeston escorted by a Higland detachment with
bagpipes and collowrs [colours] (p. 41).
One [i.e. on] Sabath morning they [Prince Charles's army] marched
off from Greenlaw with pypers playing &c towards Peebles. (p. 84).
A poor Italian prince C. Stewart, from Lochqwaber in the obscurest
corner of Britain, with any [an?] ill-armed mobb of Highlanders
and a bankrupt Twedall (Tweed-dale) laird his secretary, and
bagpypes surprising Edinburgh o'rrunning Scotland at Cockeny,
defeating a Royall armie, penetrating in to the heart of England . . .
(p. 88).
A popish Italian prince with the oddest crue Britain could produce
came all with plaids, bagpips and bairbuttocks, from the Prince to
the bagage man (p. 3).

The composition of *pìobaireachd* in the '45 was not a monopoly of the
Stuart side. Donald Bàin MacCrimmon served with the Hanoverians and
was killed in the skirmish known as the Rout of Moy – the only casualty
suffered on either side. At the Battle of Inverurie, two months earlier,
he had been taken prisoner by the Jacobites. The pipers of the Jacobite
army, many of whom had been the pupils of Donald Bàin, promptly went
on strike, and refused to play until he was released. Thus, unfortunately,
it was possible for him to be present and to meet his death in the Rout of
Moy. Donald Bàin had a premonition of his fate, so strong and vivid that

he felt the urge and inspiration, some days before the skirmish, to compose a lament for his own coming death. This was the famous *'Cha Till Mac Cruimein'* ('MacCrimmon Will Never Return'). His death inspired also the 'Lament for Donald Bàin MacCrimmon' by his brother Malcolm. Donald Bàin and Malcolm were both sons of Patrick Og.

On the occasion of the Prince's entry into Edinburgh on 17 September 1745, it is recounted that the piper played 'The King Shall Enjoy his Own Again'. It was an English tune, dating back to the days of the Commonwealth and inspired by a longing for the Restoration.*

Of the march south of the Prince's army following his victory at Prestonpans, the *Chronicles of the Atholl and Tullibardine Families* (vol. 3, p. 95) contain the entry, *'Monday, the 18th November 1745: His Royal Highness made his entry into Carlisle seated on a white charger and preceded by no less than a hundred pipers.'* Here we have the due authority for Baroness Nairne's famous song (composed long after the rising) 'Wi' a Hundred Pipers an' a' an' a' '.†

It is said of the Duke of Cumberland, on seeing for the first time the bagpipes of the Highland pipers under his own prospective command (Argyll Militia, independent companies, and others), that he asked cuttingly, 'What are these men going to do with such bundles of sticks? I can give them better weapons of war than these!' He was soon enlightened.

## Culloden

> 'The pipes will play when the Cannon begin.'
> (Prince Charles Stuart's Army Orders of the Day)

> 'Gin [if] they had a' fouchten [fought] as they pipet [piped] there wad be anither tale to tell!'
>
> (Popular saying of the time)‡

The line-up of the armies for the Battle of Culloden was the occasion for the proud playing of the various Gathering *pìobaireachd* of the clans. The Clan Stewart pipers are said to have played the ancient MacCrimmon *pìobaireachd*, 'The Lament for Rory Mór (MacLeod)'.[73] This was curious

---

* In its original form the tune is not particularly suited to the pipes, but it was evidently altered to suit; see James Hogg, *Jacobite Relics*, vol. 1, song no. 1.
† The *Chronicles* give as their authority *Carlisle in 1745: An Account of the Occupation by Prince Charles Edward Stuart*, ed. G. G. Mounsey, London, 1846. According to Walter Blaikie's *Itinerary of Prince Charles Edward Stuart* (published by the Scottish History Society as a supplement to *Lyon in Mourning*) Prince Charles entered Carlisle on 17, not 18, November. These authorities say nothing about the hundred pipers.
‡ The saying is unjust. The Highland clans of the Jacobite army displayed enormous courage despite a disastrously ill-chosen battleground.

because the MacLeods of Dunvegan had refused to join Prince Charles, and also because the Stuart march was an old and honourable pipe-tune, going back, it is said, to the Battle of Pinkie (1547) at least.[74] Amongst the pipers, too, was Iain Beag, who carried the fabled Black Chanter of the Clan Chisholm, 'The Maiden of the Sandal'.* Prince Charles himself had a particular interest in the pipes, being himself a player.† He was to find solace in playing them during the grim and drear wanderings that lay ahead of him.

The subsequent tale of the pipers at Culloden may be read at its most vivid in the pathetic lists of prisoners taken after the battle and during the flickering remainder of the rising. These include James Campbell, piper to Glengyle's Regiment; Nicholas Carr, piper to Glenbucket; Robert Jameson, piper to the Duke of Perth's; and the town piper of Arbroath, John Sinclair, a piper in Ogilvie's Regiment, who successfully pleaded at his trial that the 'rebels' had forced him to act as piper, and that he had deserted from the Jacobite army after being kept by them against his will for seventeen days. Among the prisoner-lists too, though it refers to those taken at the previous battle of Falkirk, appears the pathetic Allan MacDougall, 'A blind Hyland Piper' who had marched with his unseeing eyes straight into the hands of the enemy.[75]

# The Disarming Act, 1747

## The effects on the chiefs

The fate of one Jacobite piper of the '45 was to have a profound effect upon the fortunes of the Highland bagpipe, its pipers and its music for many a year afterwards. He was James Reid from the county of Angus, one of the pipers in Ogilvie's Regiment (which boasted quite a number of pipers).

Reid was among the Highlanders who garrisoned Carlisle when the Prince's army marched further south. At the subsequent recapture of Carlisle by the Hanoverian army he was amongst the prisoners taken when the garrison surrendered. At his trial at York, on 2 October 1746, he advanced the plea that he did not bear arms, but was a piper.

The court's judgment was that 'No regiment ever marched without musical instruments such as drums, trumpets and the like': and that 'a

---

* John Prebble, *Culloden*, p. 72. He relates a legend that the Chisholm chanter develops a crack when the chief of the clan is about to die. The *Maighdean a' Chuarain* ('Maiden of the Buskin' as Angus MacKay translates it in *A Collection of Ancient Pìobaireachd . . .*, notes, p. 7, no. XVI) is said to have been brought by an early chief of the Clan Chisholm from Rome.

† Flood (*The Story of the Bagpipe*, p. 144) tells us that the Prince's favourite set of pipes was sold in 1807 with the effects of his brother Prince Henry, Cardinal of York. They passed to Richard Lees of Galashiels.

Highland regiment never marched without a piper'; and that 'therefore his bagpipe, in the eye of the law, was an instrument of war'.[76] The jury recommended mercy, but their recommendation was ignored. He was executed on 30 November 1746.

The full effect of James Reid's execution upon the use of the bagpipe in the Highlands has to be assessed in conjunction with the Disarming Act of 1747 which formed the sequel, *fort et dur* to the suppression of the rising.

Both the risings of 1715 and 1745 – each of them ending in failure – were followed by Disarming Acts; but whereas the Act following the '15 was stern, that following the '45 was vicious and vindictive. Not only did it penalize the carrying or hiding of arms, which was understandable; but it forbade the wearing of Highland dress, even to the use of tartan or any 'party-coloured Plaid or Stuff' in any form of dress at all. The provision of the Act as to the carrying or possessing of arms applied throughout the whole of the Highland areas, and to all the Highland clans, whether they had been in rebellion against the government or not; the wearing of the tartan, however, was proscribed throughout the *whole* of 'that part of Great Britain called Scotland'.*

The Disarming Act did not actually proscribe the use of the bagpipe. Indeed, nowhere in the Act is the instrument mentioned at all. But it had been adjudged in the High Court to be an instrument of war, and the Act laid down heavy penalties for carrying or hiding an instrument of war.† As long as Cumberland's military regime policed the Highlands, an offender against any provision of the Act was quite likely to be shot on sight. A few individuals were killed thus for no more heinous a crime than wearing tartan.[77]

As far as the bagpipe was concerned, there was of course a world of difference between playing the pipes peacefully in one's own Highland glen and having been taken in active rebellion as a piper with the Jacobite army, as James Reid was. Probably if the peaceful piper in the glen were to be hauled before the magistrates or the Justice of the Peace, and his playing made the subject of a criminal court case, it might not be judged as meriting penalties, even if it could be argued on the strength of the York trial that it was in contravention of case law at least. But who was going to be the first to 'try it out' by submitting himself as a test case, at the risk of transportation across the seas?

---

* The soldiers called upon to enforce the provisions of the Act regarding the wearing of the tartan were said to be furiously ashamed at having to chase 'shawlie-wifies' (women wearing tartan head-shawls) up and down the streets, and arrest them.
† The penalty was 'transportation to any of His Majesty's Plantations beyond the Seas, there to remain for the space of seven years'. In practical terms this could mean an indefinite period if the prisoner did not have the means to return home at the end of his sentence.

The effect of the Disarming Act upon piping has probably been to some extent exaggerated. Even if the Great Highland pipe was still thought too risky in certain areas, there was always the practice-chanter, which by any stretch of imagination could hardly come into the category of 'a weapon of war'. The small-pipes, so often described in the traditional Gaelic songs of the Highlands, could also be played. They surely would have escaped classification as an offensive weapon – except in the would-be witticism of the facetious Lowlander!

Much would depend, doubtless, on which side a chief or laird had fought in the rising – although theoretically the Disarming Act applied to Jacobite and Hanoverian clans alike. The Chief of MacLeod, for example, had favoured the Hanoverian cause, and had raised several of the Independent Companies for the policing of the Highlands immediately prior to the outbreak of the rising. Afterwards he continued, for a time at least, to maintain his hereditary pipers, the MacCrimmons.

What did have a drastic effect on piping, however, was the impoverishment of many of the chiefs by the forfeiture of their estates. No longer could they afford to send their pipers for a seven-year course at the MacCrimmon College; indeed, many of the chiefs had fled to France. The chiefs' power had also declined because their hereditary jurisdiction over their clans had been abolished as part of the government's measures following the rebellion.

The Highland chief, as the owner of a feudal estate, had awesome powers over his tenants and their sub-tenants – powers which he did not hesitate to exercise.* His was a figure that commanded obedience and respect. Captain Edward Burt, who wrote in 1726, tells us that when he travelled furth of his own clan territory his retinue consisted of his henchman (his foster-brother with whom, as an infant, he had been reared, and who became his personal and faithful bodyguard); his bard, to sing his prowess in battle and the greatness of his ancestors; his spokesman or *bladair*, who acted as his advocate in discussion and argument, and who undertook the duties of routine speeches and introductions which social occasion required; his *gille mór* or sword-bearer; his *gille-cas-fhliuch*, whose duty it was to carry the chief on his back over the streams and fords so that he might cross dry-shod; his *gille-comh-sreathainn* to 'lead his horse in rough and dangerous ways'; his *gille-truis-àirneis* or carrier of his baggage; his piper, and the piper's *gille*, who carried the bagpipe; a number of his kinsmen to bear him company; and in addition, 'a number of the common sort, who have no particular employment, but follow the Chief only to partake of the cheer' – and probably to provide a strong arm with

---

* Dr J. L. Campbell of Canna tells me that a chief had no such power over a clansman living on someone else's land. When for example, the Argyll family took over the estates of the MacLeans of Duart through foreclosure in the 1670s they became possessed of this power in Mull and Tiree; the Duart family lost it over their MacLean clansmen.

*Plate 19* Sketch thought to have been made on the battlefield at the Battle of Ballyshannon (1595). Edward Bunting (*Ancient Music of Ireland*, p. 56) believes the drawing to have been the work of a soldier in the English army. It is of interest as appearing to show that the two drones of the Irish pipes did not issue from a common stock, but were attached to the bag separately. The question must really be considered as unresolved. See footnote on p. 115.

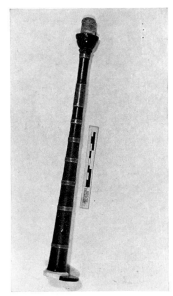

*Plate 20* (a) left.   The MacCrimmon bagpipes (the *Pìob Bhreac*, i.e. *speckled pipe*) in Dunvegan Castle. The chanter and top sections of the drones are thought to be original, the remaining parts being replacements.
The original bagpipes are said to have been played by Patrick Mór MacCrimmon in the seventeenth century.
(b) right. The chanter of the MacCrimmon bagpipes, showing metal repair bands. Photograph by the School of Scottish Studies.

*Plate 21*   James Livingston (1708–88), Town Piper of Haddington with Andrew Simpson, town drummer, and Harry Burray, a simpleton; from an engraving by George Mabon of a coloured drawing by Robert Mabon, a local artist, c. 1770. The original drawing bears the words *Robt. Mabon Del. ad vivum*, i.e. drawn from life. By courtesy of the Newton Port Museum and Public Library, which houses both original and engraving. Photograph by John Tully-Jackson, Haddington. The Museum also possesses a half-length portrait in oils of James Livingston by an unknown artist.

sword, dirk and gun, should anyone attempt to interfere with the chief
on his journey.*

The ceremonial approach of the chief, his piper playing before him,
must have been felt by clansman and stranger alike as an occasion not to
be treated lightly. To be summoned to appear before him must have
alarmed the clansman who had been up to mischief, or who had been the
cause of affront or humiliation, fancied or otherwise, to his chief.

When, following Culloden, the power of jurisdiction over the members
of their clan was taken away from the chiefs, their personal importance
and impressiveness were considerably diminished. Such a decline in the
power of the chief must of course have brought a corresponding decline
in the status of the piper who went before him.† This was reflected in the
ancient Colleges of Piping, whose prosperity began to wilt. By the end of
the 1770s, within a short time of each other, they had closed down.

Nevertheless, though the hated Disarming Act was to run for thirty-six
years, the art of *pìobaireachd*, upon which the strength of the Highland
piping tradition depended, was never in danger of dying out. Help was
soon to come with the formation of the Highland regiments, who were
allowed to keep the tartan and the pipes, and in which the playing of
*pìobaireachd* was to be encouraged and, indeed, required. This was a great
dispensation, for without the bastion of *ceòl mór*, from which Highland
piping drew its strength, it is quite likely that the Highland bagpipe might
have gone the way of the English one, and failed to survive.

### The Highland regiments after Culloden

There was a great difference between the various Highland companies used
mostly to police the Highlands and to keep the Jacobites in check following
the 1715 rising and the new Highland regiments raised in the years after
the passions of the '45 had subsided. Until then, Highlanders had been
used against their fellow Highlanders, but now a new idea was born – of
channelling the warlike nature and bravery and inborn loyalty of the
Highlander into the defence of the country as a whole against its enemies
abroad. The inspiration was William Pitt's; in 1757, eleven years after

* Captain Edward Burt, *Letters from a Gentleman in the North of Scotland:
 likewise An Account of the Highlanders* (London, 1754), vol. 2, Letter 21, p. 143.
 The spelling of the Gaelic words in the account has been edited to conform
 with modern practice.
† Dr J. L. Campbell of Canna makes an interesting observation (personal
 communication): 'I don't think the loss of this power would have affected the
 attitude of the chiefs towards their pipers. I am sure that what did, and what
 was meant to weaken their attachment to Gaelic customs, was their education
 at English public schools, which began around 1770. And it is significant that
 a letter exists at Dunvegan dated 12 April 1769 from General Fraser to
 MacLeod urging him to remove his son from Edinburgh to Harrow to be
 followed by Oxford or Cambridge. *Book of Dunvegan*, II, 45.'

Culloden, he set about raising regiments from among the Highlanders irrespective of which side they had fought on in the attempt to restore the House of Stuart.*

To quote an anonymous writer of the period,[78]

> The call to arms was responded to by the clans; and battalions
> on battalions were raised in the remotest parts of the Highlands,
> among those who a few years before were devoted to, and followed
> the fate of the race of the Stuarts. Frasers, MacDonalds, Camerons,
> MacLeans, MacPhersons and others of disaffected names and clans,
> were enrolled; their Chiefs or connections obtained commissions;
> the clansmen, always ready to follow, with eagerness endeavoured
> who should be first listed.

The first of the Highland regiments to be raised as the fruits of Pitt's vision was Montgomery's Highlanders in 1757. The regiment, which numbered 1,460 men, had on its strength thirty pipers and drummers.† In the same year were raised Fraser's Highlanders; the latter were commanded by Simon Fraser, son of 'The old fox' of the '45, Lord Lovat, executed for the part he had played in the rising. Keith's Highlanders followed in 1759. The year 1760 saw the raising of Johnstone's Highlanders and Campbell's Highlanders. Others raised before the end of the century were MacLeod's, MacDonald's, Athole, Seaforth, Argyll, and Gordon Highlanders. These regiments were fully supplied with pipers. They all very quickly distinguished themselves in foreign service.

### Evasion of the Act

The men of the Highland regiments were the only people in Scotland, men or women, allowed to wear the tartan in any form; and their pipers were free of the eleven-year-old ban, or implied ban, on their beloved pipes. Even if the only opportunity of playing the pipes had lain within the ranks of these new Highland regiments of the regular army, it was sufficient to save the ancient art of *pìobaireachd* from fading out and perishing of disuse.

* Nine years afterwards, in 1766, Pitt declared in Parliament: 'I sought for merit
  wherever it could be found. It is my boast that I was the first minister to look
  for it, and found it in the mountains of the north. I called it forth, and drew
  into your service a hardy and intrepid race of men. They served with fidelity,
  as they fought with valour, and conquered for you in every quarter of the
  world', *The Parliamentary History of England*, vol. 16, 1765–71, (Hansard),
  London, 1813.
† A set of small-pipes evidently belonging to this regiment or one of its officers
  is described in Gilbert Askew, 'The origins of the Northumbrian bagpipe',
  *Archaeologia Aeliana*, 4th series, vol. 9 (1932). It is curious that, although they
  were free from all the inhibitions of the detested Disarming Act concerning the
  great Highland bagpipe and its status as a weapon of war, the regiment should
  have deigned to have in its possession this set of miniature bagpipes.

There were at least two other groups which could play the pipes without risk of breaking the law besides the Highland regiments – and one of them allowed the wearing of the tartan as well.

First, there were the Fencibles, the eighteenth-century forerunners of the later Volunteers and of the still later Territorial Army. These were, like their later counterparts, a civilian force, which could only be embodied in time of the threat of war. The Fencibles had their pipers and presumably were allowed to wear the tartan when on duty, as part of their uniform. Their regimental music, like that of the regular Highland regiments, was *pìobaireachd* – for the pipe-march or quickstep, in time to become known as 'the best music in the world for marching to', was not yet born.

The Western Fencible Regiment, drawn from Argyll and the neighbouring counties, was embodied for defence of the Clyde and the west coast during the American War of Independence. An interesting manuscript exists entitled 'Regimental Orders of the Western Fencible Regiment and Captain James Campbell's Company commencing the 8th July 1778'. It mentions not only its pipers ('pippers') but the tunes they were to play for the day's duty calls. These were all *pìobaireachd*. The order sheet runs as follows:[79]

July 25th 1778

Paroll Silesea*

Regimental Orders

Lieu$^t$ Loghan one Serg$^t$ two Corp$^{lls}$ one Drumer one Fiffor

Eighteen men Main guard –

One Corp$^{ll}$ and foure men whith Side Arms for the Hospdell Guard – – –

The two Pippers are to take the dutty day about and and [*sic*] are

to play ther† Following tunes Viz$^t$

Gathering

Coagive & Shea

---

Revellee

Glaisvair

---

The Troop

Bodachnabrigishin

---

Retreat

Gillychristie

---

Tatoo

Mollachdephit Mahary

---

\* I.e. the password.

† 'Ther' may be the Scots word 'this', meaning 'these'.

The Gathering is the *pìobaireachd 'Cogadh no Sith'* ('War or Peace', also called 'The Gathering of the Clans'). The reveille is *'A' Ghlas Mheur'* ('The Finger Lock'). The troop is *'Bodaich nam Briogais'* ('The Carles with the Breeks') and the retreat, *'Cill Chrìosda'*, or *'Killechrist'*. The extra-ordinary-looking name of the *pìobaireachd* for the tattoo, *Mollachdephit Mahary*, appears to stand for *'Moladh do Ghibht Mairi'*, or 'Mary's Praise for her Gift', more usually shortened to 'Mary's Praise', or *'Moladh Mairi'*.

## The cattle drovers

There seems to have been another class of Highlander (and quite a numerous class it was) who, in theory at least, found it possible during the dangerous years to flaunt and play the bagpipes in the face of the law without fear of the consequences. This was the cattle drover. They came from all over the Highlands with their cattle to markets further south; for they, practically alone among the civilian population of the Highlands, were exempt from the decrees of the Disarming Act in that they were allowed under permit to carry arms for the defence of their cattle and of themselves, against cattle-thieves, for which the Highlands had always been notorious. Therefore, if the law ruled that the bagpipe was a weapon, the drovers could carry it openly as such.

Licences to carry arms were valid for two years. Statistics for the years immediately following the '45 are not readily available, but it is known that within the period of the 1715 Disarming Act, namely in 1725, General Wade issued 230 such licences to 'the forresters, drovers and dealers in cattle and other merchandise belonging to the several Clans who have surrendered their arms, permitting them to carry arms'. It is known, too, that these permits continued to be granted to the drovers even *during* the 1745 rising and throughout the years following.[80]

The cattle drovers of over twenty years later would certainly not be less numerous than those of 1725; one can reasonably surmise that it would not be within human nature if the drover or his men did not 'cock a snook' at the government and the detested Disarming Act by playing a defiant *pìobaireachd* or two on the long journey south through the Highlands.*

In the hey-day of eighteenth-century cattle-droving, the drovers and their assistants could be numbered in hundreds. A drove of cattle usually consisted of anything from 100 to 300 beasts, and there was a drover for every fifty or so. With a large drove the drovers might therefore have six or seven men. These included a 'topsman' as he was called, whose duty it was to ride ahead and spy out convenient spots for grazing and for stop-ping for the night – as well as to keep his eyes open for the approach of bands of cattle-thieves or other disturbers of their rightful business.

* This is my own guess; it is supported by the choice of the **Falkirk Tryst** (cattle market) as the venue for *pìobaireachd* competitions.

It was, by the nature of it, a leisurely business, for the cattle could not be hurried if they were to arrive at the market in good condition; and ten to twelve miles was reckoned a good day's journey with the drove. There must have been plenty of time for a bit of piping, both actually *en route*, and at the end of the day, either under the open sky or at the inns where the drovers foregathered when circumstances allowed.

The great cattle-market was the Falkirk Tryst; but the Scottish drovers went further afield than Falkirk, driving their cattle far into England, both via Carlisle and the west, and through Northumberland by the valleys of North Tyne and Coquet in the east.[81] In East Harlsey near Northallerton in Yorkshire, on the direct droving route, there still exists the Cat and Bagpipe Inn, where Scottish drovers put up for the night, and, as the name suggests, made the night 'shortsome' with the strains of their national instrument of music. The present owner of the inn, Mrs J. Ball, informs me of a local tradition that the original name of the inn was 'The Catern (cateran) and Bagpipes', and that the road fronting the inn was, for obvious reasons, known as 'Greasy Lane'. The tradition confirms that the 'caterns' here were cattle drovers with their herds.

Other ports of call on the English side of the Border were the Drovers' Inn at Boroughbridge, the inn of the same name at Wetherby, the Drovers' Rest in Cumberland, the Drovers' Call between Gainsborough and Lincoln, the Highland Laddie at Nottingham, and an inn with the same name near Norwich, at St Faiths.

At all these places no doubt the sound of the bagpipe was to be heard without restraint beyond some expressions of displeasure by the English inhabitants – and all this was within the period when the pipes were, generally speaking, discreetly silent in the Scottish glens themselves.

It should perhaps be remarked for the sake of completeness that the prohibition from carrying arms was only in force north of the Highland line. In theory, if a Highlander was very anxious to be a piper but not a soldier (or a drover) he could go and live in the southern part of Scotland, a solution perhaps not so easy in practice; or he could emigrate – and many, as we know, did.

### The effects on piping

Perhaps the hardest hit by the changed conditions were the great teacher-composers of the bagpipe, who had made piping the art it was. The days were fast ending when the centuries-old colleges of piping were thronged by eager pupils, sent there by their clan chiefs for a seven-year apprenticeship.

The college of the Rankines, pipers to the MacLeans of Duart, was the first to fold. It came to an end in 1760. By 1772, Pennant, in his *Voyage to the Hebrides*, was to write of both the MacArthur and MacCrimmon Colleges in the past tense.

The College of the MacCrimmons, whose 'diploma'* was the *sine qua non* of the accomplished piper, actually came to its end over a dispute about the raising of the rent of the holding of Boreraig, where it was situated. The date was 1770. Donald Ruadh MacCrimmon was then the principal or 'professor' of the College, and it was he who held the lease of Boreraig. The value of land had risen many times since the sixteenth century when the Chief of MacLeod had bestowed it at a nominal rent on his hereditary piper (Finlay of the White Plaid as we may suppose it to be). Now it was six or seven times its former value. Money was tight for the Highland chiefs after the '45.

MacLeod proposed that he should give MacCrimmon a free lease of *half* the holding of Boreraig, and that he should take back the other half for letting at increased rental. Donald Ruadh, whose forefathers had had the complete holding for centuries practically rent free in return for their piping and the glory it brought to Dunvegan, took the proposal as an insult. He not only threw up the lease, thus breaking up the ancient piping establishment, but, equally unfortunately, is said to have sworn an oath that henceforth no child of his would learn to play the bagpipes.†

Curiously enough, confirmation of this last resolve may be found in the diary of Sir Walter Scott, who visited Dunvegan in 1814, during the lifetime of Donald Ruadh. Scott writes of him,[82] 'He is an old man, a lieutenant in the Army, and a most capital piper, possessing about 200 tunes and "pibrochs", most of which will probably die with him, as he declines to have any of his sons instructed in his art.'

Dr I. F. Grant, in *The MacLeods: The History of a Clan*, gives it as her opinion, however, that it was probably a lack of pupils as much as

* Miss E. Carmichael, in 'Never was piping so sad and never was piping so gay', *Celtic Review*, vol. 2, p. 76 (July 1905), makes the following statement: 'It is said that in later days the MacCrimmons gave diplomas to successful graduates. These diplomas had on them pictures of Dunvegan Castle, of the galley of Macleod, and of various musical instruments, a seal, and the name of the holder, with the dates of entrance to and departure from the college.' She adds the note: 'a family of the name of Robertson in Inverness – whether town or county I do not know – is said to possess one of these certificates.'

One is forced to observe that the account, interesting though it is, must be treated with the utmost reserve. The writer gives no source for her information and I can find no confirmation of it from any other quarter. Gaelic scholars think it is unlikely that the MacCrimmons were able to write; the reproduction of a pictorial design such as is described, by any form of printing, may well be ruled out. Seumas MacNeill, Principal of the College of Piping, tells me that all attempts to find a copy of the MacCrimmon Diploma have been unsuccessful. Considering the number of piper pupils who must have studied under the MacCrimmons at their college at Boreraig over the space of 300 years, it is unreasonable to suppose that, if such a diploma existed in documentary form, not a single copy survives and can be produced. Pipers and scholars alike doubt the existence of the MacCrimmon Diploma except in the abstract sense (as it is used above).

† This tradition was mentioned to me by William MacLean of Kilcreggan.

the raising of his rent which caused Donald Ruadh to close the College.*

Donald Ruadh emigrated for a time to America. His brother Iain Dubh MacCrimmon took the farm, increased though the rent was, and obtained a new lease in 1771. But he did not carry on with the College, which makes one think that Dr Grant is probably right in her surmise about the scarcity of pupils. The ancient art of piping was in decline.

Iain Dubh MacCrimmon in his turn eventually quarrelled with his landlord, MacLeod of Dunvegan.† He left Boreraig in consequence, in 1795, intending, like his brother Donald, to emigrate to America. He actually set out on the journey, but by the time he arrived at Greenock he felt so homesick that he could not go further. He returned to Skye, but not, apparently, to Boreraig.

In the meantime, Donald Ruadh had returned from America, having there acquired a commission as lieutenant in the army.‡ He again became piper to MacLeod.


# The Highland Society

## Pìobaireachd competitions

The stultifying effect of the Disarming Act continued on its miserable way; but a group of Scotsmen living in London cared enough for the old ways of their native country to band themselves together to do something actively to preserve them. They formed the Highland Society of London, one of whose objects was 'the preservation of the Music of the Highlands'.[83] The Society decided to institute annual competitions for the best performer on the Highland bagpipe. It was decided that 'a Pipe and Flag' be given annually. The 'Pipe' was a new set of bagpipes 'of the best make and finish' made by Hugh Robertson, a popular pipe-maker in Edinburgh.[84] The pipes bore a silver plate with the name of the winner engraved upon it, and they were carried round the streets of the town in triumph after the competition. The flag took the form of a pipe-banner bearing the device of a thistle. In addition, the winner received 40 Scots merks (about £2 6s 3d).

The obvious venue for the competitions was Falkirk, during the Falkirk Tryst or cattle-market. Many Highlanders converged there from all over the Highlands with their droves of cattle, and they, as a civilian class licensed to carry 'arms', had a legal right to play the bagpipe. The

---

* Sir Eneas Mackintosh of Macintosh in his *Notes on Strathdearn* (written about 1774–83 and privately printed) says: 'Pipers turn scarce and if encouragement is not soon given, none will be found in the country'; quoted by I. F. Grant, *The MacLeods: The History of a Clan*, p. 559 and note.
† Norman MacLeod, 23rd Chief (1772–1801, cf. ibid., p. 499).
‡ He was commissioned in a 'corps of loyalist Scotsmen' in 1778; it was disbanded in 1808, 'Notices of pipers', *Piping Times*, vol. 22, no. 8 (May 1970).

Falkirk Tryst in those days must have taken on much of the appearance of a Highland Gathering, even though the wearing of tartan was still banned.

The first of these competitions was held in 1781. Although it was thirty-five years since the bagpipe came under a cloud, it was at once apparent that the art of *pìobaireachd* had not been forgotten. Practically all the winners of the early competitions came from among the older pipers who carried the memory of their art from before the '45.

The winner of the first competition was Patrick MacGregor of the *Clann an Sgeulaiche*,* the ancient race of story-tellers and pipers from Glenlyon in Perthshire. The runner-up was a MacArthur and the third prizewinner was old John MacGregor who had been personal piper and attendant upon Prince Charles himself, and who had been wounded at Culloden. Piper now to Campbell of Glenlyon, he was aged seventy-three. Next year the old man tried again and won second prize.†

Other prizewinners from the old famous piping families included Donald MacIntyre, then aged seventy-five, of the MacIntyres from Rannoch, hereditary pipers to the Clan Menzies (he also had fought at Culloden on the Stuart side); and one of the Campbell pipers from Nether Lorn, pipers to the Campbells of Mochaster, Argyll.

In 1783 the Highland Society of London appointed old John MacGregor to be their own official piper. Patrick MacGregor, the winner of the first competition mentioned above, was in all probability his son.[85] He was piper to Henry Balneaves of Edradour, who was married to a daughter of Glenlyon.

Before the competition, a 'rehearsal' was held to select the best competitors. At this rehearsal the competitor was required to play a specified *pìobaireachd*, but at the competition proper he was allowed to play one of his own choice. The panel of nearly thirty judges apparently contained few, if any, competent pipers; it consisted of, to quote Archibald Campbell of Kilberry, 'peers, baronets, lairds, retired army officers, and Edinburgh professional men'.[86] This, indeed, was one of the reasons why the Society appointed John MacGregor to be their official piper, to be 'an intermediate person between the judges and competitors'.[87]

The competence of such a body to judge the playing of music as specialized as *pìobaireachd* was extremely doubtful. It was such a panel of judges, who, in 1816, failed to understand or to comprehend the value of the precious book of *canntaireachd* brought for their inspection by John Campbell from Nether Lorn (see pp. 158–9). It was small wonder that their decisions were not always acceptable to the pipers, many of whom were highly professional. At the competition of 1824 one competitor,

---

* Members of the *Clann an Sgeulaiche* were among the prizewinners in almost every competition for the first thirty-five years.
† Competitors in succeeding competitions were eligible only for a higher prize than they had already won.

Kenneth MacRae, declined to accept a Highland powder-horn as a sort of extra second prize, because he himself felt that he should have been awarded the first prize, the coveted set of prize pipes.

Things came to a head at the third annual competition, held at the Falkirk Tryst in 1783. The competitors were so dissatisfied with the adjudications of the panel that they hived off and held their own competition in Edinburgh the following week. It was decided to form an Edinburgh Highland Society which would henceforth run the competitions in the capital city itself, though it consented to do so under the 'patronage' of the Highland Society of London. The new Society later became the Highland Society of Scotland; its concerns were broadened to include Scottish agriculture as well as Scottish music.*

The *pìobaireachd* competitions continued as an annual event in Edinburgh until 1826; after that they were held every third year. In 1844 the competitions lapsed, and there was a hiatus of some fifteen years. They were eventually revived at Inverness in 1859, being merged with the Northern Meeting, a major piping event which is still held yearly at Inverness.

Originally the piping competitions at Falkirk were strictly confined to the playing of *ceòl mór*, i.e. *pìobaireachd*; it was to preserve this that the Highland Society of London had been formed. This was fitting, for the ancient masters of piping, emanating from the MacCrimmons, had always disapproved of the playing of light music (*ceòl eutrom* or *ceòl beag*), and it was forbidden within their teaching establishments.[88] It seems to have been a prejudice shared by the chiefs and lairds regarding their own private pipers, for it is recounted that a laird of Coll, returning home unexpectedly and hearing his piper playing a piece of *ceòl beag* (light music), promptly dismissed the piper from his service.[89]

Joseph MacDonald, in his *Treatise on the Great Highland Bagpipe*, compiled in 1760, does mention that reels and jigs were 'played to good effect on the greater pipe'. He observes also that 'the smaller bagpipe, the same in form with the greater, is used for Dancing Music alone'.

Pipe tunes for marching – quicksteps as they were called in piping language – were unknown in the older repertoire, for the simple reason that there were no roads in the Highlands fit to march on. General Wade made the first roads during the second quarter of the eighteenth century, starting in 1726. In Wade's first report from Scotland on 10 December 1724 he compares the Highlands with the Cevennes in France and the 'Catalans' in Spain; 'The Highlands of Scotland are still more impracticable, from the want of Roads and Bridges'. In 1726 he writes of his road-

---

* This was the start of the present-day Royal Highland and Agricultural Society of Scotland which annually runs the great agricultural Highland Show. It can truthfully be said to have stemmed directly from the dissatisfaction of a group of pipers with the decision of the judges at a competition of piping at the Falkirk Tryst in the eighteenth century!

making plans, now in hand: 'Before midsummer next, there will be a good coach road [from Killichiumen]* to Fort William which before was not passable on horseback in many places.'⁹⁰ Wade's roads, however, were primarily for military purposes, and were likely for that reason to be avoided by the native Highlanders, particularly those with Jacobite propensities; for they would have had no desire to encounter the military before 'the hour had struck'. The typical Highlanders would certainly prefer to pick their way, as they had done from time immemorial, along the heather tracks and amid the rocks of their native straths and passes among the hills. As a means of beguiling the journey, *pìobaireachd* was the ideal music. The comparatively free rhythm of the *adagio* of the *pìobaire-achd* did not tempt the walkers to keep step, but allowed each man to pick his way as the uneven ground permitted, while at the same time enjoying the music. Joseph MacDonald calls *pìobaireachd* 'marches', but that these were not for marching in the modern military sense may be deduced from his remark that 'they are the slowest species of Pipe-Music'.

The pipe-march for marching in the modern sense was probably devised in the newly raised Highland regiments serving abroad, where there were proper roads to march on. Such roads called for the lilt of a tune in suitable tempo; and doubtless it was not long before the magic powers of the Scottish pipes to shorten the miles was realized.

To return to the subject of the piping competitions at Falkirk and Edinburgh: though these were, to begin with, strictly confined to *pìobaireachd*, Highland dancing as an extra entertainment in the form of an interlude was early introduced into the proceedings, between the more serious *pìobaireachd* items. Dalyell mentions it as early as 1783. The music for these dancing interludes was not provided by the competing pipers, who would have scorned the task, but by a band of 'ordinary musicians', fiddlers and bellows-pipers with the usual violon-cello for a bass.

From 1826 onwards, the playing on the pipes of reels and strathspeys seem to have been permitted as an extra item on the programme, but did not find a place in the actual competitions. In 1852 the Highland Society of Scotland attempted to introduce a competition for the playing of reels and strathspeys. The Society wrote a letter (still in existence) to their opposite and senior number, the Highland Society of London (whose 'patronage' they still acknowledged), suggesting such a competition.

The letter, an extract from which Archibald Campbell quotes in his *Ceòl Mór*, contains a frank admission; it is strikingly atavistic, but gives a vivid glimpse of the older piper's opinion. Such music was 'a branch of the art which the Highland piper viewed with feelings approaching to contempt . . . from a belief that the practice of it was incompatible with anything like perfection in the older and more important strains with which he is wont to salute his chief and his friends, or to summon his

* Wade's spelling: the correct Gaelic spelling is Cille Chumain.

countrymen to battle'. The letter goes on to say that in the opinion of
the Society 'this is an unfounded prejudice' and that, 'the occasional
practice of reel and strathspey musick does give an ease and freedom to
the fingering in Pibrochs'.[91]

The reply to the letter from the Highland Society of London is not on
record, but it was evidently unfavourable. Nevertheless it was an innovation that had to come sooner or later. It came after a lapse in the competitions for some years in 1844. At their revival at the Northern Meeting
of Inverness in 1859, prizes were given for reel and strathspey playing.
Marches were apparently included in the competitions at about the
same time.

An interesting sidelight on the competitions, and one which had more
impact on the general morale of the piper than one might think, concerns
the wearing of the tartan. The first competition, in 1781, was still within
the period of proscription; for the Disarming Act was not repealed until
one year later.* It seems unlikely that anyone would have dared directly
to flout the law in that year, or even in the years immediately following.
Dalyell says in two telling paragraphs:[92]

> We may question whether the musical competitors did not at first
> enter the lists in very homely attire; for the managers of the
> performance at Edinburgh in October 1783 apologise to the public
> for the deficiency of dress, as the competitors, having no prospect
> of appearing 'before so magnificent and great a company' had
> nothing in view on quitting their distant dwellings, but the
> competition at Falkirk, where their instruments alone were
> essential.
>
> The fact must have attracted attention, for among the premiums
> awarded in that year, namely in October 1783, were 'an elegant
> Highland dress, with silver epaulettes, double silver loops, buttons,
> and feathers in their new bonnets'.

The ancient glory had returned! From 1785 onwards, the competitors
were required to appear dressed in 'the Highland habit'; and it continued
so from henceforth.

## The pipers

We have seen how the long break of thirty years following the '45 was
bridged initially by the great masters of *pìobaireachd* who had survived
Culloden, and who were still alive at the end of this period, aged though
some of them were.

---

* The proclamation repealing the Act read: 'This is declaring to every man, young
and old, Commons and Gentles, that they may after this put on and wear the
Trews, the little Kilt, the Doublet and Hose, along with the Tartan Kilt,
without fear of the Law of the Land or the jealousy of enemies . . .'; quoted in
Prebble, *Culloden*, p. 330.

One name was missing from the lists of those appearing in the resurgence of the ancient art – the name of MacCrimmon. Iain Dubh MacCrimmon, still in the service of MacLeod of Dunvegan, was only fifty years of age in the year of the first competition. When Donald Ruadh, his brother, returned to Dunvegan from America in 1795 or thereabouts, he was only fifty-three. One can perhaps understand the feelings of the MacCrimmons: it would be against the dignity of their name to enter a competition against pipers nearly all of whose playing stemmed from their own teaching. If Donald Ruadh MacCrimmon had not so impetuously and bitterly declared that no child of his would henceforth touch the pipes, one could have looked for the younger MacCrimmons among the competitors. But such was not to be; the MacCrimmon story was nearing its end.

It is this that makes two competitors of more than ordinary interest; for the mantle of the MacCrimmons fell upon their shoulders and the future of Scottish piping depended on them. They were father and son, John MacKay and his son Angus, and they came from Raasay. John MacKay took the first prize at Edinburgh in 1792 when he was twenty-five. Young Angus won the fourth prize at the age of thirteen in 1826 – by which time his father was approximately fifty. Angus went on to win the first prize in 1838.

John MacKay had been a herd-boy in the service of Captain Malcolm MacLeod, 9th of Raasay, and he used to while away the hours of cattle-herding on the hillside by practising on his chanter. Malcolm MacLeod, who had held the rank of captain in the army of Prince Charles Stuart, was himself a keen piper and the composer of a fine *piobaireachd*, 'Prince Charles' Lament', composed to the Prince as a farewell on his escape to France. Overhearing the boy play, Malcolm MacLeod realized that his was no ordinary talent. He gave him lessons himself, and then sent him to the MacCrimmons; the young John MacKay studied with them for three terms of six months. It was about the year 1767, and he must have been one of the last pupils at the MacCrimmon College, then in the hands of Iain Dubh MacCrimmon, before it closed.

On the closing of the College, Captain MacLeod sent the boy to be taught by the son of the famous Iain Dall MacKay. Iain Dall had been the pupil and life-long friend of Patrick Og MacCrimmon (and his junior by only eleven years). He is said to have been the equal of Patrick Og both as a piper and a composer.

By a curious coincidence, Iain (Dall)* MacKay bore the same name as his son's pupil John MacKay, for Iain is the Gaelic form of John. Iain Dall's son was named Angus, and in due course the young John was to name his son Angus also, possibly after his teacher. There are therefore two John MacKays and two Angus MacKays, each pair being father and son. The Johns are easily to be distinguished from each other, for the elder

* '*Dall*' is Gaelic for 'blind'.

man is always known as Iain Dall from his blindness; but the two Angus MacKays are easily confused.

For the purposes of distinction, therefore, Ian Dall and his son Angus (and his grandson John Roy) are known as the MacKays of Gairloch, as they dwelt there in the capacity of pipers to the MacKenzies of Gairloch. The John MacKay and his son Angus whom we are now discussing are known as the MacKays of Raasay.* There is no known blood relationship between the families.

John MacKay of Raasay imbibed his knowledge of *pìobaireachd* both directly from the MacCrimmons at Boreraig in the person of Iain Dubh; and at one remove from the greatest of all teachers, Patrick Og MacCrimmon, through the son of Patrick's pupil and friend Iain Dall MacKay of Gairloch.

John MacKay of Raasay is said to have known about 250 *pìobaireachd*,[93] all of which he transmitted to his sons, of which Angus was the third. All the sons were pipers of merit.

Archibald Campbell of Kilberry says that 'present day *pìobaireachd* playing is derived from John MacKay, Raasay'.[94] Seumas MacNeill adds[95] that John MacKay of Raasay was looked upon as the greatest piper and authority on piping of his time, and that 'every first-class *pìobaireachd* player derives his knowledge of the MacCrimmon music through him'.

Angus MacKay, his son, was a noted teacher in his turn; but he is chiefly known for his writings about *pìobaireachd* and about the history of the hereditary pipers and *pìobaireachd* composers. Above everything, he is remembered for his noting of *pìobaireachd* in staff notation, from the *canntaireachd* transmitted to him by his father John.

## The third drone

The form of the bagpipe, as used up to and during the revival of piping after the long hiatus caused by the Disarming Act, probably included both the two-drone and three-drone pipes. It is difficult to establish when the third, the bass drone or 'great drone', came into use. Different writers suggest 1600,[96] 1700,[97] to 1800.†

We have a clue, if not a very precise one, in the Gaelic poem in dispraise of the pipes by Niall MacVurich, the last of the hereditary bards to

---

* Strictly speaking it is incorrect to use the term 'of Gairloch' of the piping MacKays. According to the strict rules of degree, 'of' followed by a place-name denotes that the holder possesses the title of laird or higher rank of the place named. In the case of the piping 'MacKays of Raasay' the appellation is one of convenience. A more correct form would be 'Angus MacKay, Gairloch'.

† Manson, *The Highland Bagpipe*, p. 52, says 'about the beginning of the nine-teenth century'. The entry on that page, however, follows the heading 'A.D. 1700' while another reference, on p. 72, gives 'about 1800'. One of the dates is obviously a slip – but which?

Clanranald.* The title is *Seanachas Sloinnidh na Pìoba bho thùs*. As has
been said earlier, the pipes were detested by the bards, as an instrument
which endangered their prestige and high position in the chief's household;
for their poems were customarily declaimed or sung to the accompaniment
of the harp, which the pipes eventually displaced (see pp. 131–2).

A version of Niall's poem is published in its original Gaelic in John
MacKenzie's *Sar Obair nam Bard Gaelach* (*The Beauties of Gaelic poetry*),
p. 67.

MacKenzie describes the '*Seanachas Sloinnidh*' as a satire occasioned
by Niall's encounter with two pipers, John and Donald MacArthur
(doubtless two of the MacArthur family who were pipers to the Mac-
Donalds of Sleat).

The following is a translation.†

The history of the pipe's pedigree from the beginning

1 An overblown pig's bladder, grunt, grunt! The [pipe's] first bag,
which was not sweet, came from the beginning of the Flood.

2 For a while it was made of a pig's bladder, blown up by every
cheek; afterwards it was made of an old wether's hide, harsh and
buzzing.

3 The bagpipe at that time had only a chanter and one opening,
and a piece of wood which would make the fundamental, which
was called the 'sumaire'.

4 A while after that, a crude invention was extended and three
poles grew on the bagpipe, one of them long, trailing and
unwieldy, with a harsh deep buzzing sound.

5 When the buzzing had been brought under control, and the reed
entirely, the contraption spread like that, squealing and grunting.

6 John MacArthur's screeching bagpipe is like a diseased heron,‡

---

* Niall MacVurich was a descendant of Lachlan Mór MacVurich, the composer of
the last *brosnachadh* or 'incitement to battle', declaimed to the clans before the
Battle of Harlaw (see pp. 19, 130–2).

† Dr J. L. Campbell of Canna has kindly translated this for me. He observes that
the poem contains a number of archaic Gaelic words, and that the existing
dictionaries and vocabularies are not sufficient to solve all the difficulties. Some
of these arise because the poem is the sole source for certain terms. He states
his translation to be tentative.

‡ It is perhaps not surprising that the seventeenth-century Scots Gaelic poet
should use the same image to disparage the sound of the bagpipes as did the
fifteenth-century Welshman, Glyn Cothe (see p. 75): the heron's cry is harsh
and unpleasant. *Reliquiae Celticae*, vol. 2, pp. 330 and 340 gives other derogatory
comparisons with the sound of the pipes as—'the crackling of geese': 'better
used as a rattle for scaring horses out of the hayfield than for inciting a host',
etc.

full of spittle, long limbed and noisy, with an infected chest like
that of a grey curlew.

7  Of the world's music Donald's pipe is a broken down outfit,
offensive to a multitude, sending forth its slaver through its rotten
bag; it was a most disgusting filthy deluge.

The bard apparently chronicles the fact that the bagpipe originally had
only one drone, but by the time he came to write the poem it had three:
the 'three poles', one the long bass drone. He makes no mention of the
extensive period during which the instrument had only two (tenor) drones.

The bard's encounter with the two pipers which occasioned the poem
is said by MacKenzie to have occurred when Niall returned to his father's
house from the College of Bards in Ireland. Presumably he had been sent
there for his bardic training, so he was still a young man. He is thought
to have been born about the 1630s,[98] which would date the satire about
mid-seventeenth century at the latest. It would seem to have been written
while the poet's father was still alive; he is said to have exclaimed, on
hearing the poem, 'Well done, my son, I see your errand to Ireland has
not been in vain.'

From the bard's definite use of the past tense in describing the development of the three drones, it would seem that this had taken place a fair
time before the poem was written. This would therefore date the advent
of the third drone, at the latest, at about 1640; or, if it came before the
poet's own day, before 1630.

We must, however, be wary because MacKenzie's statements in *Sar
Obair* are not unassailable; and the story of Niall's father praising the
poem is admittedly only a hearsay anecdote set down by MacKenzie.
It is therefore also possible that the poem was written in the poet's old
age, for Niall MacVurich is known to have been composing poems in his
eighties.* This would extend the possible date of the development of the
third drone to, let us say, the year 1700.

Whether or not we accept MacKenzie's assignment of Niall MacVurich's
poem to the period of the bard's youth (if we are to accept the poem
as evidence at all) there is a wide latitude of date for the third drone,
namely, almost any time from the early seventeenth to the early
eighteenth century. The probability of such other evidence as we have
does, however, seem to favour the early seventeenth century.

Whenever it was that the great drone was introduced, it was not met
with unanimous approval by the pipers. Iain Dubh MacCrimmon lived
until 1822, and a set of pipes in Dunvegan Castle said to have belonged
to him has only two drones. On the other hand there is a more ancient set,
also at Dunvegan, with the renowned chanter known as the *Pìob Bhreac*

---

* He composed a bardic elegy on his patron, Allan of Clanranald, who was killed
  at Sheriffmuir in 1715, when he himself must have been nearing the age of
  eighty-five.

(speckled pipe); it is said to have belonged to Patrick Mór MacCrimmon, who died in 1670, and it has three drones. One must add, however, that this set, at one point in its history, was reconditioned, and almost remade; it is said that only the tops of the original three drones survive, though the chanter is ancient.*

If the three drone tops are genuine, and if we accept the evidence of Iain Dubh's two-drone pipes of a later date, it would appear that both three-drone pipes and two-drone pipes were in use at the same time for a considerable number of years – indeed, for over a century and a half. Even after the third drone was introduced in the days of Patrick Mór in the seventeenth century, it must have been discarded by later pipers of the MacCrimmon family during the eighteenth and well into the nineteenth century.

The account books of the MacLeods of Dunvegan for 1711 show the item of '2 pypes bought to MacCrimmon, MacLeod's principal pyper'; for the year 1765 there is 'a pair of Highland pipes' bought from R. Robertson, turner, Edinburgh, for £2 10s 0d. The terms '2 pypes', and 'a pair of Highland pipes' have been taken by more than one writer to mean a two-drone bagpipe. While this is feasible, it can be accepted, at best, as conjecture; for one cannot rule out that 'a pair' may have become a stereotyped term for a set of bagpipes, irrespective of the number of drones. It could indeed have been used with equal propriety for a one-drone bagpipe, for the chanter and the drone could be held to constitute the pair, both being 'speaking' pipes.

It is useful to read what Joseph MacDonald has to say on the subject, writing in 1760:[99]

> Besides the smaller Drones of the Highland Bagpipe (two in number) there was, and still is, in use, with the Pipers in the North Highlands particularly, a Great Drone, double the Length and Thickness of the smaller, and in sound just an octave below them, which adds vastly to its grandeur, both in sound and show.
>
> This Drone may be properly termed the Bass Drone, and, in proportion to the simplicity of the instrument, has a good deal of the nature of a bass accompaniment, Insomuch that to Persons of true Taste, accustomed to it; the want of it makes a most capital Defect in the martial Strain of Pipe music.
>
> The reason given by the Pipers of the West Highlands for laying aside the use of the great Drone, was frivolous and unfounded, namely that the loudness of it drowned the sound of the Chanter music; But this is a mistake, and should it happen so, it is easily rectified by weakening the reed of the great Drone.'

* Seton Gordon, in the *Piping Times*, vol. 20, no. 9, quotes a letter from a correspondent who says that the drone tops were long in the possession of a Skye family of MacPhersons before they finally came into his possession; this correspondent helped to recondition the pipes, and sent them to Dunvegan Castle.

We can assume that by 'the Pipers of the West Highlands', MacDonald meant the pipers of the Isles, including Skye (and therefore, seemingly, the MacCrimmons); but it would be interesting to know who 'the Pipers in the North Highlands' were, to whom he refers as persisting in the innovation of the bass drone.

It is curious to find that after 1821 *two*-drone pipes were barred from the Highland Society's competitions, on the ground that 'they were thought for some reason to confer an unfair advantage on the competitor'.*

Both two-drone and three-drone pipes appear to have been present at Culloden. A set of three-drone pipes, said to have been played during the rising, is illustrated in Dalyell's *Memoirs*; he remarks that 'it could be heard at the distance of eight miles'.†

There are a number of examples and of contemporary pictures of the old two-drone pipes. There is a fine set at Blair Castle in Perthshire which visitors may see in the Castle museum. Another set is displayed at the Scottish Museum of Antiquities in Edinburgh. The eighteenth-century Edinburgh music publisher, Domenico Corri, published his *Musical Collection of Scots Airs* some time between 1780 and 1790; it has an illustration of a two-drone bagpipe, described as 'the Scotch bagpipe'. One of the prints of the Scottish artist George Cattermole, in his *Scotland Delineated* (1847), shows a piper in the Lawn Market in Edinburgh playing on a well-drawn set of two-drone pipes.‡

One unexpected contribution to the subject of the three-drone bagpipe actually comes from south of the Border. This is the sculpture of 'The Bagpipe Boy' (already referred to on p. 114) by Caius Gabriel Cibber (1630–1700). Cibber was born in Denmark and came to England during the Protectorate, or in the early years of the Restoration; in the reign of William of Orange he became Carver to the King's Closet. The bagpipe modelled in the statue has three drones, all of which have the bell-shaped ends typical of the English bagpipe of the seventeenth and eighteenth

---

* Sic – two-droned. Dalyell, *Musical Memoirs of Scotland*, p. 7. General Dalyell adjudicated at a number of the competitions.

† If Dalyell's observation is correct and the *pìob mhór* could be heard over a distance of eight miles, the chief of MacLeod at Dunvegan Castle must have been able to hear the pipes from the MacCrimmon's College of Piping at Boreraig at the outer end of Loch Dunvegan.

‡ The term 'two-drone pipes' generally means pipes with two tenor drones. A form of bagpipe which had one tenor and one bass drone seems to have been known, though it may not have belonged to the Scottish Highlands. Such an instrument is illustrated in a well-known drawing of Piper MacDonald, one of the leaders of the famous Mutiny of the Black Watch against being sent abroad (contrary to the terms of their enlistment) in 1743. If this was the only illustration of this instrument one might ascribe it to the inaccuracy of the artist, who was probably English (the mutiny took place in London). But there is another drawing, almost certainly of the same piper in a different pose, in which the details of the two drones are the same. The end of the bigger drone is uncharacteristic of the Scottish form, and has the trumpet-like bell-ending of

centuries; but as far as is known, the typical English bagpipe of the period possessed only two drones. If the pipes of the statue are representative, which seems doubtful, the date of the sculpture would place the introduction of the third drone in the English pipe some years before 1700. A photographic reproduction of Cibber's sculpture may be seen in Percy Scholes's *Oxford Companion to Music*.[100]

# The nineteenth century

## Staff notation

Since about the beginning of the nineteenth century, the Highland Society of London had been trying to encourage the writing down of *pìobaireachd*; for the music did not exist in any written form. It was still precariously dependent on its transmission by master to pupil, either by sung *canntaireachd* or by playing it on the chanter – just as it had always been since its beginnings in the seventeenth century or perhaps earlier.

It was therefore a noted landmark in Highland piping when at the competition of 1806 the Society voted a special prize or 'premium' to John MacDonald (son of Donald MacDonald, a well-known bagpipe maker in Edinburgh) for 'producing the greatest number of ancient pipe-tunes set to music [i.e. transcribed into staff notation] by himself'. In 1808 he received a further 'premium' for doing the same. In 1822 Donald MacDonald himself received five guineas for a similar task, and young John was again given two guineas for his work in the same field.

The year 1822 saw also the first publication of *pìobaireachd*, by this same Donald MacDonald: *The Ancient Martial Music of Caledonia Called Pìobaireachd*. It contained twenty-three *pìobaireachd* in staff notation. MacDonald says in his preface that, to accomplish the task, he

---

the English bagpipe. The smaller drone, obviously of tenor length in ratio to the other, is a slim pipe resembling the drone of the Northumbrian small-pipe. Altogether the details in the picture seem unlikely to be a true delineation of the Highland bagpipe of any period. It is possible that the details of the bagpipe may have been put in, possibly from an English bagpipe, after the portrait of the piper was completed. The drawings are reproduced respectively in C. A. Malcolm, *The Piper in Peace and War*, p. 94, and P. Hume Brown, *History of Scotland*, vol. 3, plate XI, p. 150.

A. Duncan Fraser, in *Some Reminiscences and the Bagpipe*, p. 398, asserts that 'there is plenty of proof that the large drone was used first on a two-drone bagpipe'; but he gives no reference, and his own extensive collection, housed in the Royal Scottish Museum in Edinburgh, contains no specimen.

The only examples of a two-drone 'Highland bagpipe' with one tenor and one bass drone which I have ever seen were some sets of pipes which were specially made for a film, *Bonnie Prince Charlie*. They were used again, and apparently played, in the television film *Culloden*. There seems to be no historical justification for them.

had 'sacrificed the leisure moments of the last fifteen years', which means that he had been at it since 1807.

His Preface contains an interesting paragraph; it gives a contemporary piper's judgment of the effect of the years of proscription upon the fortunes of the national instrument. It confirms the impression that the secrets of the piper's art at the beginning of the competitions lay largely in the hands of those who had been hereditary professional pipers thirty-five years before, when piping had been a highly honourable profession:

> It may be mentioned, that a considerable difficulty attended the recovery of many of the ancient tunes contained in the following pages. After the Battle of Culloden, a powerful check was given to the spirit of the Highlanders; and with their arms and garb, the Bagpipe was, for a long time, almost completely laid aside. In this interval much of the Music was neglected and lost. Afterwards, when the internal commotions of the country had completely subsided, and the slumbering spirit and prejudices of our countrymen awakened under the new order of things, the principal, nay only, records of our ancient *Piobaireachd*, were the memories of those Patriarchs who had proudly sounded them at the unfortunate 'Rising'. Many who attempted to take down the tunes from the directions of these Minstrels being ignorant of music, could only describe the sounds by words, which, though rewarded by the Highland Society, as evincing a laudable ambition for the preservation of those relics of our ancestors, it need not be said, would afford little satisfaction to those who wished to know the true character of these Airs. Indeed, so little idea seemed formerly to exist of the mystery of noting down the Pipe Music, that in a sort of College or Academy for instruction on the Great Highland Bag-pipe, existing not many years ago in the Island of Skye, 'the teachers made use of pins stuck into the ground instead of musical notes'.

A second volume by Donald MacDonald was prepared for publication, but it remains in manuscript, now in the National Library of Scotland. In his first volume he promised that,

> should he be encouraged in his first attempt, it is his utmost ambition not only to submit to the public the remainder, but to travel through the Highlands for the purpose of obtaining information of their history [i.e. of the *piobaireachd*]. . . . Almost all of them, unlike the silly occasions of Modern Airs, have had their origin in glorious achievements and romantic adventures, and if a second volume is called for, these interesting particulars will be communicated.

In his second volume, unpublished though it is, he is as good as his word, and gives nine pages of historical notes on the *piobaireachd* therein

full of blood-and-guts, drownings, piping fingers cruelly cut off, etc. As
with Angus MacKay, his notes are probably picturesque rather than
truly historical, but they make entertaining reading. Regretfully, he
does not include in his second volume any notes regarding the *pìobaireachd*
published in his first.

Donald MacDonald's and his son's attempts to write down *pìobaireachd*
on the music-stave were not the first. There is in existence a manuscript
transcription known as 'The MacArthur Manuscript', written about 1800,
containing thirty tunes in musical notation.[101] However, the notes are
not written at their proper pitch but are transposed down a fifth; thus
the lowest note of the chanter, G is written as middle C, and the top note
of the scale (A) written as D, a ninth above middle C.* A note inside the
cover of the manuscript states that twelve of the thirty tunes were
dictated by Angus MacArthur and written by John MacGregor. This is
probably the John MacGregor of the *Clann an Sgeulaiche* who became
piper to the Highland Society of London.

Angus Charles MacArthur followed his family tradition by becoming
piper to the MacDonalds, in the person of Sir Alexander MacDonald, later
Lord MacDonald of Sleat, who was severely castigated by Johnson and
Boswell for being so untypical of the Highland chief in his ways and
outlook.[102] Boswell observes, 'Sir Alexander's piper plays below stairs
both at breakfast and dinner, which is the only circumstance of a chief
to be found about him'.

Angus MacArthur went with Lord MacDonald to London about 1796,
where he lived until his death sometime early in the nineteenth century.
It must therefore have been in London that he dictated the 'MacArthur
Manuscript'. He was the last of the MacArthur hereditary pipers to the
MacDonalds of Sleat.

We also have the *pìobaireachd* manuscripts and published collections
of Angus MacKay of Raasay.[103] In 1838 (the same year that he won the
prize pipes) he published his celebrated book, *A Collection of Ancient
Pìobaireachd, or Highland Pipe Music*, containing sixty-one tunes. In his
preface, he apologizes for the long delay in the book's appearance, 'far
beyond the period when its completion was anticipated . . . the more to be
deplored inasmuch it has prevented him the distinguished honour of
dedicating the volume to His Late Majesty [William IV]'.

Perhaps the most interesting part of Angus MacKay's book is the
information he sets down on so many aspects of the subject of *pìobaireachd*
and pipers, their traditions and history – which, without his account,
would be largely unknown. Particularly interesting are his notes on the
history and traditions of the MacCrimmons; as we have seen, his father,

---

* This is the method used by the classical composers for the notation of the
'transposing instruments' of the orchestra, clarinets, trumpets and horns. It
may perhaps be taken as an indication that the Highland pipers were not
ignorant of other forms of music.

John MacKay of Raasay, had been among the last of their pupils at
Boreraig. Interesting too are his notes on the MacArthurs, pipers to the
Lords of the Isles; the Rankines, pipers to the MacLeans of Coll; the
Gairloch MacKays, among whom was his father's other teacher, Angus,
son of Iain Dall MacKay; the Campbells, pipers to the Campbells of
Mochaster; the MacIntyres, pipers to the Chiefs of Menzies, and possessors
of the famed 'Bannockburn Pipes'.

MacKay's 'Historical and Traditional Notes on the Pìobaireachds' at
the end of his *Collection of Ancient Pìobaireachd* contains much information
about the composers of the various *pìobaireachd* in the book, and the
supposed circumstances of their composition, although much of it is
traditional rather than accurately historical. We can assuredly say that
without Angus MacKay and Donald MacDonald the history and tradition
of *pìobaireachd* would be largely a lost subject – perhaps, without their
work it would be attributed to the fairies!

In all, Angus MacKay left 183 *pìobaireachd* in manuscript, in staff
notation. His notation of the *pìobaireachd* made his book the piper's bible
for many years to come. Campbell of Kilberry has said that 'the prestige
of Angus MacKay's book still stands higher than that of any other book
of pipe music'; and rightly adds 'Not a bad effort on the part of a youth
in his early twenties'.[104]

We must remember that the notation of *pìobaireachd* was still a totally
new skill. There was no one to teach it, and nothing to guide the young
musician but his own musical acumen and intelligence.

### The last MacCrimmons

We have said that the name of MacCrimmon was absent from the lists
of competitors at the Highland Society's *pìobaireachd* competitions.
These were, of course, strictly male events. 'Girl pipers' though they
certainly existed, were relegated to the background.

It was not unknown, however, for a member of the fair sex to enliven
the proceedings at the competitions with an exhibition of Highland
dancing. In 1799 Madame Frederick of the Theatre Royal, Edinburgh,
'dressed in an appropriate garb, danced Strathspeys, Jiggs, and other
dances, with her accustomed dexterity and effect'.[105]

The ban on girls competing was perhaps unfortunate for the
MacCrimmons. Iain Dubh's daughter Effie, one of his twelve children by
two marriages, is said to have been 'a proficient player on the pipes'.*

---

\* F. T. MacLeod, *The MacCrimmons of Skye*, p. 48. Effie was not the first of the
MacCrimmon daughters to play the pipes; according to Angus MacKay,
tradition has it that the daughters of one of the earlier MacCrimmons, possibly
Patrick Og, used to steal out to the *Uamh nan Calman* (Pigeon's Cave) near
the College of Piping. They would take with them the *binseach*, their father's
favourite set of pipes, and play a *pìobaireachd*. MacKay adds that they were
proficient enough to be able, in their father's absence, to take over the teaching.

Doubtless she had her father's style of playing, even if she had only picked it up by ear without being taught.

Though the two surviving brothers of the MacCrimmon pipers did not enter the competitions, they were probably interested in and knew about the success or otherwise of the competitors; for there were of course many of their own pupils amongst them. In 1808 the Highland Society of London suggested that a College of Piping be re-established at Fort Augustus, with Lieutenant Donald Ruadh MacCrimmon as its principal. For this, they urged upon the government that Donald Ruadh should be promoted to permanent rank on full pay, on the grounds that 'pipe-music was necessary for the Highland Regiments'.[106] Regrettably, nothing came of the proposal; and the failure of it unfortunately caused Donald Ruadh 'some mortification', as we shall see presently.

The two MacCrimmon brothers advanced gracefully and quietly into old age. In 1815 we find Donald Ruadh telling Alexander Campbell that his brother Iain Dubh was now, by reason of his old age, unable to perform. He would then be eighty-four. The Rev. Dr Norman MacLeod, *Caraid nan Gàidheal* (friend of the Gael), has left a description in Gaelic of Iain Dubh in his old age:[107]

> He died in 1822 at the age of 91 years. When owing to the infirmity of age, he could not play the Warpipe, he would sit in a sheltered spot, facing the sun but sheltered from the wind, with his stick in his hand, and playing upon it with his fingers; and with a sad *Crònan*,* he played thus the tunes he used to play in his young days.

Seton Gordon, in *The Charm of Skye*, confirms the picture of the old man with an account from his friend the Rev. Niall Ross of Glendale in Skye, whose grandmother knew Iain Dubh. She recounted that 'up to the last, when too frail to play, he used to sit by the fire and finger his stick as though it had been his beloved chanter'.

Of Donald Ruadh, Iain Dubh's younger brother, we have two equally vivid accounts. The first is by Alexander Campbell, who in 1815 (ten years before Donald Ruadh's death) was commissioned by the Highland Society of Scotland to collect the music of Gaelic Scotland.† Alexander Campbell was a trained musician, the organist at an Episcopal chapel in Edinburgh, and a native Gaelic speaker; he came from near Loch Lubnaig in Perthshire.

In the course of his tour he was entertained by Captain Neil MacLeod of Gesto (author of the lost book on the MacCrimmons) (see p. 143), at

---

* Here 'crònan' means 'crooning or humming'.

† His work was published in 1816–18 in Alexander Campbell's *Albyn's Anthology*. It included verses by Sir Walter Scott, translations of the Gaelic and original verses in English or Lowland Scots, to go with the tunes.

his home in Skye. From Gesto, Campbell obtained an introduction to Lieutenant Donald Ruadh MacCrimmon. Donald Ruadh had by then, at a date unknown, moved from the ancient MacCrimmon home at Boreraig, and was living on the mainland, at Glenelg, opposite Skye.

In October 1814 Campbell crossed over from Skye to the mainland for his visit. He has left an account of this, as of the rest of his tour, in a manuscript diary entitled 'A Slight Sketch of a Journey made through parts of the Highlands and Hebrides; undertaken to collect materials for *Albyn's Anthology*':

I made a hearty breakfast at the ferry house, the Skye side of the Kyle, after which I passed over and proceeded to Glenelg, now the property of Mr Bruce, on a farm belonging to whom I was to find Lieut. Donald MacCrimmon, the celebrated performer on the Great Highland Bagpipe, to whom I had letters of introduction from two of his principal friends, the sheriff of Uist and Captain MacLeod of Guesto [*sic*].

Lieut. MacCrimmon's present residence is Kirktoun, near Bernera Barracks, Glenelg. When I called, I found that he was at his farm in Glenbeg, a *long mile's* [Campbell's italics] distance from his present place of abode. I had little time to spare and, rather than await his homecoming, I set out to find him. On my coming to the spot, I found him leading-in his corn with the assistance of some neighbours of his own name, amongst whom he is a sort of Chieftain. He is upwards of 'three-score and ten'; rather thin, stoops a little – is about the middle size – has all the appearance of having been in his earlier years handsome; his countenance, tho' not very animated, is pleasing; and when he had the use of an eye the sight of which was lost in action, his features, one can easily imagine, must have occasionally assumed great animation.

We walked home together – on our way the conversation naturally turned to the subject of my present pursuits. Altho' conversible and polite, I did not find him very zealously inclined to enter, all at once, into my views; for, as I understood afterwards, he had but lately experienced disappointment and mortification in some projects of a similar nature to that which I have undertaken; consequently his enthusiasm has suffered a wound the recovery from which is very doubtful; which is to be much lamented indeed.

His family consists of his wife and daughter, with whom we dined. As I had come such a distance to hear him perform on his favourite instrument, and converse with him concerning the theory and practice of the Great Highland Bagpipe, he sent for Alexander Bruce, Piper of Glenelg, a favourite pupil of his own, who played several pieces in a stile of excellence that, while it excited applause, reflected much credit on his able Preceptor, who encouraged him occasionally with approbation. After a few glasses of his own toddy, MacCrummin seized the pipe, *put on his hat* (his usual custom),* breathed into the bag, tuned the drones to the chanter, gave a prelude in a stile of brilliancy that flashed like lightning, and commenced '*Failte Phrionnsah*'† in tones that spoke to the ear and affected the heart. Thro' the whole of this fine salute, he showed a masterly command of the instrument, and the manner in which he moves his fingers seems peculiar to himself; the effects he produces by this means are admirable – there is not a sound lost – not the quickest appogiatura, how rapid soever the movement or the variation – and the regular return to the subject or theme of the piece is in fine contrast with the more intricate passages. Are the talents of MacCrimmon doomed to decay in solitude? This veteran, in a *double sense*, is the seventh in succession of the MacCrummons [*sic*] of Skye – his brother John‡ is older than he – but is now, by reason of his great age, unable to perform.

After taking leave of MacCrimmon and his family, I retired to my quarters in the public-house at the end of the village. Alexander Bruce,§ the Piper of Glenelg, came along with me, and over a glass he communicated to me many interesting particulars regarding the mode of training pipers by his celebrated Preceptor which I have taken notes of and may hereafter prove useful.¶ Sandy Bruce and I parted about midnight after which I lay down to enjoy a few hours sleep.

The 'disappointment and mortification' to which Campbell refers was doubtless due to the failure of the Highland Society's proposal to appoint Lieutenant Donald Ruadh as principal of a new College of Piping to be established at Fort Augustus.

A week or two before his meeting with Donald Ruadh in September, Alexander Campbell had transcribed two *pìobaireachd*, '*Cruinneach nan Griogarach*' ('The MacGregor's Gathering'), and '*Pìobaireachd Dhomhnuill*

---

* It is a curious fact that the Highland piper formally put on his bonnet to play, but the *sgeulaiche* or reciter of folktales formally took off his bonnet before reciting the great heroic ballads of Ossian or Cú Chulainn. The first probably originated as an assertion of the piper's proud position in the hierarchy of the chief's household. The second was a tribute to the ancient mythical Celtic heroes. See Collinson, *The Traditional and National Music of Scotland*, p. 49.

† I.e. 'The Prince's Salute'. Angus MacKay in his unpublished manuscript, now in the National Library of Scotland, says that it was composed by John MacIntyre, Rannoch, in 1715. The prince in question would be James III and VIII, the 'Old Pretender'.

‡ I.e. Iain Dubh MacCrimmon.

§ Alexander Bruce's brother became piper to Sir Walter Scott, who describes him as 'John of Skye'. See J. G. Lockhart, *Memoirs of the Life of Sir Walter Scott*, vol. 4, p. 189.

¶ Unfortunately these have not survived.

*Duibh'* ('Black Donald's March to the Isles'). *Mac Dhomhnuill Duibh* is the Gaelic patronymic of Cameron of Lochiel.*

It has been mistakenly averred by one writer that Alexander Campbell took down the *Pìobaireachd Dhomhnuill Duibh* directly from the playing of Iain Dubh MacCrimmon. In *Albyn's Anthology*, however, Campbell states specifically of the two *pìobaireachd*:[108]

> The melody to which the above verses is adapted [i.e. 'The MacGregors' Gathering'] was taken down, with all possible care, from Captain Neil McLeod of Guesto's [*sic*] MS Collection of Pibrochs, as performed by the celebrated MacCrimmons of Skye; the melody to *Pibroch of Donuil Duibh* was taken down at the same time, i.e. September 1815 – the process was tedious and exceedingly troublesome. The Editor had to translate, as it were, the syllabic jargon of illiterate pipers (which was distinctively enough joted [*sic*] down in Captain McLeod's own way) into musical characters, which, when correctly done, he found to his astonishment to coincide exactly with regular notation!

It should be added that wherever Campbell noted down songs or tunes on his tour, he got the local Justice of the Peace or some other trustworthy person to certify that he had noted the song in his presence from the singer named, as a precaution against any possible charge of imposture. At Gesto this service was performed for him by Captain MacLeod himself; and in Campbell's manuscript of the *pìobaireachd* there is a note on the first page of the music in Gesto's handwriting which reads:

> *Pìoberach Dhomnuill Duibh* or Cameron's Gathering
> Gesto, Sky [*sic*] 29 Septr. 1815.
> On the following ten pages is a genuine sett of the Camerons Gathering in sylables [*sic*] as taught by the MacCrimmons of Sky to their Pupils as nearly as I could possibly write it from MacCrimmon's repeating it, and first noted by Miss Jean Campbell at Gesto and now copied and noted down more scientifically in my presence by Alexr Campbell of Albyn's Anthology.
> 
> Niel MacLeod, J.P., Capt. ½ Pay.

Captain MacLeod of Gesto's manuscript of *pìobaireachd* in *canntaireachd* was later published at Edinburgh under a long title commencing *A Collection of twenty Pìobaireachd or pipe tunes as verbally taught by the McCrummen Pipers in the Isle of Skye to their apprentices. Taken from John McCrummen, Piper to the Old Laird of MacLeod . . .*[109]

Gesto says that the *pìobaireachd* were 'taken' from Iain Dubh; but this certainly does not mean that he noted the tunes from Iain Dubh's playing of them on the bagpipe, or even piecemeal on the practice-chanter. It is much more likely that Iain Dubh would have sung them to Gesto in

* Gesto gives the *pìobaireachd* the title of 'Cameron's Gathering'; see pp. 139–40.

*canntaireachd*, the form in which Gesto wrote them down. Even in this there has been some doubt among piping authorities. The Rev. Alexander MacGregor, 'Alasdair Ruadh' who was a recognized authority on pipe-music of the mid-nineteenth century, and himself an excellent piper, says in a letter that Gesto 'was crazy about *pìobaireachd*, but did not play himself'.

From this, William MacLean* observes,[110]

> Here then, one should think, is clear proof that Captain MacLeod did not write the tunes, as some have maintained, from the chanting of MacCrimmon. There is really no question that it is beyond the capability of anyone not thoroughly versed in the intricacies of *pìobaireachd* and himself not a piper, to record the *canntaireachd* accurately. Gesto, as he himself stated, 'took' the tunes from John MacCrimmon, and they are undoubtedly extracts from the MSS of these celebrated composers. . . .

It should be added that neither of the two *pìobaireachd* transcribed by Alexander Campbell is among the twenty published by Gesto. The Rev. Alexander MacGregor estimates, in his letter, that Gesto's manuscript would contain 'upward of two hundred *pìobaireachds* from the bulk of it'.

The other account of Lieutenant Donald Ruadh in his old age is of a meeting with him by Sir Walter Scott when, in 1814, Scott was invited to join a voyage round Scotland of the 'Commissioners of the Northern Lights'.† Scott writes, in his diary of the voyage[111] (after having witnessed a 'waulking of the cloth' near Dunvegan):

> Return to the castle, take our luncheon, and go aboard at three – MacLeod accompanying us in proper style with his piper. We take leave of the castle, where we have been so kindly entertained, with a salute of seven guns. The chief returns ashore, with his piper playing 'the MacLeod's gathering', heard to advantage along the calm and placid loch, and dying as it retreated from us. . . .
>
> MacLeod's hereditary piper is called MacCrimmon, but the present holder of the office has risen above his profession.‡ He is an old

---

* I copied this letter from a typewritten copy in the possession of Pipe-major William MacLean, Kilcreggan. For the full text, see Collinson, *The Traditional and National Music of Scotland*, p. 193.

† Now the Lighthouse Commissioners.

‡ Sir Walter Scott remarked that Donald Ruadh MacCrimmon, the last of a long hereditary line of musicians and composers whose members had been almost princes in their own sphere for over three hundred years, had 'risen above his profession' by becoming a junior army officer; this is a comment on the social values of the period. The observant Captain Burt says, in *Letters from a Gentleman in the North of Scotland* (1754), letter 21, p. 143, that in the years before the '45 the piper to the chief was a figure of importance in the Highland hierarchy, with his own gillie to carry the proud instrument of his profession – in Burt's own words, 'A gentleman'.

man, a lieutenant in the army, and a most capital piper, possessing about 200 tunes and pibrochs, most of which will probably die with him, as he declines to have any of his sons instructed in his art. He plays to MacLeod and his lady, but only in the same room, and maintains his minstrel privilege by putting on his bonnet so soon as he begins to play.

These MacCrimmons formerly kept a college in Skye for teaching the pipe-music. Macleod's present piper is of the name, but scarcely as yet a deacon of his craft.* He played every day at dinner.

It is interesting to find confirmation in Scott's account of the ancient custom of the piper putting on his bonnet to play, as Alexander Campbell had noted of Donald Ruadh. A further example of this is to be found in Lockhart's *Memoirs of the Life of Sir Walter Scott*.[112] Lockhart is describing his first visit to Abbotsford, in October 1818:

When the cloth was drawn, and the never-failing salver of *quaighs* introduced, John of Skye, upon some well-known signal, entered the room, but *en militaire*, without removing his bonnet, and taking his station behind the landlord, received from his hand the largest of the Celtic bickers brimful of Glenlivet. The man saluted the company in his own dialect, tipped off the contents (probably a quarter of an English pint of raw *aqua vitae*) at a gulp, wheeled about as solemnly as if the whole ceremony had been a movement on parade, and forthwith recommenced his pibrochs and gatherings, which continued until long after the ladies had left the table, and the autumnal moon was streaming in upon us so brightly as to dim the candles.

## Pipers abroad

Some of the best players were often absent from the Highland Society's *pìobaireachd* competitions, because they were on service abroad with the Highland regiments. This state of things was remarked on by Sir John Sinclair, the president, or *preses*, of the judges, in his opening speech at the competition in 1813.[113]

Although they were not present to show their piping prowess at the competitions, they were painting a more enduring picture of the Highland piper of the regiment on active service – that of the piper's outstanding bravery in battle. This had been shown many times before in Scotland's history, at Philiphaugh, at Bothwell Bridge and the other places we have already chronicled. Already it had been manifested many times since the early years of the formation of the Highland regiments: in Canada; in what

* He is stated to have been Donald MacCrimmon, a grandson of Patrick Og; see 'Notices of pipers', *Piping Times*, vol. 22, no. 10 (July 1970).

was later to become the USA; and throughout the years of the struggle for British supremacy in India.

The theme of the bravery of the Scottish piper in battle (and we must now say Scottish rather than Highland, for the theme embraces the Lowland regiments also) is so recurrent that a chronicle of all such incidents would be impossibly repetitive.

Let us therefore take one example as typical. It is the story of a piper at the battle of Quatre Bras, Kenneth MacKay of the 19th Cameron Highlanders.

The Highlanders had 'formed square' to withstand a cavalry charge from the French. The approach of charging cavalry must always have been in war a supreme moment of test for footsoldiers. There was nothing to stop the thundering horses and their riders, with lances couched or swords slashing, but the resolute holding of their own thin fence of fixed bayonets; and nerves must have been taut.

At the critical moment, Piper Kenneth MacKay stepped *outside the shelter of the square of bayonets*, and, in full view of the approaching cavalry at the charge, started to play the ancient battle *pìobaireachd* of '*Cogadh no sith*' ('War or Peace, The Gathering of the Clans').[114]

Commencing as most *pìobaireachd* do with the slow calm *adagio* strains of the *ùrlar*, this breath-taking act of bravery brings us nearly full-cycle in our saga of the pipes; for it calls to mind the calm music of the Spartan pipers as described by Thucydides in an earlier chapter.

MacKay came through unscathed, and the whole country thrilled to the incident. The king, George III, expressed the nation's feelings by presenting to him a new silver-mounted set of pipes. After Waterloo, during the meetings of international rulers and diplomats in Paris, the Czar of Russia heard the story; he expressed a wish to hear the *pìobaireachd*, and Kenneth MacKay was asked by the British ambassador to play it for him.

In the best tradition of bagpipe stories it was laconically reported that 'the Czar did not ask for an encore'!

The courage of Piper Kenneth MacKay in the face of the enemy has been repeated many times – one could almost say countless times – in Britain's battles since Waterloo. During World War II the sound of the pipes on the battlefields was brought to us over the radio, the first time in the history of war that such a thing had happened. Who, among those who heard it, will forget the thrill of the sound of the bagpipes at the fall of Tripoli on 23 January 1943? Pages were written of that moment in the newspapers. Let us content ourselves with three brief sentences by a historian and war leader sprung from the aristocracy of England, 'the auld enemy'. The writer is Sir Winston Churchill:[115]

> I spent two days at Tripoli, and witnessed the magnificent entry
> of the Eighth Army through its stately streets. At their head were

the pipers of the 51st Highland Division. Spick and span they looked after all their marching and fighting.

## The present

We are nearing the end of our saga. The piping MacCrimmons have gone, but their music and their ways of playing it have come down to us through their pupils. From Iain Dubh, the teaching descends through Angus MacKay of Raasay and John Bain MacKenzie, both pupils of Iain Dubh. To this stream of piping the MacKays of Gairloch brought the heritage of the greatest of all teachers of *pìobaireachd*, Patrick Og MacCrimmon. It is easy to trace the descent of teaching downwards from Angus MacKay and John Bain MacKenzie to the present day.

From the other brother, Donald Ruadh MacCrimmon, there is another line of descent through his pupils the Bruces. It embraces four generations of piping MacPhersons, including *Calum Pìobaire* (Malcolm MacPherson, Badenoch) and his son Angus MacPherson. The two streams seem to have possessed their individual characteristics of interpretation; but there has been some intermixing, notably in the playing of the late John Mac-Donald, Inverness, who studied with representatives of both. He was much sought after as a teacher; to have studied with him was regarded as a piper's accolade.

Up to very recent times, there has been no way for the non-piping musician to study this great Scots music except by listening to performances, preferably at the annual piping competitions at Oban, Inverness and elsewhere. The published versions of *pìobaireachd* in staff-notation are not much help, for they only approximate to what the piper actually plays. Seumas MacNeill,[116] discussing the dangers of a growing tendency among young players of *ceòl mór* to rely too much on the printed score, remarks that 'a listener to *pìobaireachd* may well miss much of the greatness of a tune if it is played as written'.

Perhaps it is for these reasons that there has been so little knowledge of this great national heritage among the musicians and composers of the ordinary world of music even in Scotland, sometimes amounting to an ignorance of the very meaning of the word *pìobaireachd* (or 'pibroch').*

* It is with some pride that I claim that my father, the late Dr T. H. Collinson, organist for fifty years of St Mary's Episcopal Cathedral in Edinburgh, was one of the exceptions. On occasions of national importance, such as memorial services to deceased royalty or to great figures of state, he used to engage the pipe-major stationed at Edinburgh Castle to play a complete *pìobaireachd* towards the end of the service. He would get the piper, as he played, to walk slowly in 'the stately step of the piper', from the chapter-house at the far end of the Cathedral up the choir aisle to the chancel, halt there for a moment or two and then walk as slowly back again, giving the effect of a gradual approach and a slow receding into the distance. The majesty of a *pìobaireachd* played in a cathedral has to be heard to be believed. It is from these occasions that the sound of *pìobaireachd* is among my earliest memories.

This situation has been completely transformed by the advent of tape recording and the long-playing record, both of which can reproduce the longest *pìobaireachd* in its entirety. I myself can claim to be one of the first to record *pìobaireachd* by tape-recorder. During the early 1950s I recorded some fifty *pìobaireachd* from the playing of a master, the late William MacLean, Kilcreggan, one-time pipe-major of the 8th Cameron Highlanders.* William MacLean through his teacher *Calum Pìobaire* was, we might say, a 'great-great-grand-pupil' of Donald Ruadh MacCrimmon; and through him, by two further steps, of Patrick Og. To record his playing, over a period of months, with all his comments and memories, was a transcending experience.

During the past few decades the Scottish Highland bagpipe and its music has enjoyed a remarkable resurgence. Once again there is a College of Piping for the teaching of *pìobaireachd*, as well as of the lighter music, *ceòl beag*, now no longer viewed by the Highland piper 'with feelings approaching to contempt' (see p. 182).

The new College is not in Skye, but in Glasgow, where so many Highlanders have made their home. A few years ago the late owner of the lands of Boreraig, Mr Ian Martin, granted the site of the old College of the MacCrimmons in Skye to the new College of Piping. It is now only an oblong depression in the turf of the hillside, some little way up from the shore of Loch Dunvegan. The annual feu-duty, it is said, is a penny and a *pìobaireachd*!

In 1967 Dame Flora, Chief of MacLeod, instituted at Dunvegan Castle an annual competition in the playing of *pìobaireachd*, under the title the MacCrimmon Memorial *Pìobaireachd* Competition. It is open only to the winners of the highest piping awards elsewhere. The entrants compete for the trophy of a beautiful silver chanter.

So, by a remarkable coincidence, our saga of the pipes opens and closes, across the space of nearly five thousand years, with a silver chanter. The first of these, the little silver pipes of Ur, the earliest known examples of the ancient divergent pipes, with their two-part music of whatever sort it may have been, spread over the whole ancient world as the *aulos* and the *tibia* and a host of earlier names. They penetrated our own island with the Roman armies up to and into the ancient territory of Caledonia, as far north as the Firth of Forth and possibly further. Then they receded like the outgoing tide; and except for a few sparsely spread examples of two-chanter bagpipes such as the *zampogna* in Italy, they have disappeared.

The silver chanter of Dunvegan typifies the surviving species, the bagpipe with the single two-handed chanter and the unvarying drone, that we have been discussing in the latter part of our story.

---

* These recordings are in the archives of the School of Scottish Studies, University of Edinburgh. Copies of them are in use at the Army School of Piping at Edinburgh Castle, in the care of Captain John MacLellan, whose use of them ensures that the MacCrimmon style and tradition of playing continues.

Of our native variety of this last species, it has been said by a very knowledgeable writer on the subject that 'Today, there is no inhabited continent where the Scottish Highland bagpipe is not played.'[117]

The world has known the sound of the pipes in one form or another for nearly five thousand years, according to archaeological dating. It is small wonder that their sound seems to possess something elemental. Is it too fantastic to imagine that, by very reason of this elementality, the world may still be hearing their sound at the end of the next five thousand years?

# Materials

Throughout the long history of the reed-sounded pipes or chanters, and of the various substances of which they have been constructed down the centuries, one material has been curiously constant: the water-reed, *Arundo donax*.

In the earlier history of the reed-pipe, both the pipe and its sounding reed were fashioned in one piece, from the same reed or cane of this or similar water-reed. The water-reed went out of use for the making of the pipe itself in the late classical and early Roman periods, but it is still used to make the reed.

In the pipe made in one piece from the water-reed, the sounding member was the single reed, which consisted of a tongue cut in the cane towards a node or knot.* At a later stage, the reed came to be a separate component, sometimes made of cane and sometimes of straw; but the pipe itself was still likely to be made of water-reed of the *Arundo donax* or similar species or, sometimes, of wood. The ancient Egyptian pipes in the Cairo Museum are listed as *'souvent en roseau* [reed] *ou en bois'*.[1] The dainty little twin chanters that belonged to the Lady Maket of ancient Egypt, about 1580–1160 B.C., which were found enclosed within their case, are of water-reeds, probably of the *Arundo donax* variety.

The earlier types of the Greek *aulos* were almost certainly made of *Arundo donax*, as were the sounding reeds of the instrument. The *aulos* is generally thought to have had a double (oboe-type) reed, though organologists are not unanimous about this.

As early as the fourth century B.C. we find a Greek writer treating the subject of musical reeds and how to make them. This is Theophrastus, who describes in his *Enquiry into the History of Plants* the growing and cutting of the reed *Kalamos zeugites*† for *aulos* reeds:[2]

---

* A good example of such a pipe, with only two fingerholes, from Cyprus is in the Pitt Rivers Museum at Oxford.

† '*Kalamos*' means simply 'reed' in the general sense; '*zeugites*' refers to the tongue of the musical reed cut from it (see *zeugos*, p. 23). '*Kalamos zeugites*' may be rendered as the species of water-reed used for making musical reeds for pipes. It can also mean the pipe itself when it is made of the plant also, as were the early Greek *auloi*.

Of the Reed, there are said to be two kinds, the one used for
making pipes and the other kind . . . One species of 'the other kind'
was used for arrows and javelins. Others do not seem to have been
of any practical use . . .

As to the reed used for [musical] pipes . . . it grows in general
whenever the lake is full . . . for they say, apparently with good
reason, that when the lake is deep, the reed increases in height,
and persisting for the next year, matures its growth; and that the
reed which thus matures is suitable for making a reed mouthpiece
. . . while that for which the water has not remained, is suitable for
making a 'cap' . . . In one kind of pipe, the performer blew, not
directly on to the reed, but into a cap in which it was enclosed;
this cap, from the resemblance in shape to a cocoon, was called
*Bombyx* . . . Such then, it is said, is the reed's way of growth.

Also it is said to differ from other reeds, to speak generally, in a
certain luxuriance of growth, being of a fuller and more fleshy
character, and, one may say, 'female' in appearance. For it is said
that even the leaf is broader and whiter, though the plume is
smaller than that of other reeds; and some have no plume at all.
These they call 'eunuch-reeds'. From these they say that the best
mouthpieces are made (though many are spoiled in the making).

From the time of Antigenidas, before which men played the pipe
in the simple style, they say that the proper season for cutting the
reeds was the month of *Boedromion* [September] about the rising of
Arcturus; for although the reed so cut did not become fit for use
for many years after and needed a great deal of preliminary playing
upon, yet the opening of the reed tongues is well closed,* which is
a good thing for the purpose of accompaniment. But when a change
was made to the more elaborate style of playing, the time of
cutting the reeds was also altered; for in their own time they cut
them in the months *Skirrophorion* [July] about the solstice or a
little earlier. And they say that the reed needs but little preliminary
playing upon, and that the reed-tongues have ample vibration,
which is essential for those who play in the elaborate style. Such,
they tell us, are the proper seasons for cutting the reed mouthpiece.

The manufacture is carried out in the following manner. Having
collected the reed stems, they lay them in the open air during the
winter, leaving on the rind; in the spring they strip this off, and,
having rubbed the reeds thoroughly, put them in the sun. Later on,

* I.e. between the free end of the vibrating 'tongue' and the body or 'lay' of the
reed mouthpiece; the instrument implied throughout is apparently one with a
single vibrating 'tongue' (reed) like a modern clarinet (translator's note). This
does not accord with much modern opinion, which favours the theory that the
*aulos* was sounded by a double reed; see Curt Sachs, *The History of Musical
Instruments*, p. 138; also Anthony Baines, *Woodwind Instruments and their
History*, p. 195.

in the summer, they cut the sections from knot to knot into
lengths, and again put them for some time in the open air. They
leave the upper knot on this intermediate section;* and the lengths
thus obtained are not less than two palms-breadths long.

Now they say that for making mouthpieces, the best lengths are
those of the middle of the reed, whereas the lengths towards the
upper growths make very soft mouthpieces and those next to the
root very hard ones. They say too that the reed-tongues made out
of the same length are of the same quality, while those made from
different lengths are not; also that the one from the length next to
the root forms a left-hand reed-tongue, and that made from the
length towards the upper growths, a right-hand reed-tongue.†
Moreover, when the length is slit, the opening of the reed-tongues
in either case is made towards the point at which the reed was
cut,‡ and, if the reed-tongues are made in any other manner, they
are not of the same quality. Such then, is the method of
manufacture.

Theophrastus next follows with a description of where the best reeds
are to be got, and in what types of soil, which we need not set down here.
The extract concludes, 'Let this suffice for an account of the growth and
character of the reed used for pipes, of the manufacture, and of its
distinctive features as compared with other reeds.' There is little doubt
that the reed of which Theophrastus wrote in c. 450 B.C. was *Arundo donax*.

*Arundo donax* is still in use for the reeds of the Scottish Highland
bagpipe, though doubtless in the earlier history of the Scottish instrument
reeds would have been made of local material. *Arundo donax* is said to
have first come to Scotland as stowage material (dunnage) for ships'
cargoes. It seems to have been through its arrival in this form that it first
came to the notice of the Scottish piper, who found it to be the ideal
material for his pipe reeds. Nowadays growing and processing *Arundo
donax* for Scottish bagpipe and other instrumental reeds has become an
industry in Spain, France and Italy.

In course of time the Greek *aulos* came to be made of other materials,
some of which were a good deal more costly than the simple river reed.
The two ancient divergent pipes known as the 'Elgin *aulos*' found in a
tomb near Athens in the fifth century, and now in the British Museum,
are of sycamore – a wood much used today in Britain for making recorders.
In other ways also the *aulos* became a more sophisticated instrument in
ancient Greece, such as in the use of movable rings for the fingerholes
(see p. 34).

* So as to make a closed end (translator's note).
† I.e. the vibrating 'tongues' for the left-hand and the right-hand pipe of the
  double-pipe, respectively (translator's note).
‡ I.e. not at the closed end, but at the end which was 'lower' when the cane was
  growing (translator's note).

To move forward by a few centuries, four *auloi* (or perhaps they should now be called by their later Latin name of *tibia*), were discovered in the ashes of Pompeii in 1867. These consist of inner tubes of ivory, encased in a metal thought by some to be silver,[3] but more generally stated to be bronze. Movable rings cover the finger-holes. These are on view in the Museo Nazionale at Naples. The Latin poet Horace, writing in his own time of the pipes of a former age, says that the chanter was 'not *as now* (my italics) bound with brass . . . but being small and plain, was useful to blow with its few holes to assist the chorus'.[4] Virgil, too, writes of the Tuscan having 'blown his ivory pipe' (*Georgics*, book II, line 192).

In an article in 1915, T. Lea Southgate[5] describes fragments of chanters of ivory and bronze found at Meroe in Egypt, and advances the fascinating theory that these originally may have belonged to a Greek virtuoso, who brought 'his own improved and esteemed instruments for performance at Meroe'; for, he says, they are not likely to have been made locally.

Such sets of chanters were extremely valuable. The Latin writer Lucian tells us that Ismenias of Thebes gave for a chanter made in Corinth a sum computed as at least £5,000 of our currency.[6] It is said that the best pipes were made at Corinth. Socrates observes that 'the best piper ought to be given the best pipes'.[7]

From ivory and metal we come to the more familiar material of wood for the making of musical pipes, of which the Elgin *aulos* mentioned above is a notable example.

Athenaeus, a Greek writer who flourished about 200 B.C. (about fifty years before Greece became a Roman province), says that the wood of the lotus thorn was used as the material for the pipes. Sir James Frazer, in his notes to the *Fasti* of Ovid, confirms the use of this wood for the large Berecynthian pipes (the 'mad pipes').* Athenaeus also quotes Virgil as writing of 'Berecynthian boxwood', in the sense of pipes made of that wood. Indeed the term 'boxwood' seems to have been used in Rome as a synonym for the pipes themselves.

Pliny the Elder (A.D. 25–79) writes at some length in his *Natural History* on the subject of river-reeds as material for both chanters and their playing reeds, though he writes in an antiquarian sense. He perished in the eruption of Vesuvius at Pompeii in A.D. 79; and as we have seen, the pipes in use at Pompeii at the time of the disaster were much more sophisticated instruments than the ancient simple tubes of river-reed.[8]

Pliny treats the subject very much in the same way as Theophrastus, whom indeed he paraphrases (without acknowledgment of his source); and it would add little to what we already read in Theophrastus to quote him at length, but the following extract is interesting:[9]

*Flute reeds: the reed of Orchomenus.*
The varieties of the reed are numerous . . . One kind of reed is

* *Furiosa tibia.* See *New Oxford History of Music*, vol. 1.

quite hollow; it is known as the syringia,* and is particularly
useful for making flutes [i.e. pipes], having neither pith in it nor
any fleshy substance.

The reed of Orchomenus has a passage in it open from one end
to the other, and is known as the *auleticon*.† This last is best for
making pipes.

He concludes with an interesting observation of his own on the use of
other materials: 'At the present time [i.e. *c*. A.D. 50] the sacrificial pipes
used by the Tuscans are made of boxwood, while those employed at the
games are made of the lotus, the bones of the ass, or else silver.'

To step forward a couple of thousand years, it may be of interest to
add the following note to me from Alexander MacAuley written in 1974:

> My grandfather who was a South Uist piper showed me a boggy
> loch, in South Uist, Lochan Skereich, where he collected the cane
> for making his reeds; but he said that it had to be a long dry
> summer before his reeds would be successful, otherwise the reed
> would not ripen. This reed that still grows in the Hebrides grows
> to a height of 4–5 feet. It also grows in the peat bogs of Ireland.
> Practice-chanter reeds that had a good tone were made in my
> boyhood; these reeds were made from the stalk of the barley – the
> lower part of the stalk above ground where it was thicker and
> stronger.

We now come to look at the Roman pipes brought over with the
invading legions to Britain – or at least (important reservation) to the
*southern half* of Britain.

There are very few specimens of Roman pipes surviving in Britain
from the Roman occupation. Such as there are may be seen at the
Guildhall Museum, London; at the London Museum,[10] and at the Castle
Museum, Norwich. Most are of bone, but one pipe of wood, with the
fingerholes still intact, is in the Guildhall Museum.

In the museum at Chesters, one of the Roman stations on Hadrian's
Wall, there is displayed a short piece of wood listed as the fragment of a
Roman 'flute' (the mistranslation persists even among the accredited
authorities!). It is about four inches long, with a cylindrical bore, hollowed
out through its length, and has two seeming 'fingerholes' in the side.
It seems to be a piece of musical pipe. The piece is, however, neatly sawn
off – not broken off – at either end. Also, the sides of the 'fingerholes' are
sharp – as sharp as the day they were bored. There is no sign of wear at
the edges, which one often sees in old chanters.

Within the past few years a number of similar pieces have been found
at Roman stations in central Europe – all sawn off, and all with the same

---

* I.e. the *Arundo donax* of Linnaeus (translator's note).
† Or pipe-reed (translator's note).

two holes bored in the side. Obviously no one in his senses would go round Roman Europe sawing musical chanters into four-inch lengths. There must be another explanation.

It has been suggested that they were parts of hinges, for use on such articles as the lids of chests, or the doors of cupboards. The 'fingerholes' would have been in fact holes for wooden pegs, for fastening the pieces of tube to one or other of the two leaves so hinged. A central rod would go through the interior of the hollowed sections, and the whole group of wooden pieces would form the hinge.*

Ireland did not suffer Roman invasion; there are not, to my knowledge, any specimens of the early Irish *cuisle*, the players of which, the *cuisleanach*, have their place and order of precedence at the feasts of Tara so exactly set down in the Irish manuscripts.

From the mouth-blown pipes, we arrive at the bagpipe, and the woods or other material used in the making of it. For a long time native woods were used for bagpipes in Britain. William Cocks[11] mentions boxwood, laburnum, walnut, sycamore, holly and fruit-woods; he adds that in Ireland the native woods are still being used for the purpose, notably crab-apple and boxwood.

We have seen that the inventory of Henry VIII's musical instruments lists 'Baggepipes with pipes of Ivorie'. Ivory is more often used for small-pipes than for the pipes of the full-sized bagpipes. Mr Cocks informs us that Northumbrian small-pipes have often been made entirely of ivory – generally elephant ivory; and he adds the observation that the ferrules on the drone-slides and stocks of the Northumbrian small-pipes are invariably of metal, while those on the Scottish small-pipes are more usually of ivory, bone or horn. This is indeed one feature by which the two national species may be distinguished from each other – for in the earlier specimens it is not always easy to differentiate them (see p. 123).

Turning to the Scottish pipes, the published account of the Bannockburn Pipes (see pp. 123–4), though it gives very precise measurements of the chanter, drone, and blowpipe, does not identify the wood of which the surviving original parts of the pipes are made. It does tell us that the single drone has a horn mounting, in the form of 'a horn band five-eighths of an inch wide'.

The famous set of Scottish Highland bagpipes known as the Glen Pipes (see pp. 134–5) has two tenor drones emerging from a common Y-shaped stock. One report describes these as made of the wood of the thorn, while another states them to be of Arabian apple-wood. But, as has been said earlier in these pages, they are not now thought to be as early as their inscribed date.

As in Ireland and in Northumberland, a number of native woods were used to make bagpipes in Scotland in earlier times, as might be expected. The well-known bagpipe-maker, Torquil MacLeod, stated that in 1924

* Information from A. D. McWhirr, Leicester.

the pipes of Donald Bàin MacCrimmon had come into his hands and that
they were made of boxwood, and mounted in horn from Highland cattle
and pewter. Mr MacLeod also said that many old sets of pipes which he
had handled or repaired were made of native laburnum wood and that he
was still at that date making sets of pipes of laburnum when asked to do
so, mounting them with stag horn.[12]

Angus MacPherson, son of *Calum Pìobaire*, tells in a tape-recording
which he made for the School of Scottish Studies, how he had seen his
father making, on occasion, a set of pipes out of laburnum wood.

Often the native woods, which are mostly light in colour, were stained
black for the bagpipes. The old Lowland and Border pipes were however
often unashamedly of light-coloured native woods in their natural state,
as can be seen in the various museums.* Many of them were of boxwood.

It must be added however that some of the recognized makers of
Highland bagpipes also manufactured Lowland bellows pipes, of which
those still in existence are mostly of the foreign black woods (still to be
described) which are now so popular for Highland pipes.

The favourite wood for the bellows of the Lowland pipes was elm.
There is an interesting passage in a poem by Hamilton of Bangour
(1704–50), entitled 'The Maid of Gallowshiels', which describes the
making of a set of bellows.[13]

> His shining steel first lopped, with dext'rous toil,
>     From a tall spreading Elm the branchy spoil,
> The clouded wood he next divides in twain,
>     And smooths them equal to an oval plane.
> Six leather folds in still connected rows,
>     To either plank conformed, the sides compose;
> The wimble perforates the bass with care,
>     A destined passage op'ning to the air;
> But once enclosed within the narrow space,
>     The opposing valve forbids the backward race.
> Fast to the swelling bag, two reeds combined
>     receive the blasts of the melodious wind.
> Round from the turning loom, with skill divine,
>     Embossed, the joints in silver circles shine.

## Foreign woods

Lastly we come to the foreign woods which have long been the favourite
material of pipe-makers and pipers alike, and have largely replaced the

* Notably in Edinburgh and at the Wilton Lodge Museum, Hawick. Concerning
these last, see Gilbert Askew, 'The Lowland bagpipes'; notes on the instruments
in Wilton Lodge Museum, 1934, *Transactions of the Hawick Archaeological
Society*, January, 1934.

native woods for the Scottish Highland bagpipe. We may list some of them here, with their colour and characteristics, and their countries of origin.

*Lignum vitae* (*Guiacum officinale* and *G. sanctum*). Native to the West Indies, north coast of South America, Bahamas, Cuba, Florida. Colour varying from yellow in some species to dark greenish-brown in others. Characteristically it is very hard (so hard as to be difficult to work), dense and durable, and so heavy that it sinks in water. It has the merit for musical instrument-making that it cannot be split.*

*Ebony* (family, *Ebenaceae*, genus, *Diospyrus*). Widely distributed in tropical countries: India, Ceylon, Tropical Africa, Jamaica, America. Colours vary according to varieties and place of origin: a yellowish grey (*Diospyrus montana*), black (East Indian ebony), hazel brown (Ceylon), black (Angola). Characteristics: very hard and of great weight. Ebony also sinks in water. Non-black ebonies can be stained black.

*Cocus, Cocuswood* (*Brya ebenus*). One finds this wood variously misspelt as Cocas, Cocoa and cocoa-wood, coca, etc.† It has nothing to do with the tree whose fruit-beans provide the popular drink of that name, which comes from the bean of *Theobroma cacao*. Cocuswood is native to the West Indies. Colour, brown. Characteristics, heavy and hard.

*Ironwood* The name would appear to be a general rather than a specific one applied to several different kinds of woods from various tropical countries, and classified botanically as belonging to different families. Found in Africa, Mauritius, West Indies, Martinique, Guiana, India, Ceylon, Burma, Australia (including Tasmania) and North America including the southern Californian Islands. Colour, dark. Characteristics, extremely hard, dense and heavy (sinks in water). Ironwood is said to have been introduced into Britain (presumably England) by a bishop of London, Bishop Compton, in 1692 (though whether for the purpose of bagpipe-making is not mentioned!).[14]

*Rosewood* (*Dalbergia nigra*). French, *palissandre*. Imported from Rio de Janeiro, Bahia, Jamiaca and Honduras. Known in Brazil as jacaranda or cabunna. Native also to East Indies (*Dalbergia latifolia*), and the Chanda District of India where it is known as *sheesham*. In colour it is reddish-brown and streaked as seen in the well-known wood of furniture, piano-fortes, etc. It varies to a much darker colour in the Indian variety.
In India this wood is used for making the Scottish Highland bagpipe.

---

* The Black Chanter of the Clan MacPherson has been said to be made of *Lignum vitae*. (See the story about this on pp. 136-7.)

† An account-book of 1838 belonging to Messrs J. & R. Glen, musical instrument makers, Edinburgh, has an entry referring to a 'cocoa-wood flute', and another to a 'cocoa-flute'.

The Scottish pipes were first introduced there for use with the old
Indian Army, and their manufacture today provides a flourishing native
industry, notably at Sialkot.

*Stinkwood*  (*Ocotea bullata*). Also known as Cape walnut and Cape
laurel; native to South Africa. Colour, dark walnut or reddish-brown to
black. Characteristics, fine grain, dense and smooth. Its name derives
from the unpleasant odour of the tree when newly felled.

*Partridge-wood* or *Pheasant-wood*  (*Andira inermis* and other botanical
species). Native to the West Indies. Colour, red with darker stripes.
Characteristics, hardness.

*African blackwood*  (a species of *Grenadilla*). Known in France as *eben*
or *mozambique* but 'not to be confused with the unresonant ebony'.[15]
Native to East Africa. Colour, black (as its name implies). This is the
favourite wood of the modern pipe-makers and pipers.

It should be added that most, if not all of these woods have been used
to make other musical instruments such as the woodwinds of the modern
orchestra. As with the bagpipes, many of these were formerly of such woods
as pear, maple or boxwood, natural or stained; but these have been largely
replaced by such woods as cocus, rosewood, and, above all, by African
blackwood.

The catalogue of the Galpin Society's Collection of several hundred
musical instruments including bagpipes, now housed at Edinburgh
University, provides useful information regarding the woods used in their
manufacture. It is significant to note that, amid such curious names as
violet wood,* there is no mention at all of *Lignum vitae*.

Baines (*Bagpipes,* p. 129) mentions a set of Northumbrian small-pipes
of amateur make in the Pitt Rivers Museum, Oxford, as having 'cocus
wood or lignum-vitae stocks and drones'.

It may also be observed from the catalogue that those woods whose
natural colour is other than black are, for bagpipe making, often stained
black.

* Used for a cor anglais. See no. 118 in the catalogue.

# Two indentures of apprenticeship

## Scotland

Indenture betwixt the Lord Lovat and David Fraser, 1743[1]
[respecting the tuition of David Fraser, servant to Lord Lovat,
as a piper by Malcolm MacCrimmon* at Boreraig, Isle of Skye]

At Beaufort the nynth day of March one thousand seven hundred
and forty three years. It is contracted and agreed upon betwixt
the Right Honourable Lord Fraser of Lovat, on the one part, and
David Fraser, his Lordship's servant brother german to William
Fraser, tacksman in Beauly, his Lordship's musician, and the said
William Fraser, as cautioner and surety for his said brother in the
other part. In manner following. That is to say, whereas the said
Simon, Lord Fraser of Lovat, has, out of his own generosity,
cloathed and maintained the said David Fraser for these severall
years past, and has also bestow'd upon him during that time for
his education as a Pyper with the now deceas't Evan MacGrigor,
his Lordship's late Pyper,† and that his Lordship is now to send
him upon his own charges to the Isle of Skye in order to have him
perfected as a Highland Pyper by the famous Malcolm MacCrimon
whom his Lordship is to reward for educating the said David Fraser.
   Therefore, and in consideration of his Lordship's great charity,
kindness and generosity, the said David and William Frasers have
become bound and hereby bind and engage themselves conjunctly
and severally, that the said David Fraser shall honestly and
faithfully serve the said Simon, Lord Fraser of Lovat, or his heir
and successor by night and day for the haill space of seven full and
compleat years from and after the term of Whit Sunday next to

---

* Malcolm MacCrimmon was one of the two sons of Patrick Og MacCrimmon,
the other being Donald Bàin, composer of the famous 'MacCrimmon's Lament',
killed at the Rout of Moy in 1746.
† Both Ewan MacGregor and his pupil David Fraser have been credited by
Archibald Campbell with the composition of the *piobaireachd* 'Lord Lovat's
Lament' (see p. 167).

come, and that he shall never do or committ anything
inconsistent with, or contrary to that duty and obedience which a
faithful servant owes to a bountifull master, but shall serve them
uprightly to the utmost of his skill and capacity. For which cause,
and on the other part, the said Simon, Lord Fraser of Lovat, binds
and obliges himself and his Lordship's heirs, executors, and
successors, whatsomever to maintain the said David Fraser, his
servant, during the space above mentioned in Bed, Board, and
Washing, and to furnish and provide him in cloaths, shoes, and
stockings, and likewise to satisfy and pay to him yearly and ilk
year the sum of Fifty marks Scots money, in name of wages during
the said space of seven years commencing from Whitsunday next,
and, in the meantime, to send him with all due convenience to the
Isle of Skie to be perfected a Highland Pyper by the above named
McCrimon. The charge and expense whereof his Lordship is to
defray as said is etc.

In witness whereof (written upon stamped paper by Hugh Fraser,
Secretary to the said Lord Lovat) his Lordship and the said
William and David Frasers have subscribed these presents,
consisting of this and the preceding page, place and date above
mentioned before witness John Forbes, servant to his Lordship
and the said Hugh Fraser.

Lovat

| | |
|---|---|
| John Forbes, witness | William Fraser |
| Hugh Fraser, witness | David Fraser |

## Egypt (13 B.C.)

Indenture between Gaius Julius and a master-piper at
Alexandria, Egypt, respecting the tuition of Narcissus, slave to
Gaius Julius, as a piper, in 13 B.C.  [From W. L. Westerman][2]

In the larger perspective of the history of the pipes, it is interesting to
cite a similar piper's indenture of apprenticeship contained in an Egyptian
papyrus from Alexandria of the year 13 B.C. The papyrus is unfortunately
mutilated and incomplete, and cannot be reproduced *in toto*. Enough of it
exists, however, to indicate that it is an indenture drawn up by Gaius
Julius, the master of a young slave of Alexandria, named Narcissus, and
a master-piper (unnamed), for instruction of the slave as a piper.

The term of apprenticeship – a good deal shorter than the seven years
of the Scottish piper – is for six months. The fee for his instruction is 100
drachmas, 50 to be paid down on the signing of the indenture, and the
remaining 50 at the end of the period of instruction.

The owner of the slave undertakes responsibility for the apprentice's
food and clothing – as in the MacCrimmon indenture also. Westerman

interprets the conditions of the contract[3] as meaning that the pupil is to master four tunes on the Lydian pipes [the divergent double-pipes of equal length – the *tibiae sarranae* of the Romans] and also five tunes on the *syrinx*,* and on other Egyptian instruments of the reed-pipe type. Westerman indicates that two of these are to be adapted as accompaniments to go with *kythara* performances for the festivals of Serapis. The list continues with four more accompaniments, and six more tunes apparently for solo performance. Two of these are for the Phrygian pipes (the divergent double-pipes of *unequal* length – the Greek *auloi elymoi*, the Roman *tibiae impares*). Two of the compositions are thought to be *arias* (κρούματα – *chromata*).

The short period of instruction would seem to imply, as Westerman observes, that the boy Narcissus already possessed some knowledge of the rudiments of music and of the instruments concerned, as well as a natural musical aptitude, before commencing his tuition. His age was probably somewhere between eleven and fifteen years, which compares closely with the twelve years of age or thereabouts at which Scots pupils used to start playing the bagpipe.†

At the end of his apprenticeship, the indenture calls for a (doubtless customary) examination of the apprentice's progress to see if he has been properly taught. This is to be undertaken by three musical examiners, of recognized musical and technical proficiency, who are to be selected by agreement between the contracting parties, the owner of the slave Narcissus and his teacher.

---

* This is interesting in the light of the seeming affinity between the bagpipes (or bag-blown drone) and the *syrinx* in Alexandria at this period. See Collinson, 'Syrinx and bagpipe: a Romano-British representation?', *Antiquity*, vol. 43, no. 172 (December 1969), and p. 48 above.

† Pipe-major William MacLean began his tuition on the pipes under *Calum Pìobaire* (Calum MacPherson), Badenoch, at the age of twelve.

# The bagpipes of other countries

*Schnick-shnack, dudelsack,*
  *Dudelsack, dudelsack,*
*Shnick-shnack, dudelsack,*
  *Unser kinder tanzen.*

(Nursery rhyme popular in Scotland
at the beginning of the century.)

The purpose of this book has been to tell the particular story of the Scottish Highland bagpipe and its possible evolution, rather than to be a comprehensive account of the instrument throughout the world. The book might nevertheless be thought to be incomplete without some mention of the bagpipes of other countries. This appendix supplies this in brief form, together with a list of authorities, with references which the reader may consult for further and more specialized information.

The most up-to-date and comprehensive work on the subject yet written is Anthony Baines, *Bagpipes*, which is essential reading. Throughout this appendix 'Baines' refers to this publication. Next comes the concise but informative article by William A. Cocks under 'Bagpipe', in *Grove's Dictionary of Music and Musicians* ('Grove 5'). Other writers and sources cited (whom see in the Bibliography) are: W. H. Stone, D. J. Blaikley and J. B. Trend in *Grove's Dictionary* as above, 4th ed., 1940, edited by H. C. Colles, under 'Bagpipe'; J. G. Dalyell, 1849; Carl Engel, 1864; W. L. Manson, 1901; A. Duncan Fraser, 1907; W. H. Grattan Flood, 1911; P. A. Scholes, *The Oxford Companion to Music*, 4th ed., 1942, under 'Bagpipe'; *Journal of the International Folk Music Council*, 1949 – continuing ('*I.F.M.C.*'); *Folk Musician and Singer*, incorporating *Folk Dancer* and *Folklorist*, H. R. Baldry, 1954–64 (*Folk Musician*).

Earlier sources referred to include M. Mersenne, 1636; M. Praetorius, 1619; and Sebastian Virdung, 1511.

*Adzaristan, Adzeheria* (Georgian Republic, Transcaucasia), see Russia (USSR).

*Africa* African bagpipe names include the *zukra* (*suqqara, zouqqarah*) and the *shkewa* (*shkeywa*). The typical African bagpipe has two parallel cane chanters similar to the ancient Egyptian mouth-blown parallel pipes, but with each chanter terminating in an animal horn. Baines (Plate II) gives pictures of Tunisian, Algerian and Egyptian bagpipes, all having this same double chanter form. Fraser has two illustrations (pp. 56, 356), with similar chanters, one having an engraved blowpipe said to be of the leg-bone of a flamingo or other bird. The bag is from the whole skin of a small doe or gazelle. The Tunisian bagpipe has a bag made of the skin of a kid with the hair outermost. The others have the bare hide to the outside.

*Algeria*   see Africa.

*Armenia*   see Russia (USSR).

*Austria*   Cocks (Grove 5) gives the Austrian bagpipe, which he does not name, as being similar to the Polish bagpipe (q.v.).

*Balearic Islands*   see Spain.

*Belgium*   The bagpipe, though formerly known in Belgium, is apparently now extinct. Flood (p. 78) mentions 'a masque of bagpipes' at Brussels in 1529. On the bard of a suit of armour belonging to Henry VIII of England, now in the Tower of London, there is engraved the picture of a piper leading a procession with his bagpipe. It is said to be Flemish work, and the bagpipe may therefore be a representation of the Flemish bagpipe. See also bagpipes in the pictures of the Flemish painters, Pieter Breughel the elder (1525–69), Jacob Jordaens (1593–1678) and David Teniers (1582–1649). These generally show the bag of the bagpipe held against the chest of the player. (For another example of this method of holding the bag, see Ireland.) The instrument, as it appears in pictures, has a conical chanter with bell ending, and having one, or sometimes two, drones.

*Belo-Russia, Byelorussia*   see Russia (USSR).

*Brittany*   see France.

*Bulgaria*   The *gayda* (*gaida, gajda, gajde*) is described by Cocks as having a chanter and single drone. Both the cylindrical and the conical chanter are to be found in Bulgaria (Baines, p. 87). The *meshnitsa* is given as an alternative name for the Bulgarian bagpipe in *Folk Musician*, vol. 5, no. 2, February 1960, with picture. Baines (p. 69) refers to the Bulgarian bagpipe as a *type* covering Macedonia (the *gaida*), eastern Rumania (the *cimpoi*), and Bulgaria itself. Cf. also Flood (pp. 78, 79), Fraser (illustration facing p. 368), *IFMC*, vol. 12 (1960), pp. 21, 33, 35, 136 (which names the chanter of the instrument as the *gaidanitza*), p. 35.

*Chuvashia*   (Central Russia), see Russia (USSR).

*Czechoslovakia*   Cocks (Grove 5) gives the Czechoslovakian bagpipe as
being similar to the Polish bagpipe (q.v.); corroborated by Baines
(p. 80). The *dudy*, said to have been in use since the early fifteenth
century, has a single chanter and drone, both of them very long
(Baines, Plate XIVd; *I.F.M.C.*, vol. 12 (1960), p. 136). Ibid., p. 33 also
gives a passing reference to the *gaida* in Slovakia, which has the same
construction as the *dudy*. See also *Folk Musician*, vol. 8 (1963–4), p. 50.

——(Moravia)   This has the *dudy* and the *gajda* (cf. Baines, pp. 74,
84, Plate XIVf); *Folk Musician*, vol. 8 (1963–4), p. 50.

——(Bohemia)   *Folk Musician*, vol. 8 (1963–4), p. 52, gives a picture
of two bagpipes from Ceske Budejovice (southern Bohemia), one of
these being bellows-filled, the other mouth-filled. Each has a cylindrical
chanter and single drone, both of which end with a large animal horn
turned upwards.

*Egypt*   see Africa.

*Finland*   Matthew Guthrie, writing in *c.* 1800 (quoted by Baines,
p. 92, and Flood, p. 79), names the bagpipe of the Finns, the *pilai*. This
name is also given by Manson (p. 62) who adds the *volynka*, which, he
suggests, is another name for the same instrument. Both writers
describe the instrument as having 'two pipes and a blowpipe'. It should
be remarked that, as Baines points out (p. 92), Guthrie is writing of the
Finns living near Petersburg 'inhabiting the conquered provinces ceded
to Russia by Sweden', and that the bagpipe is not now played in
Finland.

*France*   The *musette* was a favourite instrument of the French Court in
the seventeenth and eighteenth centuries, but went out of use towards
the end of the latter period. It had originally one chanter, the *grand
chalumeau*. A second chanter, the *petit chalumeau*, was added in the
seventeenth century. Four drones were contained in a cylindrical
shuttle or barrel. The bag, which was bellows-filled, was covered with
rich silken cloth. Pipes and barrel were often both made of ivory. The
chief authority is Borjon; others are Cocks, Flood (p. 121 *passim*,
illustration, p. 125), Baines (Plate XII), Fraser (p. 248) and Manson
(p. 63), most of whom give pictures of the instrument; see also
Mersenne.
     The *cornemuse*, a name also used as the basic term for a bagpipe in
French, was the bagpipe of the French peasantry. It was frequently
played in conjunction with the *vielle* (hurdy-gurdy). It is now nearly,
but not quite, extinct, being, according to Baines, still to be heard in
western France (p. 104 *passim*). The bag, which is mouth-filled, is
covered with cloth, often velvet. It has a conical chanter with double
reed, and a tenor drone (the *petit bourdon*) springing from the same

stock. A bass drone (*grand bourdon*) emerges from the bag separately. Chanter and drones are often of ivory. See Grove 4, Cocks and Baines (Plate IX). Fraser (p. 96) gives pictures of carved wooden models of French peasant bagpipe players with their bagpipes, and (p. 244) a photograph of a two-droned French *chalumeau* (probably a *cornemuse*).

——(Auvergne)   This province has its own bagpipe, the *cabrette*, a name we have met in its older form *chevrette* (meaning kid) referring to the material of the bag. The *cabrette* is bellows-filled. It has the same arrangement as the *cornemuse*, of conical chanter and tenor drone emerging from the same stock, a feature which Baines (p. 105) relates to a form of instrument illustrated in the thirteenth-century Spanish manuscript, *Las Cantigas*, and to a probable ancestry derived from the ancient mouth-blown double-pipe. Authorities are Scholes 'Bagpipe' and Baines (Plates IX, XV).

——(Brittany)   The immensely popular bagpipe of Brittany is the *biniou*. This has a remarkably short chanter with double reed, and a single bass drone with single reed. The bag is of sheepskin, and is mouth-filled. The *biniou* is played together with the *bombarde*, a bag-less mouth-blown pipe blown by a second player. The true Breton *biniou* is rapidly being displaced by the Scottish form of bagpipe, made in the *biniou* key of B flat, which is played in concert with the *bombarde* as heretofore. The Breton band of *biniou*, *bombarde* and drums is known as the *bagad* (*Folklorist*, vol. 7, part 4 (1962). The *biniou* is pictured in Cocks and Baines (Plate IX). Cf. also *I.F.M.C.*, vol. XIII (1961), p. 128 for an interesting review of *Ar Soner*, the Breton Pipers' journal, no. 117, Lorient, Morbihan, June 1960.

*Germany*   The general name for the bagpipe in Germany is *Dudelsack*, or, alternatively, *Sackpfeife*. Cocks says that the bagpipe has almost died out in Germany, but still lingers on in the southern part of the Black Forest. According to Flood (p. 79), the *Dudelsack* is also found in Hungary, though most sources give the *duda* for the Hungarian bagpipe. An interesting feature of the *Dudelsack* is the square-section form of the pipes, both in chanter and drones (it may be remembered that the semi-legendary Bannockburn Pipes of Scotland are said to have had a blowpipe of square section, merging into the round at the mouth end). Praetorius gives descriptions with drawings of five varieties of German bagpipe: (1) the *Bock*, (2) the *grosser Bock*, (3) the small *Hümmelchen*, (4) the *Dudey* and (5) the *Schäferpfeife* (shepherd's pipe). Cocks gives also the *Magdeburg bagpipe*. See also, Baines (p. 118), Manson (drawings facing p. 60) and Flood (p. 79).

*Greece*   Macedonia has the *gajda*, which is similar in type to the Bulgarian bagpipe (q.v.). See *I.F.M.C.*, vol. 13 (1961), p. 78, where the Macedonian bagpipe is described as a *Dudelsack*, also Scholes and Baines

(Plate XIVf). There is a good picture of the Greek bagpipe on the cover of *Musical Events*, April 1971.

——(Crete)   Crete has the *mandoura*, also called *askomandoura*. Baines gives a picture (Plate III).

——(Greek islands)   The bagpipe of the Greek islands is the *tsambouna* or *sampouna*, with parallel double-chanters of cane, which terminate in a single animal horn. In Crete, the parallel chanters end in a yoke of distinctive shape. See Baines for picture (Plate III) of the bagpipes of Crete and the Greek islands.

*Holland* (The Netherlands)   The bagpipe is now extinct in the Netherlands. An incidental reference is to be found under *cornemuse* in the article on 'Bagpipe' in Grove 4. See also Belgium (above) for reference to paintings by Flemish artists showing the bagpipes of the Low Countries.

*Hungary*   Accounts are conflicting regarding the exact form of the Hungarian bagpipe. Cocks describes it as similar to the Bulgarian one, which has a chanter and a bass drone but no tenor drone. Baines (pp. 77, 79) gives Hungary as one of the countries possessing the *duda*, which has this construction; also a Hungarian bagpipe with a diple (i.e. twin-bore) chanter, one bore of which gives a variable drone, the bagpipe having a bass drone in addition. Robert Bright in *Travels through Lower Hungary* (1818), quoted by Flood (p. 79), describes a Hungarian bagpipe as having *two* drones and a chanter [all?] of square section (in other words, the *Dudelsack*). Bright goes on to describe the *Dudelsack* as playing the national music of Hungary. See Manson (p. 64) and Dalyell (p. 45). Fraser (p. 243) has a picture of a Hungarian bagpipe with one chanter and one drone of medium length, probably a bass drone. It seems possible that all these forms of the instrument may be in use.

*India*   North India has the *mashag, mashac* or *moshag*, consisting of a bag of goatskin, a chanter and a blowpipe only. The chanter may be used either to play a melody, or, more often, simply a single drone note as the accompaniment to another wind instrument of the shawm type. Baines (p. 56) mentions a remarkable specimen of a similar pipe with two chanters of cane set in a yoke, one of which is stopped up and rendered silent, the other pipe obviously having been used as a *mashag* to provide a drone, as described above. He also mentions (p. 30) reports of a single-chanter bagpipe in Afghanistan and in Azerbaijan. See also Flood, p. 10.

——(Southern India)   Southern India has the *s'ruti upanga*, a single-chanter bagpipe used, like the *mashag* of the north, to accompany a second instrumentalist playing a shawm. See Cocks and Baines (Fig. 9,

p. 30). Cocks also gives the name *bhazanr-s'ruti*. Flood gives both names (p. 10). Baines has a picture (Plate I). The *titty, tourti,* or *tutli* mentioned as a bagpipe by Engel (p. 78) is probably a mouth-blown pipe of the shawm type. See Baines, p. 30.

*Iran*   (Persia) The bagpipe of Iran is the *nay amban* or *nei ambanah* from *nay*, meaning a pipe and *amban* (*ambanah*) meaning a bag (Engel, p. 78; Dalyell, p. 48). Baines (p. 57) mentions a bagpipe from Linga on the Persian Gulf (with drawing of the chanter).

*Iraq*   (Mesopotamia) There the bagpipe is similar to those of Egypt and Syria; i.e. having twin cane chanters terminating in animal horns. See Baines, p. 38.

*Ireland*   As Kathleen Schlesinger remarks (*Encyclopaedia Britannica*, 11th ed, 'Bagpipe') very little is known about the old Irish bagpipe, the war-pipe or *piob mhór*; information is limited to what can be gleaned from the woodcut in Derricke (1578–81) and from a contemporary sketch said to have been made by an English soldier at the Battle of Ballyshannon (1595). The instrument is shown as a mouth-filled bagpipe with a large bag,* a long chanter and two drones. Derricke's drawing seems to suggest that the two drones emerge from a single stock, though this is not clear, as the stock is obscured by the head of the player; the soldier's sketch of 1595 shows the two drones clearly issuing separately from the bag. The player in Derricke's woodcut holds the bag in front of him, pressing it to his chest, in the manner of pipers in pictures by the Flemish School of Painters.

   The *union* or *uilleann* pipes. These are bellows-filled, and have a chanter with keys which gives a fully chromatic scale of two octaves. Three drones sounding in octaves issue from one stock. Extra pipes known as regulators, also springing from the drone-stock, have special keys which are depressed by the wrist of the player to sound simple chords which may be used to accompany the melody. Regulators have increased in number successively from one in the late eighteenth century to three and sometimes four in the nineteenth. The player plays the instrument seated, with the pipes laid across his knee. Descriptions with pictures may be found in Cocks, Baines (p. 120, Plate XI), Fraser (p. 392), Flood (pp. 146 ff) and Scholes. Fraser gives a picture (facing p. 40) which he captions 'Old Irish Bagpipe'.† It has *four* drones (the true ancient Irish *piob mhór* had only two drones). From the shape of the insufflation tube stock, this is almost certainly a bellows-pipe, of which the bellows is missing; it is hardly likely therefore to be a true specimen of the Irish *piob mhór*. This pipe is now in the Royal Scottish Museum in Edinburgh with the rest of the Fraser Collection of bagpipes.

* See also note from Alexander MacAuley, p. 115.

† Fraser continues the caption: 'It was of this set that the late Professor Goodman wrote, "No such pipe has been played in Ireland for at least 200 years".'

*Italy*   The bagpipe of southern Italy is the *zampogna*. It has two chanters, each played with one hand, and two drones. Both chanters and drones have double reeds. This is the bagpipe of the *pifferari*, who come in from the country to play in the towns at Christmas. (Handel's 'Pastoral Symphony' from the *Messiah* is almost certainly modelled or perhaps actually borrowed from a tune of the *pifferari* and in the score he heads the symphony '*piva*', which is the name of a bagpipe of *northern* Italy.) The *zampogna* is generally used as an accompanying instrument to the melody played on the *ciaramella*, a mouth-blown bagless chanter played by a second instrumentalist. The accompaniment on the two chanters of the *zampogna* is usually in the form of two melodic lines below the melody, often in thirds and octaves with it, while the two drones below sound the interval of a twelfth, thus making a double-pedal to the whole. Baines (Plate XV), Fraser (p. 216), Cocks, Grove 4, and Scholes all give pictures. (The last-named is incorrectly labelled 'Italian cornemuse'.) See also the painting by David Allan (Plate 24). Baines (p. 99) gives an example of the music.

——(Northern Italy)   Northern Italy has the *piva*, now nearly extinct. This has a conical chanter and one drone. See Cocks, Baines (p. 99) and Fraser (picture facing p. 232).

——(Naples)   Naples had its own local bagpipe, the *surdelina*, though this seems now to be extinct. It was bellows-filled, and had two chanters of cylindrical form and bore. It is described by Mersenne; modern authorities are Cocks, Manson (p. 63) and Dalyell (Plate XIII).

*Latvia*   see Russia (USSR).

*Lithuania*   see Russia (USSR).

*Malta*   The bagpipe is the *zampogna*, abbreviated to *zapp* (*Piping and Dancing*, Ardrossan, May 1939, quoted by Baines, p. 46). Despite the name, the instrument bears no resemblance to the Italian *zampogna*, but has two parallel cane chanters in a yoke, terminating in a cowhorn, similar to the bagpipes of Crete and the Greek islands.

*Netherlands*   see Holland.

*Norway*   The *penbrock* is given by Scholes as a Norwegian bagpipe, but this must be regarded as doubtful, as it is not included in the authoritative booklet *Norwegian Folk Instruments*, published by *Norsk Folkemusikklag* for the International Folk Music Conference in Norway in 1955. Baines makes no mention of a Norwegian bagpipe.

*Poland*   The bagpipes of Poland are the *dudy* and the *koza* or *kozial*. Cocks says that both the mouth-filled and bellows-filled bagpipes are found. Baines (p. 92, quoting Matthew Guthrie) gives also the *volynka* as a name derived from Volyn, a province in the northern Ukraine within the boundaries of Poland. *Folk Musician*, vol 8 (1963–4), mentions the bagpipe in Polish Silesia. Scholes adds the *Polnischer Bock* ('Polish goat') as another bagpipe name, and gives a picture of it, showing the chanter stock ornamented with wooden horns and carved in the form of a goat's head. The bag is of sheepskin.

*Portugal*   Baines (p. 111) says that the bagpipe in use in northern Portugal is similar to the *gaita asturiana* of Spain (q.v.).

*Rumania*   Rumania has the *dutka*, a bagpipe with conical chanter and single drone; and the *cimpoi* (*cimponi* or *ciumpoi*) said to be of similar construction to the *dutka*. Authorities are Cocks, Baines (p. 69 ff, Plate VI), *Folk Musician*, vol. 8 (1963–4), p. 52 and *I.F.M.C.*, vol. 12, 1960, frontispiece.

*Russia*   (USSR) The *volynka*. Flood (p. 79), Manson and Dalyell (p. 62) quote Matthew Guthrie, writing in *c.* 1800, as saying that the *volynka* is another name for the *pilai*, a bagpipe having 'two tubes and a mouthpiece all apart, inserted in a raw hairy goatskin, found in some provinces, but [that it is] more the appropriate instrument of the Finns'. Baines (p. 92) also quotes the passage, but he says (p. 80) that *volynka* is 'the Russian literary word for a bagpipe'. Another Russian bagpipe is the *koza* (given also under Poland), having a chanter and bass drone. Cocks gives the *zurna* for the Caucasus, but does not give constructional details. Possibly this is the same instrument as the *zurla*, qualified by Baines (pp. 89, 93) as a shawm and not a bagpipe. The *shyabur* of Cheremiss Russia (i.e. the area 300–800 miles east of Moscow) has two double parallel chanters of metal, one of these providing a variable drone. Baines gives an excellent picture of it (Plate IV).

——(Ukraine)   The Ukraine is said by Cocks to possess an enormous bagpipe, having a chanter and single drone, of which the latter is about ten feet in length. Baines (p. 80) gives the *meshin* as another Ukrainian bagpipe name. *Piping Times*, vol. 9, no. 10 (July 1957) publishes an important article (unsigned) based on information received from K. A. Vertkov of the State Institute of Scientific Research on the Theatre and Music (USSR). He gives two main varieties of bagpipe for Russia. The first 'has two metal (lead) playing pipes fixed in a wooden base' [i.e. a yoke] 'and a sound disperser of cow's horn. The first pipe is melodic and has three to four holes. The scale is diatonic. The second is a drone with two holes' (i.e. a variable drone). The description corresponds closely to the details of the Cheremiss bagpipe as pictured and described by Baines. Of the second main variety of bagpipes, Vertkov says, 'they have a melodic pipe and two drones, tuned to the fifth and octave'. He gives the names and distribution of these as follows: Armenia, the *tik*, the *parakapusuk*; Adzaristan, Adzeria (Transcaucasia), the *chiboni*; Azerbaidzan (Caucasus), the *tulum*; Byelorussia, the *duda*; Chuvashia (central Russia), the *sarnai*; Georgia, the *stviri* (Baines, *striviri*); Lithuania, the *duda*, the *labanoru*.

Other states of the USSR having bagpipes are Estonia, the *toropill* (Baines, drawing on p. 91); Latvia, the *toropill*, the *suomo duda* (Baines, drawing on p. 91). The subject of the Russian bagpipes is both poorly documented and complicated, merging as it does with both the names and types of neighbouring states, and authorities do not always agree. The best of these are Baines and Cocks, whose works should be consulted.

*Spain*   The Spanish bagpipe is the *gaita* (*gheeyita* – Fraser, drawing facing p. 32), of which Galicia has its own variety, the *gaita gallega*; and Asturia, the *gaita asturiana*. It is a single-drone bagpipe with conical chanter and bass drone. Baines (p. 111) gives also a Catalan bagpipe, the *cornamusa*, but remarks that it is now extinct. Authorities are Cocks, Baines (pp. 108–11, drawing, p. 109), Fraser (p. 369 and drawing facing p. 32) and *I.F.M.C.*, vol. 6 (1954), p. 26. See also 'The bagpipe in Asturia', Raphael Mere, *Piping Times*, vol. 8, no. 10 (July 1956).

——(Balearic Islands)   The bagpipe is the *zampona*, of which sole mention is to be found in Baines (pp. 103, 111), who gives a picture of it from Minorca (Plate XV). See also articles on the mouth-blown single and twin pipes of Ibiza, 'Las Xeremies de la Isla de Ibiza', by C. Garcia Matos in *Instrumentos musicales folkloricos de Espana* (reviewed in *I.F.M.C.*, vol. 10 (1958), p. 104).

*Sweden*   Both Flood (p. 79) and Baines (p. 92) mention an unnamed Swedish bagpipe with cylindrical chanter and two (sometimes one) drone. See also *I.F.M.C.*, vol. 4 (1952), p. 97 for a passing reference.

*Switzerland*   The Swiss bagpipe has long been extinct. It receives a passing reference in Baines, p. 118.

*Syria*   Baines has a picture (Plate II) of a Syrian (Bedouin) bagpipe unnamed. This shows a goatskin bag and blowpipe with two parallel cane chanters terminating in animal horns. There is no drone.

*Turkey*   Cocks gives the *ghaida* (*gaida*, *gajde*). Baines, citing L. E. R. Picken ('Instrumental polyphonic folk music in Asia Minor', *Proc. Royal Mus. Assoc.*, London, April 1954), adds the *tulum* (with a drawing), as a bagpipe with parallel cane chanters in a yoke, the latter terminating in an unusual square bell, fashioned from the wood of the yoke itself. The lower end of this is serrated.

*Wales*   The bagpipe is now extinct, but see drawings from Welsh manuscripts in Baines (p. 40). Cocks says that the use of the bagpipe in Wales did not cease until the nineteenth century.

*Yugoslavia*   Bagpipe names are the *gaida*, *gajde*, *dudey*, *dudy*. Cocks says that the Yugoslavian bagpipe is similar to the Bulgarian (i.e. with cylindrical chanter, often possessing double bores; and bass drone). It should be remarked, however, that Bulgaria has the *conical* chanter also. Authorities are Baines (p. 87, Plate V), Flood (p. 78), *Folk Musician*, vol. 4 (1956) (picture). There are brief references in *I.F.M.C.*, vol. 5 (1953), p. 82, and vol. 20 (1968), p. 24. Bartok remarks on the contrapuntal facility of the Yugoslav bagpipes. See B. Suchoff (referring to Bartok's *Microkosmos*, nos 40 and 138), *Guide to Bartok's 'Microkosmos'*, reviewed, *Musical Times*, London, November 1971, p. 1173.

# Bagpipe components and other terms connected with musical reed-pipes

*Arundo donax*   A species of marsh reed-plant of which the cane is much used for the reeds of musical wind instruments, including the bagpipe. See Appendix I.

*The bag*   The air reservoir from which air is forced out under pressure of the arm to sound the reeds of the bagpipe. As its name implies, it consists of a flexible bag, which can be fashioned from a number of materials. These include the whole skin of a sheep, dog, goat or kid. The hair of the two latter may be either displayed on the outside of the bag, or turned to the inside. Other materials include animal bladders such as that of a cow or the stomach of a seal; or the bag may in modern times be made of rubber or synthetic equivalents. Sometimes, as in Poland, Hungary and Bohemia, the chanter stock at the front or neck of the bag is ornamented with small wooden horns to imitate animal horns, so that the chanter appears to issue from the head of a horned animal. The bag of the Scottish Highland bagpipe is of sheepskin cut to a special shape and sewn together. Sometimes the bag is enclosed in a cloth or velvet cover, that of the Scottish Highland bagpipe often being of tartan.

*Bellows*   Small bellows of wood and leather are used in some bagpipes to fill the bag instead of filling it with the breath from the lungs via a blowpipe. The bellows are strapped under the opposite arm to that which holds and controls the bag. A flexible leather tube is joined to the bellows and crosses the player's chest to connect with the bag under the other arm. This tube usually terminates in a wooden end-pipe which can be pushed into a stock in the bag for the purpose of inflating the latter.

*The blowpipe, 'blowstick', or insufflation tube*   This is a pipe, generally of wood, though it may be of other material such as bone or ivory. It is connected to the bag of the bagpipe by a stock, and through it the bag is inflated by the breath. It usually has a non-return air valve at the inner end, i.e. nearest the bag, consisting of a hinged disc or strap of leather. In some countries this valve is lacking, the player closing the outer end of the blowpipe with his tongue between inflations.

*The chanter*   This may be defined briefly as a reed-sounded musical pipe on which a scale or melody may be played by means of fingerholes bored in it. Chanters may be made of wood, metal, ivory or bone, including the bones of birds or animals *au naturel*, particularly in prehistoric times. Some chanters are conical in bore, some are cylindrical. Cylindrical-bore chanters are usually played with a single reed. Broadly speaking, such chanters of cylindrical bore and single reed are more characteristic of the eastern than the western half of the old world, embracing eastern Europe, south-western Asia and India. Conical chanters, played with a double reed, are found in central and western Europe, including the British Isles. The Scottish Highland bagpipe has a conical chanter. Curiously enough the cylindrical chanter is found in Northumberland (stemming from the French *musette*) and (formerly) in Scotland, in the 'small-pipes'. Northumbrian small-pipes are, however, played with a double reed, as were probably also the Scottish small-pipes. Although the chanter of the Scottish small-pipes might have had a conical shape externally, it still had a cylindrical bore.

A chanter of conical bore gives both the even- and the odd-numbered harmonics, and is therefore capable of sounding the octave harmonic by over-blowing, while the chanter of cylindrical bore cannot. A cylindrical chanter has the acoustical properties of a 'stopped pipe' and gives the odd-numbered harmonics only. Generally speaking, the conical chanter produces a brighter, more incisive tone-quality than the cylindrical, which characteristically has the softer, veiled tone of the clarinet (also an instrument of cylindrical bore); though as Baines observes (*Bagpipes*, p. 9), other factors in the fashioning of the instrument and of the reed may affect the tone-quality.

Some bagpipes, mostly to be found in eastern countries, have double-chanters, formed of two cylindrical pipes or canes bound or joined together in parallel. In some species, such double-chanters are made as twin bores in the same pipe. In these, each pair of coinciding fingerholes is normally covered by the same finger. Such double-chanters, whether of two pipes or bored within the same pipe, will be fingered by the fingers of both hands, one hand above the other. Italy possesses a bagpipe with two chanters which are not bound together in parallel, but separate, issuing divergently from a common stock (which is common also to the two drones). Such divergent chanters were common in the mouth-blown divergent double-pipes of antiquity. In the case of bagpipes they seem to have been more common formerly than now, for many early church carvings throughout Britain depict bagpipes of this type.

Some chanters, including that of the Scottish Highland bagpipe, have a thumbhole at the back, covered and uncovered by the thumb of the upper hand, as well as the usual fingerholes – which in the Scottish type number seven. The chanter of the Scottish Highland bagpipe has also two vent-holes, positioned across the pipe below the lowest fingerhole.

*The practice chanter*   This is a bagless chanter blown directly by the mouth. It has a double reed which is covered by a wooden chamber or cap in the manner of the ancient Scottish stock-and-horn, or hornpipe. The pipe is of the same length as the chanter of the bagpipe, but being of cylindrical bore in contrast to the conical bore of the chanter it sounds an octave lower. An exact standard of pitch is not maintained in manufacture. It is an essential instrument in Scottish piping. The practice chanter is also found in Spain, though Baines thinks this may have stemmed from Scottish influence which, as far as bagpipes and piping are concerned, is increasing in Spain. In Scotland, the practice chanter or *feadan*, the much used Gaelic name for it, is second in importance only to the pipes themselves. It is used not only extensively in teaching, particularly the complicated and often arbitrary rhythms of *pìobaireachd*, but in the piper's daily practice, which is done quite as much on the practice chanter as on the pipes themselves, particularly in the study of a new piece. It is equally used in demonstration and discussion of tunes, phrasing, etc., between fully accomplished pipers, and is by no means merely a learner's instrument. Many Scottish pipers, particularly of the older schools, use the ancient method of nasal inhalation in playing the *feadan*, and are able to play long dance-tunes, or even the ground or other movement of a *pìobaireachd* on it, without a break for breath. Research does not seem to have been done to any extent on the history of the practice chanter. In its resemblance and possible relationship to the hornpipe, it could be very ancient.

*Double-pipes*   The term is used for two chanters played simultaneously by the same player, whether directly by the mouth, or on a double-chanter bagpipe. In antiquity there were two kinds of double-pipes, the *parallel*, probably originating in Egypt, and the earlier *divergent* double-pipes from further east, i.e. Sumeria and Babylonia. Today, with one exception, only the parallel pipes remain. The two chanters of the double-pipes may still be blown by the mouth as a bagless instrument, as with the hornpipe; or they may be sounded by means of a bag, i.e. as a bagpipe. The parallel double-pipes, whether mouth-blown or bag-blown, are fingered with both hands on the two pipes, one hand above the other, as in the modern west European single-chanter bagpipe. With the divergent pipes, however, one chanter was held to the mouth in each hand and fingered independently. They were held so as to issue from the mouth divergently, in the form of a V, the apex formed by the end with the reeds, which were close together in the player's mouth. The sole surviving example of divergent pipes is the Italian *zampogna*,

a double-chanter bagpipe. Other double-chanter bagpipes did exist in
Italy until a century or so ago, notably in the Neapolitan *surdelina*, and
in the Italian or Sicilian 'peasant bagpipe' both illustrated by Dalyell
in his *Musical Memoirs*, citing the seventeenth-century writer Mersenne
as his authority.

*Drone, drones*    The term 'drone' has two meanings: (a) a single musical
note used as a monotone-accompaniment to the melody – usually,
though not invariably, lower than the melody in pitch; and (b) the pipe
which produces such note. Which meaning came first would be difficult
to say. The *Oxford English Dictionary* favours the *sound* as the
originating term, and the *pipe*, a transference from it. In some bagpipes
the drone note can be varied during performance, in which case the pipe
is positioned in order to be under the control of the fingers. A change of
drone note may also, in some pipe species, be set beforehand by
mechanical means. The bagpipe drone is usually a pipe of cylindrical
bore sounded by a single reed, though there are exceptions to both
features.

The number of drones may vary from one to five or six, though all
these are not usually allowed to sound at once, some being shut off by
end-stoppers or other means. Drones may issue separately from
differently positioned stocks in the bag, or they may be grouped
together in a single stock as in the Northumbrian small-pipes. The
Scottish Highland bagpipe has three drones – two tenor-drones sounding
in unison an octave below the low A of the chanter; and a bass-drone
sounding an octave below the tenor-drones. Very many different drone
tunings are found throughout the world of the bagpipe. The commonest
forms are the tonic alone, the tonic with its octave below, and the
octave tonic with the fifth between.

*Drone-sliders*    These are polished metal tubes joining the sections of
pipe forming the drone – two sections in the average tenor-drone, and
three in the bass-drone. The drones can be tuned by sliding the external
wooden pipe sections along the metal tubes, either inwards or outwards.

*The hornpipe*    A bagless musical reed-pipe blown directly with the
mouth. The pipe of the hornpipe terminates in an animal horn, which
may have originated more as a cult-symbol than for acoustical purposes.
Often the reed or reeds are also contained in a chamber or cap made of
a horn, or segment of horn, into which the player blows with his mouth.
In such case, it will be seen that the instrument takes the form of a
chanter or pipe with a horn or segment of horn at either end. A good
example may be seen in the Basque hornpipe, the *alboka*.

With rare exceptions, notably from India and Egypt, most hornpipes
throughout the old world have two parallel chanters. These terminate
either in two animal horns or in a single horn common to both pipes.

The fingerholes in such double-chanter hornpipes may either coincide in position, in which case each pair will normally be covered with the same finger (though there are exceptions to this); or the fingerholes may differ in number and position. In the latter case, one pipe may have only one fingerhole, sounding a drone; or two or three fingerholes, to make a variable drone. Baines observes (*Bagpipes*, p. 41) that double-chanters with an unequal number of fingerholes are not found in hornpipes terminating in double horns, but occur when both pipes share the same horn. Sometimes double-chanter hornpipes are fashioned as two bores within the same pipe, in which case they are known as 'diple' hornpipes. Some hornpipes, paradoxically, lack the animal-horn ending. With rare exceptions, most hornpipes have enough fingerholes to require both hands upon the chanter to cover them. Thus we may see the relationship between the fingering of the bag-blown hornpipe and that of the two-handed chanter of the true bagpipe, while the fingering of the ancient *divergent* pipes, in which each hand fingers its own chanter, is unlike either. The whole subject of the hornpipe is dealt with in detail by Baines (*Bagpipes*, chapters II and II) whose book is essential reading in the subject.

*Nasal inhalation*   This is a method by which the puffed-out cheeks were used as an air reservoir for sounding a musical reed-pipe directly with the mouth, many centuries before the bag was devised. It is never used in playing the *bagpipe*, the bag rendering the method superfluous, but may be used in playing the Scottish practice-chanter, or the bagless hornpipe or other musical reed-pipes. In practice, the cheeks are distended, and the air is directed through the pipe by the pressure of the cheek muscles. As the air stored in the cheeks is used up, a fresh supply of air is taken in through the nose and transferred from the back of the mouth-cavity to the distended cheeks. Nasal inhalation is of great antiquity. It was certainly used by the ancient Greeks, as may be seen in pictures or vase decoration of players of the *aulos*. They are depicted playing with cheeks distended, often wearing a cheek-strap or *phorbeia* to prevent overstrain of the cheek muscles. The method may however be much older than the days of ancient Greece, and may well have been used from the earliest age of the musical pipes, in Sumeria, Egypt, Syria and other ancient civilizations.

*The reed*   A tongue or pair of tongues of cane, straw, metal or thin wood, etc., which are caused to vibrate by a stream of air being blown over or between them. This vibration of the reed-tongue or tongues is imparted to the air-stream, which gives rise to the musical sound.

As far as the bagpipe is concerned, reeds can be divided into two classes, the single or beating reed, and the double reed. (A third class, the 'free reed' made of metal, is found only in instruments of the harmonium and accordion type and does not concern us here.)

The beating or single reed consists of a single tongue or 'blade' of this flexible material (usually of cane), which covers a slot cut in a tube, often also of cane. One end of the tongue is attached to the outside of this tube, the other being left free to vibrate over the slot. The tube of the reed must be closed at one end. In a cane reed, the closure is usually effected by the node of the cane. Tubes of other material may be closed with a stopper of wax or resin. The first reeds of this type consisted of a tongue cut in the side of the river-reed which formed the musical pipe. Nowadays the reed is formed as a separate unit which is inserted into the end of the resonating pipe nearest the bag (or on a bagless pipe, the end of the pipe nearest the mouth of the player). The tongue of the reed may be cut either towards or away from the closed end of the tube. If cut towards the closure, it is said to be 'up-cut'; cut away from the closure, 'down-cut' (see Fig. 3, p. 4). The single reed is of the same general type as that used in the orchestral clarinet and saxophone. Curt Sachs indeed refers (in *The History of Musical Instruments*, New York, 1940, p. 91) to the single reed, even in the pipes of antiquity, as a 'clarinet reed', and to such pipes of antiquity themselves as 'ancient clarinets'; but in fact, as the most cursory glance will show, the single reed of antiquity and that of the modern bagpipe does not, except in the most general sense, resemble that of the clarinet with its wide blade. Instead of a single blade beating against the sides of its bed or slot in a tube, a reed may take the form of two blades laid close to each other. The blades are cut narrower towards the foot, where they are fastened together, either by being bound with a ligature, or more frequently by means of a metal staple. The double reed is of the type used in the orchestral oboe and bassoon, and the double reed of the bagpipe closely resembles these. Modern reeds, whether single or double, are usually made from the cane of *Arundo donax*. The reed in the drone of the bagpipe is almost always a single reed, though there are exceptions. The double reed is more often used for the chanter, but here again, there are exceptions, and a number of chanters throughout the old world use the single reed.

*The stock*   This is a hollow wooden socket which penetrates a hole cut for it in the bag, into which it is tied. Into this socket is pushed the end of the pipe, which may be detached from it as required. Sometimes, as in the Scottish Highland bagpipe, each of the pipes – chanter, drones and blowpipe – has its own stock. In other bagpipes, such as the Northumbrian, the drones may all issue from a common stock. The chanter is usually fixed into an independent stock (sometimes ornamented to resemble the head of a horned animal) at the front of the bag; though in some countries, such as Italy and France, the chanter may issue from a common stock together with the drones.

*Yoke*   A piece of wood roughly of 'D' section, with the flat part of the

D uppermost. This flat surface is hollowed out to receive the two pipes of a double-chanter hornpipe, which are often bedded into the yoke with wax. Sometimes the upper end (nearest the mouth) of the yoke, instead of being 'D' section, is left circular, and is bored to take the upper ends of the chanters. The outer circumference of the round part of the yoke may have a groove cut in it all round, for the purpose of tying it into a bag. A good illustration may be seen in Fig. 11, p. 75.

With a bag attached, this kind of hornpipe in a yoke becomes, of course, a bagpipe, though still belonging to the hornpipe species – i.e. with double-chanters and, in most cases terminating, in the fashion of the species, in an animal's horn or horns.

# References

**Preface**

1 See W. Keller (trans. W. Neil), *The Bible as History*, p. 51.

**Chapter one    Antiquity**

1 See Hans Hickmann, 'Instruments de musique', nos 69201–852.
2 *Catalogue général des antiquités égyptiennes du Musée du Caire*, p. 139.
3 *The History of Musical Instruments*, p. 72.
4 Lord Carnarvon and Howard Carter, *Five Years' Exploration at Thebes*, Oxford, 1912, p. 55.
5 *Catalogue général . . .*, no. 69836, p. 136n.
6 Baines, *Bagpipes*, p. 78.
7 Ibid., pp. 30, 45, 47; H. Balfour, 'The old British "pibcorn" or "hornpipe" and its affinities', *Journal of the Anthropological Institute*, vol. 20 (1890).
8 Op. cit., p. 91.
9 *Ur Excavations*, p. 258.
10 Sachs, *The History of Musical Instruments*, p. 72–3.
11 *Ur Excavations*, p. 227.
12 *Bulletin of the American Schools of Oriental Research*, nos 77 and 88 (1940, 1942).
13 Op. cit., p. 72
14 *New Oxford History of Music*, vol. 1, p. 241.
15 Op. cit., p. 258
16 *Antiquaries Journal of London*, vol. 5, Plate XLVII.
17 Op. cit., p. 143.
18 Ibid., p. 239.
19 Ibid.
20 *The Greek Aulos*, p. 73.
21 *The Music of the Sumerians*, p. 19.
22 Ibid., p. 17.
23 Op. cit., p. 115.
24 Op. cit., p. 92.
25 Translation from Loeb Classical Library.
26 A. A. Howard, 'The aulos or tibia', *Harvard Studies in Classical Philology*, vol. 4 (1893).
27 Curt Sachs, op. cit., p. 141.
28 Ibid., p. 142.
29 H. G. Farmer in *New Oxford History of Music*, vol. 1, p. 443.
30 Plutarch, *De Musica*, V; and Pollux, *Onomasticon*, IV, 74, Basle, 1541, facsimile ed., Stuttgart, 1967.
31 Op. cit., p. 139.
32 Aulus Gellius, *Noctes Atticae*, book XV, 17, trans. John C. Rolfe, Loeb's Classical Library.
33 Cf. Robert Graves, *The Greek Myths*, Penguin, 1955, vol. 1, p. 77.
34 Op. cit., p. 138.
35 Penguin edition, Introduction, p. 21.
36 Baines, *Bagpipes*, p. 63.
37 Aulus Gellius, *Noctes Atticae*, I. xi, 1–5.
38 Plutarch's *Lives: Lycurgus*, trans. Dryden (revised A. H. Clough).
39 *Geography of Strabo*, ix.3.10.
40 Ibid.
41 Pausanias, VI, 14, 9; and X, 7, 4.

42 Kathleen Schlesinger, op. cit., p. 79.
43 VI, 622.
44 Plutarch's *Lives: Numa Pompilius*, trans. Dryden (revised Clough).
45 Cicero, *De Legibus*, II, xxiii, trans. Clinton Walker Keys, Loeb's Classical Library.
46 Ibid., II, xxiii, ix, xx.
47 Notes to Ovid's *Fasti* by Sir James G. Fraser, Macmillan, 1929, and Loeb Classical Library.
48 Ovid, *Fasti*, VI, Ides of June; Livy, IX, 30; Plutarch, *Quaestiones Romanae*, 55; Quintilian, V, xi, 9.
49 Varro, I. ii, 14–17, trans. Roland G. Kent, Loeb's Classical Library.
50 Horace, *Satires*, II, trans. H. Rushton Fairclough, Loeb's Classical Library.
51 John Garstang, *The Land of the Hittites*, London, 1910, p. 260.
52 Hans Hickman, *Musikgeschichte in Bildern*, vol. 2, p. 94.
53 Dio Chrysostom, *Orationes*, 7.xxi.9, trans. H. Lamar Crosby, Loeb's Classical Library.
54 Martial, *Epigrams*, x.3.8, Loeb's Classical Library.
55 *The Story of the Bagpipe*, p. 16.
56 Aristoxenus, *Harm.*, cited by A. A. Howard, 'The aulos or tibia', *Harvard Studies* . . ., p. 30n.
57 *Art in Britain under the Romans*, p. 167.
58 Collinson, 'Syrinx and Bagpipe': a Romano-British representation?', *Antiquity*, vol. 43, no. 172, December 1969.
59 Baines says for another six centuries, *Bagpipes*, p. 67.
60 Dio Cassius, *Roman History*, book LI.6.4. Translation by Ernest Cary on the basis of Herbert Baldwin Foster, Loeb Classical Library, vol. 6, p. 17.
61 'Roman inscribed and sculptured stones preserved at Tullie House, Carlisle', Notes from Cumberland and Westmorland Society, *Transactions*, vol. 15 (1896–9), p. 109, and Plate IX.
62 Meibomius, 'Aristides Quintilianus, *De Musica*, Book 2', *Antiquae musicae Septem Graece et Latinae*, Amsterdam, 1652, p. 73.
63 *The Highland Bagpipe*, p. 34.
64 London Museum catalogue, *London in Roman Times*, under 'Flutes' (!).
65 Op. cit., p. 138.
66 I. A. Richmond, *Roman and Native in North Britain*, pp. 57ff, 109.
67 Op. cit., p. 98.
68 Cf. Keller, op. cit., p. 121
69 Baines, *Bagpipes*, p. 30.
70 Baines, *Woodwind Instruments and their History*, 1957, p. 234; *Musical Instruments through the Ages*, p. 224; *Bagpipes*, pp. 57, 61.
71 Sir J. G. Frazer, *The Golden Bough* ('fire', 'sun').

## Chapter two   Britain after the Romans

1 I. A. Richmond, *Roman and Native in North Britain*, p. 109; also Anthony Birley, *Life in Roman Britain*, pp. 22, 51.
2 Grove, *Dictionary of Music and Musicians* (4th ed.), Plate LXIV; also Galpin, *Old English Instruments of Music*, Plate XX.
3 O'Curry, *On the Manners and Customs of the Ancient Irish*, vol. 3, pp. 246, 377–80.
4 George Petrie, 'On the antiquities of Tara Hill', *Transactions of the Royal Irish Academy*, vol. 18 (1839), p. 38.
5 P. W. Joyce, *A Smaller Social History of Ancient Ireland*. See also *Encyclopaedia Britannica* (14th ed.), 'Brehon Laws' and Introduction to the Laws.
6 Ibid.
7 *Encyclopaedia Britannica* (14th ed.), 'Brehon Laws'.
8 *The Ancient Laws of Ireland*, Brehon Law Tracts, Dublin (1879), p. 339, published under the direction of the Commissioners for publishing the ancient Laws and Institutes of Ireland. Cf. also the edition of the Brehon Laws published by the Brehon Law Commission, Dublin (1852), vol. 5,

(Dublin 1865), pp. 108–20.

9 Joyce, op. cit., p. 35.

10 *The Story of the Bagpipe*, ch. IV *passim*.

11 Ibid., p. 20.

12 From George Petrie, op. cit., pp. 148–9.

13 *A Description of the Western Islands of Scotland*, pp. 148–9.

14 In the deeds of the Priory of Holy Trinity (Christ Church Cathedral), Dublin (Flood, op. cit., p. 24).

15 Flood, op. cit., p. 27. He omits, however, to give references for pipers at the battle of Crecy.

16 Ed. and trans. by Whitley Stokes, *Revue Celtique*, vol. 19 (1898), pp. 154–5.

17 Verse and translation from W. S. Gwynn Williams, *Welsh National Music and Dance*, p. 41.

18 '*Nyd amken a telyn yhun a crud yarall a pyben yr tredyt*', ibid., p. 28.

19 *Man*, vol. 47, no. 17 (1947), pp. 17–40.

20 Baines, *Bagpipes*, pp. 40–1.

21 *Bagpipes*, p. 40.

22 *The History of Musical Instruments*, p. 281.

23 *Bagpipes*, p. 67.

24 P. L. Migne, *Patrologia Latinae*, xxx, p. 221, Epistola xxiii, ad Dardanum: *De diversus generibus musicorum*.

25 '*Synagogae antiquis temporibus fuit chorus quoque simplex pellis cum duabus cicutis aereis: et per primam inspiratur, per secondam vocem emittit*.'

26 See woodcut in John Derricke, *The Image of Ireland*; also Pieter Breughel's two 'Wedding Dance' paintings and his 'Peasant Dance'.

27 C. R. Day, *Musical Instruments of Southern India and the Deccan*, London, 1891, Plate XVI.

28 Sir Robert Ker Porter, *Travels in Georgia, 1817–80*, vol. 2, Plate 64.

29 Rep.II.144a; cf. Edward Buhle, *Die Blasinstrumente des frühen Mittelalters*, Leipzig, 1903.

30 Lat. 6705. Cf. Buhle, op. cit., Plate B, Dudelsack und Platerspiel.

31 Bodleian no. 964, completed 1344. Cf. J. Strutt, *Sports and Pastimes of the People of England*, p. 309.

32 See Sachs, op. cit., pp. 308–9, for a fuller description.

33 Royal Library (British Museum) MSS. 14 E iii and 14 B v. Cf. Strutt, op. cit., pp. 314, 315.

34 Royal Library, 14 B v.

35 Dalyell, *Musical Memoirs of Scotland*, Plate VIII.

36 Cf. Dauney, *Ancient Scottish Melodies*, p. 125n.

37 Ibid.

38 The poem is published in full in the original Anglo-Saxon and in modern English by Ronald Sutherland in *Piping Times*, vol. 19, no. 4 (1967).

39 Giraldus Cambrensis: *Topographia Hiberniae*, Tertio distinctio, cap.XI. Rolls Series, ed. J. S. Brewer (London, 1861–91), cf. Dalyell, op. cit., p. 47n. The passage is quoted in most of the works on early music of Britain; cf. for instance Dauney (p. 121 and note) who gives the reference as, Giraldus Top.Hib. lib.ii, c.12.

40 Flood, op. cit., p. 31.

41 Baines, *Bagpipes*, p. 104.

42 Dauney, op. cit., p. 125.

43 'Liber de Computis Garderobae', BM, MS. Cott. Nero C viii, vol. 82.

44 Flood, op. cit., p. 37.

45 Joannis de Fordun, *Scotichronicon cum supplementis et continuatione*, Walter Boweri, vol. ii, Edinburgh, 1775, p. 504, bk XVI, ch. xxviii.

46 The interpreted drawing (Plate II,1) is copied from the Bannatyne Club's publication, *The Sculptured Stones of Scotland*, Edinburgh, 1867.

47 Dalyell, op. cit., Plate VIII.

48 *Bagpipes*, p. 102.

49 *Oxford Companion to English Literature*.

50 William Chappell, *Popular Music of the Olden Time*, p. 34n (the trial of William Thorpe).

51 *Oxford Companion to English Literature*.

52 *The Works of James the First*,

*King of Scotland;* and *A Dissertation on Scottish Music,* Edinburgh,
1825 (editor not named), pp. 201,
209.

53  Allan Ramsay, *The Ever Green,
Being a Collection of Scots Poems,
wrote by the ingenious before 1600,*
vol. 2, p. 76, Edinburgh, 1724.
The original source is *The Bannatyne MS,* ed. W. Tod Ritchie,
Scottish Text Society, Edinburgh,
1928–32.

54  *The Bannatyne MS,* vol. 4, p. 279.

55  *The Accounts of the Great Chamberlains of Scotland . . . rendered
at the Exchequer, 1326–1370,* vol. 1;
published by the Bannatyne Club,
Edinburgh, 1817.

56  *Liber de Computis Garderobae,*
Nero C viii, vol. 82. (See also
Strutt, op. cit., p. 277.)

57  *A History of Music in Scotland,*
p. 41.

58  Ibid., p. 39; see also Chappell,
op. cit., p. 5.

59  Farmer, op. cit., p. 39.

60  Andrew Lang, *A History of
Scotland,* vol. 1, p. 105; also James
Taylor, *The Pictorial History of
Scotland,* London (n.d.), vol. 1,
p. 314; also H. G. Farmer, *History
of Music in Scotland,* p. 39. I have,
however, been unable to find the
reference in Ailred's account.

61  MS. Harl. 266. Cf. Ritson, *Ancient
Songs,* p. xiii.

62  H. G. Farmer, *Music in Mediaeval
Scotland,* London, 1930, p. 12.

63  Dublin, 1943.

64  MS. Cott. Lib. Nero C viii fol. 269.

65  C. E. Borjon, *Traité de la musette.*

66  *Robin Hood's Garland,* quoted in
Ritson, *Ancient Songs,* p. ix.

67  Chappell, op. cit., p. 38 and note.

68  Strutt, op. cit.

69  Monstrelet, quoted by Chappell,
op. cit., p. 38.

70  Chappell, op. cit., p. 40.

71  Liber Niger, p. 598.

72  Farmer, *Music in Mediaeval
Scotland,* p. 20.

73  Ibid., p. 17

74  John Hawkins, *A General History
of the Science and Practice of Music,*

London, 1875, vol. 1, p. 271.

75  Ibid., p. 272.

76  *Accounts of the Lord High Treasurers
of Scotland,* 4 vols, ed. T. Dickson
and Sir J. Balfour Paul, Edinburgh,
1877–1902.

77  Cf. John Leyden, Introduction to
*The Complaynt of Scotland,* p. 142.

78  Chappell, op. cit., p. 48, who cites
Harl. MS. 433.

79  Ibid., p. 49.

80  Hawkins, op. cit., p. 271.

81  Holinshed's *Chronicles . . .,* in
6 vols. London, 1808, vol. 3,
p. 577.

82  B.M. Add. MS. 31922, the so-
called 'Henry VIII's Manuscript';
published as 'Music at the Court
of Henry VIII', *Musica Britannica,*
18, 1969.

83  Harl. MS. 1419, fol. 200; and see
F. W. Galpin, *Old English Instruments of Music,* p. 215.

84  Article on 'Waits' by Lyndesay G.
Langwill in *Grove's Dictionary of
Music and Musicians* (5th ed.).

85  Manson, *The Highland Bagpipe,*
pp. 171–2.

86  Extract from *Records of the Royal
Burgh of Lanark A.D. 1150–1722,*
published Glasgow, 1893; reprinted
in *Hamilton Advertiser,* 21 January
1939.

87  Ibid.

88  Manson, op. cit., p. 171.

89  London, 1861.

90  Op. cit.

91  Quoted from an article by Hugh
Macphee in *Radio Times,* 9 November 1956.

92  Reprinted in Watson's *Choice
Collection of Comic and Serious
Scots Poems* (1706), reprinted
Glasgow, 1869.

93  *Robert Burns,* London, 1952, p. 13.

94  Manson, op. cit., p. 47; Flood,
op. cit., p. 50.

95  Flood, op. cit., p. 50.

96  John Knox, *History of the
Reformation in Scotland,* vol. 1,
p. 127.

97  'The records of Elgin', *New Spalding Club,* Aberdeen, 1908, vol. 2,
p. 76.

98 J. L. Campbell and F. Collinson, *Hebridean Folk Songs*, pp. 68–9, line 280.

99 Michael Drayton, *The Poly-Olbion*, London, 1613, song no. 4.

100 *Letters from Kenilworth*, ed. F. J. Furnivall, London and New York, 1907.

101 For the complete words and tune of the ballad, see Chappell, op. cit., vol. 1, pp. 299–300.

102 'The Countryman's Ramble through Bartholomew Fair', Thomas Durfey, *Pills to Purge Melancholy*, editions 1699–1714, vol. 1; see also Chappell, op. cit., vol. 2, p. 585.

103 Brand, *Popular Antiquities*, vol. 2, p. 81, London, 1777.

104 Dalyell, op. cit., p. 31.

105 Chappell, op. cit., p. 580.

106 London, 1857.

107 Surtees, op. cit., vol. 2, p. 122, note (f).

108 Ibid., p. 122.

109 *Popular Music of Olden Time*, p. 84.

110 Ibid., vol. 2, p. 545.

111 For further information see R. D. Cannon, 'English bagpipe music', *Folk Music Journal*, vol. 2, no. 3 (1972), pp. 176–219, which appeared after the above was written. Cf. also ibid., no. 2 (1971).

112 Flood, op. cit., p. 102.

113 Quoted in Percy A. Scholes, *The Oxford Companion to Music*, 4th ed.

114 Dalyell, op. cit., p. 31.

115 J. Leyden, Introduction to *The Complaynt of Scotland* (1548), Edinburgh, 1801, p. 151. Leyden is quoting from an un-named mid-seventeenth-century 'MS. cantus'.

116 Alexander MacAuley, 'The Battle of Cremona', *Piping Times*, vol. 21, no. 2 (1968–9).

117 Vincenzo Galilei, *Dialogo della musica antica e moderna*, Florence, 1581. As the book is now withdrawn from the National Library in Edinburgh I have referred to the translation given by Flood, op. cit., p. 92.

118 Grove, op. cit., 'Bagpipe'.

119 Flood, op. cit., p. 95; *Grove's*, 5th ed., 'Northumbrian Minstrelsy', iv.

120 The mis-statement is repeated by W. Gillies Whittaker in 'The folk-music of north-eastern England', in his *Collected Essays*, London, 1940, p. 38.

121 G. Askew, 'The origins of the Northumbrian bagpipe', *Archaeologia Aeliana*, 4th series, vol. 9, 1932.

122 W. Cocks and J. F. Bryan, *The Northumbrian Bagpipes*, p. 13.

123 Borjon, op. cit.

124 Cocks and Bryan, op. cit., p. 13.

125 Ibid., Introduction.

126 *The Traditional Music of Scotland*, pp. 167–8.

127 Op. cit.

128 J. S. Keltie, *The Scottish Highlands, Highland Clans and Highland Regiments*, 1879, vol. 2, p. 453.

### Chapter three   The Great Highland bagpipe

1 John Barbour (ed. W. W. Skeat), *The Bruce*, 1894, book 19, lines 696–745.

2 *Chronicles of England, France, Spain, and the adjoining Countries*, by Sir John Froissart, trans. from the French eds by Thomas Johnes, London, 1839, vol. 1, p. 23, and vol. 2, p. 375. Cf. also *Froissart Chronicles*, ed. G. Brereton, Penguin, Harmondsworth, 1968, pp. 51, 347.

3 Tacitus, *Agricola* 30 (Galgacus's address to his army before the battle of Mons Graupius). Penguin ed., p. 80.

4 John Gunn, *An Historical Enquiry Respecting Performance on the Harp in Scotland*, p. 51.

5 Edinburgh, 1811, vol. 2, p. 201.

6 'Notes on the "Bannockburn" bagpipes of Menzies', *Proceedings of the Society of Antiquaries of Scotland*, vol. 5, 3rd series, 1894–5.

7 Manson, *The Highland Bagpipe*, p. 39.

8 'The ancient musical instruments of Scotland', *Proceedings of the*

*Society of Antiquaries of Scotland,*
vol. 14, 1879–80.

9  Baines, *Bagpipes,* p. 116.

10 *Encyclopaedia Britannica,* 'Lignum
   vitae'.

11 *Creag Dhubh,* the annual [journal]
   of the Clan MacPherson Association,
   Newtonmore, Inverness-shire,
   no. 15, 1963, pp. 15, 17.

12 Sir Walter Scott, notes to *The
   Fair Maid of Perth,* note 22, p. 687.
   See also Androw (*sic*) Wyntoun,
   *The Orygynale Cronykil of Scotland,*
   ed. David Laing, Edinburgh, 1872.

13 Ibid. Also, in *The Buik of the
   Croniclis of Scotland, a Metrical
   Version of the History of Hector
   Boece* by William Stewart, ed.
   William B. Turnbull, London,
   1858, col. 3, p. 452. there is no
   mention of either bagpipes or
   trumpets. The version quoted by
   Scott in his notes is by John
   Bellenden and is entitled *The
   History and Chroniklis of Scotland,*
   Edinburgh, 1636.

14 Vol. 6, p. 528, 1853 ed., notes p. 447.

15 Glen, *Early Scottish Melodies,* p. 219.

16 *The Story of the Bagpipe,* p. 54.

17 Child, *The English and Scottish
   Popular Ballads,* Boston, 1882–98,
   no. 163, vol. 3, p. 318, version A,
   stanza 1.

18 *Ancient Scottish Melodies,* p. 120.

19 Cf. Derick S. Thomson, 'The
   Harlaw *Brosnachadh,* an early
   fifteenth-century curio', *Celtic
   Studies,* 1968, p. 147.

20 J. F. Campbell, *Popular Tales of
   the West Highlands,* vol. 4, p. 56,
   Edinburgh, 1862.

21 Vol. 1, ch. 33.

22 John Monipennie, *A Summary of
   the Scottish Chronicle; an abridgement of the Black Book of Paisley;
   Of The Isles of Scotland in General,*
   p. 136.

23 Op. cit., p. 51.

24 For further information on the
   origin of the MacLeods, see the
   important note (p. 107) in William
   Matheson, *The Blind Harper,*
   Edinburgh, 1970, Gaelic Texts
   Society, published since the above

was written.

25 Seton Gordon, *The Charm of Skye,*
   London, 1929, p. 112.

26 Roderick Ross, *Binneas is Boreraig,*
   vol. 1, Introduction, p. ii.

27 Ibid.; also R. C. MacLeod of
   MacLeod, *The MacLeods of
   Dunvegan,* p. 160; G. C. B. Poulter
   and C. P. Fisher, *The MacCrimmon Family,* Camberley, 1936,
   p. 8; and Neil Ross, 'Ceòl Mór',
   *Transactions of the Gaelic Society
   of Inverness,* 1925, vol. 32, p. 162.

28 I. F. Grant, *The MacLeods: the
   History of a Clan,* p. 29.

29 Poulter and Fisher, op. cit., p. 6.

30 Ibid., p. 8, and see note 31.

31 *Piping Times,* Vol. 5, nos 4–10
   (1952–3).

32 Poulter and Fisher, op. cit., p. 7.

33 *Piping Times,* vol. 22, no. 11
   (August 1970).

34 Angus MacKay, *A Collection of
   Ancient Pìobaireachd,* pp. 2, 3n.

35 For further details of these and
   later members of the MacCrimmon
   family, as well as of other pipers,
   see 'Notices of pipers', *Piping
   Times,* vol. 22, nos 8, 10 and 11
   (1970–1) and other numbers of
   this informative series of articles;
   also Seumas MacNeill,
   *Pìobaireachd,* p. 41.

36 Daniel Dow, *A Collection of
   Ancient Scots Music,* p. 28;
   'Battle of Hardlaw'; James
   Johnson, *The Scots Musical
   Museum,* vol. 4, p. 447.

37 C. S. Thomason, *Ceòl Mór,* p. ix.

38 Donald MacDonald, *Ancient
   Martial Music of Caledonia called
   Pìobaireachd.*

39 Ibid.

40 Angus MacKay, op. cit., p. 21;
   Thomason, op. cit., p. 188.

41 MacKay, op. cit., p. 21; Thomason,
   op. cit., p. 96.

42 MacKay, op. cit., p. 37; Thomason,
   op. cit., p. 157.

43 MacKay, op. cit., p. 162.

44 I. F. Grant, *The MacLeods,*
   pp. 137–9.

45 See note 64, below.

46 The above translation of the Latin

of Giraldus, I have compressed and edited from John Gunn, *An Historical Enquiry Respecting Performance on the Harp in Scotland*, and John J. O'Meara (trs.), *The First Version of the Topography of Ireland by Giraldus Cambrensis* (Dundalk, 1951).

47 Cf. Angus MacKay, op. cit., notes, p. 13.

48 Scottish History Society, *Chronicles of the Frasers*, vol. 47, Edinburgh, 1905.

49 James E. Scott, 'I kissed the king's hand', *Piping Times*, vol. 6, no. 12 (1953–4); also other articles on the subject in the same journal at various times.

50 Op. cit., p. 5.

51 Thomas Pennant, *A Tour in Scotland and Voyage to the Hebrides, 1772*, Chester, 1774, vol. 2, p. 301.

52 Angus MacKay, op. cit., p. 7.

53 This interesting indenture was published with notes by Archibald Campbell of Kilberry in *Piping Times*, vol. 16, no. 5 (1963–4) where it may be read in full, and see Appendix II above.

54 Archibald Campbell, 'The MacGregor pipers of the *Clann an Sgeulaiche*', *Piping Times*, vol. 2, no. 10 (1949–50).

55 J. F. Campbell of Islay.

56 Grove, op. cit. (4th ed.), under 'Guido d'Arezzo', 'Solmisation'.

57 Poulter and Fisher, op. cit., p. 7.

58 J. P. Grant, 'Canntaireachd', *The Pipes of War*, p. 179.

59 Archibald Campbell, *The Kilberry Book of Ceòl Mór*, p. 11.

60 Ibid.

61 Ibid.

62 J. P. Grant, op. cit., p. 187.

63 G. F. Ross, *Some Pìobaireachd Studies*, p. 9.

64 For a fuller explanation of the structure of *pìobaireachd* see Collinson, *The Traditional and National Music of Scotland*, p. 174, and, for a more advanced study, Seumas MacNeill, *Pìobaireachd*, p. 42. Seumas MacNeill is Principal of the College of Piping, Glasgow,

and his work is authoritative.

65 The official guide to pronunciation of the Nether Lorn *canntaireachd* as revised by Colonel J. P. Grant of Rothiemurchus is set out in no. 11 of the Pìobaireachd Society's books of tunes, *Pìobaireachd*, 1966.

66 A reference to two or three of the MacArthur vocables may be found in an article by William Gray, 'The Lost Pìobaireachd, by Patrick Mór MacCrimmon', *Piping Times*, vol. 11, part 10 (1958–9).

67 Manson, op. cit., p. 117, quoting from *Trans. Soc. Antiq. Scot.* without giving the date or number of the issue of the *Transactions*. Cf. also 'Roll of MacNachtane's Soldieris schipped at Lochkerran, 11th December 1627', Scottish History Society, *Highland Papers*, vol. 1, p. 114, Edinburgh (1914).

68 John Buchan, *Montrose*, p. 120. (Buchan modernizes the spelling as in the quotation above.)

69 Ibid., pp. 221, 225.

70 Cf. J. B. Salmond, *Wade in Scotland*, chapter 4, 'The Highland Companies'. The author puts the phrase in quotation marks but does not give his source.

71 Ibid.

72 *A Narrative of Events in Edinburgh and District during the Jacobite Occupation, September to November 1745*. Printed from original papers in the possession of C. F. S. Chambers, Edinburgh (Chambers, Edinburgh, 1907).

73 John Prebble, *Culloden*, p. 69.

74 Manson, op. cit., p. 347.

75 Prebble, op. cit., p. 247.

76 *Baga de Secretis*, Appendix 2 to the fifth report of the Deputy Keeper of the Public Records, London, lxix, p. 193.

77 Prebble, op. cit., p. 329.

78 See *The Parliamentary History of England*, vol. 16 (Hansard), p. 98 and J. S. Keltie, *A History of the Scottish Highlands, Highland Clans and Highland Regiments*, vol. 2, pp. 345n and 453.

79  I am indebted to Dr J. S. Campbell of Canna, direct descendant of Captain James Campbell of the Western Fencibles (later Sir James Campbell of Inverneill), for the Regimental Order Sheet here quoted.

80  A. R. B. Haldane, *The Drove Roads of Scotland*, p. 25.

81  Ibid., pp. 103, 180.

82  J. G. Lockhart, *Memoirs of the Life of Sir Walter Scott*, vol. 3, p. 231.

83  Dalyell, *Musical Memoirs of Scotland*, p. 93, gives 1778 as the year of the Society's formation. Andrew Lang gives 1803.

84  Ibid., pp. 102–3.

85  Archibald Campbell, 'The MacGregor pipers of the *Clann an Sgeulaiche*', *Piping Times*, vol. 2, no. 10 (1949–50).

86  *Ceòl Mór*, p. 8.

87  Angus MacKay, *Ancient Pìobaireachd*, p. 9.

88  Ibid., p. 16.

89  Seton Gordon, *The Charm of Skye*, p. 111.

90  J. B. Salmond, *Wade in Scotland*, pp. 48, 113.

91  *Ceòl Mór*, p. 8.

92  Op. cit., p. 107.

93  Seumas MacNeill, *Pìobaireachd*, p. 38.

94  Archibald Campbell, *Ceòl Mór*, p. 10.

95  Seumas MacNeill, op. cit., p. 37.

96  Roderick Ross, *Binneas is Boreraig*, vols 3 and 4, Introduction.

97  Flood, op. cit., pp. 128, 135; also William Cocks, 'Bagpipe', in Grove, op. cit., 5th ed.

98  Derick Thomson, 'The Mac-Mhuirich Bardic Family', *Transactions of the Gaelic Society of Inverness*, vol. 43 (1960–3), p. 276.

99  Joseph MacDonald, *A Compleat Theory of the Scots Highland Bagpipe*, compiled 1760–3, first published, Edinburgh, 1803, reprinted Inverness, 1927. MS. in Edinburgh University Library.

100  4th ed. (1942), facing p. 62.

101  Cf. Archibald Campbell, *Ceòl Mór*, p. 11. The MS. is now in the National Library of Scotland.

102  Boswell's *Journey to the Hebrides*, p. 115 and *passim*.

103  See the article by John MacLellan in *Piping Times*, vol. 18, no. 6 (1965–6).

104  Archibald Campbell of Kilberry, 'The History and Art of Angus MacKay', *Piping Times*, vol. 2 (three articles) (1949–50).

105  Angus MacKay's account, *Ancient Pìobaireachd*, p. 11.

106  *Inverness Journal*, 30 December 1808.

107  Article by Dr Norman MacLeod in the *Messenger*, 1835. The translation, taken from Dr I. F. Grant, *The MacLeods*, p. 561, is by Alick Morrison, Bernera.

108  *Albyn's Anthology*, notes, vol. 1, p. 90.

109  For the full title, 86 words in length, see Collinson, *The Traditional and National Music of Scotland*, p. 193.

110  'Transliteration of the Gesto *Canntaireachd*' by William MacLean, unpublished. (From my notes made from the typescript.)

111  J. G. Lockhart, *Memoirs of the Life of Sir Walter Scott*, vol. 3, p. 231.

112  Ibid., vol. 4, p. 189.

113  Angus MacKay's account, *Ancient Pìobaireachd*, p. 12.

114  Robert Jameson, *Historical Record of the 79th* [Regiment of Foot] *or Cameron Highlanders*, Edinburgh, 1863, p. 55n.

115  *The Second World War*, vol. 4, pp. 644–5, London, 1951.

116  Op. cit., p. 30.

117  Baines, *Bagpipes*, p. 114.

## Appendix I  Materials

1  Hans Hickmann, 'Instruments de musique', *Catalogue général des antiquités égyptiennes du Musée du Caire*, p. 139.

2 Translation by Sir Arthur Hort, Loeb's Classical Library, pp. 369–75.
3 A. A. Howard, 'The aulos or tibia' *Harvard Studies in Classical Philology*, vol. 4 (1893).
4 *Ars Poetica*, I, 202–5.
5 'Ancient flutes from Egypt', *Hellenic Studies*, vol. 35 (1915).
6 'Remarks addressed to an illiterate book fancier' (*Adversus indoctum*, iii).
7 Socrates quoted by Aristotle, *Politics*, III, 2–4, Loeb ed., p. 233.
8 *Natural History*. Trans. J. Bostock and H. T. Riley, Loeb's Classical Library, London, 1892.
9 Pliny's chapter LXVI.
10 Catalogue no. 3 (1946).
11 William Cocks, *The Northumbrian Bagpipes, their Development and Makers*, Newcastle-upon-Tyne, 1933.
12 Information extracted from a letter from A. C. Hunter in an early number of *Piping Times*.
13 William Hamilton of Bangour, manuscript volume in Laing MSS III, 451, University of Edinburgh Library; and see also Nelson S. Bushnell, *William Hamilton of Bangour*, Aberdeen, 1957.
14 W. J. Bean, *Trees and Shrubs*, London, 1914, vol. 2, p. 116.
15 Baines, *Musical Instruments through the Ages*, p. 253.

## Appendix II   Two indentures of apprenticeship

1 *Piping Times*, vol. 21, no. 3 (1968–9), by kind permission.
2 W. L. Westerman, 'Apprenticeship contracts and the apprenticeship system in Roman Egypt', *Classical Philology*, vol. 9, 1914, pp. 295ff.
3 W. L. Westerman, 'The castanet dancers of Arsinoe', *Journal of Egyptian Archaeology*, vol. 10 (1924), p. 143. The details given respecting this indenture are extracted from these articles, with acknowledgment.

ALBRIGHT, W. F., 'New light on the history of western Asia in the second millennium', *Bulletin of the American Schools of Oriental Research*, no. 77, Baghdad (1940), p. 20.

ALBRIGHT, W. F., 'A third revision of the early chronology of western Asia', ibid., no. 88, Baghdad (1942), p. 28.

ASKEW, GILBERT, 'The origins of the Northumbrian bagpipe', *Archaeologia Aeliana*, 4th series, vol. 9, Newcastle-upon-Tyne (1932).

ASKEW, GILBERT, *A Bibliography of the Bagpipe*, Newcastle-upon-Tyne, 1932.

ATKINSON, J. C., *The History of Cleveland, Yorkshire*, vol. 1, Barrow-in-Furness, 1874.

BAILEY, CHARLES T. P., *Knives and Forks*, London, 1927.

BAINES, ANTHONY, *Bagpipes*, Oxford, 1960.

BAINES, ANTHONY, *Musical Instruments through the Ages*, Harmondsworth, 1961.

BAINES, ANTHONY, *Woodwind Instruments and their History*, London, 1957.

BALFOUR, HENRY, 'The old British "pibcorn" or "hornpipe" and its affinities', *Journal of the Anthropological Institute*, vol. 20 (1890).

BANNATYNE CLUB, *The Accounts of the Great Chamberlains of Scotland . . . rendered at the Exchequer, 1326–1370*, vol. 1, Edinburgh, 1817–45.

BARBOUR, JOHN (ed. W. W. Skeat), *The Bruce*, London, 1894.

BENTLEY, WILLIAM, 'Notes on the musical instruments in the windows of the Beauchamp Chapel, St. Mary's Warwick', *Transactions of the Birmingham Archaeological Society*, vol. 53 (1928), p. 168.

BENTZON, A. F. W., *The Launeddas, a Sardinian Folk Music Instrument*, Copenhagen, 1969.

BIANCHINI (or Blanchini), FRANCESCO VERONENSIS, *De Tribus Generibus Instrumentorum Musicae Veterum*, Rome, 1742.

BIRLEY, ANTHONY, *Life in Roman Britain*, London, 1964.

BORJON, C. E., *Traité de la musette*, Lyons, 1672.

BOSWELL, JAMES, *Journal of a Tour to the Hebrides with Samuel Johnson* (1773), modern edition, Pottle & Bennett (eds), London, 1963.

BOYS, WILLIAM, *Collections for a History of Sandwich*, Canterbury, 1792.

BREHON LAW COMMISSION, *The Ancient Laws of Ireland*, ed. D. A. Binchey et al., vol. 5, Dublin, 1852.

BRITISH MUSEUM, *Catalogue of the Greek and Etruscan Vases in the British Museum*, vol. 2, H. B. Walters, London, 1893.

BRITISH MUSEUM, ibid., vol. 3, Cecil H. Smith, London, 1896.

BUCHAN, JOHN, *Montrose*, Edinburgh, 1928.

BUCHANAN, GEORGE, *Rerum Scoticarum Historia*, Frankfurt, 1582.

BUHLE, EDWARD, *Die musikalischen Instrumente in den Miniaturen des frühen Mittelalters*, Leipzig, 1903.

BUNTING, EDWARD, *The Ancient Music of Ireland*, Dublin, 1840.

BURNEY, CHARLES, *A General History of Music*, London, 1776–89.

CAMPBELL, ALEXANDER, 'A Slight Sketch of a Journey made through parts of the Highlands and Hebrides; undertaken to collect materials for *Albyn's Anthology*' (1815), MS., Edinburgh University Library.

CAMPBELL, ALEXANDER, *Albyn's Anthology, or A Select Collection of the Melodies and Vocal Poetry peculiar to Scotland and the Isles*, 2 vols, Edinburgh, 1816.

CAMPBELL, ARCHIBALD (of Kilberry), *The Kilberry Book of Ceòl Mór* (2nd ed.), Glasgow, 1953.

CAMPBELL, ARCHIBALD (of Kilberry), 'The MacGregor pipers of the *Clann an Sgeulaiche*', *Piping Times*, vol. 2, part 10, Glasgow, 1950.

CAMPBELL, JAMES, 'Regimental Orders of the Western Fencible Regiment and Captain James Campbell's Company Commencing the 8th July 1778', Inverneil MS. no. 18, privately owned by J. L. Campbell of Canna.

CAMPBELL, J. F. (of Islay), *Canntaireachd: Articulate Music*, Glasgow, 1880.

CAMPBELL, J. L. and COLLINSON, FRANCIS, *Hebridean Folk Songs: The MacCormick Collection of Waulking Songs*, London, 1969.

CANNON, R. D., 'English Bagpipe Music', *Folk Music Journal*, vol. 2, no. 3 (1972), pp. 176–219, English Folk Dance and Song Society.

CARNARVON, LORD, and CARTER, HOWARD, *Five Years' Exploration at Thebes*, Oxford, 1912.

CARTER, JOHN, *Specimens of the Ancient Sculpture now remaining in this Kingdom from the earliest period to the reign of Henry VIII*, London, 1780. *Catalogue général des antiquités égyptiennes du Musée du Caire*, see Hickmann.

CHAPPELL, WILLIAM, *Popular Music of the Olden Time*, 2 vols, London, 1855–9.

CHARLTON, G. V. B., 'The Northumbrian Bagpipes', *Archaeologia Aeliana*, 4th series, vol. 7, Newcastle-upon-Tyne (1930).

*Chronicles of the Atholl and Tullibardine Families*, collected and arranged by John, seventh Duke of Atholl, privately printed, Edinburgh, 1908.

COCKS, WILLIAM A., 'Bagpipe' in Eric Blom (ed.), Grove, *Dictionary of Music and Musicians* (5th ed.), London, 1954.

COCKS, WILLIAM A., *The Northumbrian Bagpipes: Their Development and Makers*, Newcastle-upon-Tyne, 1933.

COCKS, WILLIAM A., and BRYAN, J. F., *The Northumbrian Bagpipes*, Newcastle-upon-Tyne, 1967.

COLES, J. M., 'Irish Bronze Age horns and their relations with northern Europe', *Proceedings of the Prehistoric Society*, new series, vol. 29 (1963).

COLLINGWOOD BRUCE, J., *Handbook of the Roman Wall* (3rd edn), London, 1887.

COLLINGWOOD BRUCE, J., and STOKOE, JOHN, *Northumbrian Minstrelsey*, Newcastle-upon-Tyne, 1882.

COLLINSON, FRANCIS, *The Traditional and National Music of Scotland*, London, 1966, Nashville, U.S.A., 1966.

COLLINSON, FRANCIS, 'Syrinx and bagpipe: a Romano-British representation?',
*Antiquity*, vol. 43 (1969).

COSSON, BARON DE, 'A brass repoussé knife-handle representing a bagpiper,
found at Glanton, Northumberland', *Proceedings of the Society of Antiquaries,
Newcastle-upon-Tyne*, vol. 5, 2nd series (1891).

DALYELL, JOHN GRAHAM, *Musical Memoirs of Scotland, with Historical
Annotations*, Edinburgh, 1849.

DAUNEY, WILLIAM, *Ancient Scottish Melodies, with an introductory inquiry
illustrative of the History of the Music of Scotland*, Edinburgh, 1838.

DERRICKE, JOHN, *The Image of Ireland*, London, 1581.

*Disarming Act of 1747: An Act for the more effectual disarming the Highlands
in Scotland and for more effectually securing the Peace of the said Highlands,
and for restraining the Use of the Highland Dress* . . . Libris, Bibliothecae
Facultatis juridical, Edinburgh, 1746 (hand-engrossed copy in the Advocates'
Library, Edinburgh).

DIXON, D. DIPPIE, 'Knife handle, curious, found at Glanton', *Whittingham
Vale, Northumberland; its history, Traditions and Folklore*, Newcastle-upon-
Tyne, 1895.

DONINGTON, ROBERT, *The Instruments of Music*, London, 1949.

DOW, DANIEL, *A Collection of Ancient Scots Music*, Edinburgh, n.d. [1783].

*Duanaire Finn* (ed. Gerard Murphy), Irish Texts Society, vols. 7, 28, 43,
London/Dublin (1908–53).

ENGEL, CARL, *The Music of the Most Ancient Nations*, London, 1864.

ENGEL, CARL, *Musical Instruments*, London, 1875.

*Exeter Book, The*, Early English Text Society, no. 194, ed. W. S. Mackie,
London (1934).

FARMER, HENRY G., *A History of Music in Scotland*, London, 1947.

FARMER, HENRY G., *Music in Mediaeval Scotland*, London, 1930.

FARMER, HENRY G., 'The music of ancient Mesopotamia' in Egon Wellesz (ed.),
*The New Oxford History of Music*, vol. 1, Oxford, 1966.

FLOOD, C. W. H. GRATTAN, *The Story of the Bagpipe*, London, 1911.

FORDUN, JOHANNIS DE, *Chronica Gentis Scotorum*, trans. F. J. H. Skene, ed.
W. F. Skene, Edinburgh, 1872.

FRASER, A. DUNCAN, *Some Reminiscences and the Bagpipe*, Edinburgh, 1907.

FRASER, SIMON (of Knockie), *Airs and Melodies Peculiar to the Highlands of
Scotland*, ed. Angus Fraser, vol. 2, part 1, Inverness, 1874. (The remainder is
in manuscript in Edinburgh University Library, 'The Angus Fraser
Manuscript'.)

FRAZER, J. G., *The Golden Bough* (Abridged ed.), London, 1941.

FRERE, A. H., manuscript copies of correspondence relating to the *pibgorn* and
Spanish *alboka*, in possession of Lyndesay G. Langwill.

FROISSART, JOHN, *Chronicles* (ed. Thomas Johnes), London, 1839.

GALILEI, VINCENZO, *Dialogo della musica antica e moderna*, Florence, 1581.

GALPIN, F. W., *The Music of the Sumerians*, London, 1937.

GALPIN, F. W., *Old English Instruments of Music*, rev. Thurston Dart, London,
1965.

GALPIN SOCIETY, *An Exhibition of European Musical Instruments* (catalogue),
ed. Graham Melville-Mason, Edinburgh, 1968.

GARSTANG, JOHN, *The Land of the Hittites*, London, 1910.

GLEN, DAVID, *A Collection of Ancient Pìobaireachd*, Edinburgh, n.d.
GLEN, J. & R. (Highland bagpipe makers), Account Book, 1838 (in manuscript), Edinburgh.
GLEN, JOHN, *Early Scottish Melodies*, Edinburgh, 1900.
GLEN, ROBERT, 'The ancient musical instruments of Scotland', *Proceedings of the Society of Antiquaries of Scotland*, vol. 14 (1879–80).
GORDON, SETON, *The Charm of Skye*, London, 1929.
GORDON, SETON, *Highways and Byways in the West Highlands*, London, 1948.
GRANT, I. F., *The MacLeods: The History of a Clan*, London, 1959.
GRANT, J. P. (of Rothiemurchus), 'Canntaireachd', chapter in Bruce Seton of Abercorn and Pipe-major John Grant, *The Pipes of War*, Glasgow, 1920.
GUNN, JOHN, *An Historical Enquiry Respecting Performance on the Harp in Scotland*, Edinburgh, 1807.
GWYNN, EDWARD, *The Metrical Dinnseanchus*, Dublin, 1903.
GWYNN WILLIAMS, W. S., *Welsh National Music and Dance*, London, 1932.
HALDANE, A. R. B., *The Drove Roads of Scotland*, Edinburgh, 1952.
*Hamilton Advertiser*, 21 January 1939, reprinted extract concerning the town and burgh minstrels, from *Records of the Royal Burgh of Lanark, 1150–1722*, Glasgow, 1893.
HARRISON, FRANK and RIMMER, JOAN, *European Musical Instruments*, London, 1964.
HAVERFIELD, F., 'Roman inscribed and sculptured stones preserved at Tullie House, Carlisle', Cumberland and Westmorland Society, *Transactions*, vol. 15 (1896–9).
HAWKINS, JOHN, *A General History of the Science and Practice of Music* (new ed.), London, 1875.
HICKMANN, HANS, 'Instruments de musique', *Catalogue général des antiquités égyptiennes du Musée du Caire*, Cairo, 1949.
HICKMANN, HANS (ed.), vol. 2, *Musikgeschichte in Bildern: Musik des Altertums*, Leipzig, 1961.
HOGG, JAMES, *Jacobite Relics* (1819), reprinted, Paisley, 1874.
HOWARD, A. A., 'The aulos or tibia', *Harvard Studies in Classical Philology*, vol. 4 (1893).
HUME BROWN, P., *History of Scotland*, Cambridge, 1911.
JOHNMAN, W. A. P., 'Bagpipes and border pipers', *Transactions of the Hawick Archaeological Society* (1913).
JOHNSON, JAMES, *The Scots Musical Museum*, new ed., with notes by William Stenhouse, additional notes by David Laing, Edinburgh, 1853.
JOYCE, P. W., *A Smaller Social History of Ancient Ireland*, London, 1908.
KELLER, W., *The Bible as History*, trans. W. Neil, London, 1956.
KELTIE, JOHN S., *A History of the Scottish Highlands, Highland Clans and Highland Regiments*, 2 vols, London, 1879.
KER PORTER, ROBERT, *Travels in Georgia, Persia, Armenia and Ancient Babylon*, vol. 2, London, 1820.
KING, EDWARD, *Munimenta Antiqua*, vol. 2, London, 1799.
KINGSLEY PORTER, A., *The Crosses and Culture of Ireland*, five lectures delivered at the Metropolitan Museum of Art, New York, 1931.
KNOX, JOHN, *History of the Reformation in Scotland*, ed. W. Croft Dickinson, vol. 1, London, 1949.

LAFONTAINE, H. C., *The King's Music*, London, 1909.

LANG, ANDREW, *A History of Scotland from the Roman Occupation*, Edinburgh, 1900.

LANGWILL, LYNDESAY G., 'The stock and horn', *Proceedings of the Society of Antiquaries of Scotland*, vol. 84 (1949–50).

LANGWILL, LYNDESAY G., manuscript material for above, in Lyndesay Langwill's possession.

LANGWILL, LYNDESAY G., *The Waits, A Short Historical Study*, London, 1952.

LANGWILL, LYNDESAY G., 'Waits', in Eric Blom (ed.), *Grove's Dictionary of Music and Musicians* (5th ed.), London, 1954.

LANGWILL, LYNDESAY G., manuscript material for the above, in Lyndesay Langwill's possession.

LANGWILL, LYNDESAY G., miscellaneous collection of manuscripts and published material on wind instruments, including bagpipes, in Lyndesay Langwill's possession.

LEDWICH, EDWARD, *The Antiquities of Ireland*, Dublin, 1790.

LEYDEN, JOHN, Introduction to *The Complaynt of Scotland*, Edinburgh, 1801.

*Liber de Computis Garderobae*, British Museum MS Cott. Lib. Nero C. viii.

LOCKHART, J. G., *Memoirs of the Life of Sir Walter Scott*, Edinburgh, 1837.

*London in Roman Times*, London Museum catalogue no. 3, with preface by R. E. Mortimer Wheeler, London, 1930.

LORIMER, R. L. C., in association with the British Council, sleeve notes to record, *Pibroch 1*, Waverley ZLP 2034, Edinburgh, 1964.

LOVILLO, JOSE GUERRERO, *Las Cantigas; Estudio arqueologico de sus miniaturas*, Seville, 1949.

MACALISTER, R. A. S., *Monasterboice, Co. Louth*, Dundalk, 1946.

MACDONALD, DONALD, *The Ancient Martial Music of Caledonia called Pìobaireachd*, vol. 1, Edinburgh, 1822. Vol. 2 in manuscript at the National Library of Scotland.

MACDONALD, JOSEPH, *A Compleat Theory of the Great Bagpipe*, compiled 1760–3, Edinburgh, 1803, reprinted Inverness, 1927. The manuscript is in Edinburgh University Library.

MACDONALD, PATRICK, *A Collection of Highland Vocal Airs/Never hitherto published./To which are added a few of the most lively/Country Dances or Reels/of the/North Highlands & Western Isles./And some Specimens of Bagpipe Music*, Edinburgh, 1784.

MACGILLIVRAY, JAMES, 'The cylindrical reed pipe from antiquity to the 20th century', *Music Libraries and Instruments*, Cambridge, 1959.

MCINTYRE NORTH, C. N., *Leabhar Comunn nan Fion Gheal* (The Book of the Club of True Highlanders), London, 1881.

MACKAY, ANGUS, *A Collection of Ancient Pìobaireachd, or Highland Pipe Music*, Edinburgh, 1838.

MACKENZIE, JOHN, *Sar Obair nam Bard Gaelach* (*The Beauties of Gaelic Poetry*), Glasgow, 1841.

MACLEOD, F. T., *The MacCrimmons of Skye*, Edinburgh, 1933.

MACLEOD, NEIL (of Gesto), *A Collection of Twenty Pìobaireachd ...*, Edinburgh, 1828.

MACLEOD, R. C. (of MacLeod), *The MacLeods of Dunvegan*, Edinburgh, 1927.

MACLEOD, R. C. (of MacLeod) (ed.), *The Book of Dunvegan*, The Third Spalding Club, no. 8, 2 vols, Aberdeen, 1938–9.

MCNEILL, F. MARIAN, *The Silver Bough*, vol. 1, Glasgow, 1957.

MACNEILL, SEUMAS, *Pìobaireachd: Classical Music of the Highland Bagpipe*, Edinburgh, 1968.

MALCOLM, C. A., *The Piper in Peace and War*, London, 1927.

MANSON, W. L., *The Highland Bagpipe*, Paisley, 1901.

MARTIN, MARTIN, *A Description of the Western Islands of Scotland, c.1695*, 1703, reprinted London, 1716, 1884. The edition quoted is ed. with introduction by Donald J. MacLeod, Stirling, 1934.

MASSON, GEORGINA, *The Companion Guide to Rome*, London, 1965.

MENZIES, D. P., 'Notes on the "Bannockburn" bagpipes of Menzies', *Proceedings of the Society of Antiquaries of Scotland*, vol. 5, 3rd series (1894–5).

MERSENNE, MARIN, *Harmonie universelle*, Paris, 1636.

MIGNE, JACQUES PAUL, 'De diversus generibus musicorum (ad Dardanum)', *Patrologiae Cursus Completus*, Paris, 1844–79.

MITCHELL, DUGALD, *The History of the Highlands and Gaelic Scotland*, Paisley, 1900.

MONIPENNIE, JOHN, *A Summary of the Scottish Chronicle, an abridgement of the Black Book of Paisley: Of the Isles of Scotland in General*, London, 1603. Reprinted Edinburgh, 1756, as *An Abridgement or Summary of the Chronicles of Scotland . . . together with A Description of the Realm of Scotland, as to its Situation, Distance and Commodities; to which is added, A Particular Account of the Isles, and of the Rarities therein.*

MONTFAUCON, BERNARD DE, *L'Antiquité expliquée et representée en figures* (supplément), Paris, 1719.

MORGAN, JACQUES DE, *Délégation en Perse*, Paris, 1900.

*Musical News*, vol. 25, articles on ancient Egyptian pipes, unsigned, probably by T. Lea Southgate (August and November, 1903).

*Musical Times*, two unsigned articles (probably by T. Lea Southgate) on the ancient Egyptian pipes discovered by Flinders Petrie (October and December 1890).

NAYLOR, E. W., *An Elizabethan Virginal Book*, London, 1905.

*New Oxford History of Music*, vol. 1, *Ancient and Oriental Music*, ed. Egon Wellesz, London, 1966.

NORTH, S. KENNEDY, 'The Northumberland small pipes', *Proceedings of the Musical Association*, vol. 56 (1929).

O'CURRY (or Curry), EUGENE, *On the Manners and Customs of the Ancient Irish*, 3 vols, London, 1873.

*Oxford History of Music, The,* original edition, introductory volume, ed. Percy C. Buck, Oxford, 1901.

PEATE, I. C., 'Welsh musical instruments', *Man*, vol. 47, no. 17 (1947), pp. 17–40.

PENNANT, THOMAS, *A Tour of Scotland and Voyage to the Hebrides*, Chester, 1774.

PETRIE, GEORGE, 'On the antiquities of Tara Hill', *Transactions of the Royal Irish Academy*, vol. 18 (1839).

PETRIE, WILLIAM FLINDERS, *Ten Years Digging in Egypt*, London, 1892.

PÌOBAIREACHD SOCIETY, *Pìobaireachd*, Glasgow, 1925.

POPE, A. UPHAM, *A Survey of Persian Art*, vol. 4, Oxford, 1938.

POULTER, G. C. B. and FISHER, C. P., *The MacCrimmon Family, 1500–1936*, Camberley, 1936.

PRAETORIUS, MICHAEL, *Syntagma musicum*, 4 vols, Wolfenbüttel, 1619.

PREBBLE, JOHN, *Culloden*, London, 1961.

PRIDEAUX, EDITH K., *The Carving of Musical Instruments in Exeter Cathedral Church*, Exeter, 1915.

RICHMOND, I. A., *Roman and Native in North Britain*, Edinburgh, 1958.

RITSON, JOSEPH, *Ancient Songs*, London, 1792.

ROSS, G. F., *Some Pìobaireachd Studies*, Glasgow, 1926.

ROSS, NEIL, 'Ceòl Mór', *Transactions of the Gaelic Society of Inverness*, vol. 32 (1929).

ROSS, RODERICK, *Binneas is Boreraig*, Edinburgh, 1959.

SACHS, CURT, *The History of Musical Instruments*, New York, 1940.

SALMOND, J. B., *Wade in Scotland*, Edinburgh, 1938.

SCHLESINGER, KATHLEEN, 'Bagpipe' in *Encyclopaedia Britannica* (11th ed.), London, 1910.

SCHLESINGER, KATHLEEN, *The Greek Aulos*, London, 1939.

SCHOLES, PERCY A., *The Oxford Companion to Music* (4th ed.), Oxford, 1942.

SCOTT, SIR WALTER, 'Voyage in the Lighthouse Yacht to Nova Zembla and the Lord knows where', in J. G. Lockhart, *Memoirs of the Life of Sir Walter Scott*, vol. 3, Edinburgh, 1837.

SCOTT, SIR WALTER, *Old Mortality*, Border ed., London, 1924.

SCOTT, SIR WALTER, *The Fair Maid of Perth*, Border ed., London, 1925.

SCOTTISH HISTORY SOCIETY, *Chronicles of the Frasers* (Wardlaw Manuscript) '*Polichronicon seu Policratica Temporum or the true Genealogy of the Frasers*', by Master James Fraser, ed. William Mackay, vol. 47, 1st series, Edinburgh, 1905.

SCOTTISH HISTORY SOCIETY, *The Prisoners of the '45*, ed. Sir Bruce Gordon Seton and Jean Gordon Arnot, vols 2 and 3, Edinburgh, 1928–9.

SKENE, WILLIAM F., *The Highlanders of Scotland*, Stirling, 1902.

SOUTHGATE. T. LEA, 'Ancient flutes from Egypt', *Journal of Hellenic Studies*, vol. 35 (1915). Cf. also under *Musical News* and *Musical Times*.

STAINER, JOHN, *The Music of the Bible*, London, 1879.

STOKES, MARGARET, *The High Crosses of Castledermot and Durrow*, Dublin, 1898.

STRUTT, JOSEPH, *Sports and Pastimes of the People of England*, ed. J. Charles Cox, London, 1801.

STUDIO, THE, London, July 1861. Illustration of the Silchester 'Flute Girl'.

SURTEES, ROBERT, *History of Durham*, 4 vols, London, 1840.

THOMASON, C. S., *Ceòl Mór: A Collection of Pìobaireachd as played on the Great Highland bagpipes: Compiled, edited and rendered in a new and easily acquired notation*, London, 1900. (Manson, 1901, p. 393, gives the index to Thomason in full.)

THOMSON, DERICK S., 'The Harlaw *Brosnachadh*, an early fifteenth-century curio', *Celtic Studies*, ed. James Carney and David Greene, London, 1968.

THOMSON, DERICK S., 'The MacMhuirich Bardic Family', *Transactions of the Gaelic Society of Inverness*, vol. 43 (1960–3).

TOYNBEE, J. M. C., *Art in Britain under the Romans*, Oxford, 1964.

VIRDUNG, SEBASTIAN, *Musica Getutscht*, Basle, 1511.

WARDLAW MANUSCRIPT, see Scottish History Society.

WALKER, JOSEPH C., *Historical Memoirs of the Irish Bards* (Appendix), Dublin, 1786.

WESTEN, STEPHEN, 'An account of a bronze figure found at Richborough in Kent, representing a Roman soldier playing on the bagpipes', *Archaeologia*, vol. 17 (1814).

WESTERMAN, W. L., 'Apprenticeship contracts and the apprenticeship system in Roman Egypt', *Classical Philology*, vol. 9 (1924).

WESTERMAN, W. L., 'The castanet dancers of Arsinoe', *Journal of Egyptian Archaeology*, vol. 10 (1924).

WINTERNITZ, E., *Musical Instruments and their Symbolism in Western Art*, London, 1967.

WOOLLEY, C. LEONARD, *Ur of the Chaldees*, London, 1929.

WOOLLEY, C. LEONARD, *Ur Excavations*, London and Philadelphia, 1933.

WYNTON, ANDREW (Androw) OF, *The Orygynale Cronykil of Scotland*, ed. David Laing, Edinburgh, 1872.